The WILEY *advantage*

Dear Valued Customer,

We realize you're a busy professional with deadlines to hit. Whether your goal is to learn a new technology or solve a critical problem, we want to be there to lend you a hand. Our primary objective is to provide you with the insight and knowledge you need to stay atop the highly competitive and ever-changing technology industry.

Wiley Publishing, Inc., offers books on a wide variety of technical categories, including security, data warehousing, software development tools, and networking — everything you need to reach your peak. Regardless of your level of expertise, the Wiley family of books has you covered.

- For Dummies® — The *fun* and *easy* way™ to learn
- The Weekend Crash Course® — The *fastest* way to learn a new tool or technology
- Visual — For those who prefer to learn a new topic *visually*
- The Bible — The *100% comprehensive* tutorial and reference
- The Wiley Professional list — *Practical* and *reliable* resources for IT professionals

The book you hold now, *Windows Server 2003 Security Bible,* is your 100% comprehensive guide to creating a secure server environment for this latest release. Whether you are new to security, or are a veteran programmer, *Windows Server 2003 Security Bible* is everything you need to build a secure system. Starting with security fundamentals such as planning and auditing and then building on with authentication and encryption methodology, our expert author guides you through multi-level security for Windows Server 2003.

Our commitment to you does not end at the last page of this book. We'd want to open a dialog with you to see what other solutions we can provide. Please be sure to visit us at www.wiley.com/compbooks to review our complete title list and explore the other resources we offer. If you have a comment, suggestion, or any other inquiry, please locate the "contact us" link at www.wiley.com.

Thank you for your support and we look forward to hearing from you and serving your needs again in the future.

Sincerely,

Richard K. Swadley

Richard K. Swadley
Vice President & Executive Group Publisher
Wiley Technology Publishing

15 HOUR WEEKEND CRASH COURSE

Visual

Bible

DUMMIES FOR

WILEY

Wiley Publishing, Inc.

Windows® Server 2003 Security Bible

Windows® Server 2003 Security Bible

Blair Rampling

WILEY

Wiley Publishing, Inc.

Windows® Server 2003 Security Bible

Published by
Wiley Publishing, Inc.
10475 Crosspoint Boulevard
Indianapolis, IN 46256
www.wiley.com

Copyright © 2003 by Wiley Publishing, Inc., Indianapolis, Indiana
Published simultaneously in Canada

Library of Congress Control Number: 2002114785

ISBN: 0-7645-4912-X

Manufactured in the United States of America

10 9 8 7 6 5 4 3 2 1

1O/QX/QU/QT/IN

About the Author

Blair Rampling is a System Administrator currently contracted to a mid-sized resource company and is responsible for the administration of a number of large servers running business applications. His past experience involves a wide array of systems, including Microsoft Windows and UNIX, in both corporate and Internet Service Provider environments.

Credits

Senior Acquisitions Editor
Sharon Cox

Project Editor
Marcia Ellett

Technical Editor
Allen L. Wyatt

Copy Editors
Susan Hobbs
Gabrielle Chosney

Contributing Writer
Diana Huggins

Editorial Manager
Mary Beth Wakefield

**Vice President & Executive
Group Publisher**
Richard Swadley

**Vice President and
Executive Publisher**
Bob Ipsen

Vice President and Publisher
Joseph B. Wikert

Executive Editorial Director
Mary Bednarek

Project Coordinator
Dale White

Graphics and Production Specialists
Beth Brooks
Amanda Carter
Jennifer Click
Jeremey Unger

Quality Control Technicians
Laura Albert
John Greenough

Proofreading and Indexing
TECHBOOKS Production Services
Brian Herrmann
Bill Barton

This book is dedicated to Christina.

Preface

Is This Book For You?

If you work with Windows Server 2003 and need more information on security issues in both theory and practice, this book is for you. This book introduces you to the theory of computer security, covers the procedures for securing Windows Server 2003, and walks you through the steps for setting up a Microsoft ISA-based firewall.

How This Book Is Organized

This book is organized into the following four parts:

- ✦ **Part I** — Security Fundamentals
- ✦ **Part II** — System Security
- ✦ **Part III** — Authentication and Encryption
- ✦ **Part IV** — Microsoft Internet Security and Acceleration Server

In addition, the book contains appendixes with information about other available security tools and resources, as well as a list of standard port assignments.

Conventions Used in the Book

Icons appear in the left margin. The following icons are used to call your attention to points that are particularly important.

 A Note icon provides extra information that you need to pay special attention to.

 A Tip icon indicates a special way of performing a particular task.

A Caution icon alerts you that you need to take special care when executing a procedure, or damage to your computer hardware or software could result.

A Cross-Reference icon is used to refer you to further information on a subject that appears in another chapter of the book.

Acknowledgments

First of all, thanks to Kathy Ivens who first connected me with this project. Without her, I wouldn't have had this opportunity. Thanks to everyone at Wiley who worked on this project through its long production process and showed an exemplary amount of patience and dedication to its completion. Nancy Stevenson and Sharon Cox were both vital in developing and maintaining the schedule and production process on the book. Marcia Ellett worked from beginning to end at developing the manuscript into a finished product. Thanks to Allen L. Wyatt who edited the book for technical accuracy and Diana Huggins who provided the last stage of review and editing. Thanks also to Susan Hobbs and Gabrielle Chosney for providing the copy edit of the final work. Finally, thanks to David Fugate for helping me through the process from proposal to completion.

Contents at a Glance

Contents

Part II: System Security   113

Part III: Authentication and Encryption   169

Security Fundamentals

◆   ◆   ◆   ◆

◆   ◆   ◆   ◆

Security Threats

In all but the smallest of computing environments, IT security has become a full-time job. System administrators must protect data, devices, and networks from a multitude of threats and vulnerabilities. And a day seldom passes without report of newly discovered threats or vulnerabilities. Security threats come in many forms — from malicious code to defaced Web sites. The damage inflicted through security breaches ranges from minimal and localized to widespread and devastating. As quickly as agile minds invent new ways to connect systems and data, others find dubious means of accessing and utilizing them.

The security administrator's job is to identify and patch system and network vulnerabilities before the bad guys use them for malicious purposes. He must also monitor systems and data for intrusions and improper access attempts. And he contends with these security needs on several levels: data, system, network, intranet, extranet, and Internet. The more users and devices added to the computing environment, the more work for the security administrator. After Internet connectivity is established, the work, the vulnerabilities, and the security threats multiply dramatically — when a system or network is connected to the Internet, it can potentially be accessed by anyone, from anywhere, at any time.

Fortunately, Windows Server 2003 administrators have a plethora of technology (NTSF, data encryption, IPSec, PPTP, and so on) for protecting all levels of the computing environment. In addition, auditing capabilities and security logs ease the burden of monitoring and reporting on intrusion attempts. Later chapters in this book provide specific information on configuring and using security tools and technologies. In this chapter, I explain the nature and origin of the security threats you are most likely to encounter both inside and outside the firewall.

Internal versus External Threats

Curiously, 80 percent of corporate security funds are spent on deterring external threats — access breaches by persons who are not authorized users on a network. But security experts estimate that 70 to 80 percent of all security incidents involve corporate insiders. Yet, perhaps because external security breaches are often highly publicized, companies focus their efforts on fighting external access attempts.

In this chapter, I introduce some of the means and methods used in internal versus external attacks. As a system administrator, you must address security threats from both inside and outside your network. Through reading this book, you will see that the processes and tools used for defending against both types of attack are often similar. A good security plan includes several layers of protection and secures resources and data from most unauthorized access — whether from corporate insiders or external attackers.

The key to getting a grasp on the security of your systems (although it sounds cliché) is to think like an attacker. If you can do this, you can better prioritize what needs to be secured and how much effort is required to do the job. Some systems may be simple to restore and may not contain any information of value to an attacker. In that case, it's better to focus your efforts somewhere else — verifying your off-site data storage, for example, and securing your Web servers against the latest worm. System security almost always involves compromises, and a good security administrator always knows how to prioritize.

Internal threat considerations

Internal threats pose the most serious problem to the security of a system or network. Often, an organization's servers and workstations reside on the same network behind a firewall, which gives the users of the workstations free access to attack the servers. In essence, a "trusted" user who already has some degree of access to a network initiates an internal attack.

Internal threats range from unskilled users to systems administrators — even the CTO. Unfortunately, every company employee must be considered a potential threat, but they cannot be treated with the same paranoia as external users. You must develop some level of perceived trust and provide convenient access for internal users, but also develop internal security. The convenience versus security debate has been raging as long as computers have existed.

Some internal security incidents are unintentional and result from carelessness, while others are the intentional work of a disgruntled employee. Still others are intentional attempts to profit from archived records — selling health and financial information, for example.

An internal user may attack a system for any number of reasons, including the following:

✦ Data theft

✦ Espionage

✦ Sabotage

✦ General malice

Curiosity about private information accounts for a very large number of internal security violations. Accounting records, such as payroll data, and e-mail are tempting targets. Most companies keep this information secured, and a curious employee becomes a network attacker when he or she decides to search for an answer to the question, "I wonder how much Joe makes?" In many cases, the curious insider discovers that he doesn't have access to the data and gives up. But others who don't have authorized access to the desired data will search for other means of access — cracking the password of a user who does have access, tricking an authorized user into revealing their password (commonly known as social engineering), or bribing an authorized user to provide the desired information.

A large number of internal attacks are initiated by disgruntled employees or former employees who want to get back at the company. This type of attacker takes many approaches:

✦ Deleting valuable corporate data

✦ Publishing or distributing private corporate data

✦ Changing administrative policy settings or passwords, or similarly disrupting the corporate network

✦ Sending offensive or inappropriate e-mail messages from the corporate messaging system

The level of damage inflicted by a trusted user largely depends on the user's computer and network skills. Those who have broader knowledge of the systems and network can literally halt the workflow of an entire company. While the scope of damage caused by a relatively unskilled user is not usually so large, the unskilled user can still cause serious harm.

The unskilled user

Consider the following situation:

One weekend, when the system administrators or tech support users are not in the office, an HR assistant decides to do some extra work. He attempts to access the payroll files, only to find that he doesn't have access. Either he is legitimately denied access, or he may not have been added to a security group by accident. The HR assistant becomes incensed, especially because he commuted all the way to the office on a Sunday morning. The assistant goes directly to his manager on Monday and makes a complaint; the manager himself complains up the chain of management until eventually an edict comes down to remove the security on all files on the network: the result of uninformed decision-making.

This relaxing of security is a worst-case scenario for the systems administrators because when the payroll data is leaked by some user who wants to know Joe's take-home pay, it is the administrator's responsibility to explain how that happened. Of course, bad decision-making by management is never a valid excuse when those managers are the ones asking questions.

By planning a proper internal security architecture, you can have a secure internal network and still maintain a level of convenience for users. It may take some measure of skill, some trial and error in the lab (trial and error on the production network is a bad idea for numerous reasons), and even some luck to get everything balanced out. However, after everything is in place, many attacks will either be impossible to carry out or finding the attacker will be easy.

Unskilled internal users may attempt to find a variety of information. For example, they may try to access software that they would not normally have access to (to make copies for home, or for other uses), view other users' e-mail for malicious purposes, or steal company secrets. This type of user is typically easy to track and generally unsuccessful on the majority of attempts. Furthermore, they will be neither familiar with the network, nor have the expertise to use network discovery tools. To track the movements of the unskilled internal user and gather evidence, you can simply add your network monitor (you have a network monitor as part of your response kit, right?) and thereby monitor the user for purposes of discipline or prosecution.

The skilled user

The second type of user posing a threat to your network security is the skilled user, of which the best example is a system administrator. Typically, the skilled user doesn't attack the network for trivial purposes, but for malicious purposes such as espionage and selling company secrets, or worse, revenge. Tracking this type of user presents two major difficulties. A skilled user will likely be competent enough to cover his tracks. He may be removing or modifying system and security logs, and attacking from a variety of hosts; he probably knows the layout of the network, including the existence of any network monitoring and intrusion detection systems. Also, after you notice a problem and respond, the skilled user may be scared off before you gather enough information to identify and prosecute him. It is very important that the attacker is not aware of the monitoring systems.

It is possible, in a number of ways, to make a "blackened" network monitor. A blackened network monitor should be able to receive all data sent on the network but not send any data onto the network. More difficult than creating the system that is logically blackened is physically hiding that system from the attacker, especially when the attacker has physical access to the data center. The attacker would notice something unusual, such as a new system or a strange connection to the network.

An internal network's layout should be configured so that users and servers are separated. The best design is one in which firewalls separate the two groups, but they should at least be on separate network subnets. More importantly, you should use an intrusion detection system (IDS) agent to watch traffic between the networks. With this layer of security, you can track intrusions from internal users.

Anatomy of an internal attack

The effect of an internal attack (by a skillful attacker) on a company can range from small inconvenience to irreparable damage. Consider, for example, that the attacker is someone who is involved with the systems on the network, such as a system administrator. As mentioned earlier in this chapter, the attacker can mount his attack for a number of reasons. Data theft is a fairly simple act; it is also undetectable in many cases — until your innovations start appearing on your competitor's products, or your competitor's sales force starts targeting your customers en masse.

Another motive for attacking a system — one where the effects may be less obvious than that of data theft, but just as damaging — is revenge. A disgruntled employee is probably the best example of an attacker with vengeful motives. He may be able to access the systems because he is given notice of his termination ahead of time, or he may be let go immediately but still have access for a brief period. In any case, he probably doesn't feel he has much to lose.

A well-planned attack will involve the theft of such items as backup tapes and system software, and possibly even hardware. By taking such items, which he knows are vital to operations, the attacker can disrupt service and possibly even cause total data loss. If nothing else drives home the importance of off-site backups, this situation should. After the attacker has removed all possibility for a quick restoration of service, he then begins the main attack against the network or data. Because he has already disabled the backup/restore devices, this portion of the attack may have devastating consequences. The attacker may have full access to many systems, so the attack could run the gamut from small and malicious to total network disablement. One of the simplest and most dangerous things that the attacker can do is format the hard disks. This makes it impossible to load the operating system or access the data stored on the hard disks.

This simple attack is complete. Data has been lost and the backups, operating system media, and application media are missing. The company has now suffered a potentially deadly attack. It will only be able to recover from it by starting from scratch.

A Network Configuration for Highly Important Data

Some government and military installations employ a network configuration that places a firewall between the user workstations and the servers. This isn't common practice in the private sector due to the difficulty of correctly configuring and maintaining the firewall to allow enough access — but not too much access. (One government administrator described such a firewall as resembling Swiss cheese when improperly configured.) This network configuration is used when the value and protection of the data on the network servers is of the utmost importance. Government, military, and financial institutions often demand this level of security.

External threat considerations

Most organizations spend a great deal of effort and money defending against external attackers, despite the fact that internal attacks are more common. Perhaps this is due to the intense publicity that some external attacks have generated. Perhaps it's because trusted employees (potential internal attackers) can't be further restricted from corporate data. Whatever the reason, more emphasis is placed on protecting systems and networks from external attackers, and internal security is often neglected as a result.

An external attack originates from outside a network's firewall. Depending on the location of your servers in the network architecture and the configuration of the firewalls at your network entry points, your servers may be vulnerable to attack from users who are not located on trusted networks under your control. The firewall separates your internal, private network from the external, public world — the Internet. In theory, users on the public networks know less about the configuration of your network and servers, so they would seem to be less of a threat; however, poor security can allow them to collect system and network information and create their own map of your systems.

Black hats, white hats, and script kiddies

External attackers' motives are usually different from those of the internal attacker. In rare cases, they are also looking for secrets and practicing espionage, but most of the time they are attempting simple Web page defacements or attacking for the thrill of it.

The most severe situation you will face involves an attacker looking for specific data on your network. This person is typically a lone wolf who is highly skilled and doesn't leave much of a trace, if any. This attacker doesn't share his attacks with anyone, reducing the likelihood of being caught (there's no "honor among thieves," as the saying goes). This type of attacker has mastered each system he intends to attack — he leaves no evidence of his presence in log files and does not destroy any data on your systems, only making copies of whatever he is looking for. He spends much time in preparation before mounting the attack, which you may never even detect. This type of attacker may also be capable of finding new vulnerabilities and coding the associated exploits, or coding new exploits for old vulnerabilities. The best defense against this type of attacker is to keep up-to-date on all vulnerabilities in your systems and their respective fixes, have a secure firewall layer, and implement a good blackened intrusion detection system (discussed later in this chapter).

The attacker who attempts Web defacements (the *script kiddie*) is a much weaker enemy. His skill set is much smaller than that of the lone wolf, as he is only capable of using what is provided to him and doesn't write his own malicious code. He launches an attack from a previously compromised system on the Internet to compromise your systems for either a Web page defacement or a staging area for his next attack. To defend against the script kiddies, keep your systems patched and your firewalls locked down as tightly as possible.

Nowadays, with millions of people connected to the Internet, the threats have changed and multiplied. The expert attackers can be categorized as *white hat* and *black hat* hackers. The white hat hackers discover security problems in systems and then work with the software vendors to fix these problems. Many of these experts believe in full disclosure—that is, releasing the information about these problems both to the software vendors and to the general public through paths such as the Bugtraq mailing list. Normally, the vendors are contacted first and given time to address and repair the problems before information about the vulnerabilities is publicly released. The black hat hacker locates problems with systems, but does not release them to the vendor or to the general public, choosing instead to exploit them for his own gain.

White hat hackers do not pose a threat to network and system security. On the contrary, they work with the software vendors to make the software that is used on a daily basis more secure, and in situations where the vendor is unresponsive, they notify the general public so that the software can be avoided. The black hat hacker is a rare threat. Most black hat hackers (remember, they know the systems thoroughly) will use the security holes they find for their own gain, through industrial espionage or outright theft. Black hat hackers are rare; you are less likely to encounter one "in the wild" than you would another type of attacker, such as the script kiddie.

Note The phrase "in the wild" refers to something you come across on the public Internet rather than in a lab environment. It is commonly used to refer to particular viruses that are commonly seen on the Internet.

You are almost guaranteed to come across a script kiddie when administrating a network connected to the Internet. Script kiddies possess no real skills and use the exploits created by expert hackers to maliciously attack systems. Everyone in the Information Technology industry looks down upon script kiddies, who simply install a copy of the Linux operating system, download a few exploits, and begin to attack systems. Most of the time, script kiddies use these attacks to facilitate Web page defacements as a way to flaunt their own skills. In most environments, it is common to see some form of attack from a script kiddie daily, even if it is only a port scan.

Human imperfection should also be considered in a discussion about security. Humans don't usually function well under stress, can be easily distracted, and may forget things. Furthermore, they become complacent when they perform the same procedures over and over again. When considering the individuals who will potentially come into contact with your network, you will probably decide that it's best not to trust anyone: internal users as well as anonymous external users. Don't take your own actions for granted either. Leaving a security hole in a system that you configure or maintain is not much different from an attacker installing a backdoor to give himself access. The process is similar, and the results are the same. Admittedly, comparing a system administrator to an attacker is an extreme way of thinking, but it guarantees the highest level of protection for your system.

> **Note**   A *backdoor* is a program installed without your knowledge that allows an attacker to re-enter a system that he has compromised. However, backdoor programs originated not with the malicious hackers, but from system developers and testers who left alternative ways into a system to facilitate their development and testing.

Anatomy of an external attack

The attack of an intruder who does not have knowledge of your network will progress in one of two ways. If the intrusion is simple, such as the compromise of a system that is not behind a firewall, he may simply attack that machine and not bother exploring any further. A more determined attacker, however, is willing to do more work. Keep in mind that the attack outlined in this section is possible with a firewall in place, although some firewalls can be configured to stop parts of the attack.

The determined attacker first attempts to get more information about your network while avoiding detection. He can obtain this information from a number of places. Protocols such as Simple Network Management Protocol (SNMP) can be queried using default passwords to get information about router and firewall configurations. Some network devices also have other vulnerabilities and will divulge information when queried the right way. These types of exploits provide the attacker with the network layout, including the following valuable information:

✦ IP addresses

✦ MAC addresses

✦ Routing information

The attacker can then begin to determine what systems exist on these networks. The most common method of finding systems is by using a port scanner such as nmap. nmap is discussed in more detail later in the book, but essentially, it scans an IP address or range of IP addresses and checks each port for a response. A number of methods can be used to check open ports, the simplest of which is to send a TCP packet and check for a response. Many of these methods are detectable by firewalls and IDSs, but some methods of scanning, known as stealth scans, are not detectable. Figure 1-1 shows a stealth port scan using nmap showing the open ports on a target system.

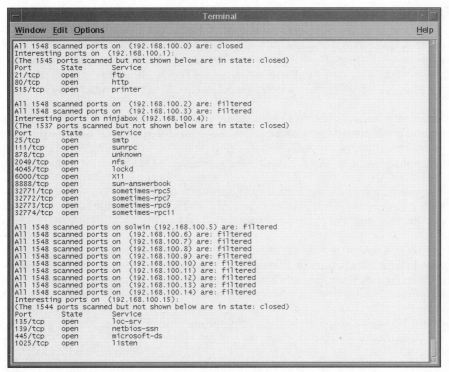

Figure 1-1: nmap is used to find the open ports on a target system.

At this point, the attacker possesses a large amount of information about the network. He queried your network devices to determine the network layout and mapped the systems with open ports. The attacker now knows what to attack, but not how to mount the attack. To determine which vulnerabilities exist and which exploits he can use, he must first determine what type of operating system is on each target machine. The best way he can do this and remain undetected is through deduction. Certain services run by default on particular operating systems. For example, a system with NetBIOS ports (137–139) or Microsoft Exchange–related ports open is most likely a Microsoft Windows system, and so on. You can configure a system in many ways so that the default ports are closed, and software config-urations exist that make one type of system look like another, such as a UNIX sys-tem running the Samba package. The attacker can also use other less stealthy methods of determining the type of system. A number of applications, such as nmap (if not using stealth scanning) and QueSO, are capable of looking at signa-tures present in the Transmission Control Protocol (TCP) stack of the target, as well as open ports, and determining the type of operating system (this is known as stack fingerprinting).

QueSO is a freeware network utility used to detect the operating system running on a host machine. QueSO works by sending a faulty TCP packet to the targeted com-puter. A Unix system and a Windows system respond differently to malformed TCP packets, so the response to the bad packet reveals the operating system of the tar-geted computer. Interestingly, the name QueSO comes from the Spanish phrase "Que Sistema Operativo?" which loosely translates to "What is the operating system?"

Nmap — or Network Mapper — is another freeware utility that is used for both port scanning and stack fingerprinting. Nmap is considered more powerful than QueSO for several reasons: it can be used for port scanning while QueSO cannot, and it can be used to scan a range of IP addresses while QueSO scans only a single address.

The nmap utility includes a variety of options (or switches). For example, the –O switch (typed nmap –O) is used to perform stack fingerprinting, while the –p switch designates which port is to be scanned.

QueSO and nmap are valuable administrative tools used by legitimate administra-tors. Unfortunately, they're also used by less principled people who use them as reconnaissance tools for gathering information about a system or network prior to an attack.

Figure 1-2 shows nmap being used to determine the operating system type with the –O switch.

Finally, the attacker has everything he needs to carry out the attack: the network layout, and a map of all the systems, including their operating systems and running software with open ports. He can now determine which tactics to use and begin to attack systems on the network. All he has to do now is compromise one internal system. One easy and commonly used exploit for the attacker is to run a program that inserts an access point by which he can freely access the system. A thorough attack will progress to using the compromised machine (or machines) to gather information about the internal network, finding all of the information about every system. The attacker essentially has free reign over the entire network now that he has a steppingstone behind the firewall.

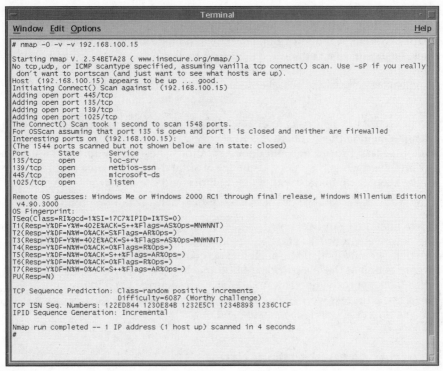

Figure 1-2: nmap can be used to determine the type of operating system on a target system through stack fingerprinting.

Anyone with a little time, a moderate amount of knowledge, a lot of determination, and little or no fear of getting caught can carry out this type of attack. With the proper pieces in place, you can prevent such attacks and limit damage if the network is compromised.

Internal versus External Security Measures

System security is widely misunderstood and often overlooked. When a new security problem is discussed in the media, many computer users — including system administrators — fail to understand the problem and its repercussions. This book will help you understand potential security problems and how to prevent and deal with their symptoms.

To simplify, you can view an effective security plan as a series of roadblocks, each roughly equal in strength and importance. If the attacker is not stopped by the first roadblock, he will likely be stopped by the second or third.

To properly secure your systems, you must follow the same type of design. A multi-layer security architecture is the most important design consideration. With proper network, system, and application security and monitoring, you are far less likely to suffer damage from an attack.

Cross-Reference   Chapter 2 discusses multilayer security architecture in detail.

System security measures can take two forms: *static* and *dynamic*. Static security measures include the installation and securing of the system, and application and development of procedures and documentation. These procedures do not change very often and when they do, the change is often minor. Dynamic security measures involve keeping up-to-date with vulnerabilities and the necessary changes required to offset them. Dynamic security is an ongoing task.

System administrators are now faced with many threats. In the past, many systems were on private networks and the only threats were internal to those networks that were tightly controlled, or through dial-up connections. As the Internet grew out of the connection of these networks to one another, the user base could not be controlled, increasing the need for greater system security. Even in the Internet's early stages, the attackers were highly trained experts who knew the operating systems (such as Unix, VMS, and MVS) inside and out.

External security measures

External threats are addressed somewhat differently from internal threats. While internal security measures focus on appropriately configuring access to data, external security measures focus on blocking access to the internal network and its systems.

External threats normally originate from attackers with no knowledge of the layout of your network (unless, of course, you're attacked from outside the firewall by a current or former employee). Before an external attacker can damage your systems or data, he must first find entry points and locate his targets on your systems or network. By configuring good security between your internal and external networks, you can limit the amount of information that an attacker can learn as well as stop many attacks at the network edge. One of the key elements to stopping external attackers is a well-secured firewall between your network and the outside. In this book, you'll learn to implement and maintain the correct security measures to protect your computer systems from an external attack.

Internal security measures

Beyond the Internet-type security provisions, more specific changes are needed to secure against an internal attacker. Many security provisions are built into Windows

Server 2003 and Windows XP, the most basic of which are Access Control Lists (ACLs). By using ACLs, you can block users from accessing files on the network that they are not supposed to access.

Group policies also allow for the specific configuration of security. You can restrict which systems or types of systems (workstations, domain controllers, and so on) that a user can log in to. You can also take more control of the desktop with the more advanced policy features. You can avoid having your internal users run unauthorized programs, which may introduce security vulnerabilities or be used to attack other internal systems.

The bottom line is that security is often more of a people problem than a system problem. Users often access files they shouldn't because they are snooping around. If you're viewing your security issues as purely technological problems, you're considering only a single element of a total security plan. Compromises can often be avoided by simply making users think that they'll be caught, and that the repercussions will be severe. This can be accomplished by writing and publishing a Computer and Network Security Policy. Some companies display a brief security statement when a user logs on to the network. Others require each employee to sign a document stating that they have read and understand the corporate security policy. Many companies do both.

Technological security comes into play for those who either don't know that what they're doing causes a security flaw, or don't care or believe that they'll be caught or that the consequences will be extreme.

Forms of Attack

There are probably as many ways to attack a computer system or network as there are reasons for attacking. With good reason, many people do not view the Internet as a safe place. They worry about using their credit card or having their personal information stolen. Take a minute to think about your attitude towards the Internet. Do you feel it is safe and has adequate security, or does its insecurity concern you?

The Internet is not inherently safe or unsafe. It all depends on the implementation of the services being used and the behavior of the user. For example, sending your credit card over a Secure Socket Layer (SSL) connection is a safe activity. E-mailing your credit card information in plain text is not.

The Internet — by design — is not secure. The protocols that are now used on the Internet were designed (with a few exceptions) in the days of *DARPAnet*, many years before the advent of the modern Internet. This early network of government, and later educational, sites is the birthplace of TCP/IP and many of the application layer protocols now in use. Originally, these protocols were designed for a network with a restricted user base; only the staff of government and educational institutions would have access to these systems. Because the user base was assumed to be trustworthy, security was not designed into these protocols.

Note   *DARPAnet* was a computer network created in 1969 that connected academic institutions, government agencies, and businesses engaged in computer research, Originally called ARPAnet and created by the Advanced Research Projects Agency (ARPA), the network was later renamed to DARPAnet when ARPA became the Defense Advanced Research Projects Agency. DARPAnet is commonly regarded as the precursor to the Internet.

The problem is becoming obvious. Since its inception, the Internet has been a series of compromises. Insecure protocols were used and protocols were modified to perform in ways that were not originally intended. For example, the layout of DARPAnet and many of the protocols used by DARPAnet were modified to allow public access, resulting in the creation of the Internet. As the Internet began to grow, additional modifications were made. During the early 1990s, the growth of the Internet exploded. The Internet protocols are now straining to handle the load of the Internet, and are still being modified to keep up with its ongoing evolution.

These protocols are so ingrained into the Internet that they cannot be easily replaced with better solutions. We are forced to work with the existing protocols, securing them so that local systems are not vulnerable to attack.

Today, administrators encounter a variety of security threats that were probably never dreamed of in the days of DARPAnet, including Trojan horses, worms, logic bombs, and viruses. The complete list is long and overwhelming.

Cross-
Reference   Chapter 2 discusses these forms of attack in detail.

Luckily, Microsoft Windows Server 2003 — the latest version in the evolution of Microsoft Windows — has become more secure over its many incarnations. Microsoft has strengthened the security of the operating system, and added additional security features in the network services as well. While numerous security flaws may still exist, as the traditional Internet protocols cannot be removed, many new security features have been implemented, such as IP Security (IPSec) and Kerberos.

Caution   Keep in mind, Windows Server 2003 is not intrinsically secure. It includes tools and settings that allow it to be secure, but the application of those tools and settings is left up to the administrator. If the administrator doesn't make the server secure, it won't be secure

A secure host or secure network can be connected to the Internet and still be considered safe. While the original, insecure Internet protocols remain a huge problem, the problem can be overcome if you have the necessary knowledge and an excellent security plan.

The rest of this chapter provides a general overview of the more common threats to the security of your network. The next chapter is more thorough in its discussion of the actual methods used by attackers.

Defacements and Web vandalism

The most basic form of attack on a Web server is defacing a Web page. Web page defacement is also the most audacious type of attack, as the attacker usually uses the defaced page to brag about his skills (ironically, very little skill is required to deface a Web page). Sometimes, Web page defacements are politically motivated; activists (often referred to as "hacktivists") use them as a way to spread their message. A "war" of Web page defacements between crackers in the United States and China has recently broken out for this reason.

Web page defacements are common among attackers working in groups. One teenage member of an infamous group defaced the White House Web site and was later convicted for the attack. The same group also declared war on Iraq and China, but later retracted their declaration.

You can find an archive of defaced Web sites at `www.attrition.org/mirror/attrition/`. However, with so many Web site defacements occurring on a daily basis, the task of maintaining the archive became overwhelming and the site is no longer actively maintained.

Because only a single page needs to be replaced (the `index.html` file), an attacker does not even need full access to a system to perform a Web page defacement, depending on the configuration of the Web server software and the system. The simplicity of this most basic security attack stresses the importance of using a proper multilevel security architecture and keeping up on the latest security patches for your operating system and applications.

Web page defacements are often preventable. Many attacks are implemented through vulnerable Common Gateway Interface (CGI) scripts such as forums and other standard "canned" code that is used on Web sites. As this code is freely distributed, the vulnerabilities are often exposed and exploits created. Certain CGI scanners even search the Web for vulnerable sites. By simply running one of these scanners, a script kiddie can find an entire list of pages that he can deface using an exploit that has already been written. The process requires almost no effort on his part, other than that of running the scanner, running the exploit, and uploading the defaced page.

Many of these vulnerabilities are widely known. It is important that you check all the software you use on your Web site for updates to prevent yourself from becoming a victim of these attacks.

In addition to CGI vulnerabilities, Web servers are often vulnerable to many of the other types of exploits, such as buffer overflows. Buffer overflow was at the root of the Code Red worm infestation that attacked many of the Microsoft IIS servers on the Internet in the year 2001. The attack was performed through a known buffer overflow vulnerability in Microsoft Index Server, for which a fix had been released six months before the actual Code Red outbreak. The fact that there was plenty of time to apply the fix or make a configuration change to prevent an attack, but that the attack still had such devastating consequences, indicates that security is not understood or taken seriously in many organizations.

Web page defacements are also one of the most obvious types of attack. While data theft can sometimes go completely undetected and Denial of Service (DoS) attacks can look like other types of traffic, Web defacements are immediately apparent.

Espionage and data theft

System and network attacks also result from industrial espionage and data theft. Almost every company possesses confidential and business-critical data. Proprietary information can be damaging to a company if it ends up in the wrong hands — their competitors', for example. Data theft can involve stealing files or e-mail messages.

The theft of proprietary files is somewhat difficult when good security practices are in place; stealing e-mail is a much easier task, because it is usually sent unencrypted across public networks when it is not intended for local recipients.

 Cross-Reference   See Chapter 8 for information on encrypting data.

Stealing files from protected systems is quite difficult. Normally, the systems where important files exist are protected behind a firewall and are not externally accessible. For internal security, important files are password protected. This lulls a user into a false sense of security. Any time you have an externally accessible system on the same network as an internal system, it can be used as a jumping off point for attacks on the internal system.

Files can be stolen in a number of ways. The most obvious way is an attack on your network. If one of your network systems is accessible from the Internet, even a Web server, it is vulnerable to attack. If the attacker manages to control that particular system, he can use it as a staging point for deeper penetration into the network. If the system is not kept strictly separate from the rest of the network, the attacker can learn the layout of the internal network and access internal systems from the initial compromised system. In the worst-case scenario, the attacker could access all your network systems. This scenario clearly outlines one of the downfalls of the traditional Microsoft Windows domain architecture of trusted authentication, where a user logged into one system on the domain has a token allowing him access to any system in the domain with his assigned privilege level. While convenient for internal users, this practice is highly insecure in the case of an attack where a domain member is compromised. By using exploits that elevate the privileges of the user, the attacker can gain administrator access to the entire domain.

Internal users have an even easier time with data theft. They can use a similar process to the one described in the preceding paragraph, with the additional advantage of being able to access the entire domain (if that architecture is in place). By finding a method to elevate their privilege level, they basically have free reign over the entire network. Without proper security implemented across the entire network, users can get any data they want.

Stealing e-mail is much simpler than stealing files. E-mail is transmitted in plain text (in most cases) and can be sniffed any time the attacker has access to any network segment over which the mail is transmitted, the sending or receiving mail servers, or the client system. As mail travels over many parts of the Internet that are not under your control, it is highly vulnerable. This reinforces the importance of using encryption for important information.

Note   *Sniffing* traffic is the practice of looking at all traffic flowing over a network connection. Normally, only the traffic destined for your system will reach it but sniffing allows you to see all traffic.

The danger of data theft and industrial espionage shows the importance of a proper multilevel security architecture from the firewall (ingress and egress points) to the client (encryption).

Denial of Service attacks

An entirely different class of attacks is known as *Denial of Service (DoS) attacks.* Instead of trying to gain access to systems (for various reasons), an attacker attempts to stop others from having normal access to the system(s) under attack.

An attacker can mount a DoS attack in a number of ways. Normally, he uses known DoS exploits in a piece of software or hardware. Many DoS attacks are performed by sending a certain type of network packet to the vulnerable system. For example, Windows 95 and Windows NT (before patches) were vulnerable to an attack called WinNuke, which is performed by sending Out of Band data to port 139 (a NetBIOS port). During a WinNuke attack, the Out of Band data occurs when the URGENT flag in the TCP header is set and the URGENT POINTER is set to the end of the frame where no more normal data occurs. This attack causes the victim machine to suffer a Blue Screen of Death (BSoD) on Windows NT (requiring a reboot), or an exception error on Windows 95, which would cause the system to stop network communications.

Many DoS attacks are found in the wild, and can attack everything from Windows 95 workstations to the large routers that run the Internet. It is important to use one of the available resources, such as the Bugtraq mailing list, to keep up-to-date on new DoS attacks to which your systems may be vulnerable. Responsive vendors usually release patches soon after the vulnerabilities are exposed, but some vendors may be less responsive, allowing vulnerabilities to exist for weeks or months.

> **Note**   *Bugtraq* is a discussion list focusing on computer security vulnerabilities and how to fix them. To subscribe to Bugtraq, simply send an e-mail to `bugtraq-subscribe@securityfocus.com`. Your message does not require any special text or subject line.

The *Distributed Denial of Service attack (DDoS)* has been used to bring down major Web sites such as Yahoo! and eBay. The steps required to perform a DDoS are fairly simple, as the necessary software has already been written. The attacker first compromises a number of systems on the Internet, installing DDoS agents on each machine. For the best performance of a DDoS, the DDoS agents should be on different network segments, preferably on different backbones. The attacker may also leave a root kit on the systems so he can access them later. (A root kit is a package of modified system files that are designed to hide an intruder's activities on your system. Using the files from the root kit, the intruder can gain access, deposit files, and run programs undetected.) A central management program then controls these agents remotely. Often, the central management point resides on an Internet Relay Chat (IRC) channel as a bot (a software agent) that the attacker can use to control the attack anonymously. The attacker launches the attack against a target from the central point and the agents begin sending spurious network traffic (usually UDP packets) to the target (often on port 80). This huge amount of traffic will bring down the target machine, and often the network link on which the target resides. Figure 1-3 shows the architecture of a DDoS attack.

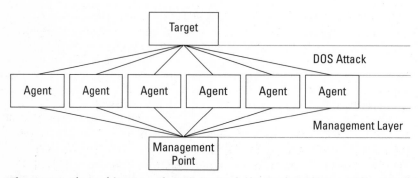

Figure 1-3: The architecture of a DDoS attack shows the agents and the central management point.

You cannot stop a DoS attack without a widely distributed effort between ISPs and backbone carriers. As the victim of a DoS, you can't do anything except try to block the traffic from the outermost network router that you control (usually an edge router, which is a router logically located at the outer edge of your network). Even after blocking the traffic, the router will suffer, as it is utilizing most of its resources just to discard packets.

DoS attacks can theoretically be stopped through a distributed joint effort between providers. With a simple DoS attack, the Internet Service Provider (ISP) providing service to the host originating the attack can cut off the network or dial-up connection from which the attack is originating. This type of procedure is simple enough to coordinate with the abuse department of the ISP in question, as long as the company is responsive. DoS attacks often originate from countries with lax computer security laws, and getting help is not an option.

To make a DoS attack even more complicated, what happens if the DoS originates from a system that has been compromised and does not belong to the attacker, such as a system at an educational or governmental institution? Since the ISP or carrier does not control the organization's internal network, it would have to disable access from the entire campus, which is obviously not an option. Another level of human contact may be brought in, the abuse department or network administrators at the organization where the attack is originating. This group may or may not be responsive and may not take responsibility for fixing the problem.

Furthermore, what happens if the attack is not a simple DoS from one system, but a DDoS from a number of systems distributed across the Internet? Your woes are now multiplied by the number of DDoS agents the attacker has employed. Each of these systems needs to be disabled. If they are on different carriers and in different organizations, you must deal with a large number of people to end the attack.

One final situation that has not yet occurred but easily could is that a really intelligent attacker could design a DDoS network that uses a larger number of agents spread widely across the Internet. The controller could dynamically change the source of the DDoS to any subset of these agents at any time. If the DDoS had a large enough pool of agents to use and was constantly changing, it would be nearly impossible to stop. Simply shutting down the network connection from one agent would not influence the overall effectiveness of the DDoS attack, as another agent would automatically take its place. It's probably just a matter of time before such an attack occurs.

Some companies are attempting to find solutions to their susceptibility to DoS attacks. Many of these solutions involve alliances with a number of companies working together to develop a product that will detect DDoS agents and stop them from attacking. The implementation of this product would most likely need to be rolled out on many devices, as the attacks will be stopped locally. For example, the product would be deployed on firewalls or routers, and if the device detected the pattern of activity identifying a DoS attack from a local system, that system would be quarantined.

Summary

The information presented in this chapter is meant to be somewhat intimidating. Computer security is an extremely broad topic, and I want you to develop a healthy regard for its complexities. Administrators must know how to protect their data from both internal and external attackers, while still providing trusted users with access to the resources necessary to perform their jobs. While remaining vigilant to attack from any direction, administrators must also learn to recognize and defend their systems from a variety of attacks. A detailed security plan, covering both internal and external security requirements, is essential for any successful administrator.

In the following chapters of this book, you'll discover a variety of tools that will help you monitor, secure, and maintain your Windows Server 2003 computer systems and network. When properly implemented and maintained, the security features available in Windows Server 2003 provide a secure connected computing environment.

✦   ✦   ✦

Network and System Security Overview

Securing a network is an extensive job that requires ongoing attention and unfaltering vigilance. One unnoticed change could cause a critical hole in your security.

You can look at the security of your network and systems many different ways. Different people have different trains of thought when it comes to the best way to secure systems. The safest way to look at security, however, is the most conservative way. If you aren't a highly experienced security expert, you really don't have much to go on unless you plan thoroughly.

The topics of planning and documentation come up repeatedly in this book (you'll get tired of hearing about it soon). The best way to have an insecure network is to implement systems without planning or documentation.

When you plan something out, whether it's an addition to the network or a total redesign, you can look at the entire situation objectively and make the best decisions based on the factors that you can predict. If you try to implement without planning first, you're rolling the systems out under stress, and you're far more likely to make mistakes or omissions.

Documentation is the other important part of planning a rollout. Nobody wants to write a system spec or an operations guide while there is other more interesting stuff to play with, such as the new Widget XP. However, getting into the habit of documenting everything properly is the most helpful thing you can do for yourself.

With more and more distributed systems and a trend towards more cheap systems rather than fewer expensive systems, implementations often happen without documentation. A contributing factor is that many of these low cost small footprint systems come preinstalled with all the software needed to get up and running. They are essentially plug and play, with only the IP address having to be configured. Few are willing to spend a few hours documenting a system when it only takes five minutes to set it up, even if the document outlines a standard that spans all of the systems. When something breaks, all that can be done is to restore the system state back to what it was when the system was new. This obviously doesn't promote security.

You will find that the more secure you attempt to make your network, the more difficult the task will become. The more ports and settings you lock down, the more that will break. You need to do extensive lab testing before making changes unless you want to cause outages and downtime.

This chapter provides an overview of the components of a secure network architecture. The information provided is not a strict guide, merely recommendations. You will need to customize a plan for your network design and the requirements of your organization.

Requirements for a Secure Network

Taking a conservative approach to securing your network demands a number of key requirements. Secure systems are only one of the requirements; others include the following:

✦ A multi-level security architecture

✦ Secure network access points

✦ Secure applications

Many networks administrators rely on a single layer of security. It is dangerous, but surprisingly common. The most common single layer to be relied upon is the firewall between the internal and public networks, but a firewall has inherent flaws. To provide access to systems inside the firewall, ports must be opened. Those open ports essentially have no security at all. Stateful inspection and application filtering provide more security on open ports, but they still provide access to the system.

 Note   Stateful inspection is a firewall process that examines incoming packets to a network connection to determine whether the packets are legitimate. Applications and protocols generate certain predictable packet information that indicates the current state of the network connection. Using stateful inspection, the firewall tracks the status of each network connection and analyzes the packets for expected connection information. For example, when a user initiates a session with an Internet Web site, the initial TCP packet from the user's computer contains certain flags that clearly indicate the packet is a request to initiate communication. The response packet from the target computer follows a predictable format as well. The packet communication between the two computers follows a predictable pattern that the firewall analyzes and tracks to determine the current state of communication between the two devices. If the firewall intercepts an incoming packet on this network connection that does not follow the predicted pattern of reply/response (in other words, the packet information is not consistent with the current state of the network connection), the firewall discards the packet and does not allow it to reach the computer on the private network.

Another problem with having only a single layer of security (a firewall in this case) is that if that layer fails, everything else is wide open. If a new exploit was discovered that opened the firewall up completely, the single layer of security would be useless and the insecure systems would be exposed.

In addition to planning the multi-level architecture, the security of each level is important. The network is made up of three sections:

✦ The public network

✦ The demilitarized zone (DMZ)

✦ The internal network

Firewalls are used to control traffic flow between each of these networks. A strong firewall policy should be in place, as no traffic should flow into the internal network, outgoing traffic from the internal network should be highly restricted, and traffic into the DMZ should be controlled so that only necessary connections can be made.

Individual system security is the next key factor. If an attacker manages to gain access to your network by disabling the firewall or by compromising another system on the same network, each system should be able to hold its own ground against an attack. Without proper system security, a compromise on one network layer would allow the compromise of all systems on that layer.

Application security is the last requirement. Application security varies based on the type of application. Database servers require strong password policies, client/server or multi-tier applications should use secure tunnels to transfer data, and all applications should have their administrative interfaces secured.

A multi-level security structure

A good way of looking at network security is as a multi-level architecture. Figure 2-1 shows a diagram of a multi-level security architecture.

When doing the planning for your network security, you should always imagine what would happen if one entire level of your multi-level structure was lost. A level could fail if it were compromised due to an attack, or even due to a misconfiguration. The failure of a single level would open up the next layer to attack, but other security layers are still providing protection. For example, if a firewall failed outside the DMZ (the outermost layer), the systems in the DMZ would be vulnerable to attack but they would still be protected by their system and application security. With the DMZ penetrated and no longer acting as a protective barrier, the internal network firewall (as the next layer of defense) would now be vulnerable to attack from the Internet. But unless this firewall is breached, the internal systems would be protected by the firewall as well as their own system and application security.

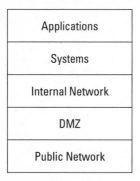

Figure 2-1: Break down your network architecture into different levels when planning for security.

In another example, if the system security failed on an internal server, it would still be protected from attack by the firewall and DMZ above, and the application would still be secure due to its own security. Other neighboring systems and applications would also still be secure with their system and application security.

This multi-level architecture is known as the *Defense-in-Depth* principle. Defense-in-Depth refers to the idea that security must be provided by several layers, and the more layers, the more security is provided. The inverse of this is that no one layer provides adequate security.

Plan your security architecture as a multi-level design, but plan the security of each level as if it was the only security on the network. By thinking like this, you can maximize the security at each level and not expect the next higher level to provide protection.

A History Lesson

Hundreds of years ago, the entrances to walled towns were protected by a gate on the outside, followed by a narrow passage, followed by another gate. If enemy troops broke through the outer gate, they were forced into the narrow passage where they were easy targets for the archers perched on the walls above, and they still had to deal with the second gate into the town. The DMZ is similar to the narrow passageway. Even if an attacker gets into the DMZ, he cannot directly access the internal network without a struggle. Unfortunately, there is no way to place archers in the DMZ.

Public network

When considering a security architecture, the outermost layer of defense is the public (or untrusted) network layer. Devices such as routers, switches, and the outside interfaces of your firewall sit on this level. Devices on the public network layer must be hardened in a number of ways.

✦ Firewalls should have remote access disabled on their public interface(s).

✦ Routers and switches should either use serial console access only (through a serial port concentrator if you have several devices) or use a secure form of remote access such as Secure Shell (SSH) if it is supported.

✦ Using telnet for remote access is not recommended because it is susceptible to packet sniffing to grab passwords as traffic is transmitted in clear text and most telnet daemons are easier to attack than SSH.

Telnet daemons are easier to attack than SSH because they use clear text user authentication and send traffic in clear text. SSH uses encrypted user authentication and encrypted host authentication and encrypts all traffic. SSH is susceptible to man-in-the-middle attacks (during which an attacker intercepts packets on a network connection), but it is extremely difficult to decrypt the data, especially if a strong key is used.

Note SSH is an application (and a protocol) used to get a shell on a remote machine, similar to telnet.

Aside from remote access, devices in the outermost layer must be kept up to date with the latest software revisions. By keeping the software on your routers, switches, and firewalls up to date, you can minimize the possibility of attacks such as Denial of Service and exploits that can be used to gain access to the units. You should never use beta code on your production devices because it has not been fully tested and secured. You should evaluate all beta code on test servers (nonproduction devices) in a lab environment. After you deem the beta code safe for use, you can introduce it on your production devices. In most cases, you should also wait for a short amount of time after the new version is released (two to four weeks is usually sufficient) before you install it, to give "white-hat" hackers time to test it and discover any major security flaws. The only time this rule should not apply is if there is a known vulnerability in the version of software you are running and you need the newly released version to fix it. You should also test the new version on a device in your lab to ensure that it does not affect any functionality and cause a service outage.

With proper system security in your DMZ and your network equipment, you will be safe from script kiddies, but skilled attackers are usually more determined.

The attacks from the public network can only be made against your systems that have exposure to the outside. This exposure can be thought of as your systems' "profile." A system providing a number of services with plenty of open ports can be thought of as having a high profile, while a server providing a single service and only one open port can be thought of as having a low profile.

High profile servers exposed to the public network are more likely to face attacks by script kiddies, just because there is a higher probability that with numerous open ports, and, thus, more potential traffic, the server will attract attention and one of the open ports will become the target of an attack. The odds of having the single port attacked on a low profile server are lower.

DMZ

The next layer is the demilitarized zone or DMZ. The DMZ is usually provided by the firewall, but a DMZ can also be provided by using two firewalls, one on the outside between the public network and the DMZ and one on the inside between the DMZ and the internal network. A router may be necessary in the DMZ if a proxy server is not in use so that the internal traffic can be routed to the Internet. Systems on the internal network behind a DMZ can often be configured to use private addresses, and the firewall can be configured for Network Address Translation (NAT) to reduce the number of public IP addresses used, especially if a proxy server is in place. With this type of configuration, there is no reason to assign each internal system a public address. Systems in the DMZ are protected by the firewall, but the DMZ has no access to the internal network.

Normally, a DMZ is a one-way proposition. Systems within the internal network can connect to the DMZ, systems on the public network can connect to the DMZ (through access controls and firewall policies), and the DMZ can connect to the public network, but the DMZ cannot connect to the internal network.

The DMZ is often used in a situation where the internal network is isolated from the public network. For example, if a corporation wanted to host its own Web site and a proxy server isolated the rest of the corporation's network, the Web server could be placed in the DMZ.

The reason for placing the Web server in the DMZ is twofold. It is protected from attacks because it is still behind the firewall, and it stops a compromise of that system from leading to compromises of other systems. If the Web server is attacked in the DMZ and successfully compromised, it can only be used to launch attacks against other systems in the DMZ.

If the Web server was on the internal network, a compromise of it (possible because it needs to be accessible from the outside) could lead to a compromise of other internal systems, such as file servers that may hold sensitive data. Placing it in the DMZ isolates it from the more sensitive systems. If the Web server were on the public network, it would be isolated from the internal systems but would be wide open to attack without protection from the firewall.

The proxy server for the internal users would also reside in the DMZ. A proxy server is used for a number of reasons, including the security of internal users and content and access control. With the proxy server on the DMZ, it is possible to implement stricter access controls for the internal network. All outgoing traffic can be blocked unless it is destined for the proxy server.

The DMZ is an important part of many networks. A number of systems are candidates for residing on the DMZ, including the following:

✦ Web Servers

✦ Mail Servers

✦ Proxy Servers

✦ DNS Servers

Some networks are not candidates for a DMZ, however. For example, for Internet service providers (ISPs), as well as other organizations with large amounts of incoming traffic, a DMZ would be cumbersome because the number of internal servers is small compared to the number of servers providing services to the outside. It would be possible to implement, but a large number of systems would be placed in the DMZ with only a few in the internal network, so it may be a wasted effort. It would probably be easier to manage firewall policies if all systems were inside.

Another location where a DMZ would be unnecessary is a data center. There are no internal systems at a data center; the whole point is to provide access to the internal systems from the public network. Firewalls are still vital, but the DMZ becomes redundant.

Internal network

The internal network consists of the switches and routers where all of your trusted (internal) servers and workstations reside. This is the most important part of the network. While you may think that a good firewall is enough protection for your internal network, that does not address the problem of internal threats, and as good as any firewall is, it is not a complete solution and may have unknown vulnerabilities or even a misconfiguration.

The internal network is ideally separate from the outside. No traffic should be allowed into the internal network at all. The safest configuration is to have all Internet traffic channeled through a proxy server. The proxy server, as discussed in the previous section, provides security and content and access control. Internet connections such as Web browsing are channeled through the proxy, and connections to servers in the DMZ such as mail servers are allowed directly to those systems. By restricting all other access, users cannot bypass the content and access controls in place on the proxy server and attackers cannot establish direct connections to the internal systems.

As mentioned earlier, the internal network is a good place to use NAT. As no connections are being made to any of the internal systems from the outside and all other connections are made through the proxy server, it is a viable option to assign only private IP addresses to the internal systems.

Note Network Address Translation (NAT) is used to translate private IP addresses on the inside of the network to public IP addresses on the outside. NAT can be used to assign a single external IP address to any number of internal systems. Configuring NAT on a Windows-based Internet Security and Acceleration (ISA) Server is discussed in Chapter 17.

NAT provides an element of security and conserves public IP addresses. The security provided by NAT is such that without any port translation from the outside, it is impossible to connect from the public network to the internal network, even if the firewalls were not in place. Connections to private IP addresses cannot be routed over the Internet so an attacker cannot reach the inside. NAT is not, however, an answer to all of your security problems because enabling port translation on the device performing the NAT allows connections to the internal network. Employing a firewall is still important.

NAT also saves precious IP addresses. IP address allocations are becoming more difficult to obtain as addresses become scarcer. The implementation of schemes with larger address spaces, such as IPv6, is taking longer than expected and the current address space is largely allocated. NAT is a temporary fix to the IP address space issue, as many of the allocated addresses would become freed if more internal networks were switched to private addresses.

The internal network should be a secure place, safe from external attackers. With a DMZ, firewalls, and NAT in place, no external attacker should be able to access your internal network (or it will at least be very difficult). The problems faced in the internal network are different.

Chapter 1 discussed the differences between internal and external threats. With all of the previously discussed security features in place to control entrance and egress from your network (such as proxy servers and firewalls), external threats should not be able to get in and internal users should not be able to get out except through the provided channels.

However, the systems with the most sensitive data, such as your file servers, are susceptible to the most common attacker, your own users.

Internal attackers have a number of advantages over external attackers. They are already trusted users, especially in the domain model of Microsoft Windows. With Active Directory (introduced in Windows 2000), access control was greatly upgraded with the introduction of group policies. With the introduction of safer authentication methods, such as Kerberos in the domain model, the internal network can be made even safer.

Note   Kerberos is an authentication protocol that uses encrypted tickets to grant access to a requested service. The name Kerberos is taken from a character in Greek mythology—the three-headed dog Kerberos guarded the gates of Hades.

Access controls are arguably the most important part of internal network security. You can control access to particular files and even specific systems. A server holding accounting data, for example, should not be accessible except to accounting personnel. Files on a generic file server belonging to accounting should have the same restrictions.

Access controls require a lot of ongoing maintenance. With the proper configuration of security groups and administrative delegation provided by Active Directory, you can ease this burden. For example, the accounting manager can be responsible for controlling access to files and setting group membership.

A number of other considerations should be made on the internal network. Password policies should be maintained. Strong passwords should be enforced along with scheduled password changes. A problem that comes along with strong passwords that are regularly changed, however, is user apathy. Users who are forced to use strong passwords and change them on a regular basis are likely to simply write their passwords on a sticky note and paste it to their monitor or under their keyboard. The protagonist in the movie "War Games" knew that his school administration wrote the password to the computer holding the grades on a note in the office and purposefully got in trouble so that he could look at the current password and change his grades.

Systems

Physical security is also important to the internal network. Most organizations house their servers and network devices in secure facilities protected by locked doors. In many cases, ID cards and access codes are required for physical access to these data centers and server rooms. But it's important that a locked door not be the only thing standing between an intruder and your valuable data.

Restricted access to the servers is essential because a number of attacks are possible when physical access is provided, such as booting another operating system from a floppy disk. There are NTFS drivers for DOS that can be used to access files that are normally protected by booting a server from a DOS disk and accessing the NTFS volume. If internal servers are not in a secure location, they should have their disk and CD-ROM drives disabled and BIOS passwords set. You can even get diskette drive locks that are inserted into the drive and locked with a key so that a disk cannot be inserted. Workstations should use the same precautions, especially if the workstations are shared between more than one user. Encrypted File System (EFS) is a partial solution with shared workstations; it allows the encryption of files on disk so that other users cannot access them, even if booting from a DOS disk with an NTFS driver.

See Chapter 8 for more information on EFS and encryption.

The systems are nearly the final layer in the security architecture. System security is usually your last line of defense against an attack. The level of security varies on individual systems on the internal network. Each type of server on your network requires its own security plan. For example, a database server requires different security hardening than a file/print server. (Server hardening is a commonly used expression to describe implementing and configure security on the servers.) For example, most workstations do not need to be as secure as file or mail servers.

Applications

The applications are the most granular level in the multi-level design. Your applications, whether they are databases or multi-tier Web applications, must all be secure.

Application security takes a number of forms, as many applications behave differently. Databases must have strong password protection and access controls, client-server or multi-tier applications should have secure data channels between each layer, DNS servers should be secured against illegal zone updates, and so on.

Entrance and egress points

Entrance and egress points refer to the logical locations where traffic passes between your internal network and the public network. In smaller networks this is often one point (the firewall), but it can be a number of different points, such as a firewall, a number of different firewalls, or one or more proxy servers. Figure 2-2 shows two networks: one complex network with multiple points of entrance and egress and one simple network with only one shared entrance/egress point.

The entrance and egress points are the "choke point" where all traffic must travel if it is transitioning between the internal and external networks. Because of this, it is an ideal point to implement a security solution. Implementing security at these points can limit the traffic that reaches your systems. This is usually the first point at which security is implemented, although sometimes security measures are implemented on the network edge routers, the next step out.

A system implemented to control traffic flow between networks, at the entrance and egress points of the network in this example, is known as a firewall.

Firewalls are discussed at length in Chapter 16.

Firewalls are simply hosts that inspect each packet traveling across their network interfaces and determine their disposition. Based on a set of rules configured in the system, packets are either allowed to pass or denied. Denied packets are normally discarded, and events can be logged when this occurs. By looking through these events for patterns, you can often locate attacks against your network. This is basically a manual implementation of an intrusion detection system.

Your entry and egress points should be controlled in a number of ways. Firewalls and proxy servers are used to control traffic flow. Working from the outside in, the firewall will block all incoming traffic except to specified ports on servers on the DMZ. These servers may provide a number of services to the public network, such as Web or mail. All other incoming traffic is discarded. This firewall will also allow outgoing traffic from the DMZ, preferably only on the specified ports. Most incoming connections will have their responses allowed out as a feature of the firewall, but the proxy server will need to be explicitly allowed access.

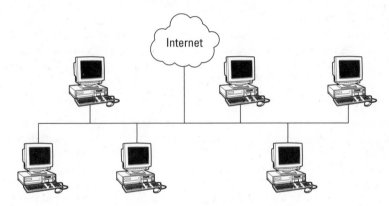

Simple Network One Ingress/Egress Point

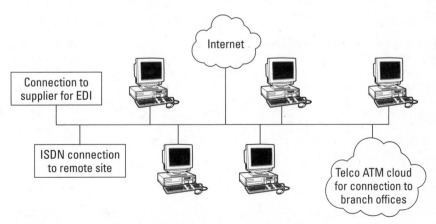

Complete Network Four Ingress/Egress Points

Figure 2-2: Some complex networks have multiple entrance and egress points while others have only one.

The point between the DMZ and the internal network will also have a firewall although the two firewalls may be integrated into one. This firewall will not allow any traffic into the internal network. It will also block all outgoing traffic from the internal network unless it is destined for the proxy server. It may also provide NAT functionality for the internal network if private IP addresses are being used.

The firewalls on the outside and inside of the DMZ control all traffic except outgoing traffic from the internal network. The proxy server controls this traffic. The proxy server runs at the application layer and inspects all traffic. By operating at the application layer, it can perform such functions as content and access control for outgoing traffic. In many networks without a proxy, most traffic is allowed out of the network and no content or access controls are in place.

With a proxy server in place, only the applications that you decide to allow can access the outside network. You will probably want to restrict "bandwidth killer" applications such as peer-to-peer file sharing, as well as "productivity killer" applications such as instant messaging programs. Many organizations have a policy in place where all but a few basic applications (Web browsing, mail, FTP) are restricted unless there is a good business case for allowing access. A deny-by-default policy can reduce administrative overhead.

In addition to access controls, proxy servers can implement content controls. Some organizations implement policies that restrict users from viewing adult or other objectionable content. You can also restrict other content that may have high bandwidth usage such as streaming media.

Some proxy servers also include content caching. With forward caching requested objects are cached to disk on the server. Subsequent requests for the content within the time to live are directed to the cache instead of to the Internet, reducing latency and bandwidth usage.

 Caching is explained in detail in Chapter 16.

Secure systems

Within the firewalls, on the internal network, traffic is usually free to travel to any other point on the network. This is obviously a problem if the firewall's security is breached. The next security step inside the firewall is security on the system itself.

A system can face attacks a number of ways, but there are three major methods through which an attack is likely to occur:

✦ **A firewall breach** — In the case of a firewall breach, which is somewhat uncommon, all systems inside that firewall are open to attack on any port. With the firewall non-functional, all traffic is free to flow in and out of the network. An attacker can locate any vulnerability on a system and exploit it to gain access.

✦ **Systems and ports open to the outside**—Without breaching the firewall, an attacker can mount attacks on systems and ports that are open to the outside. For example, a Web server will allow incoming traffic on TCP port 80. On many firewalls, any traffic would be allowed to reach that server on TCP port 80, legitimate or malicious. By attacking on open ports, the attacker can send any data and exploit any vulnerabilities existing on the services running on those ports. These vulnerabilities can include out-of-band traffic such as a buffer overflow, but can also involve legitimate data as in the case of a CGI vulnerability in any scripts running on a Web server.

✦ **Compromised systems on the internal network**—Attacks through open ports lead into the next possible attack, which is that mounted from a system on the internal network that has been compromised through other means. If an attacker were to compromise one system through an open port and gain full control of that machine, he could use it as a staging point to attack other systems that are not open to the outside, as is commonly the case with file servers.

Each of these situations stresses the importance of having secure systems. Simply having one layer of security, such as a firewall, cannot guarantee that the systems will not face attacks. Even the best firewalls cannot protect against every attack, especially those disguised in legitimate traffic.

Having secure systems is not an easy process. The key to securing systems is to reduce their profile. Although it is not feasible, other than being disconnected from the network, the most secure system is that with no services running. With no services running, the system has no profile (that is, it cannot be seen on the network). Opening only one service exposes the system to attack. Each additional service opened creates more potential security vulnerabilities are exposed to attack.

Cross-Reference You can find further discussion on securing systems in Chapters 3, 6, and 7.

You can reduce a system's profile through two methods. The first method occurs during the initial installation of the system and is known as *minimization*. The goal of minimization is to install the absolute least number of software and operating system components possible. Fewer components equal fewer potential security vulnerabilities in the future.

The second method is by disabling unnecessary services. Through the process of minimization, a number of services are installed that cannot be deselected. These services that are not needed can be disabled to reduce the profile of the system.

There are often a number of services that can be disabled depending on the role of the server. An application or mail server may not require file and print sharing to be enabled. Likewise, a number of other services such as the print spooler and remote registry services can be disabled. The key is to have the minimum possible number of components installed and the minimum number of services enabled.

Another aspect of securing the system is determining its trust relationships. Adding a system to a domain is convenient for users and administrators alike but causes a number of problems. Systems in a domain are inherently trusted and also trust other systems. Domain logins will work on any system in the domain. After an attacker gains administrative access to a domain system, he essentially has that access across the entire domain.

With a file or print server, which provides services to internal users, domain membership is important. That inherent trust allows the configuration of Access Control Lists (ACLs) that function for all domain users and all users can access the server as long as they're not denied that access. A Web server that is serving intranet content would also be part of the domain. The intranet will most likely be secured by username and password, and by being on the domain, the intranet server will allow login using the users' regular domain login.

There are a number of applications that you do not want on servers that are domain members. Any applications that do not have a requirement for domain authentication should not be on domain member servers; they should be on standalone servers. The administrative overhead of using standalone servers is higher than that for domain servers because you must maintain local user accounts and local policies. Domain policies and user accounts will obviously not function on a standalone server because it is not a member of a domain. The higher overhead comes with the advantage of having systems that are not trusted by other systems and cannot be used for attacks on other domain members as easily.

The rule for servers should be that if a server does not require domain authentication, it should not be a domain member. The same password policies should apply to the standalone servers, however, and strong passwords and password changes should be enforced.

Secure applications

Applications can come under attack in a number of ways. Unfortunately, many applications are shoddily coded or coded by programmers without the knowledge or experience required to write secure software. This leaves many programs open to the same common vulnerabilities, such as format string vulnerabilities and directory traversal vulnerabilities, especially Web-based applications. (A format string vulnerability is a malformed line of programming code through which an attacker can gain access to or take control of a system. A directory traversal vulnerability allows an attacker to traverse directories on a hard drive or Web site, also allowing access to the data files stored in those directories.) Even worse, Web-based applications are often in an insecure multi-tier or client-server layout, which leaves the database and middleware open to attack as well. An attack on an e-commerce Web site with such a design would be especially damaging because credit card and other customer data could be lost.

Each application has its own requirements for security and some cannot be secured at all.

Cross-Reference Application security for some general applications is discussed in Chapter 7.

Each application has different methods of making it secure; however some commonalities exist across most applications available today. Many applications include a separate user interface for administration. Some of these interfaces integrate with Windows domain authentication or local user authentication (on a standalone system), but others require their own usernames and passwords. This can be an advantage because an attacker with a domain login cannot use that information to compromise the application. Applications should follow the same password policy as regular domain and local users. Strong passwords and regular password changes should be enforced. Each user accessing the interface should have their own username for auditing purposes, if possible.

This policy is even more relevant to database servers. While some database servers use an integrated Windows authentication scheme, others use a separate username and password set. It is very important to maintain separate logins for each user accessing the system as well as enabling auditing so that in the event of an anomaly, it can be traced to the offending user. Access control lists (ACLs) are also important with database servers. Maintaining good ACLs prevents users from accessing databases or writing to tables that they shouldn't be.

Database servers and multi-tier applications use some sort of data transfer protocol. Database servers usually have a proprietary protocol and many multi-tier Web applications use protocols such as XML over HTTP connections. You should also secure these communication methods.

Some database communication protocols provide secure communications between hosts by default. But with some Web applications, data is often passed between client and server (often a database server) in readable formats, such as XML carried over HTTP. To secure this data, you can change the communication protocol to an encrypted form such as HTTPS (which uses a secure connection to pass data between client and server) or use a secure data format such as Security Services Markup Language (S2ML), a yet-to-be-standardized secure version of XML. Security becomes even more important to these applications when the data is shared outside the organization such as in a business-to-business (B2B) or Electronic Data Interchange (EDI) situation. Both B2B and EDI involve transferring data between two organizations across a network. Transferring data to an untrusted party or over an untrusted link is always a dangerous situation and using a secure transport and secure data format will reduce the peril.

Note HTTPS is essentially HTTP running over an SSL connection. SSL (Secure Sockets Layer protocol) uses public key encryption to create a secure communication channel between client and server.

S2ML (Security Services Markup Language) is a common markup language that allows companies to securely transmit authentication and authorization information in e-commerce transactions.

Another method exists for securing data transfer between tiers in an application. Using encryption significantly taxes a system's resources and may not always be a viable alternative. You can obtain security on such links by isolating them. If you use a dedicated point-to-point private network such as a simple Ethernet crossover cable between dedicated network adapters in each tier and use private addressing, it makes it much more difficult for the data to be stolen in transfer and also makes for a faster connection.

Other applications, such as DNS, require security. If you are running an authoritative DNS server (at an ISP for example, or for your company's domain) there are a number of steps you should take for security. Restricting zone transfers and zone updates is important to avoid illegal zone update attacks or zone transfers where an attacker can learn the entire layout of your network.

Web and FTP servers also require their own security considerations. It is important to ensure that they are not vulnerable to common attacks such as directory traversal. You should also ensure that file and directory permissions are set correctly and that anonymous FTP has the proper restrictions so that unauthorized users cannot access or overwrite files.

Note   Every application has its particular quirks when it comes to configuring it securely. It is important to refer to the application's documentation as well as using your own common sense.

Methods for Compromising a System

For you to gain a full understanding of system security, you should understand the methods by which a system can be compromised. After you are familiar with these vulnerabilities, you will be better prepared to protect against them, in addition to having a better understanding of the internals of your systems and applications.

There are many different ways to exploit weaknesses in a target system. New exploits are found every day, but the discovery of a new class of vulnerability is rare. Almost every vulnerability is the result of either poor programming or something being overlooked in the program design.

Most vulnerability disclosure announcements include proof-of-concept code to demonstrate how to take advantage of a vulnerability. For example, when a string format vulnerability is documented, the author includes sample code so that the reader can see how the vulnerability works (proving the concept) and how to correct the code to prevent the vulnerability. Most of these vulnerability announcements are made to the Bugtraq mailing list, which is an excellent list to subscribe to.

Cross-Reference   See Appendix B for more information on Bugtraq.

White-hat hackers working for security companies discover most of these vulnerabilities. These experts usually notify the software vendor prior to releasing information about the vulnerability to the public. This gives the software vendor time to devise a patch or fix for the vulnerability and communicate it to their customers. When news of the vulnerability is released, the white-hats include proof-of-concept code. This code is rarely a complete exploit that can be copied and used against a target system. But malicious attackers modify the proof-of-concept code to create exploits that they publish to Web sites or distribute via e-mail. Now everyone from black-hat hackers to script kiddies have access to a fully packaged exploit that they use to launch malicious attacks.

 The merits of full disclosure are discussed elsewhere in this book, but stopping full disclosure would not stop the development of exploits.

Most known attacks fit into one of the following categories:

✦ Information leaks

✦ Brute force attacks

✦ Buffer overflows

✦ Format string vulnerabilities

✦ Directory traversal vulnerabilities

✦ Man-in-the-middle attacks

✦ Social engineering

Information leaks

A leak of information about the configuration of your systems and network will often precipitate an attack. A number of exploits for various pieces of software and hardware allow an attacker to view configuration information on that device.

Information leaks most often come from firewalls and network equipment. Any time an attacker can gain information about the inside of your network, he has the basis to begin an attack. For example, a well-known information leak vulnerability in certain versions of the BIND DNS server discloses environment variables. Similarly, tools such as nmap and QueSO (discussed in Chapter 1) reveal operating system and port information. Information leaks come in various forms — in fact, some attackers gather information from messages innocently posted on administrative support forums.

Many network devices and firewalls come with SNMP enabled and the SNMP read-only community string set to "public" by default. An attacker could use an SNMP management system to poll your devices for information (a common occurrence). Many devices also come with the default SNMP read/write string set to "private," which can be even more damaging in the hands of a skilled attacker as he can now write information to the SNMP object. It is considered best practice for network managers to change all the community strings to a value that is not easily guessed. As well, vendors are getting better at addressing such defaults and disabling these features or making them accessible from only the inside interface of the device.

Note   SNMP stands for Simple Network Management Protocol. It is used for network management and is capable of reading and writing configuration data on a number of devices including routers, firewalls, and servers.

Even if you attempt to prevent information leaks, there are still ways to get information about your network by looking at routing information on the Internet and so on. These things can't be avoided. It is best to just take all the steps you can to avoid these vulnerabilities and not be concerned with those you can't. Hopefully, the other layers of security that you've implemented will take care of any shortcomings.

Brute force attacks

Many people immediately think of password cracking when they think of security vulnerabilities. Password cracking is a brute force attack in which a hacker tries a combination of usernames and passwords until he eventually gains access to a system. Although best practices for password policy are widely known, many organizations are too lax or too intimidated to implement them. For example, some companies don't require an eight-character password because the users are accustomed to four-character passwords and the users got upset when administrators tried to implement the change. Or password history policies are too short and allow the same passwords to be used repeatedly because changing passwords is considered inconvenient. Really! It happens more often than you'd imagine.

A brute force attack through password cracking is one of the first methods any attacker—whether black-hat or script kiddie—may try. With lax security policies so widespread, the odds are pretty good that an attacker can gain access using a list of commonly known IDs and passwords. For example, if an attacker wants access to a Windows XP system he encounters on the Internet, it's very likely that Administrator or Guest will be valid usernames. And it's just as likely that a handful of commonly used passwords (such as "administrator," "password," or "football") will be valid as well. Best practice dictates changing the name of default accounts such as Administrator and Guest so that an attacker cannot guess them. But surprisingly few administrators actually follow this practice.

While it might initially seem unlikely that an attacker would target your lowly Windows XP home computer, rest assured that you're a prime target. Your home system probably contains several tidbits that an attacker might want—your social security number, address, bank account information, and so on. Or the attacker might want access to your machine to use as an unwitting host in a Denial of Service (DoS) attack, which I describe later in this section.

If you aren't monitoring your systems for failed logon attempts, the brute force attacker has an infinite amount of time to find a valid ID/password combination. As well, the attacker can use one of several widely available password-cracking applications to automate his brute force attempts and be logged on to the system in minutes. The use of these applications is more common when the targeted system or network is widely known or high profile, such as a corporate or government entity. Or an attacker may turn to a password cracking application when you implement strong security on your system and he is unable to easily guess his way in. Thus, properly configured audit logs are an important security device as well. An audit log showing a sequence of failed logon attempts reveals the evidence of a brute force attack. (It also reveals the identity of those users who just never remember their password — but you're probably well acquainted with them already.)

A second form of brute force attack that has become quite widely known is the Denial of Service (DoS) attack or Distributed Denial of Service attack (DDoS). (For brevity, I refer to them both as a DoS attack.) The DoS attack is a bit different from most attacks in that the attacker isn't trying to gain access to the system, but is instead attempting to bring the server or Web site down (thus denying access to all users). DoS attacks are commonly launched against government or political sites or against very popular sites such as Yahoo! or eBay. A Denial of Service attack sends a continuous stream of malformed service requests to a target computer or Web site. The target is overcome with the requests for service and becomes non-responsive or "crashes." A DDoS is similar, but the attack is launched from a series of hijacked computers distributed across the Internet. The attacker first compromises a number of systems, planting a program that will later send malformed service requests to a targeted host. (Sometimes these systems are compromised manually, but many times the attacker writes and distributes a virus to spread the DDoS payload.) After the attacker feels he has a sufficient number of computers involved, he initiates the attack against his target. Again, this is a brute force technique designed to render the targeted site inactive. DDoS attacks are often coordinated by organized groups who consider themselves activists and attack a site or server in the name of a political cause.

Buffer overflows

Buffer overflows are an extremely common type of exploit. A buffer overflow occurs when an application has a fixed input buffer and no proper exception-handling method when more data is input than the buffer can handle. For example, an application may accept 128 characters for the "name" field, which the system stores at a designated memory address. If an attacker enters more than 128 characters, an exception occurs within the program. If no proper handling exists for this exception, the extra characters may also be stored in adjacent system memory addresses. An attacker simply adds executable code within those extra character strings, thus passing commands to the system that allow him to gain access.

One of the primary causes of buffer overflows is that the C and C++ programming languages have no automatic bounds checking on array and pointer references. These checks must be added by the programmer — a step that is often overlooked. Several standard string functions also allow buffer overflows.

Those with programming experience may be familiar with a stack, but for the uninitiated, the stack is a location in memory where data can be stored temporarily. Data is placed and removed from the top of the stack (first in last out, or FILO).

Normally, the data in the buffer is placed on the top of the stack, which is usually used for variable storage. The problem with a buffer overflow happens when so much data is placed into the buffer that the data takes up more space in the stack than is expected. The attack data can overwrite legitimate stack data such as the value of other variables.

The most extreme type of buffer overflow is called *stack smashing*. While a normal buffer overflow can be used to change the execution of a program, stack smashing can be used to execute arbitrary code.

The stack always contains a return address. The return address is set when a program executes a function. It is a memory pointer that directs the execution of the program back to the main code when the function is complete. Modifying the return address in the stack can cause the program to return to some arbitrary code placed in the stack. This can be used to launch a shell or backdoor program with which the attacker can gain access to the system.

A similar type of buffer overflow is called a *heap overflow*. The heap is somewhat similar to the stack in its operation, but it holds different types of data and is allocated differently. A heap overflow attack is more difficult to execute than stack smashing because the attacker is required to locate a security-critical variable. This is difficult without the program source code.

A buffer overflow exploit generally works as follows:

  ✦ The attacker identifies a vulnerability to exploit.

  ✦ The attacker writes and compiles the exploit code, or obtains the code on the Internet. There are a number of sources to get this code on the Internet; it has been written for a number of platforms.

  ✦ The attacker runs the code, which pads the buffer with enough characters to fill it and moves the overflow characters (which contain the malicious code) into the memory stack, and the system runs the malicious code.

Buffer overflow vulnerabilities in various applications are well documented on the Internet — the attacker has many to choose from. Unless programmers routinely adopt bounds checking (comparing the length of the character string to be stored against the size of the buffer) or other reliable methods of handling character strings, exploiting buffer overflow vulnerabilities will continue to be a widespread problem. Some modern programming languages now include bounds checking routines and thus prevent buffer overflow vulnerabilities. But as long as legacy applications with buffer overflow problems are in use, attackers will continue to use this form of attack.

Format string vulnerabilities

A format string vulnerability is a class of exploit that first appeared in 1999. A little familiarity with C code helps to understand the format string vulnerability. Consider the proper method of printing a string in C:

```
printf("%s", str);
```

This piece of code uses the format string %s to instruct the program to print a single string, "str." The %s format string means simply "print string." Another, yet incorrect, method of printing the same string, which may be implemented by a less savvy programmer, is as follows:

```
printf(str);
```

By eliminating the format string from the printf function, the specified string is interpreted as if it were the format string. If you assume that the input to that string can be controlled by the user, a malicious attacker could specify a string such as "%x %x %x %x %x" (%x being the format string for "unsigned hexadecimal integer"). This input would cause the program to print the first five values from the top of the stack.

A person can arbitrarily read data from the stack using a format string vulnerability, but that is generally not very useful. An attacker needs to be able to place data onto the stack or alter data on the stack to take control of a program or system. A format string bug (a coding error in a format string of a software program) can allow that to happen as well. Using a format string exploit, it is possible to place any value into any memory location.

The first step is to determine the memory location into which to write the value. This can normally be done using a debugger. The %n format string can be used to write any arbitrary data to the stack. As with a stack smashing attack, a format string bug can be used to change the return address in the stack and point it to another value in the stack. By placing malicious code in the stack and changing the return address, arbitrary code can be executed. This leads to the potential compromise of the entire system.

Directory traversal vulnerabilities

Directory traversal vulnerabilities have been around for many years and are present in many different types of software. Directory traversal vulnerabilities are common on Web and FTP servers, among other services. A directory traversal vulnerability allows an attacker to gain access to a directory on a system to which he is not explicitly granted permission. For example, assume a user has followed a series of hyperlinks to reach a Web page with the following URL, www.foo.tld/ food/breads/breakfast/recipes/. Looking for additional information on this Web site, the user edits the URL to read www.foo.tld/food/breads/breakfast to move from the recipes directory to the breakfast directory. Because security isn't properly configured, the user suddenly sees a directory listing showing all the files in the breakfast directory. The user can access all of the files in the directory, and can initiate a command on the host system by modifying the URL to read `www.foo.tld/food/breads/breakfast/recipes/anycommand.exe`. This vulnerability has a number of limitations, but with the correct information or trial and error, the attacker can gain full access to a system by installing a backdoor.

Directory traversals are common in Web and FTP servers (and other software using directories) for the same reason that buffer overflows proliferate. Programmers often leave out important bounds checking and the user of a program is allowed to do things that were never expected. A Web server should never let you access files below the Web root, but as has been proven several times, some do.

Man-in-the-middle attacks

A man-in-the-middle attack is not an attack on a system, but on the data that a system is transferring. A man-in-the-middle attack is the basis for some cryptographic attacks against protocols such as SSH and SSL and is also a method of stealing information. This type of attack is essentially a way for an attacker to get a copy of all data transferred between a source and target host.

A man-in-the-middle attack is most commonly performed by the attacker spoofing his IP address so that the source host requests are routed to him. The attacker then makes a copy of the information, and forwards the request to the original destination while changing the source address to his own. The target host processes the request and returns the response to the attacker. The attacker copies that data and then forwards the response back to the source host with the original destination's source address.

The client in this scenario has no idea that his session is being routed through the attacker. The attacker is making copies of all of the transmitted data for later consumption. Because the unsuspecting user has no idea that something is amiss — he is receiving the expected responses to his requests — it is usually not necessary to hide the attack from the target host, but it is possible.

While the ability to copy all of the data in the session is an obvious advantage, there are usually easier ways to steal unencrypted data. The man-in-the-middle attack becomes more useful when the attacker is not on a network through which the traffic is passing and regular eavesdropping will not work.

Using this type of attack will result in the attacker having a copy of the entire session. A common use of this type of attack is to steal SSL or SSH sessions. While forcefully decrypting these types of sessions on the fly is not possible, the attacker can use cryptographic attacks against the copies of the sessions and, if successful, have the plaintext information contained within.

Social engineering

Social engineering is a different kind of attack all together. Social engineering refers to an attacker who will contact an unsuspecting user and convince them to provide their password or other information.

A hypothetical social engineering attack might first involve the attacker finding out information about the target company. Good information to get includes the names of people in the IT department, and the names of some people working in non-technical jobs in the company. This information can be discovered through a number of means, including the following:

✦ Simply phoning the company and asking for the information will often work

✦ Reading newspaper or magazine articles or the company annual report

✦ Posing as a salesperson and actually meeting with people inside the company

Information about people in the IT department can even come from information leaks in network devices.

After the attacker has this information, he can use it to his advantage. He only needs to phone a non-technical user in the company posing as someone from the IT department. He then claims there is a problem with the network and requests that user's password. Unsuspecting users are often more than willing to share that information, especially when they think that it is an IT department member on the other end of the line. This can be especially dangerous if the target is someone with access to sensitive data, such as an executive assistant. And this is only the tip of what social engineering involves.

Dumpster diving

The strict definition of social engineering can be expanded to involve physical intrusions as well. Years ago, dumpster diving was common. *Phone phreaks* (attackers who targeted the telephone system) would go to the telephone company offices and literally dive into their dumpsters and look for information. Most printouts and other documentation were not shredded, just thrown out. These phreaks would find miles of line printer paper covered with the information they were looking for, such as maintenance information and passwords. Dumpster diving is less common today because shredders have proliferated.

Gaining physical access

Another example of a physical attack would be gaining access to an office somehow, possibly through another social engineering attack. If the attacker could gain access as an electrician or mover, he would have prime access to information. As much as system administrators try to stop it, many users still write their passwords down and put them in a drawer, under their keyboard, or even stick them to their monitor. By finding the user associated with these passwords, which is as simple as finding a nametag or business card, the attacker can gain a whole list of accounts with which to access your network.

 Note   This attack works just as well for an internal user, who can use the information to launch attacks, making them appear to come from someone else.

Viruses and worms

Another more rampant type of social engineering attack is an e-mail virus or worm. Many of these worms have some way of enticing the recipient to open the e-mail or attachment, such as the promise of something cute or access to adult content. When the user opens the e-mail or attachment, the computer is infected. A well thought out worm will be able to trick many users into opening the message, rapidly spreading it. These worms are getting slightly less common now that several prominent ones have gone around, but there are still an incredibly high number of users who will open messages and attachments without considering the possibility of a virus.

Social engineering is a type of attack that rarely gets coverage in the media and rarely gets addressed by administrators; however, making users aware of social engineering is important because attackers are very aware of it. The only way to possibly secure against a social engineering attack is to train the user base. They should be told what social engineering is, and policies should be in place so that they are instructed never to give out information over the phone and never to leave their passwords written down. The penalties for a violation of such policy should be severe, as the resulting damage from an attack can be severe.

Root Kits and Trojans

After a system is compromised, an attacker will often leave a door open for himself so that he can access the system in the future without going through the process of exploiting the system again. This back door may take many forms, most of which are through "*Trojanned" binaries*. A Trojanned binary is a normal program that has been modified to provide a secret back door to the attacker. This Trojan will replace the standard file and provide the same functionality except for the addition of the back door.

A root kit is a collection of Trojanned binaries that are automatically installed by way of a script onto a system. Root kits are commonly available for most operating systems, including Windows and most versions of Unix.

One of the most famous Trojans (although not a root kit by the strict definition) is BackOrifice. Developed by hackers and now slowly becoming obsolete as a Trojan, it was installed by unsuspecting users running infected files and allowed access to the infected system on a specific TCP port (12345 or 31337 depending on the version). BackOrifice provides remote desktop access as well as access to files on the system.

Root kits are the most common residue left behind after an attack. Many of the binaries in root kits will attach to specific TCP ports so the attacker can later reconnect. Some even contain DDoS agents.

Detecting root kits

You can detect root kits and Trojanned binaries in a number of ways. The most basic but least accurate of these is through your own observations. When connecting to a system, you should be familiar with how the system normally functions and you should be able to notice any differences, although many root kits are fairly clean and do not look obvious.

The next method of detecting root kits and Trojans is through scanning your systems using a security scanner or port mapper. You should maintain a list of the ports that should be open on each of your servers (by doing a baseline scan after the initial build and after any changes are made—see Chapter 4). By doing periodic scans on your systems, you will notice any ports open that are not on your maintained list. These could be indications of root kits in use.

The final and most accurate way to detect a root kit is by using a system state scanner such as Tripwire. Tripwire is available for a number of operating systems, including Windows and Unix. Tripwire is used to create a system state database containing all of the static files on a system such as binaries. This initial state database is encrypted and stored, often offline. On a regular basis, the files on the system are compared to the database created on the fresh system. Any changes are reported.

Other toolkits can also detect root kits. Some virus and security scanners have this capability and specific root kit detection programs are also available. These are usually less helpful than a full system state database system, such as Tripwire, because they are only capable of detecting the root kits for which they are written. Tripwire will detect any change in the system files.

Cleaning up

The only viable option after a compromise where root kits or trojanned binaries have been installed or for any compromise is to reinstall the operating system and all applications.

It is possible to clean up without reinstalling, but you need to think about the consequences. By using Tripwire or comparing the files on the compromised system, you will most likely find the binaries that have been changed and copy the originals from a known good system. You will probably get most, if not all, of the bad files.

The problem occurs when you miss a file or two. The attacker will still have access to your system.

The extra expenditure of effort is more than worth the extra security gained by performing a fresh installation on the compromised system.

Summary

In this chapter, you learned that good security architecture involves multiple layers of defense and includes system security, application security, internal network security, firewalls, and possibly a DMZ. To adequately protect all your data and devices, each security layer functions independently. Thus, if an intruder breaches your network's firewall, good application and system security remain barriers to further damage. Similarly, if a system is breached, strong password policy and ACLs still protect data stored on the system.

To fully understand how to better protect computer systems from attack, administrators learn about system vulnerabilities and common methods of exploiting them. Intruders use a number of techniques to attack a system or network, including:

✦ Buffer overflows

✦ Brute force attacks

✦ Format string vulnerabilities

✦ Directory traversal vulnerabilities

✦ Man-in-the-middle attacks

Finally, if all layers of security are breached, an intruder often leaves behind a destructive payload — root kits, Trojans, and viruses. Cleaning up after a security breach is time consuming and often involves completely reinstalling the operating system and applications. Unless you implement the appropriate security architecture to protect your computing environment, rebuilding compromised systems will become a too common occurrence.

In Chapter 3, you'll learn to design a multi-level security architecture for your environment. Subsequent chapters show you how to implement the security architecture using the features found in Windows Server 2003.

✦   ✦   ✦

Security Architecture Planning

C H A P T E R

3

Planning and implementing a secure environment for
your servers is a complex process and must be meticu-
lously documented. Without documentation and the appropriate policies to follow the documented processes, any security
architecture is worthless. Planning a secure environment will
seem simple compared to maintaining secure systems, especially when you have more than one person with administrative access to those systems.

The concept of *standardization* appears frequently in this
chapter, and includes all parts of your systems from hardware
to operating system configuration to application configuration. In some cases, standardization is not possible, and it is
not a requirement for system security. In actuality, system
security has few requirements. Standardization, among other
security procedures in this book, facilitates the maintenance
of security. In most cases, you can obtain a secure system in
more than one way. What is offered in this book is the best
way to obtain secure systems and, most importantly, to keep
those systems secure through day-to-day operation.

The first step is to design the initial security for your systems.
This design will include the initial server build and the steps
you will take to secure the system before it is put into production. These steps will become the build document used to
build all new servers that have the same function (that is,
Web servers or mail servers).

The next planning phase is building an operational plan that
will enable you to maintain server security on a day-to-day
basis. This is the most difficult part of planning a complete
security architecture. Making minor changes to systems, such

as the addition of new services, can drastically affect the system's security. Making these changes without considering the security implications is a common occurrence when a number of system administrators have access to the same systems.

The final stage of planning is to implement a proper change control procedure. Implementing change control is often difficult because buy-in is needed from a number of groups. Front line system administrators are often resistant to implementing change control because doing so seems to make their jobs more difficult. What they don't realize is that their jobs actually get easier because problem solving is facilitated by the documentation of all changes previously made.

You gain two advantages by implementing all three stages of planning. The first advantage is consistency. All systems built to your specifications should be secure, as they should all be configured the same. As an extra benefit, administration is made easier when the systems are consistent. Instead of having to remember each system separately, the system administrators only need to remember one configuration with a few specific changes for each system, such as applications.

The second benefit of well-documented systems design is that almost anyone can build a system to the specifications. When building systems, most people have different ways of building the same type of system. These differences can lead to security lapses and more difficult administration for other admins who would have built the system a different way. A specific design requires everyone to learn only one configuration instead of having to deal with a different setup by each person.

 Note   The documentation and planning in this chapter does not apply specifically to security. Most of what is discussed is standard design and operational procedures. The focus can be on security, stability, or the reduction of administrative overhead, but the planning and documentation is the same.

Following a proper planning and operational procedure, as laid out in this chapter, will not only create a more secure environment, but will also reduce downtime and administration across all systems.

Secure Server Architecture Design

The first thing to remember when you're designing your security architecture is to document the entire process. The final version of the document you create will become the procedural guide for anyone creating a new system that will go on your network. The document should be clear and concise, and you should make sure it is understandable by anyone you foresee building systems for your network. It should contain a step-by-step process for everything to be done to a new system, as well as some description of what's going on. A thorough design document should contain the following:

- ✦ Title page
- ✦ Introduction
- ✦ Nomenclature
- ✦ Hardware specifications
- ✦ Step-by-step operating system installation procedures
- ✦ Step-by-step application installation procedures
- ✦ Step-by-step post-installation security procedures
- ✦ Final verification procedures

The design of a secure server architecture should begin with the hardware specifications. As unrelated as it sounds to system security, you should standardize your hardware to simplify problem solving further down the road. Hardware is becoming so inexpensive, you may as well standardize on a small number of system specifications, rather than have a large number of different configurations, as well as standardize on a single vendor.

The next step is to install the operating system on the new system. Quite often OEM-type hardware from large vendors is provided with the operating system preinstalled. This may be convenient, but you seldom know exactly what components are installed. The simplest way to start is with a fresh installation, because you know exactly what is selected to be installed. It is possible to modify a preinstalled system, but it is usually faster to do a new install.

Minimization

One of the keys to a secure system is minimization. You always want the absolute minimum amount of software installed on a server so that the server can still perform its function. This reduces the number of potential vulnerabilities and simplifies administration.

Minimization is simple. During the operating system installation, Setup will automatically install a number of core components. A number of optional components can also be installed after Setup is complete.

After Windows Server 2003 is installed and you log in as the administrator for the first time, you are presented with the Manage Your Server window. The Manage Your Server window can be used to configure the server roles such as DNS server, Web server, and Mail server. You can configure a server for a specific role by launching the Configure Your Server Wizard. To launch the wizard, click Add or remove a role. The first step in the wizard outlines the preliminary steps that should be completed before configuring a server role. Click Next after reviewing the information to continue.

The next step, as shown in Figure 3-1, is to select a server role. In this case, the server is being configured as a Web Application Server. Click Next to continue.

Your selection here will determine which services and components are installed, and will automatically start their installation. Because Internet Information Services (IIS) is installed during the initial installation, you have the option of removing IIS or you can click back to select a different server role.

After you close the Configure Your Server Wizard, the initial installation of Windows Server 2003 and its components is complete. The next step is to make changes to the installed system to make it more secure.

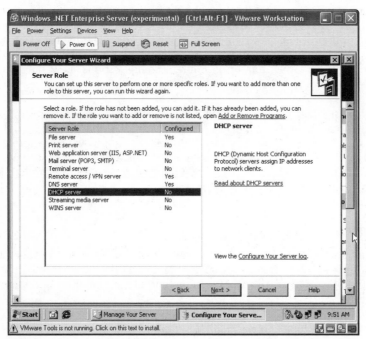

Figure 3-1: The Configure Your Server Wizard is used to set the role of the server.

Disabling unnecessary services

You should now have a fully functioning Windows Server 2003 installation with a Web server component. By default, Windows Server 2003 enables a number of services that are unnecessary for a pure Web server. Using a UNIX-based tool called Nmap, you can make a list of the open ports on the server. This tool is called a *portmapper* because it makes a map of all open ports on a given system (or a group of systems). Each network service on the system has a specific port to which clients connect. For example, connections to the Web server are made to TCP port 80. Keep in mind that just as you can use a tool such as Nmap, so can malicious attackers if your system is not behind a firewall (which is often the case with Web servers).

Nmap also shows its estimation of the operating system running on the remote machine based on a number of factors, such as the tcp sequence numbers. The open ports on this default installation include port 80 and 443, which are both bound to the Web server (http and https respectively). Ports 135, 139, and 445 are NetBIOS-related ports used for file and print sharing and Windows Networking. Port 3389 is used for Microsoft Remote Desktop Protocol, for connecting to a Microsoft Terminal Server. Port 1025 is bound to the remote file sharing listener. Port 1026 is bound to the Distributed Transaction Coordinator. Finally, port 5000 is bound to Free Internet Chess Server (fics).

Any of the aforementioned ports are all potential security risks. An attacker can attempt to use exploits against any of these ports, or find new exploits against these services. By disabling the services that open these ports, you vastly reduce your security risks by reducing your profile to attackers. Think of a server with a large number of open ports as a large target for an attacker, while a server with only one or two open ports is a much smaller target.

To begin disabling unnecessary services, open the Services MMC snap-in by selecting Start ➪ Administrative Tools ➪ Services and then expand the window. Figure 3-2 shows the open Services snap-in.

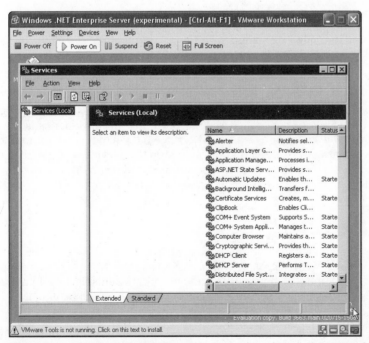

Figure 3-2: The Services MMC snap-in is used to change the state of services and their behavior at system startup.

You can now begin to disable services. Depending on the type of server and the configuration and design of your application, you may not require the Distributed Transaction Coordinator (DTC). You can assume that if you aren't using distributed databases or distributed file systems (which you likely aren't on a Web server), it's not required. Right-click the Distributed Transaction Coordinator, and select Properties. The Properties dialog box is shown in Figure 3-3.

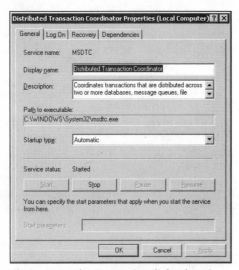

Figure 3-3: The Properties dialog box for a service can be used to change the startup behavior as well as start and stop the service.

To disable the service, select Disabled from the Startup Type drop-down box. This change will prevent the service from starting the next time the server starts. You will also see a third Startup type called Manual. Selecting this option means the service can be started by a user or a dependent service but will not start automatically when the system starts. Click the Stop button to stop the service, and click OK to close the dialog box. The DTC service is now stopped and disabled. You're on your way to securing the open ports and unnecessary services on your server.

Patching the system

Another important step when building a new system is to apply all relevant patches and software updates. With Microsoft Windows Server 2003, the process is simple for operating system updates. If you use Windows Update and select (at least) the critical updates, the necessary security patches and bug fixes will be installed automatically.

To use the Windows Update site, do the following:

1. Select Windows Update from the Start ⇨ All Programs menu, or go to `http://windowsupdate.microsoft.com` in your Web browser. Figure 3-4 shows the Windows Update site.

2. Click Scan for updates to have the site scan the installed components on your system and determine the required updates.

   When you click Scan for updates for the first time, the Windows Update site automatically installs an ActiveX component to scan your system. You may be prompted to accept the component, which is signed by Microsoft for security purposes.

3. When the scan is complete, you are presented with a list of available updates. Select the updates you want to install and begin the installation.

Note Some updates must be installed separately from any others. You can install other updates after these are complete.

Windows Server 2003 includes a technology called Windows Automatic Updates, which is disabled by default. To access the settings for Automatic Updates, right-click the My Computer icon on the desktop and select Properties. Click the Automatic Updates tab, as shown in Figure 3-5.

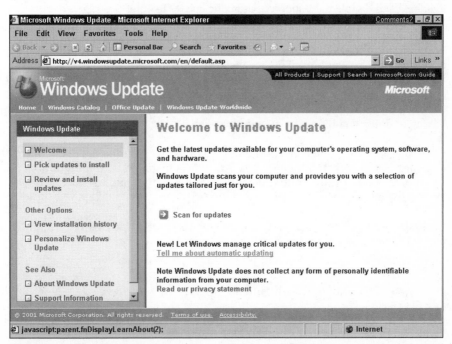

Figure 3-4: The Windows Update site is used to download patches for the Windows operating system components.

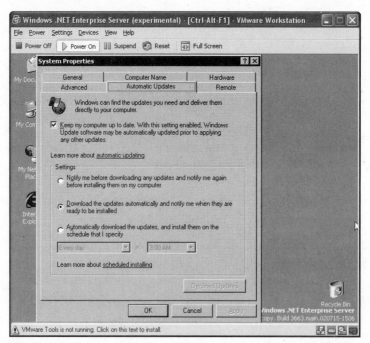

Figure 3-5: The System Properties' Automatic Updates tab is used to enable and disable the Windows automatic update feature.

Three options are available for automatic update notifications. By default, all automatic updates are enabled. This means updates will be downloaded automatically and you will be notified when they are ready to be installed. You can also select one of the other two options. You can configure Windows Update to notify you before downloading updates and again before installing them. You also have the option of having updates installed on a specific schedule.

When updates are available, a notification icon appears in the taskbar. Clicking the icon allows you to install the updates. Nothing is installed without interaction, but depending on your Automatic Updates preferences, the updates may be downloaded to your system.

Clicking the icon in the taskbar launches the Automatic Updates Wizard. The first page of the wizard allows you to choose from the following:

✦ Install the updates

✦ View details about the updates

✦ Delay the installation of the updates

Clicking the Details button shows a list of the updates that will be installed. You can select or deselect specific updates as well as read more information about each update by clicking Read This First. Clicking the Settings button opens the Automatic Updates configuration dialog.

Clicking Install begins the installation of the selected updates. Figure 3-6 shows the status window that displays the installation's progress. The updates will be downloaded if required.

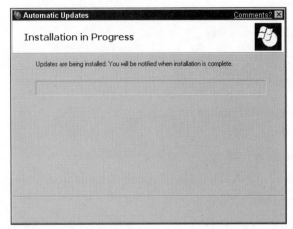

Figure 3-6: The status window is displayed as installation progresses.

Some updates may require a reboot as shown in Figure 3-7. Click Yes to restart the system.

Figure 3-7: Some updates require a reboot of the system.

While Windows Update and Automatic Updates apply the patches to the operating system, applications often do not have such a service. You should go through the appropriate channels (usually a Web site) for each application installed on the system to download and install any relevant security patches and bug fixes.

Application updates are normally available from the application vendor's Web site. In most cases, you need to download the update package and install it manually. Some applications do have an automatic update feature, although these are the minority.

New system documentation

After the new system is built and patches and updates are applied, documentation should be assembled. This documentation should contain detailed information about the system, including the following:

- ✦ The initial operating system installation
- ✦ Installed applications
- ✦ Installed security patches and bug fixes
- ✦ Documentation can also contain network settings, passwords, and other data about the system

The primary reason to have documentation about a new system is to have a reference when working on the system in the future. With this documentation, anyone can sit down and work on the system without having to explore and discover what is installed on the system and how it is configured. This documentation will be organized by system and will be combined with the Change Control archive (discussed later in this chapter) to provide a detailed history of a system.

The new system documentation is different from the design document. The new system documentation documents any deviation from the plan within the design document. The system documentation contains items such as the specific network configuration of the system as well as any installed applications and their configuration.

Network architecture

There's more to a secure server architecture than just the security of the particular system, although that is a large part. The architecture of systems and their interoperation must also be considered.

A number of principles can help to create a more secure environment. One of the primary design goals is to minimize the number of possible vulnerable points. This goes against many of the schools of thought in system architecture design that teach the practice of scaling out (adding more systems) to add both resources and redundancy.

By minimizing the number of vulnerable points, you can lessen your chances of an attack. You only have one system to secure rather than several. When you need more resources to dedicate to an application, scaling up (adding more hardware resources or switching to a larger system) is, in theory, more secure than scaling out, which entails adding additional systems.

For example, if you have an application running on a single system with one processor and a certain amount of memory, and so on, which is reaching its limitations with those resources, you may want to scale the system. Assume that you know the growth rate of the load on the application. Instead of scaling to twice the resources, you will scale to four times the resources as the growth rate is probably also growing. There are now two options. You can add three more systems and distribute the application (a common architectural practice), or you can add three processors and expand the memory in the existing system (or change the motherboard if that is not supported).

If you were to expand to four distributed systems, you'd have four times the potential for mistakes. Maintaining security on the single system is simpler than on a group of four disparate systems. Imagine if you had 10 applications with the same user base. You would be expanding from 10 to 40 servers with the scaling out situation instead of 1 to 4. The potential for vulnerabilities becomes greater as you scale out higher numbers of servers.

Other than scaling a single application, there is another advantage to consolidation. Securing a number of applications consolidated on a single server is easier than securing a number of servers each with a single application. While each application still has its own potential problems, there is only one system with one operating system to secure. Consolidation is also known to reduce administrative overhead.

However, a disadvantage exists to consolidation that almost outweighs the added security from having only a single system. If the system is compromised, a number of applications are compromised instead of just one. The advantage of having the applications distributed is to slow an attacker and to limit the damage done in the event of a compromise.

Now that consolidation has been touted as a method of increasing security, I'm going to say the exact opposite. Scaling out means distributing the load across more than one server and scaling out to distributed systems can increase security in certain situations.

Take the same assumptions as in the previous example. Your user base is expanding and you are going to scale the application server fourfold. The previous example implied that the user base was all in one location. In this example, assume the user base is distributed evenly across four locations that are all equal users of the application (in a perfect world). Now, instead of scaling the application server up in its existing location, scaling it out and adding a server at each location may be the most secure plan.

While there is now four times the number of potential vulnerabilities, one server is located at each site. The client data is no longer traveling over the wide area network (WAN). The network connection between sites will have more potential for attack than the extra system added to the remote site. A WAN connection has a fair amount of network equipment with potential vulnerabilities and also passes through a telecommunications company, an untrusted party.

Another advantage to having the systems distributed across remote sites is that the client connections will be faster and will not be vulnerable to failure in the event that the WAN connection fails.

A number of different, and contradictory, viewpoints have been presented, and all are perfectly valid. All are not, however, valid for all environments and for all situations.

The key is that you must determine what the best architecture is in your environment. The principles laid out in this section are all valid and can hopefully help you to reach an acceptable design, but when it comes to finalizing your architecture, a lot of it comes down to common sense. The point of presenting this information isn't to guide you through designing your environment, but to tell you how to approach the task. Without specific information about your network, nobody can tell you the best way to secure it because every network is different, and the differences are often vast.

Design an Operational Plan for Maintaining Security

The key to keeping your secure systems secure is having a plan. A very common sight is a system that was originally built to a secure specification, but with months of use and changes, is now vulnerable. Good planning can help you avoid this situation.

The plan will provide steps for an administrator to follow on a day-to-day basis to ensure that systems are still secure. This will include auditing and updating. The plan should contain a schedule for performing audits and checking for updates.

The operational plan for security can also be integrated with your disaster recovery planning and other operational documentation.

Maintaining security on a day-to-day basis

Maintaining security on a day-to-day basis is one of the most difficult tasks you will face. As discussed later in the "Change Control" section of this chapter, most environments have many fingers in the same pie. There may be any number of systems administrators with access to any and all of the systems in your network. Not every administrator is expected to be well versed in security (although some basics should be a requirement) and that can lead to security compromises.

Define a schedule for audits and updates. For example, certain tasks, such as inspecting log files, should be done on a daily or weekly schedule. Other tasks, such as security auditing, can be slated on a monthly schedule or every three months. A yearly schedule for a large-scale security review would also be prudent.

These schedules, especially the shorter schedules such as auditing, should be staggered. This allows the tasks to be done in smaller increments instead of having to be done all at once. Checking one system per day is far easier than checking 5 systems every Friday, or 10 systems every second Tuesday, and so on.

Keeping up to date with security problems and fixes

New security problems are constantly being exposed. Hackers, both legitimate and illegitimate, look at different aspects of widely deployed software and search for vulnerabilities. Many of these hackers believe their work is beneficial because they believe in full disclosure. Remember, however, that these hackers are not a trusted source.

Full disclosure is the belief that releasing the details of a security vulnerability to everyone is more advantageous than keeping it to oneself or releasing it to only the software vendor. In most cases, the person who discovers the vulnerability notifies the vendor and gives it a decent amount of time in which to generate a fix. After this time has passed, the vulnerability is fully disclosed, whether or not a patch exists.

Overall, full disclosure seems to be the best method of notifying users of vulnerabilities. Full disclosure is made on the assumption that if one person has found a vulnerability and is willing to disclose it, there may be any number of others who have discovered it and do not disclose it. Those people can exploit the vulnerability without anyone else knowing it exists. The major advantages of full disclosure include the fact that system administrators know about the vulnerability and can patch the software if there is a fix or take other steps if no fix exists, such as changing software or disabling the service. Full disclosure also places pressure on the software vendors to create a fix quickly, and to create more secure software the next time around.

While full disclosure has many advantages, it also has one glaring disadvantage. Disclosing the vulnerability, which is often done with proof-of-concept exploit code (a proof-of-concept exploit code is a sample of the code used by the hacker) means that not just the discoverer has it anymore; anyone can get it. This opens up the vulnerability to anyone with access to the forum where it has been disclosed.

The disadvantage to releasing a vulnerability only to the software vendor is that the vendor can choose to ignore the vulnerability and not release a fix. There is nobody to put pressure on the vendor for a fix because nobody knows about the vulnerability. Apathetic vendors can leave security holes open indefinitely.

Due to the full disclosure policy of most hackers, many vulnerabilities are released to the public, often with fixes provided by the vendors at the same time or soon after. By watching for these vulnerabilities and fixes, you can keep your systems secure. A number of different resources exist for the disclosure of vulnerabilities and the notification of fixes, and it is important to monitor all of these. A more thorough list of resources is contained in Appendix B, but the following are the most important:

✦ **Bugtraq** — a moderated mailing list with a medium volume. It can be found at `www.securityfocus.com`. On that site, you can both subscribe to the mailing list and view and search the archives. Bugtraq is used for the release of vulnerabilities for everything from operating systems to network equipment and beyond.

✦ **NTBugtraq** — a mailing list similar to the original Bugtraq list but more specific to Microsoft Windows. NTBugtraq is found at `www.ntbugtraq.com`. The discussions on NTBugtraq pertain only to Microsoft Windows-specific security issues; other types of discussions are not allowed.

✦ **Microsoft Security Notification Service** — Microsoft publishes its own security bulletins whenever a new vulnerability and fix is published. The security bulletins are published in TechNet and can be accessed at `www.microsoft.com/technet/treeview/default.asp?url=/technet/security/current.asp`. In addition to the Web site, the Microsoft Security Notification Service will e-mail the Microsoft security bulletins to you when they are released. Subscribe by sending an e-mail to `microsoft_security-subscribe-request@announce.microsoft.com`.

Change Control

Assume for a moment that there are five system administrators on a team. Imagine that you are the member of that team who is the security specialist. This is not to say, however, that other members of the team are not responsible for security.

You spend several hours securing and auditing a given system. You determine that the system is fully secure and release it into production. As there are four other administrators, they will also have access to the system. What happens if one of these administrators adds a Web server to the system without any notification? There is now a system with potential security flaws on the network that you (as the security specialist) are unaware of.

Change control is all about communication. Any time a change is made to any production system on the network, all parties involved with that system (especially security) must be notified.

Note   Notifying others (not necessarily involved with a specific system that is changing) of changes to the network itself is equally important. New systems/servers, new routers, and new gateways can all affect security.

Security is not the only driver for implementing change control. Change control can also be driven by uptime requirements. If a systems administrator decides to add a piece of software to the system without realizing that the software is incompatible, it can cause a service disruption. Change control provides a method of allowing all of those who maintain the systems to preview changes that will be applied to them.

Change control can be implemented in a number of ways, but generally works as follows. Everyone is forbidden to make any changes to systems without filing a change request. Occasionally, restricting changes must be done using somewhat draconian measures as some people will ignore the change control measures and continue making changes without communication.

The Change Request should include the following information:

✦ Date submitted

✦ Name

✦ System or device to which the change is applicable

✦ Proposed date and time of change

✦ Length of time of change

✦ Change description

✦ Potential problems

✦ Rollback plan

✦ Results

Multiple changes can be compiled on to a single change request if they are for the same system or device and are being done at the same time.

After the change request is filled out, it is forwarded to all parties involved with the system to which the change is being made. In the preceding example, all five system administrators would receive the change request. The change control process should also have a coordinator, a central point who will aggregate information and approve the change request.

The review process is the most important step in the change control process. During the review process, a number of people can look at the proposed change and find problems, either with the change itself, with incompatibilities with existing software or configurations on the system, or with security including potential vulnerabilities. During the review process, the reviewers forward their comments to the change request author and/or coordinator. If problems are found, the change should either be cancelled, or the change request should be reworked to address the issues and then resubmitted for review.

Approving the change does not complete the process. The change must be performed and the results recorded. The results of the change should be sent around to the same group who reviewed the change request. The importance of this step is that those who will be working on the system should know what changes have been applied, and which have failed. With this information, they will have an overview of the state of the system.

The final step is to archive the change documentation. By keeping a detailed record of the change requests (organized preferably by system), tracking the source of a problem can be simplified. Instead of jumping right in to the troubleshooting process, the change records for a given system can be referenced to the approximate time when the problem began. If there were changes made at that time, those changes can be addressed first when troubleshooting.

The change control records are also useful for security purposes. Records will exist when patches are applied and software is updated. If a new security vulnerability is revealed, you can check the original build documentation of each system along with their change control records to determine if they are vulnerable. If systems are compromised, the change control records will assist with determining how the compromise occurred.

Contingency Planning

You should have a final plan in place, although an administrator hopes he must never use it. A contingency plan outlines what is to be done in the event of a system or network compromise.

The contingency plan must outline a few stages of the response to an attack:

- ✦ Immediate response
- ✦ Forensics/evidence gathering
- ✦ Cleanup

The plan should have a step-by-step process for performing these tasks. Anyone should be able to follow the process because an attack may happen at any time. You may be sleeping or on vacation, and whoever is on duty must be able to, at the very least, halt the attack.

Immediate response

When you notice a system has been compromised, you essentially have two options. The option taken by most is to immediately disconnect the compromised system from the network and move to the next steps, forensics and cleanup. This is often the best plan because it immediately halts the attack, and can stop the attacker from gaining further access into your network. This method has a big advantage in that the attacker cannot remove evidence when he is caught because he immediately loses access to the system. The most common method for this is to simply unplug the network cable.

The other option available at your discretion is to attempt to isolate the system from the rest of your network while allowing the attacker to continue accessing the system. This option can be advantageous if there is no vital data on the system and it can be isolated. This is a dangerous option, however. If you begin to make changes to the network that the attacker notices, he is likely to remove the evidence from the system (possibly by removing ALL data from the system) and cease his attack. While this method can allow more evidence to be captured, only a highly skilled security expert should attempt it.

Forensics/evidence gathering

There are two reasons to perform forensics on a system: one is for your benefit, and the other is in case you want to pursue criminal charges against the attacker. By performing a forensic audit on the system, you can learn exactly how the attacker gained access, and you can also learn a bit about the attacker's mind.

The forensics stage of the contingency plan is by far the most complex. Becoming a computer forensics expert takes a huge amount of dedication and training and these experts charge high prices for their services. If you have a major compromise and do want to pursue legal action, the best plan is to bring in forensics experts.

Forensics in a computer environment (as in other environments) is so vastly complex because the evidence needs to be collected without being disturbed. If the evidence looks to have been tampered with, it will not be admissible in any legal proceedings.

If legal action is not your goal, there are a few things you can do to collect evidence yourself and do some investigation into the attack. In doing so you can learn how to better secure your systems the next time.

One of the key locations where evidence will be stored is in logs. The Windows event log will track any anomalies in the operating system and any applications that log to the Application log. Some applications may also log to files.

Anomalies in logs may take many forms. Some stand out, such as those associated with buffer overflows. These entries will contain errors that show extremely long strings being entered into applications. Others are far less obvious and more difficult to identify, such as anomalies in performance or processes running on a server due to unauthorized activity.

The best log entries are those recorded by the auditing features of Microsoft Windows. With auditing enabled, you can record a number of events, such as logons, logoffs, and file changes.

 Cross-Reference   Working with auditing is discussed further in Chapter 6.

Other logs that may be of interest are those from firewalls and routers. Depending on your environment, you may keep firewall access logs and access logs on the router. By looking at these logs, you may be able to track when the attacker accessed your network and possibly even track the attacks that they used to gain access.

By far the most useful logs, however, come from the Intrusion Detection System (IDS), if you have one. The IDS will notice many types of attacks even if they do not fit a specific stored pattern. These attacks will be noted in the IDS logs and, depending on the system, the entire session by that attacker may be logged.

If you have some sort of access log or IDS logs that show the source address of the attack, you should attempt to determine where the attack originated. If you find that the attack is originating from a specific organization or Internet service provider (ISP), you should notify its abuse department. Although the IT departments of educational institutions are notorious for their apathy towards attacks originating from their networks, many Internet Service Providers (ISPs) are far more vigilant.

 Caution   Do not EVER use illigitimate means to determine the origin of an attacker or retaliate against the attacker. There are numerous problems with this approach (which I've even seen happen in corporations), not the least of which is that you would be breaking the law and liable to prosecution. While the attacker against whom you are retaliating or trying to find may not prosecute, the telephone company whose resource you are using or any other organizations whose network you cross could.

Cleanup

Cleanup is the last step after an attack. The importance of formatting the drive in the compromised system and performing a complete reinstall cannot be stressed enough. You must always take this step; closing the security holes and re-deploying the system is not enough. The main reason for this step is to remove any files containing backdoors that the attacker may have left behind. Even when using a file integrity checker such as tripwire, the extra step of reinstalling a clean system is worthwhile.

Honeypots

A honeypot is an advanced security subject, a system that is built to lure attackers in so that they can be observed. After you become good at performing forensics and auditing compromised systems, a honeypot can be an interesting experiment.

Caution This information is provided for informational purposes only. Honeypots are in a legal and ethical "gray area" for reasons discussed in this section.

Honeypots and honeynets (entire networks of honeypots) are said by some to be unethical or even illegal, because they are used to lure attackers and capture private information, including their conversations and movements. They are a gray area because the attackers are accessing the systems illegally anyway and the systems belong to you, so it should be acceptable for you to monitor any activities on the system; however, electronic evidence has been ruled inadmissible in court when the attacker was not somehow notified that he was being monitored. This was deemed illegal surveillance.

I'm not going to delve into an ethical or legal debate, as I'm not a lawyer nor an ethics professor. You can make your own decisions on the subject and decide if you want to build a honeypot or not.

Honeypots and honeynets are built for research purposes. It is easy to build a system, make it secure or insecure to any level you please, and put it on the Internet (isolated from your other systems). You can then monitor any attacks on the system, and it is only a matter of time before they occur. Honeypots should be blocked from sending outgoing traffic though, so that they cannot be used to attack other systems.

The difference between a honeypot and a regular system is that with a honeypot you are not under any pressure to repair the compromised system. As the attacks occur and the attackers take over the system, you can sit back and watch what happens.

The ideal method for monitoring a honeypot is to use an undetectable network monitor (a "blackened" system) on the network connection to the system. You can also set the system up to log everything both locally and to a secure external location so copies of the logs are not lost when the attacker attempts to cover his tracks.

The best honeypot is one that looks just like a regular server. Early honeypots were simulations of a system and were somewhat easy to detect. If you were to build a

DNS server system that even had DNS data on it, however, the attacker would think the system was simply a normal system. The honeypot does not need to have real data on it, nor does it have to be referenced from anywhere else, as long as it looks like a legitimate system.

A honeypot can be an interesting project if you have the knowledge and experience to interpret the accumulated data. If not, it is essentially a waste of time and resources. Setting up a honeypot can teach you a lot about the patterns of attackers and their behavior. You can be better prepared to see the "calling card" of an attacker on your production network if you can see it firsthand in a safe environment.

An organized honeynet project exists at `http://project.honeynet.org`. An interesting feature on this site is the scan of the month section, where they post signatures of specific types of scans so that you can see what different types of scans look like in a packet capture utility. The site has much useful information about attackers for those interested in security.

Summary

The focus of this chapter was on security architecture planning. Two important areas must be considered when looking at security: securing the individual server, and securing the network environment.

The chapter offered several tips on how to secure a server, from disabling unnecessary services to keeping up to date with operating system service packs and security updates. Using the Windows Update feature, Windows Server 2003 makes it simpler to keep a server current with all the latest service packs and patches.

A number of steps can be taken to secure the network environment, such as minimizing the number of access points. After a secure environment is established, it also must be maintained. This entails performing security tasks such as viewing security logs on a regular basis and keeping up to date with known security problems and updates. To maintain security, some form of change control should be enforced so administrators follow the appropriate channels before making changes to the existing environment. A contingency plan should also be in place outlining the process that will occur in the event that a system or network is compromised.

✦   ✦   ✦

Basic Security Auditing

Security auditing is an important part of your network security strategy. Security auditing consists of testing your network's security through a number of means, including security scanners, port scanners, penetration testing, and other less common tools.

Security scanners are programs that use a set of canned scripts to test systems for a set of known security vulnerabilities. This set of vulnerabilities is updated as new vulnerabilities are discovered.

Port scanners allow you to look at your network and see what systems have what ports open. This is an indication of what services are running on the system, and what potential vulnerabilities exist.

Penetration testing is used to determine if your network is penetrable by a determined attacker, and is usually performed by a security expert who attempts to gain access to the network.

It's usually best to have an expert perform security auditing if you want to ensure the maximum level of security. Nonprofessional security auditing may miss vulnerabilities on your network. If you are comfortable with this fact, performing your own audits is far cheaper than employing professional auditors. You may, however, be lulled into a false sense of security if you don't find any holes.

System Audit Planning

System audits should be done on new systems before they are placed in a production role where users will access them and then performed on a regular basis. You should also create a comprehensive plan for auditing that includes the auditing process as well as the schedule. The schedule should be an ongoing rotation where a small number of systems are audited each week or on a similar rotation. The rotation should ensure that each system is audited on a regular basis.

The schedule on which every system is audited will vary depending on your needs. Auditing more often will catch vulnerabilities sooner, and will theoretically increase security. The tradeoff is found in the increased amount of time spent performing audits. You can manipulate the schedule so that more vulnerable systems are audited more often than less vulnerable ones. More vulnerable systems include firewalls and Web servers exposed directly to Internet traffic, for example. Less vulnerable systems would include systems accessible only from the internal network and those housing non-critical data.

The most important time to audit a system is following any changes; making changes to a system can inadvertently open security vulnerabilities, and can occur with the change of only one small configuration setting.

When you schedule specific auditing times, new vulnerabilities can be discovered on a regular basis. You may be using an application or portion of an operating system for which a new vulnerability has been found. If you miss the notification for that vulnerability, it will be found when the signatures for your security scanner are updated, if you keep the scanner up to date.

Windows-Based Auditing

Windows-based security auditing is somewhat limited. Traditionally, Windows has not allowed direct communication with "raw sockets" as UNIX does, so security tools are somewhat more difficult to build for Windows. Raw sockets allow any network traffic to be sent by an application. If raw sockets are not implemented, only the network traffic restricted by the operating system can be sent by an application. This allows the operating system vendor to disallow an application programmer to develop malicious programs.

Stating that Windows has had no raw sockets support is an oversimplification because raw sockets were available to users with administrator access or at the system level in Windows NT 4.0 and Windows 2000, but the raw sockets implementation was not complete. In Windows Server 2003, the raw sockets implementation is complete and compatible with the Berkeley raw sockets implementation in most versions of UNIX.

A number of auditing tools are available for Windows, including security scanners, port scanners, and packet sniffers. The packet sniffer tool, Network Monitor, is included with Windows Server 2003.

Raw Sockets in Windows Server 2003

Much discussion has taken place over Microsoft's decision to include a full implementation of raw sockets in Windows Server 2003 and Windows XP. First, an explanation of raw sockets is warranted.

A socket is simply a logical object that provides a network connection to another host. In most cases, sockets are accessed through an application programming interface (API), which provides a controlled set of functions.

Raw sockets typically refer to the Berkeley implementation of sockets originally implemented in the Berkeley UNIX system. In this case, it is possible to access sockets at a lower level, bypassing the controls implemented in a strict API. An API is still used, but the new API is much more flexible.

The controversy surrounding raw sockets in Windows XP and Windows Server 2003 is somewhat confusing. On one hand, many in the technical media are claiming that raw sockets in Windows will cause the Internet to collapse because the development of malicious hacking tools will be simplified and such tools will become more widespread. On the other hand, Microsoft claims that there will be no detrimental effects on computer security. Only a few individuals are actually driving this controversy. The truth is somewhere in the middle and will probably not be known completely for some time.

As stated previously, raw socket access is available in earlier versions of Windows, and has been available for 20 years in UNIX. While DDoS attacks (discussed in Chapter 1) can be launched from any system, they will show a source IP address in the packet header that can be used to block the attacks. Raw sockets allow the spoofing of the source IP address so that the packet cannot be blocked because the real source IP is unknown.

While raw sockets are available in many other operating systems, all of the controversy stems from the fact that raw sockets are now implemented in the Windows XP Home edition. This operating system will have a wide installed base, replacing Windows 95, 98, and Me, none of which have raw socket implementations. Users also have administrative access by default in Windows XP Home, and can access raw sockets. If these systems are compromised, and DDoS agents are installed on them, raw sockets will make it possible for the source IP address in the DDoS packets to be spoofed and make the attack unblockable.

The raw sockets implementation is not as troublesome as it has been made out to be in some cases, but is somewhat of a concern. The problem is not with raw sockets, per se, but with the fact that there is no feasible way to block DDoS attacks with spoofed source IP addresses. The shortcoming is in the TCP/IP protocol itself. When the protocol was designed, these situations were not considered because the protocol was designed for private networks.

Raw sockets are not hackers' evil tools. They allow the implementation of Windows features such as the Internet Connection Firewall (ICF) and IP Security (IPSec).

General security audits

A few tools are available for performing general security scans on Windows. Most of these are fairly expensive; however, if you choose to use a commercial Windows-based security scanner, they are typically easy to use.

Microsoft often provides security scanning tools for Windows. These normally provide scanning for a specific vulnerability rather than a general scan of the entire system. These tools can be found at `www.microsoft.com/technet/treeview/default.asp?url=/technet/security/tools/tools.asp`.

Microsoft does provide a general scanning tool called the Microsoft Personal Security Advisor. This tool is only for Windows NT 4.0 or Windows 2000 Professional workstations, and cannot be used for servers. It does not yet support Windows XP.

The tools on the Microsoft site include those for checking which patches are installed on a system and maintaining IIS security, among others.

Most security scanners for Windows are point and shoot. You specify a host to scan, start the scan process, and a list of vulnerabilities will be shown. These reports are often available in a number of formats, including HTML.

Figure 4-1 shows an example of a report generated by a commercial scanner. This report was generated using the Cisco Secure Scanner. The default report view is shown with the vulnerabilities for each host listed (only one host was scanned). It is also possible to view the collected data in a number of ways, including by operating system and by service.

Figure 4-2 shows a scan completed on the same host by the WebTrends NetIQ Security Analyzer. One medium risk and three low risk vulnerabilities were found. A number of the vulnerabilities found by the previous scan were not found in this scan. This scan was done without updating the signature files to show the importance of having the scanner current.

Security scanning tools are useful if they are kept current with the latest updates from the vendor. The software vendor must also keep the signature files current. Without these two steps, security scans are almost useless.

Packet sniffing in Windows

A few packet sniffing tools are available for Windows. The primary packet sniffing tool for Windows is Network Monitor, which is included with the operating system. Network Monitor is not installed by default. The version of Network Monitor, included with Windows Server 2003, can only capture data traveling to or from the local system.

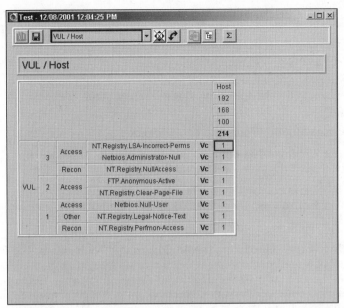

Figure 4-1: The Cisco Secure Scanner scans a Windows Server, and shows the security vulnerabilities discovered.

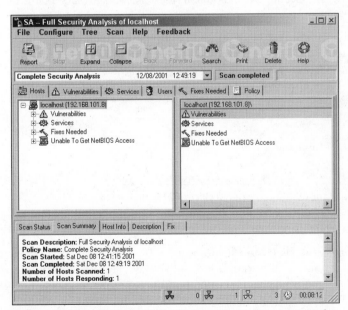

Figure 4-2: The WebTrends NetIQ Security Analyzer scanned the same system without up-to-date signature files, and didn't find the same vulnerabilities as the Cisco Secure Scanner.

To install Network Monitor, do the following:

1. Open Add or Remove Programs from the Control Panel, and click the Add/Remove Windows Components icon.

2. Click Management and Monitoring Tools from the list in the Windows Components Wizard (do not select the check box) and then click the Details button.

3. Select the Network Monitor Tools box and click OK.

4. Click Next in the Windows Components Wizard to install the Network Monitor. You will need the Windows Server 2003 CD.

5. After the installation is complete, click Finish to close the Windows Components Wizard. You can then close the Add or Remove Programs dialog box.

You can now open Network Monitor from the Administrative Tools menu. The first time you open Network Monitor, you must select the default network on which to capture data if more than one is installed. Figure 4-3 shows the Select a Network dialog box used to select a network adapter. You must know the MAC address for your network adapter to select it from the list. You can find the MAC address using the **ipconfig /all** command from the command prompt.

Note   In the output of the ipconfig /all command, the MAC address is shown in the Physical Address field.

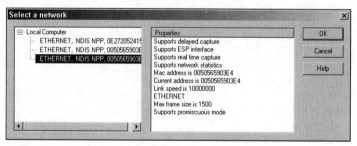

Figure 4-3: If you have more than one network connection, you must select a connection from the list and then click OK.

To begin a capture session, click the Start Capture button. By default, all traffic in and out of the local system is captured. Figure 4-4 shows a capture in progress. The statistics show the amount of traffic traveling over the network interface. A list of source and destinations for captured frames is also shown.

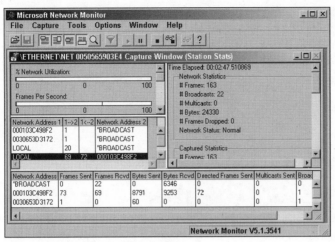

Figure 4-4: A capture is in progress.

 To stop a capture, click the Stop Capture button. The captured data can be viewed by using the Display Captured Data button. The captured data is displayed in a new window within the Network Monitor. It is also possible to click the Stop and View Capture button to stop the capture, and display the captured data in one step. You can now review this data.

It is also possible to review each frame in detail by double clicking a frame in the list. The upper pane shows the frame in the same view type as the summary. The middle pane shows detailed information about the frame at each level of encapsulation. For example, expanding the ETHERNET entry will show detailed information about the Ethernet section of the frame. Likewise, expanding the TCP section will show the TCP protocol information in the frame. Finally, the bottom pane shows the actual data contained in the frame in hexadecimal and ASCII forms.

Network Monitor also includes filters that can be used to filter the capture or the display. To filter what data is captured, ensure that you are not viewing any captured data and then click the Edit Capture Filter button. The default capture filter is shown in Figure 4-5.

The capture can be filtered based on a number of criteria, the most common being by address. By selecting the (Address Pairs) entry and then clicking the Address button to open the Address Expression dialog box, you can specify a source and/or destination MAC address for the filter, as shown in Figure 4-6. The address can be either included in the capture or excluded. You can also specify the direction of the traffic to or from a specific address. This is useful if you want to capture data communicating with a specific system, or to exclude a particularly chatty system from the capture.

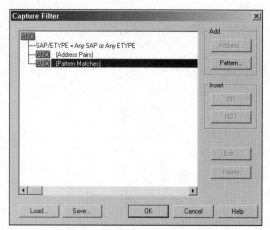

Figure 4-5: The default capture filter captures all data.

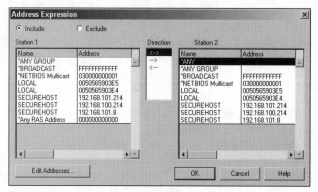

Figure 4-6: The Address Expression dialog box is used to filter data to or from a specific system.

You can also filter traffic based on a pattern contained within the packet or frame. Click the (Pattern Matches) entry and then click the Pattern button to open the Pattern Match dialog box, shown in Figure 4-7. You must specify a pattern to match in hexadecimal (hex) or ASCII format, and an offset value. The offset value specifies how far from the beginning of the frame or the end of the topology header to look for the pattern specified in hex.

With a pattern filter, you can also use the OR or NOT buttons, which are used to specify more pattern filters. It is possible to filter on a number of patterns with the OR function, and exclude certain patterns using NOT.

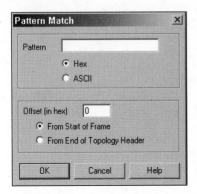

Figure 4-7: Data can be filtered based on a specific hex or ASCII pattern in a frame.

The final filter, shown in Figure 4-8, is the SAP or ETYPE filter. This filters specific protocols. All protocols are enabled by default. If you have a heterogeneous network with more than one type of network protocol and want to view one or a few types of traffic, they can be filtered by selecting the protocols and then clicking the Enable or Disable button.

Filtering the display of traffic is similar. While displaying a capture, click the Edit Display Filter button to open the Display Filter dialog box shown in Figure 4-9. The display filter is more flexible than the capture filter because you can filter based on a wider range of expressions. All captured packets are displayed by default.

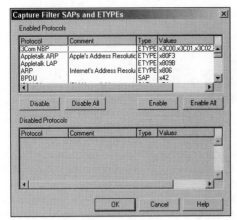

Figure 4-8: Traffic can be filtered based on the type of protocol contained in the frame.

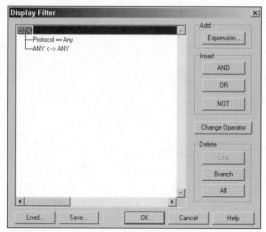

Figure 4-9: The Display Filter dialog box is used to filter data that has already been captured.

Click the Expression button to open the Expression dialog box, shown in Figure 4-10, and add an expression on which to filter. By selecting the Address, Protocol, or Property tabs of the dialog box, you can filter based on address. This is similar to the capture filter, filter based on protocol (with more granularity than the SAP or ETYPE capture filter), or filter based on a specific protocol property.

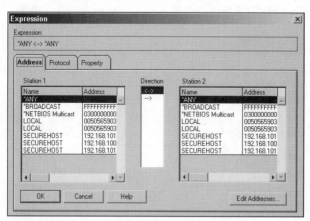

Figure 4-10: The Expression dialog box is used to define display filters.

With display filters, you can insert AND, OR, or NOT operators. These allow more granularity in inclusion and exclusion of filter expressions. You can also edit and delete existing filter expressions.

Another packet capture utility for Windows, WinDump, is a Windows port of the common UNIX packet capture tool, tcpdump. WinDump can be found at `http://windump.polito.it`. The advantage of WinDump over Network Monitor is that all traffic is captured rather than just traffic to and from the local machine.

Note   A version of Network Monitor that captures all data is included with Microsoft Systems Management Server.

There are two steps to installing WinDump. You must first install the WinPcap driver used for packet capture and then install WinDump itself. Download the WinPcap driver from `http://winpcap.polito.it` and then run the downloaded file to install. The install process is simple; no intervention is needed except to click Next to begin and Finish to close the program. For Windows Server 2003 or Windows XP, you must use at least version 2.3 of the WinPcap driver.

Download WinDump to a location on your hard drive, preferably in your default path, as defined by the PATH environment variable. WinDump comes as an executable file, so no special installation is necessary. Open a command prompt window to run WinDump in the same manner as tcpdump (explained in the following section).

In addition, Ethereal is also available for Windows. Similar to WinDump but unlike the Windows Server 2003 version of Network Monitor, Ethereal captures all data on the network. Although functionally almost identical, the UNIX version performs far better than the Windows version. Ethereal also requires the WinPcap driver. For information on using Ethereal, see "Packet Sniffing in UNIX" in the next section.

Auditing from a UNIX System

Auditing from a UNIX system is often easier than auditing from a Windows system because far more tools are available. UNIX also has an advantage because it traditionally has direct socket access for network programming.

Another big advantage to using a UNIX system for auditing is that almost all of the security tools for UNIX are free, while almost all of the security tools for Windows cost money—a lot of money, in some cases. It is fairly easy for anyone to download a copy of Linux, install it on a PC, and start using security tools.

General audits

A number of security scanners are available for UNIX. One of the most feature-packed and friendly scanners is Nessus, a freeware, two-part system with a Nessus client and server. See the Nessus Web site at www.nessus.org for installation instructions. It is critical to keep these applications current; otherwise, newly discovered vulnerabilities cannot be scanned.

Configuring Nessus

The Nessus daemon must first be started as root on the Nessus server. This can be configured to start automatically, but must be started manually by default. As root, run the nessusd command.

1. The first time you run Nessus, you must add a user. Run the nessus-adduser command. When adding a user, you must specify the following:

   • User name

   • The authentication method of either cipher or plaintext

   • An IP address or range to limit access to the account

   • A one-time password

   • Any rules for the user that control what features of Nessus the user is allowed to use

   Press Ctrl-D to accept the default and allow the user full access. You can then review and accept your selections. The simplest method is to add a username that is the same as your system login. You may be asked if the specified user is a local account on the system. Specifying Yes means the default logon credentials for that account will be used.

2. You can now run Nessus by typing **nessus** at the shell prompt.

3. Specify a passphrase to protect your private key. (Private keys are discussed in detail later in the book.) You can set a passphrase for increased security, or leave the passphrase blank if you need to run Nessus in an automated fashion from a script or a cron job. If a passphrase is entered, it will be required every time you start Nessus. Click OK to continue.

4. Figure 4-11 shows the initial Nessus window. Specify the host running the Nessus server in the Nessusd host box. This will be the default setting of localhost if the Nessus server is running on the local system. Enter the username you specified during the nessus-useradd process in the Login box and then click the Log In button. It is recommended that you use the same username that you use to log on to the system as your Nessus username.

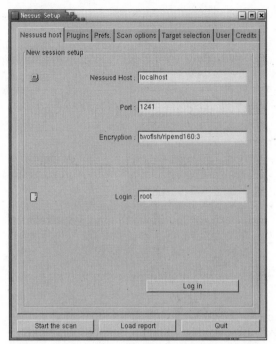

Figure 4-11: You must log in to Nessus from the initial dialog box.

5. When you log in to Nessus, you are notified that any plugins that have the capability to crash a target server are disabled, as shown in Figure 4-12. This is done by default so that you do not inadvertently crash any production target servers. Click OK.

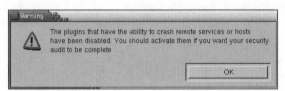

Figure 4-12: You are notified that dangerous plugins are disabled by default.

6. Plugins are individual components added to Nessus that provide the actual security scans. Plugins are used so that new scans can be written and added easily. When you have logged in and clicked OK to close the notification dialog box, the Plugins tab of the Nessus Setup dialog box is shown as in Figure 4-13. The different classes are shown in the upper pane. By clicking one of these, you can select individual plugins in the lower window. Clicking the selection box for the plugin classes in the upper pane will select or deselect the entire class.

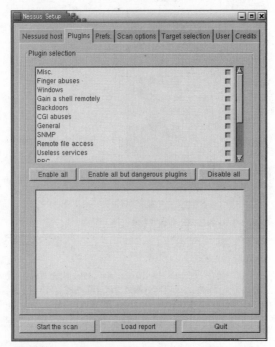

Figure 4-13: The Plugins tab of the Nessus Setup dialog box is used to select or deselect scanning plugins.

Figure 4-14 shows how the dangerous plugins are disabled by default in the lower pane. Dangerous plugins are marked with an exclamation mark icon. These plugins are dangerous because they can crash a target system. Some can crash a system that is vulnerable to the attack that they are scanning for and others can crash any system. You can manually enable these plugins, if you want. This is recommended if the system is in use and must not go down.

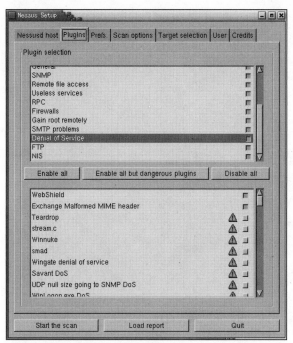

Figure 4-14: Dangerous plugins, marked with an exclamation mark icon, are disabled by default in the Plugins tab.

It is simple to go straight to a scan in Nessus, but there are two other tabs used for configuration in the Nessus Setup dialog box: Prefs. and Scan Options. You don't need to change anything on these tabs unless you have a special requirement. You may need to change the scan options if your scan is passing through a firewall, for example. Regardless of whether or not you need to change these settings, you should familiarize yourself with them. Figure 4-15 shows the Prefs. tab. The upper half of this tab is used to set the ping options for the scan. By default, Nessus does both a TCP and ICMP ping. The lower half sets the Nmap scanning technique. Nessus automatically performs an Nmap scan to determine open ports on the target system. (Nmap is discussed later in the chapter.) The default scan technique is connect( ), which is easily detected by firewalls and intrusion detection systems.

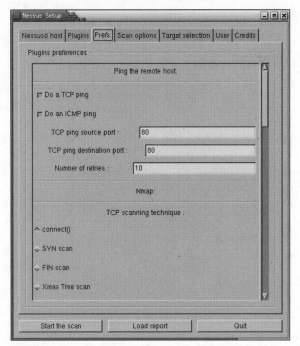

Figure 4-15: The Prefs. tab is used to configure ping and Nmap scan options.

Figure 4-16 shows the Scan Options tab. This tab is used to set the scan behavior, including the following:

✦ **Port range** — defines the range of ports that are scanned on remote hosts. Scanning more ports takes longer, while scanning fewer ports can result in vulnerabilities being missed. The default setting of 1-15,000 is normally fine.

✦ **The Max Threads option** — defines how many threads can be used for scanning. Each remote system scan uses one thread, so this setting defines the number of concurrent scans that can occur. The default is 8. On more powerful systems, or those with more network bandwidth, this number can be increased. It may need to be decreased on less powerful systems.

✦ **The Path to the CGIs option** — used to instruct Nessus where to look for CGI applications on scanned Web sites. If you know of specific directories on Web servers being scanned, they can be added. Only the /cgi-bin directory on target servers is scanned by default.

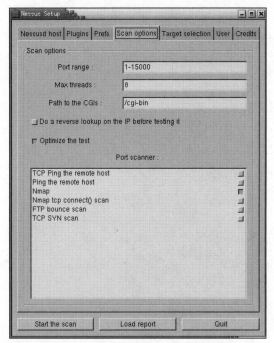

Figure 4-16: The Scan Options tab sets the scanning behavior of Nessus.

✦ **The Do a Reverse Lookup on the IP Before Testing It option** — causes a reverse DNS lookup to be done on the host to verify the host name. This can cause the scan to run slower, and is disabled by default.

✦ **The Optimize the Test option** — causes Nessus to only run certain tests based on specific criteria. For example, specific tests will be run only if a certain port is open. If this option is disabled, all tests will run regardless. It is possible, though unlikely, that a vulnerability could be missed due to this behavior. This option can be disabled to increase security at the cost of speed.

The remaining options are used to set the port scanning behavior of Nessus. By default, only a standard Nmap scan is done. You can also enable TCP, ICMP pings, and other types of port scans.

Using Nessus

Now that Nessus is configured to your liking, you can begin scanning target hosts.

1. Click the Target Selection tab (shown in Figure 4-17).

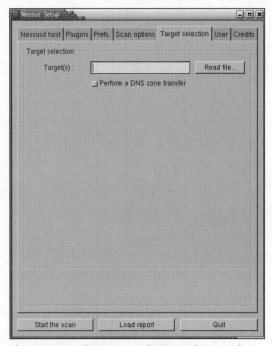

Figure 4-17: The Target Selection tab is used to specify which hosts will be scanned.

2. Enter the targets you want to scan in the Target(s) box. A comma can separate target hosts. You can also click the Read file button to read target hosts from a text file. In addition, it is possible to enter a domain name in the Target box and then select the Perform a DNS zone transfer option. This will cause a zone transfer attempt, and all hosts in the zone for that domain will be scanned. The DNS server, however, may not allow zone transfers to unknown hosts.

3. Click the Start the Scan button at the bottom of the Nessus Setup dialog box. The scan will proceed as shown in Figure 4-18. Each host being scanned as well as its progress will appear in the list. You can stop individual scans, or you can stop the whole test, if necessary.

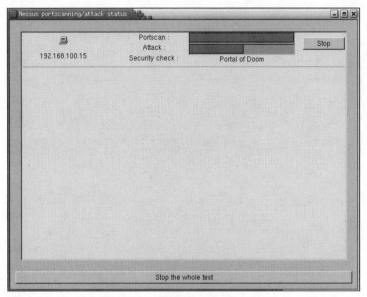

Figure 4-18: The Nessus scan is in progress.

After the scans are complete, the Nessus Report dialog box is displayed. The list of scanned hosts is shown in the left pane. The upper left pane shows the summary of statistics for the entire scan, including the number of hosts scanned and the number of security holes, warnings, and notes found. Click a host in the left pane to display the scan details in the right pane, as shown in Figure 4-19.

Each security hole (red), warning (orange), and note (yellow) for the host is shown in the right pane. Expanding each entry displays details about the security flaw including a description, solution, and risk factor.

Security holes are the most vital to repair. These indicate a major well-known problem in the system that, if exploited, can lead to a compromise. These should be fixed immediately. Security warnings are less important. Usually the problem cited in a warning makes other attacks less difficult, rather than being subject to attack itself as with a security hole. Security notes simply give information about the system.

You can save the Nessus report in other formats, such as HTML. This allows you to place the report directly into a Web site, and even include graphs. Use the Save As drop down box to select the format in which to save the report, and click the Save as button to specify the location.

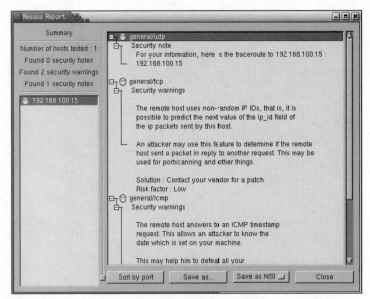

Figure 4-19: Clicking a host in the left pane of the Nessus Report dialog box brings up the results for that host in the right pane.

Port scanning

Port scanning is a more basic form of scanning used to view only the open ports on a system. This will tell you what services are running on the system, and which ports are open to attack. Port scans are almost always performed by general security scanners, but can also be performed on their own using specialized tools.

Port scanning tools are more prevalent on UNIX systems. Nmap, the most common port scanning tool, was originally developed on UNIX, and is now being ported to Windows. Nmap has been used a few times throughout this book already to show the open ports on a system.

For instructions on installing Nmap, see the Nmap Web site at `www.insecure.org/nmap`. After Nmap is installed, for the simplest scan type with no options, type `nmap <host>` where host is a hostname or IP address.

Using the -O option, Nmap can also identify the operating system type of the remote host.

Another useful Nmap option is -v. The verbose option causes more information about the scan to be displayed. With this option you can see how Nmap works. It first checks to see if the host is alive, performs the port scan (connect( ) in this case), and finishes with the remote operating system type scan. It is also possible to specify the -v option more than once in the Nmap command line to enable even more verbosity.

Many other options are available for Nmap, and you should reference the Nmap command line help and manual page (using the man nmap command) for these options. Nmap provides a number of different scan types, including methods that can be used to avoid tripping intrusion detection systems and ways of performing Nmap scans through certain firewalls. You can also output the Nmap results to a log file, and use a file containing target hosts as input.

Packet sniffing in UNIX

A number of packet sniffing utilities are available for UNIX. Sun Solaris, for example, comes with a packet sniffing program called Snoop. This program captures all data on the network link to which it is connected.

tcpdump

One of the most common packet sniffing programs for UNIX is tcpdump, which can be downloaded from www.tcpdump.org. In addition to the tcpdump program, a packet capture library is also required on some platforms. This library, called libpcap, can also be downloaded from the tcpdump Web site. Tcpdump is free software, and installation instructions are provided.

Simply run tcpdump with no options, and it will capture all packets on the first network interface, as shown in Figure 4-20. To stop capturing, press Ctrl-C. If you want to capture data from an interface other than the first, use the -i <interface> option where <interface> is the interface name.

Figure 4-21 shows an example of the output from a tcpdump session. This output is streamed to the console by default, so you may want to pipe it to a text file. On a busy network, there may be a large amount of data being captured. Filtering data with tcpdump is fairly easy; data is filtered using expressions. Expressions consist of a primitive, which is a term that describes what to filter, such as "port" or "proto." The expression also requires a value on which to filter.

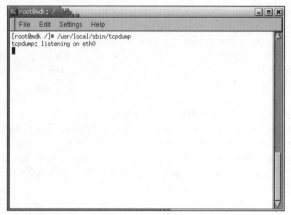

Figure 4-20: Running tcpdump with no options captures all packets on the first network interface in the system.

Figure 4-21: The data output from a tcpdump session shows the network traffic passing a network interface.

Tcpdump is flexible, and has a wide range of expressions that can be used for filtering (see the tcpdump man page for details). For example, you may want to see data only to or from a specific host. The host primitive is used in this case. The command is `tcpdump host <host>` where <host> is the name or IP address of the host for which to filter data. If you want to see only data coming from that host, the command is `tcpdump src host <host>`. It is impossible to list all of the available primitives for tcpdump, but you should now have a basic understanding of how they are combined to filter specific data from reading this section.

Ethereal

Another common UNIX packet sniffer is Ethereal, which is free and available for download at `www.ethereal.com`. Follow the instructions to install and start Ethereal. Unlike tcpdump, Ethereal is a graphical program. To begin capturing data with Ethereal, select Start from the Capture menu to open the Capture Preferences dialog box, as shown in Figure 4-22.

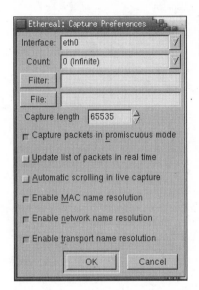

Figure 4-22: The Capture Preferences dialog box is used to configure the packet capture session before it starts.

✦ **Interface** — specifies the network interface on which Ethereal will listen.

✦ **Count** — used to specify the number of packets to capture. The default value of 0 specifies no limit.

✦ **Filter** — used to specify a filter for the capture. You can type a filter name, or click the Filter button to use the Filter dialog box to create a filter entry. The default of no filter will capture all packets.

✦ **File** — used to specify the file to which the capture results will later be saved. This can be specified later using Save As from the File menu.

✦ **Capture length** — specifies the maximum amount of data captured per packet. This must be at least as big as the Maximum Transmission Unit (MTU) for your network protocols. The default setting is more than sufficient for most.

Note   The MTU is the largest allowable size for a packet on the network. Ethernet uses an MTU of 1500 bytes by default.

There are a number of selectable options as well, including the following:

✦ **Capture packets set in promiscuous mode** — specify whether all packets (selected) or only packets to the local machine (deselected) are captured.

✦ **Update list of packets in real time** — if this is not selected as the default, captured packets are only shown after the capture is stopped. Enabling this will cause packets to be displayed as they are captured. They are added to the end of the list unless the next option is selected.

✦ **Automatic Scrolling in Live Capture** — if this option is enabled in concert with the previous Update list option, the last packet captured is always shown.

The final three options control how name resolution occurs.

✦ **MAC name** — causes the manufacturer of the network device to be resolved.

✦ **Network name** — causes DNS resolution to occur.

✦ **Transport name** — resolves protocol names to captured port numbers.

Click OK to begin capturing packets. A statistics dialog box is displayed, as shown in Figure 4-23. This shows how many packets have been captured as the scan progresses. If the Update List of Packets in Real Time option was selected in the Capture Preferences dialog box, the captured packets will be shown in the Ethereal window.

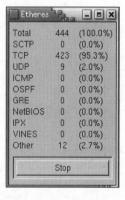

Figure 4-23: Statistics for the captured packets are shown as the capture progresses.

Click Stop to stop the capture. The captured packets are displayed in the upper pane of Ethereal, as shown in Figure 4-24. Selecting a packet in the upper pane displays details, such as information on encapsulated lower-level packets in the middle pane, and the actual packet data in hexadecimal and ASCII is shown in the lower pane. This is similar to Microsoft Network Monitor's detailed view of a packet.

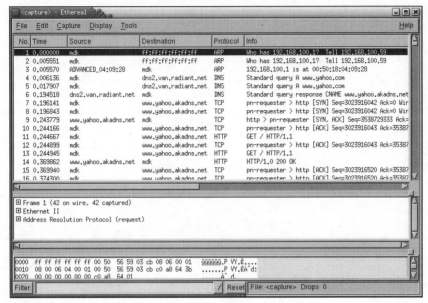

Figure 4-24: A list of captured packets is shown in Ethereal.

dsniff

dsniff is a powerful collection of utilities in one package. This package is available from `www.monkey.org/~dugsong/dsniff`. The advantage of dsniff is that a number of the utilities can be used to sniff application-specific data, rather than packet-level data. Mailsnarf, for example, captures all mail sent over the network. In addition to sniffing capabilities, it includes a number of spoofing utilities that can be used to spoof arp and DNS entries on a network for a man-in-the-middle attack. In addition, a number of documents on the dsniff Web site relate to preventing dsniff style sniffing and spoofing attacks against your network like those discussed here.

Caution   The dsniff package can get you into trouble. There are laws against stealing other people's e-mail; therefore, make sure if you are using these tools for any reason that you are not breaking any laws. Consult a lawyer before sniffing any traffic.

The dsniff utility included in the dsniff package is a password sniffer that can be used to sniff passwords for a large number of applications from FTP to Oracle. Figure 4-25 shows dsniff at work. By simply listening on the network, dsniff will pick up all password traffic, and all plaintext authentications will be displayed. You can also pipe this data to a file.

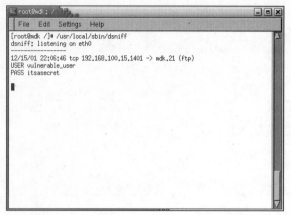

Figure 4-25: dsniff is being used to sniff passwords from the network.

Other utilities within the dsniff package include the following:

- **mailsnarf** — sniffs POP and SMTP mail on the network.

- **msgsnarf** — sniffs instant messaging traffic.

- **filesnarf** — sniffs NFS traffic.

- **sshmitm** — can be used for man-in-the-middle attacks against SSH version 1 to capture password logins and hijack sessions.

- **Webspy** — requires you to specify a host. After you run `webspy <host>`, any Web pages visited by the host system will be displayed in your local Web browser in real time.

Dsniff is a dangerous tool. If you are sniffing passwords from your network, could someone else be doing the same? You aren't safe with a switched network, either, because the arpspoof utility can be used to spoof arp replies from the default gateway, and all systems will talk through the local system. Using arpspoof will only capture data sent to remote networks, though, and not to other local machines. It is also possible to use a mirrored monitoring port on the switch to capture all data.

Most administrators and users are probably not even aware of the existence of dsniff and other sniffing tools. Dsniff just filters the data captured from the network and arranges it in a readable format. The dsniff suite of tools is not just useful for hacking either; it has legitimate uses. Packet sniffers are important to network administrators when problems are occurring and Dsniff is useful for auditing.

The answer to the problem of this type of tool being used for malicious purposes is not to ban applications such as dsniff, because the applications would still exist, only they would be harder for legitimate users to find. The only way to fight tools such as this is by changing your network to be more secure. If you need security on FTP sites, you can use a Kerberized version of FTP, or use SFTP (secure FTP), which is similar to SSH and uses encryption.

Cross-
Reference

For more information on Kerberos authentication, refer to Chapter 11.

You can circumvent all of these tools using encryption. If everyone encrypted their e-mail, mailsnarf would be useless. Encryption of all traffic would make sniffing attacks useless; however, encryption is not the absolute solution to all security problems. It is vulnerable to certain attacks, but is a step in the right direction.

The best way to secure your network from attackers is to attack it yourself using the same tools that they would use. This is known as penetration testing. Penetration testing is a common way of verifying the security of a network. The auditing techniques listed in this chapter are part of a full penetration test, but, in fact, a penetration test goes further than auditing, as described here. Penetration testing goes as far as to actually launch malicious attacks against your network to determine how and where the network is vulnerable. Penetration testing is usually done by a consultant who is a security expert with a lot of experience in this field, and is not usually something you can or should do yourself.

Summary

This chapter discussed security auditing of your network. You should have learned how auditing is performed and how to use the available auditing tools for both Microsoft Windows and UNIX/Linux platforms.

A full deep security audit of your entire network is something best left to experts, but security auditing is something that you should be doing on a regular basis as an administrator. Security auditing gives you an indication of any major security problems in your systems before an attacker can exploit them.

✦　　✦　　✦

Windows Server 2003 Security Provisions

CHAPTER

5

Windows Server 2003 provides a number of provisions for securing your operating system and applications. Some of these provisions such as Access Control Lists (ACLs) have been carried over from earlier versions of Windows (Windows NT Server 4.0 and Windows 2000 Server), while some are new, such as Internet Connection Firewall.

Before the actual security features in Windows Server are discussed in detail, some background on the architecture of Windows Server and its subsystems is given. Chapter 6 explains how to implement some of these features to secure your system.

Windows Server Architecture

Windows is a modular operating system. It looks integrated on the surface, but it is, in fact, made up of a number of components. A number of levels of modularity exist, each more granular than the last.

The least granular modules in the Windows Server 2003 architecture are the memory modes. Everything in Windows runs in one of two memory modes, as shown in Figure 5-1: User mode, in which all user programs and applications (in essence, everything that is not a device driver or operating system component) run, and Kernel mode, in which operating system services, such as the Windows kernel, and device drivers run.

The components running in Kernel mode have direct hardware access and direct memory access to almost the entire memory space. Programs running in User mode memory cannot directly access Kernel mode memory. Keep this in mind because it is an important factor in security.

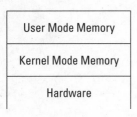

Figure 5-1: User mode and Kernel mode memory

The difference between User mode and Kernel mode is important when it comes to Windows Server security. Imagine if there were no restrictions on what memory space programs ran in, and operating system components and user applications shared the same space. An attacker could easily write an application to access system memory and steal passwords, for example. The separation between the two memory modes avoids such attacks because important values such as passwords are protected in the Kernel mode memory, which is not accessible by user applications. Other vulnerabilities exist, but this is the first step to designing a secure operating system.

The next level of granularity exists in the modules within the Windows kernel itself. These modules include components such as the Process Manager, which controls processes and threads, and the I/O Manager, which controls access to hardware through device drivers. These are known as *executive services*.

Now that you know a little about the architecture of Windows, you may be wondering how applications bridge the gap between User mode and Kernel mode so they can access hardware and write to disk or access the network. Application access is strictly controlled though a number of gateways, including the Win32 subsystem and the Local Security Authority (LSA). Figure 5-2 shows how these gateways allow access to applications.

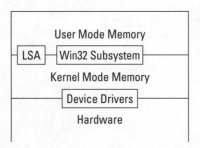

Figure 5-2: Bridging between User mode and Kernel mode

The Win32 Subsystem is responsible for most access to hardware and other kernel services by applications. In Windows Server, almost everything is considered an object, including files, processes, and so on. These objects may only be accessed directly by the operating system. A number of Application Programming Interfaces (APIs) are provided that programmers can use for this access. The advantage of limiting direct hardware access is clear. All access is controlled by the operating system, which avoids the circumvention of the operating system-level security services. Application developers do not need to be concerned about authentication within their software, as the standard Windows authentication mechanism can be used. Users may only access an object to which they have permissions.

The LSA is another gateway between the operating system and the user environment. Rather than providing access to objects for user applications, however, it performs security validation for those accesses. The LSA is the main component in the Windows security subsystem. Most other security components connect to the LSA. The LSA is responsible for user authentication and for granting access tokens, as well as managing local security policies. The LSA is the component in the Windows architecture that provides access to users when they are accessing a resource on the local system.

The LSA uses a number of external components to grant or deny access. User databases such as the Security Accounts Manager (SAM), which is the database of local users, and the Active Directory feed information into authentication protocols such as Kerberos and NT LAN Manager (NTLM), which connect to the LSA for access control. These authentication protocols are decided on by a component called the Multiple Authentication Provider (MAP). The MAP controls what type of authentication is used, such as Kerberos, an external authentication mechanism for clients that support it, or NTLM for downlevel (older) clients that do not support newer protocols such as Kerberos.

The LSA does not interface directly into the operating system either. The LSA is the hub of security activity on the system, but it uses a component called the Security Reference Monitor (SRM) for actual kernel-level operations. The SRM is responsible for the actual access control operation, as well as auditing object access.

Security Features in Windows Server

Windows Server introduces a number of new security features, some of which are shared with Windows XP. A few of these features are completely new, such as the Internet Connection Firewall (ICF), while some are vastly updated versions of existing features, such as Encrypting File System (EFS).

Windows Server has many more security features than it appears to at first. Most of these features are not apparent until you begin to roll out Windows networks on a larger scale, and move out of the workgroup model and into the domain/Active Directory architecture.

What's new in Windows Server?

Most of the new security features in Windows Server have been carried over from Windows 2000 and updated. New features include the Internet Connection Firewall (ICF), Session Initiation Protocol (SIP) service, blank password restrictions, and software restriction policies.

Internet Connection Firewall

Internet Connection Firewall (ICF) is a personal firewall application. A personal firewall is designed to protect only the local computer from attacks. In a network with a number of computers, a true firewall protecting the entire network is a more effective solution because configuration changes are only made in one place. On a small network, however, it is sometimes more cost-effective to have a personal firewall such as ICF on each system. Full hardware firewalls are now available for small networks in the $500 to $1,000 range, so the usefulness of a personal firewall is limited to single Internet-connected systems, but some may choose to use ICF rather than a small firewall solution.

ICF secures a single system. It is installed by default, and needs only to be enabled and configured. ICF can be used to configure both outgoing and incoming connections. Configuration for outgoing connections is limited. All outgoing traffic is allowed, except for some ICMP traffic, which can be allowed or denied.

 Cross-Reference   Working with ICF is covered in Chapter 6.

Incoming traffic settings are more configurable. ICF's main purpose is to control incoming traffic. By default, no traffic is allowed into the system. Different types of traffic can be enabled, such as FTP, Web, or Ping requests. Custom services can also be defined if a service you require is not defined by default.

In addition to traffic control, ICF also has logging capabilities. This allows you to log either successful or unsuccessful connections, or both. These logs can be used to detect attacks against the system and view other network traffic.

Session Initiation Protocol (SIP) service

The Session Initiation Protocol (SIP) is used for applications such as Instant Messaging (IM) and other real-time communications applications such as videoconferencing. The SIP service provides a consistent and secure pathway for these applications.

These applications (IM, for example) are fairly insecure. Features such as file transfer allow untrusted files to reach your network without being scanned for viruses as they would in e-mail. You can't limit this functionality without disabling IM across the entire network. With SIP, tighter controls can be implemented on this type of traffic.

Blank password restrictions

By default, in Windows Server, you cannot log on to a system remotely using a local account with a blank password. For example, if the local administrator account has a blank password, you can log in to the system from the console with no problems. You cannot, however, log in remotely using that account. Remote logins would include connections to a local Web server or shared file.

This behavior is designed to avoid attacks from the Internet if the system has a blank password. If an account had a blank password and this security measure was not in effect, anyone could remotely access resources on the system.

The inability to log on remotely can be avoided in two ways. All accounts should be protected by a strong password. When a password is set, the account can be used remotely. It is also possible — but not recommended — to disable this security feature in a policy.

Software restriction policies

Software restriction policies are used to isolate potentially dangerous programs so that no damage is done to the system when they are executed. A common problem is viruses or worms received in e-mail or through other methods. When these programs are executed, they launch malicious code that often spreads itself automatically and sometimes causes damage to the system.

By configuring software restriction policies in a group policy, untrusted programs are isolated to protect the system from any harmful effects. These programs can be restricted from running entirely or strictly restricted so that they can be run in an isolated environment to check for negative effects.

Programs can be isolated in e-mail attachment directories, Internet links, and ActiveX controls, as these are the most common locations for malicious programs. Programs can also be restricted based on a hash (a signature of the file) and specific Internet zones.

Existing Windows security provisions

A number of features have been carried over from older versions of Windows, such as NT 3.5, 3.51, and 4.0. Windows 2000 took the next step towards being a secure operating system, and implemented a large number of new security features in the base operating system, especially with the introduction of Active Directory (AD). Active Directory allowed security policies to be applied to users and groups in a far more efficient and granular method than was previously possible.

Users and groups

While this seems like an obvious feature in a multi-user operating system, users and groups are an important security feature. Having individual user accounts and groups allows you to use other access control and authentication methods. Everything from logins to cryptographic key pairs is user-based. Without user accounts, anyone could log into the system and access all system resources.

Each user account in Windows Server is assigned a security identifier (SID). The SID is a unique number that identifies the account to the operating system. Items such as the name fields and even the user name are simply attributes. Only the SID is used to identify the account by the operating system.

On the surface, a group is simply a container in which user accounts are stored. A group provides an easier way to grant access to a resource than providing each user access individually. Groups become complex in terms of their scope. There are a number of different types of groups, each with a different scope. Local groups are local to the system and can only be used on the local system. They can contain both local users and others, such as domain users.

Domain local groups are valid only in the local domain. They can contain any user, as well as other groups. *Domain global groups* are similar to domain local groups, except they can be used outside the local domain. They can contain domain users and other domain global groups if the domain is configured to run in Native mode. Native mode is used in Active Directory when there are no pre-Windows 2000 domain controllers. Native mode allows more functionality as it does not need to be backwards compatible.

The final group type is a Universal group. This group is valid anywhere in the Active Directory domain *forest* and can contain any users, domain global groups, or other universal groups. A forest contains a number of domains that share configuration information and a single Global Catalog in AD.

Access Control Lists

Access Control Lists (ACLs) are a major security feature in Windows Server. An ACL is an attribute of an object that specifies what type of access users or groups have to an object, if any. This type of ACL is called a Discretionary ACL (DACL). In addition to the ACL on the object, it is also possible in some cases to allow ACLs on specific object properties. In this case, specific access can be allowed or denied to the property rather than the entire object, allowing for more granularity in access control.

Auditing

Windows Server also provides auditing for object accesses. As many objects exist in the Windows system (such as user accounts and files), events such as logins, logouts, and file access can be audited. Objects have a second ACL, called a system ACL (SACL), that controls auditing.

User rights

User rights are similar to ACLs except that instead of allowing a user access to an object, they allow a user permission to perform an action. User rights are specific to the local system. In a domain model, user rights are assigned through group policies. A number of rights can be granted to a user, including the following:

✦ Rights for changing the time on the system

✦ Rights for shutting down the system

✦ Rights specific to logon actions

Users can be restricted from logging on locally or accessing the local system from the network, for example.

Group policies

Group policies are implemented in Active Directory. A group policy is applied to a specific group of users or computers or to the entire domain, and defines a set of policies for those users or computers. This is similar to the policy editor utility in Windows NT 4.0, but greatly expanded.

Group policies are a major security feature in Windows Server 2003. They are used to control a number of security features, such as password policies and Kerberos configuration. Group policies are a powerful tool in securing your network. In addition to customized group policies, a number of group policy templates are included with Windows Server that allow you to set the security level of the system without having to understand every setting that needs to be changed. The template can be applied and all required changes made automatically.

NT File System

The NT File System (NTFS) is a replacement for the DOS File Allocation Table (FAT) file system used in some other versions of Windows and in DOS. Unlike FAT, NTFS provides the capability to support ACLs. This is the key feature leading to the widespread use of NTFS in Windows installations. Assigning permissions on file objects in a FAT file system is not possible. NTFS is also advantageous in the way the file system drivers work, giving it better performance than FAT.

Encrypting File System

The Encrypting File System (EFS) is used to encrypt files on an NTFS disk partition. Essentially, EFS uses a combination of public key and symmetric encryption to encrypt files. Only the user who encrypted the file or an administrator can decrypt the files. EFS is totally transparent to the user; all operations are performed at the file system driver level.

 The Encrypting File System is discussed in detail in Chapter 8.

When encrypting a file using EFS, the data is encrypted using a randomly generated file encryption key (FEK). EFS then employs a user's certificate, which is created automatically through Windows Server's PKI auto-enrollment feature, to encrypt the FEK. The encrypted FEK is stored as an attribute of the file. The decryption process is the opposite. You decrypt the FEK using the user's private key and then decrypt the file using the FEK.

 Public Key Infrastructure is discussed in Chapter 12.

Kerberos authentication

By default, Windows Server uses Kerberos for authentication when configured in a domain model. Kerberos is much more secure than the traditional NTLM authentication method because it uses full public key cryptography rather than a simple one-way hash. Kerberos has been used for many years as a highly secure authentication mechanism.

 An overview of Kerberos authentication is given in Chapter 10, and a detailed description is provided in Chapter 11.

Virtual Private Networks

Virtual Private Networks (VPNs) are a method of creating a secure connection from one network to another over a public network such as the Internet. You can implement VPNs in Windows Server in several ways. Point-to-Point Tunneling Protocol (PPTP), Layer 2 Tunneling Protocol (L2TP), and IP Security (IPSec) are all supported protocols. VPNs are proliferating because the cost of high-speed Internet connections is dropping and the cost for point-to-point network connections is staying relatively consistent. For many lower-speed, point-to-point connections such as T1 (1.544 Mbps), it is far more cost-effective to implement a VPN over an SDSL Internet connection or something similar. Higher-speed connections have not experienced a sufficient price drop to be considered more effective than VPNs. In addition, the hardware required to run a VPN over a high-speed connection (100 Mbps+) is expensive.

The most basic VPN implementation in Windows Server is a PPTP VPN. This is the original VPN protocol to be supported in Windows, and is still the simplest. PPTP is not as secure as IPSec, but for many applications it is good enough.

L2TP and IPSec are often combined to form a more secure VPN tunnel. IPSec is a common protocol implemented across many platforms. IPSec is a standard VPN protocol designed to allow equipment from multiple vendors to interconnect.

The implementation of IPSec in Windows Server is theoretically compatible with all standard IPSec protocol implementations, so it can connect to third-party VPN devices and firewalls. This is not always true in practice, but will work in most cases.

PKI and certificate services

Windows Server provides the services of a PKI through a number of methods, including certificate services. A PKI provides a central location for the storage of keys and certificates used for encryption and authentication. A certificate is essentially a public key that has been verified as authentic. With the PKI in place, key sharing and trust relationships are simplified, and encryption and authentication can take place more securely.

Certificate services is a Windows component used for the generation and maintenance of certificates in the domain. These certificates are used for a number of things, from Secure Sockets Layer-encrypted (SSL-encrypted) Web pages, to IPSec, to EFS. A wide variety of applications exist for certificates, and certificate services enables these applications.

Windows Server also provides certificate services autoenrollment, which allows users and computers to automatically enroll in the certificate authority and receive certificates for certain features, such as IPSec and EFS, without any user intervention.

Cross-Reference
A PKI is a complex subject that is discussed in detail in Chapter 12. Chapter 13 explains the use of certificate services.

Delegation

The ability to delegate permissions to perform certain tasks is a useful security feature in Windows Server. Active Directory enables you to delegate permissions for certain tasks to other users without giving them full administrative access. This is useful if you want to delegate the management of user accounts to Human Resources or to the department manager. Even more advantageous is the ability to delegate permissions on a per-OU basis. An *Organizational Unit (OU)* is essentially a set of objects grouped together for management purposes. This allows a department manager to have permission to manage users in only his department, for example. In addition to specific tasks that can be delegated, it is also possible to delegate custom tasks. Custom tasks can be used to delegate permissions on specific properties of an object.

External authentication methods

Windows Server supports external authentication using smart cards. The *smart card* is a device similar to a credit card, except that instead of using a magnetic strip, it contains circuitry that can store data. In the case of Windows Server authentication, the smart card contains certificates and private keys. When you authenticate, Windows uses the keys on the smart card to authenticate to the Kerberos Key Distribution Center (KDC).

A smart card provides an extra level of security over password authentication. With password authentication, you only need a user's password to access the system as that user in most cases. Smart card authentication, on the other hand, requires both the physical card and the personal identification number (PIN) associated with that card for access as that user.

C2 security

C2 security has always been a big buzzword around Microsoft Windows. Windows NT 4.0 has been "C2-capable" for quite some time. What does that mean though? The C2 security level is a standard defined by the United States Department of Defense and is granted through the National Computer Security Center (NCSC). Both Windows NT 3.5 and Windows NT 4.0 have been certified to the C2 standard by the NCSC in some configurations.

While not specifically C2-certified by the NCSC, Windows Server (along with Windows 2000 and Windows XP) is C2-capable. The C2 level of security has a number of requirements and is known as *discretionary security*. Only an overview of some of the requirements for C2 follows. This is by no means a comprehensive list.

✦ Each user must log on with a unique user name and password to the system.

✦ Protection against data theft must be in place. The Ctrl+Alt+Delete login sequence in Windows is in place for this reason.

✦ Auditing and accountability must be in place. It must be possible for any task performed by a user to be audited.

✦ Both files and memory space must be protected so that lingering data cannot be recovered. Deleted files on an NTFS partition cannot be recovered, and Windows reinitializes memory space when a program releases it.

✦ The system state must be protected. This is why the Windows kernel runs in Kernel mode memory. External processes cannot change the running system state.

✦ Users with administrative privileges cannot access files to which they do not have permission. They must first take ownership of the file, which notifies the user that the file has been accessed.

Security with Active Directory

Active Directory is a Lightweight Directory Access Protocol (LDAP)-based directory that contains all information about a domain. LDAP is simply a standard protocol for a directory. Active Directory servers essentially take the place of domain controllers in a Windows NT 4.0 network. Active Directory does not simply provide authentication like a domain controller, however. Many more features are available.

Active Directory provides a point for integration with other applications. A perfect example is Microsoft Exchange. In a Windows NT 4.0 environment with Exchange 5.5, the Exchange environment and Windows domain were essentially separate. The only integration was for authentication. With Active Directory and Exchange 2000, the Exchange directory is integrated into the Active Directory schema. The AD *schema* defines the layout of how information is stored in the directory. Instead of having a user account in the domain and a separate Exchange mailbox, all the information is stored in the Active Directory. The physical mailbox still resides in the Exchange mailbox store, but all the user attributes are stored in the AD.

Active Directory architecture

Active Directory is fairly simple in its architecture. You need one or more Active Directory servers; more are better from a redundancy and scalability standpoint. In addition, you need one or more Global Catalog servers. The Global Catalog (GC) is stored by default on the first domain controller (AD server) created. The GC is used for logon and for searching the directory. In addition, one AD server must be the Operations Master, which is also the first AD server by default.

Active Directory removes the parent/child relationship from the domain model that was present with Windows NT 4.0. That model used one Primary Domain Controller (PDC) to which changes were made, and any number of Backup Domain Controllers (BDC) to which the changes were replicated. The BDCs were read-only. In an Active Directory implementation, the Active Directory servers are peers. Any server can accept changes and they are replicated to the other AD servers. There is, however, an exception to this rule, which is where the Operations Master comes into play.

Certain changes to the AD cannot be made through any AD server. These changes, such as schema updates, must be made through the Operations Master. Five Operations Master roles can be dispersed among AD servers, but that is outside the scope of this book.

Turning now from the AD server architecture to the AD internals, the discussion becomes somewhat more complex. AD is a directory based on LDAP. If you are familiar with directory servers or even databases, you will be familiar with a schema. The schema is basically an outline of what data can be stored in the directory. The advantage of the AD is that the schema can be modified to enable the storage of any data. Any piece of software can modify the schema to store its data in the directory. This is how the integration of Exchange into the AD works.

The directory is meant to hold objects. Users, groups, and computers are all objects stored in AD. Objects have names that define them in the directory, and they also have attributes. The attributes are all of the settings and so on that are configured in the Properties dialog box when working with a user, group, or similar object.

The directory would become a mess if all objects were stored in a flat space. The directory is divided into OUs and domains. OUs are used to separate objects logically. An OU could be created for each department, each branch office, or any other logical division you choose.

You will find logical divisions above OUs in the hierarchy. The next step up is a domain, the highest level at which you can set policies. Just as individual OUs can have policies that apply only to the OU, the domain can also have a domain-wide policy. This policy applies to all OUs unless a more specific policy is set at the OU level. While you can have multiple OUs in a domain, you can only have one domain on each AD server; however, there can be more than one AD server in a domain.

Above domains are trees, which contain domains, and forests, which contain trees. These hierarchical levels are only used to establish trust relationships across multiple domains. Policies cannot be applied at the tree or forest level.

How Active Directory provides security

When it comes to security, AD is primarily responsible for authentication and policies. As in the Windows NT 4.0 domain model, AD maintains the user database for authentication. Authentication is performed using Kerberos for Windows Server, XP, and Windows 2000 clients, and defaults to NTLM for other clients. In addition to standard authentication through Kerberos or NTLM, external authentication through smart cards or other hardware devices is supported.

 Cross-Reference Authentication is covered in detail in Chapter 10.

The second main security feature of AD is group policies. Group policies, as previously discussed, provide a way to apply specific configuration settings to a group of users. In addition to general desktop settings, a number of security-specific settings can be configured in group policies.

AD also provides two additional security-related features: trusts and delegation of authority. Trusts are configured between domains to allow users from one domain to access resources in another domain and vice versa, depending on the direction of the trust.

Delegation of authority is used to allow certain users administrative access to specific areas of the directory without global administrative access. For example, a department manager can be assigned access to add and remove users from his department group.

Microsoft CryptoAPI

Cryptography is the process of encrypting plain text information so that it can only be decrypted with the appropriate key using the appropriate cryptographic algorithm. Cryptography is used often on the Internet to protect sensitive data such as credit card information or e-mail. Cryptographic algorithms are implemented in Windows Server, which can be used by any application with the CryptoAPI.

 Cross-Reference Cryptography is discussed in detail in Chapter 8.

The Microsoft CryptoAPI is an API that is used to interface applications with a cryptographic service provider (CSP). The CryptoAPI is used each time a cryptographic operation is needed within Windows. The CryptoAPI provides all cryptographic functions, from key and certificate management to encryption and decryption. It provides an interface layer so that any software can use these functions without writing the required code.

The CryptoAPI is a set of features in itself for key management, as well as an abstraction layer between the application and the CSP. The CSP is a modular component that performs the actual cryptographic functions of manipulating data. It is possible to have a number of CSPs installed, one each for RSA, DSA, and smart cards, for example; however, only one CSP is used at a time. The CSP is never accessed directly by an application, but always through the CryptoAPI.

IPSec

Typically, traffic over a TCP/IP connection is sent in plain text. Anyone with a packet sniffer and access to any network link between the source and destination hosts can read this data because the IP packets are in a standard form. Encryption is done, if at all, at the Application layer. Even if encrypted data is being sent in the Application layer, much information can still be gathered from the lower layers of the packet. If the traffic is not encrypted at the Application layer, it is readable by anyone sniffing the packets.

IP Security (IPSec) is a protocol used to secure TCP/IP traffic below the Transport layer. It is a public key-based system in which public key encryption is used to share a session key that is then used to symmetrically encrypt the actual data.

IPSec is often used for creating VPNs over Internet links, but can also be used to secure local links between computers to avoid sniffing or spoofing attacks. This is essentially a short-haul VPN.

In Windows Server, IPSec policies can be defined to control connections to other systems. Connections to other IPSec-compatible systems can be configured to use IPSec, while connections to non-IPSec-compatible systems default to non-IPSec connections.

In addition, Windows Server supports some extra features with IPSec. It is possible to implement network load balancing (NLB) for IPSec connections, which allows VPN services to load balance and provide failover for VPN servers. If a VPN server fails, another can automatically take its place. This feature can be used to make IPSec-based VPN services more robust.

IPSec can also pass traffic over a connection using network address translation (NAT). This can be used to establish a VPN tunnel to a branch office or home network using NAT and private addresses.

Another added feature to IPSec in Windows Server is support for 128-bit Internet Key Exchange (IKE) keys. This longer IKE key ensures the security of the IPSec key exchange process and increases the security of the entire IPSec connection.

ISA Server

Microsoft Internet Security and Acceleration (ISA) Server is an external product that provides firewall and caching services. Traditionally, these products would have been purchased from a third party, but they are now available directly from Microsoft and integrate into Windows Server 2003 or Windows 2000 Server.

The ISA Server provides two services: firewall and caching. The firewall service is used to control traffic passing through the ingress and egress points of your network. The caching service is used to cache certain objects to speed up incoming and outgoing connections.

 Cross-Reference ISA Server is discussed in detail in Chapters 16, 17, and 18.

What do the ISA Server services do?

The ISA Server firewall service is a fully stateful firewall with application filtering capabilities. A stateful firewall inspects the contents of all packets passing though the firewall. Firewalls without stateful inspection inspect only the packet headers.

The firewall can be configured in a number of ways. Several types of filtering can be performed, including basic packet filtering, stateful inspection, and application filtering.

Using ISA Server, you can tightly control the traffic entering and leaving your network.

The acceleration component of ISA Server allows you to cache incoming and outgoing Web and FTP content. Caching outgoing connections, or *forward caching*, reduces the bandwidth usage on your Internet link and speeds access to content for internal users. Caching incoming connections, or *reverse caching*, speeds the access to content on your Web servers for external users. Load on those Web servers is also reduced.

How does ISA Server provide security?

ISA Server's firewall components provide security by controlling the network traffic traveling in and out of your network. Chapter 2 introduced the principle of network ingress and egress points — points where network traffic enters or leaves the network under your control to or from a public network. A firewall should, by default, block all traffic between the two networks. You then open the firewall to allow only the traffic that is required to pass. For example, you will probably want to allow internal users to surf the Web. You may also have a Web server on the internal network and open the firewall to provide access to that from the outside.

A firewall's entire responsibility is to control the movement of traffic in and out of your network. Essentially, three levels of filtering can be used:

✦ The most basic level is *packet filtering*. Packet filtering simply inspects the IP and TCP packet headers to determine if the packet should be allowed through the firewall.

✦ The next level of inspection is *stateful inspection*. Stateful inspection uses more of the packet headers to determine whether or not to allow it. It is called stateful inspection because it keeps track of whether or not each packet is part of a proper exchange of data (its state). An added level of security is gained by inspecting the packet contents and tracking incoming and outgoing packets. Stateful inspection ensures that sessions are completed properly and gives some insurance against session hijacking.

✦ The most detailed level of inspection, but also the most costly, is *application filtering*. Application filtering inspects the packet data at the application level to ensure that hostile data is not included. Application filters are also known as *proxies*. One big advantage to application filtering is the ability to control content. While other types of filtering only control the source and destination of packets, application filtering can block packets based on their content. This allows blocking of hostile content, such as e-mail worms and malicious Web code, as well as objectionable content.

 Cross-Reference Chapter 16 provides a detailed overview of the exact methods used by the firewall to control traffic in and out of your network.

Summary

In this chapter, you learned about the security features included in Windows Server 2003. Windows Server security features are range all the way from protecting your network from rogue packets with ISA Server to maintaining the security of LAN resources with ACLs. In addition, Windows Server includes a number of authentication methods and provisions for encrypting your data.

✦   ✦   ✦

System Security

◆   ◆   ◆   ◆

Securing Windows Server 2003

After covering the theories and procedural aspects of security, the practical aspects of Windows Server 2003 security can be addressed.

As discussed in Chapter 5, the security arena has advanced a number of steps from Microsoft Windows NT 4.0 through Windows 2000 and now Windows Server 2003. Plenty of progress has been made in all aspects of security, such as authentication with the move to Kerberos for domain authentication.

You can take a number of measures to increase your systems' security, including those in the following list, which this chapter discusses in detail:

  ✦ Hardware configuration

  ✦ Installation of the operating system

  ✦ Setting file permissions

  ✦ Configuring auditing

  ✦ Setting policies

Taking these measures can lead to a secure system if you take the potential gaps in security into account. You should be familiar with your network configuration, as well as Windows Server 2003, to fully secure a system.

Hardware Security

The first thing to take into account when securing a Windows Server 2003 is the security of the hardware. It may sound unrelated, but having secure hardware is an important step in overall system security.

Insecure hardware can lead to the complete compromise of protected files or the compromise of an entire system. With the default security of most hardware platforms, anyone can edit the system BIOS and boot from a floppy disk.

One major potential flaw exists with this scenario. NTFS file systems are available for both the DOS and Linux operating systems. By booting off of a floppy disk-based DOS or Linux operating system (several exist) with an NTFS file system, you make all of the files on that system accessible because these file system drivers ignore Access Control Lists (ACLs). The ACLs are ignored because there is no Windows authentication mechanism in DOS or Linux to provide an access token. These file systems are useful for recovery and compatibility purposes, and their existence necessitates security on the hardware and BIOS.

Using one of these file system drivers and booting from a disk makes everything on the system hard drives accessible (unless certain software RAID configurations are in place for those drives, although that is no measure of security). An attacker can edit system files and even the Registry and SAM database to change passwords or otherwise gain system access. Other files on the drive are also accessible, such as confidential documents on a file server. Another possible problem is the attacker's ability to install a new operating system. If the attacker were to install a fresh copy of Windows Server 2003, he could overwrite the ACLs on existing files as the local administrator and access those files.

You can stop an attack at the hardware level in a few ways. The most basic way to stop the system from booting from a floppy disk or CD-ROM is to physically lock the machine. Floppy drive locks are available that insert into the drive and lock with a key. Systems equipped with locking covers also exist. If the system is installed in a cabinet, you can physically lock the cabinet, and the data center or server room can also be secured. All of this physical security should be in place, with only trusted people having access, such as the system administrators. The floppy drives and CD-ROM drives should also be removed from systems after operating systems are installed. Software can then be installed from network shares, such as your workstation.

Obtain the next level of security by editing the BIOS parameters. The BIOS must first be password protected so that an attacker cannot change the configuration. Figure 6-1 shows the configuration of a BIOS supervisor password on an example system. On most systems, the supervisor BIOS password is used for access to the BIOS configuration utility.

Many different BIOS manufacturers exist, and the BIOS configuration often varies by hardware type. Although the specifics are different, almost all of them have the configuration options discussed here.

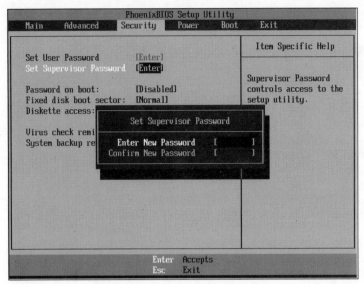

Figure 6-1: The BIOS supervisor password or access password
limits access to the BIOS configuration utility.

The specific BIOS configuration in this example also allows you to set a user password. The system can be configured so that the user or supervisor passwords are needed to boot the system. A related option allows disk drive access to be limited to those with the BIOS supervisor password so that only those individuals can use the drive.

Normally, however, on systems without this configuration option, only a supervisor password or BIOS access password is set, and the disk and CD-ROM drives are disabled in the BIOS configuration. Figure 6-2 shows the BIOS configuration option that allows you to disable the floppy drive.

To boot from the floppy drive, someone with the BIOS access password must enter the BIOS configuration and enable the floppy drive. Disabling the CD-ROM drive can be more difficult. To disable the CD-ROM drive, you can disable the IDE channel to which the drive is connected if it is the only drive on the bus. If another drive exists on the bus or the CD-ROM is connected to an SCSI bus that cannot be disabled, you may have to remove the drive.

The other way to disable an attacker's ability to boot from a floppy or CD-ROM drive is to change the boot order in the BIOS configuration. This does not prevent someone from using the drive when the system is running, but it does prevent the booting of another operating system. Figure 6-3 shows the system's default boot order.

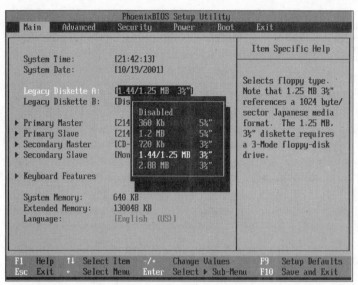

Figure 6-2: The floppy drive should be disabled in the BIOS configuration utility.

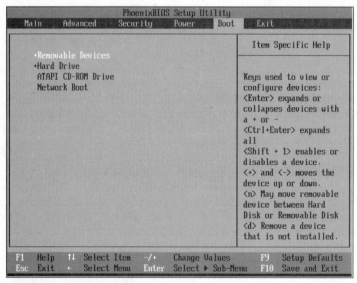

Figure 6-3: The system's default boot order allows booting from removable devices and the CD-ROM drive.

By default, this system first attempts to boot from the removable devices, such as a floppy drive. It then attempts to boot from the system hard drive, from a CD-ROM, and finally from the network. An attacker can boot this system from the floppy disk by default (if it is enabled), and by disconnecting the system disk, he can boot from a CD-ROM or network boot server. Even though the system drive is disabled, he can still access other drives on the system. By changing the drive configuration, an attacker can also make it unbootable and access the files on that drive. After he makes the necessary changes to gain access to the system, he can reconfigure the drive and make it bootable again.

For reasons previously discussed, simply changing the boot order so that the hard drive boots first is not enough. Disabling booting from the external devices, as shown in Figure 6-4, is imperative. In this BIOS, the exclamation mark indicates that a device is disabled and cannot be used to boot the system.

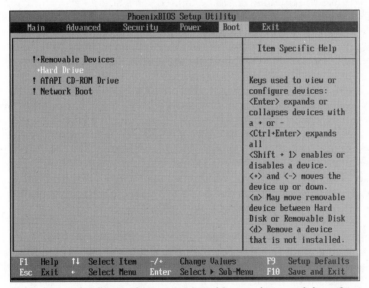

Figure 6-4: The floppy drive, CD-ROM drive, and network have been disabled in the boot order and cannot be used to boot the system.

The system should now be secure at the hardware level. Keep in mind that good password control is important, because the only way an attacker can boot the system from a disk or otherwise attack the system at a hardware level is with the password or by replacing the BIOS chip on the motherboard. Replacing the BIOS chip is an extreme but possible measure for a determined attacker. This emphasizes the need for physical security in the data center as well.

Going back to the security in layers model, the BIOS protection and disabled boot devices are one layer of security, and locks on the data center, cabinet, and computer are other layers of security. Even removing the disk and CD-ROM drives is not foolproof because the attacker could easily bring his own drives. Each of these layers can guarantee only to slow down a determined attacker or thwart an attacker who is less willing to spend the required time to gain access to the system on a physical level.

Securing the Operating System

After the hardware has been secured, you can install the operating system. An important step is to ensure that the operating system media you are using is authentic. A copy of the original CD, either created in-house or a forged pirate version meant to look like the original, could be tainted. This sounds like an extreme measure, but the original CDs created by the duplication facility used by Microsoft are controlled by security and created from only a known, good master CD. Newer Microsoft software CDs are inscribed with a number of holographic markings that are difficult to duplicate so that you can verify the authenticity of the disc.

In some cases, the operating system is installed on your system before it is delivered to you. In many cases, system administrators will reinstall the operating system when the system arrives, both for security and so that they know exactly how the install was done for the purposes of future administration. In extreme cases, very large servers and the high-end version of Windows Server 2003 (Datacenter Edition) can be obtained only with the operating system pre-installed on the system. In this case, verify that the server vendor is an authorized reseller. You may also want to ensure that a bonded carrier is used to ship the system to minimize the chances that it could be tampered with on the way to your location.

Copies of the installation media can be easily infected with binaries containing backdoors. Even if an employee copies the CD, that employee could add a Trojan binary to the original. This is a little paranoid, but it is so simple to avoid that the risk is not worth it. Ensuring that the CD is a known, good copy protects the system against security holes from the start.

A number of other measures that you can take to secure the operating system through the installation and initial configuration phases include the following:

✦ Minimizing the operating system during installation

✦ Disabling unnecessary services immediately following installation

✦ Setting proper file permissions

✦ Configuring auditing on the system

✦ Using policies to enforce system security

When installing Windows Server 2003, you should always install the system on an NTFS partition for security and never on a file allocation table (FAT) partition. FAT partitions do not provide the security features such as ACLs and EFS that are available with NTFS.

Caution   The FAT file system should never be used for any disk partitions on a production Windows Server 2003.

When performing the initial system installation, create the system partition and select the NTFS format for the partition, as shown in Figure 6-5.

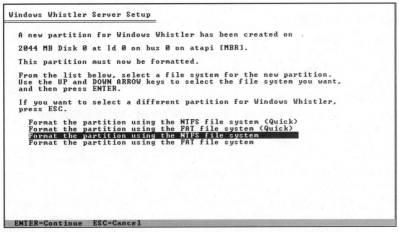

Figure 6-5: Choose the NTFS format for your system partition during the initial installation phase of Windows Server 2003 for increased security.

Operating system minimization

Operating system minimization, as discussed in Chapter 3, is a method of reducing the number of potential places for a security vulnerability to occur. This has been referred to earlier in the book as reducing the system's profile. Each application or service is another location where a buffer overflow, format string bug, or other vulnerability could be located. If this vulnerability is discovered in the future and you are not aware of it, an attacker could gain access to the system locally or, in the case of services that accept network connections, remotely.

Minimizing Windows components

Unlike earlier versions of Microsoft Windows, such as Windows 2000 Server and Windows NT 4.0 Server, Windows Server 2003 does not give you the option of which components to add during the operating system installation process. By default, Windows Server 2003 installs with the minimal required components for security. Windows Server 2003 continues to the network installation section after you set the following:

- ✦ System locale
- ✦ Personalization information
- ✦ Product key
- ✦ Licensing mode
- ✦ Computer name
- ✦ Administrator password
- ✦ Date and time

The network installation procedure in Windows Server 2003 provides a default configuration good for a basic system. Dynamic Host Configuration Protocol (DHCP) is used to assign IP addresses and the default network services are enabled. In most cases, however, you will want to set the network configuration manually. This allows you to assign your own IP addresses and decide which network services to enable.

Click Custom Settings and then click Next to continue.

The default network settings are displayed. The Client for Microsoft Networks should be enabled, as should TCP/IP unless your network uses a different protocol. The important decision to make at this stage is whether or not to enable File and Printer Sharing for Microsoft Networks.

If this server will not be used as a file or print server, disable the File and Printer Sharing. Having this service enabled can lead to security vulnerabilities through insufficient file permissions and through vulnerabilities in the service itself. A dedicated Web or mail server has no reason to be running File and Printer Sharing. If you choose to disable the service, deselect it. You can also configure TCP/IP and then click Next to continue.

Decide whether the server will be a domain member or reside in a workgroup.

A server that is a domain member allows access from domain users and will trust other systems in the domain. Traditionally, servers that do not require domain membership, such as Web servers or some types of mail servers, are not added to the domain. If a server that is a domain member is compromised, it can lead to the compromise of other systems in the domain due to the inherent trust of domain users by member servers.

If a server is a domain member, there are a number of advantages in ease of use. Instead of maintaining a user database on each server, as is required with servers not in the domain, access can simply be granted to users or groups in the domain. This advantage has led many administrators to make Web servers and other servers that do not use the domain for user authentication members of the domain. However, such servers should never be domain members because, if they are compromised, they can lead to the compromise of other systems.

Some systems must be domain members, assuming that a domain has been implemented for workstation authentication and so on. File and print servers are perfect examples. If a file server were not a domain member, a user database would need to be maintained on the server that mirrored the domain user database for the purpose of ACLs on files. Domains were created to alleviate just this problem. When the file server is a domain member, domain users and groups can be used in the ACLs, and there are no problems with passwords that are not synchronized or user accounts that are missing.

Some mail applications or, more specifically, groupware applications, such as Microsoft Exchange, require domain membership for user authentication. Some Web servers should also be domain members, such as intranet servers that provide internal access only. Users would then use their domain accounts to access content on the server.

When you decide whether your application for this system requires domain membership or not, specify the domain or workgroup name and then click Next to continue installation. After this step is complete, Windows Server 2003 finishes the installation process by copying files and setting the system configuration.

Disabling and customizing services

You should now have a functioning basic Windows Server 2003 installation. The next step is to work with the system's default services to customize it to fit your application.

The first time you log into a new installation of Windows Server 2003, the Manage Your Server utility is displayed, as shown in Figure 6-6. The Manage Your Server utility is used to set up the server for specific roles. *Roles* are set packages of files and services that each add a specific function to the system, such as a DNS server or Active Directory.

1. To add a role to your system, click Add or remove a role.

   Ensure that you have done all of the preliminary steps shown on the first page of the Configure Your Server Wizard. These steps include configuring the system's network connection and the addition of all peripherals. Click Next to continue.

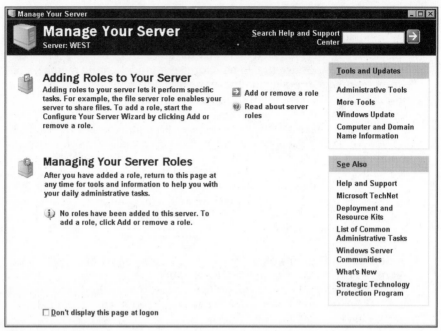

Figure 6-6: The Manage Your Server utility will automatically configure the system for certain roles.

2. Figure 6-7 shows the next step in the Configure Your Server Wizard. Using the Typical configuration for a first server option will configure the server as the first domain controller in a new domain and install the associated services.

   The Custom setup option, also shown in Figure 6-7, allows you to customize the configuration of the server to a specific application or as a domain controller. Select Custom Setup and then click Next.

3. The wizard allows you to choose from a variety of roles for the server. Each of the options shown in Figure 6-8 will customize the server in a different way. Selecting Application server, for example, adds Internet Information Server (IIS) and ASP.NET for Web applications. Selecting Streaming media server installs Windows Media Services automatically; selecting Mail server installs SMTP and POP3; and so on.

   If you want to use the Configure Your Server Wizard to configure the system for your application, select the type of server from the list and click Next to continue the process. Clicking Cancel will close the Configure Your Server Wizard without making any changes, and you can continue to the next steps in securing the system. You can also install any applications you want at this point.

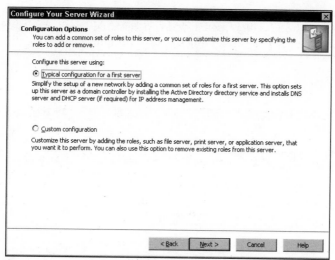

Figure 6-7: Using the Express setup option in the Configure Your Server Wizard installs the services necessary to make the server the first domain controller in a new domain.

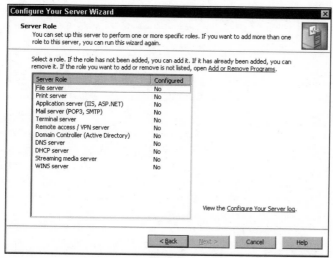

Figure 6-8: Selecting a Custom configuration in the Configure Your Server Wizard allows you to choose from a variety of applications for which the server will be optimized and the respective services will be installed.

The next step after customizing the system is to disable any unnecessary services. The default services and applications have been installed on the system, but a number of other services will still be running by default on the system. Click Start, select Administrative Tools, and then Services. The Services MMC snap-in opens, as shown in Figure 6-9.

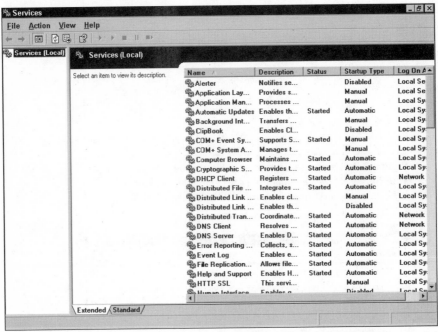

Figure 6-9: The Services MMC snap-in is used to enable and disable Windows services.

Looking at the Services snap-in, you see that each service has the following:

✦ Name

✦ Description

✦ Status

✦ Startup type

✦ Logon information

The status reflects whether or not the service is currently running, and the logon information specifies the account that the service uses for authentication.

A service's startup type can be one of the following three:

✦ **Automatic** — A service configured to start automatically will be started when Windows initially boots.

✦ **Manual** — A service set to start manually will start either automatically when it is called from another program or service or when it is selected in the Services snap-in and the Start button is clicked.

✦ **Disabled** — A service set to Disabled will never start.

Setting a service to Disabled is the most secure method of disabling unnecessary services because the service cannot be restarted by another process.

The list of services is large and grows when certain applications are installed that add services of their own. The goal is to learn the purpose of each service and determine whether or not it should be disabled.

A simple example is the DHCP Client service. The DHCP Client service is responsible for requesting addressing information from a DHCP server when a network interface in the system is configured to use DHCP. Because none of the interfaces in the example system use DHCP (servers are often configured with static IP addresses to avoid DHCP problems), the service can be disabled.

1. Right-click the DHCP Client service and select Properties. The Properties dialog box is displayed for the service.

2. Change the Startup type to Disabled and then click the Stop button, as shown in Figure 6-10.

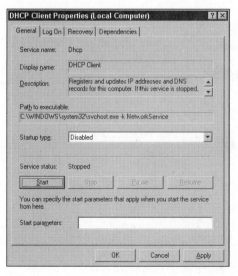

Figure 6-10: The service has been set to a Startup type of Disabled and has been stopped.

3. Click OK to close the Properties dialog box.

The service is now stopped and will not restart, and the change is reflected in the right pane of the Services snap-in.

A lot of services in Windows Server 2003 do not need to be running but are enabled by default. Your application and your environment will dictate which services can be disabled.

File permissions

File permissions are an important part of security in Windows Server 2003. You can apply file permissions both to files stored by users on the system and to system files themselves.

In previous versions of Windows, important files and directories, such as the Windows system files, were not adequately protected. This problem has been solved in Windows Server 2003.

The most common reason for changing file permissions is to protect files on a file server. For example, you can assume that the accounting group requires a location to store sensitive accounting data on the file server. The first step is to create the directory normally.

1. When the folder has been created, right-click it and then select Properties.

2. Click the Security tab. The default permissions are shown in Figure 6-11.

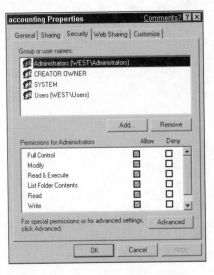

Figure 6-11: The default permissions on a folder allow read access to any authenticated user.

3. By default, the domain Administrators group and the System account have full access to the folder. The domain Users group has read access to the folder. In this example, the domain Administrators and System will keep full access, but the domain Users will have no access, while the Accounting group will have read and write access. Select the domain Users group and then click the Remove button to remove that group's access. By default, access is denied so that any user or group not explicitly granted access would have no access. You will most likely not be able to remove the Users group from the Security tab because it is inheriting permissions from the parent folder. You must first disable permission inheritance.

4. Click the Advanced button on the Security tab to display the Advanced Security Settings dialog box, as shown in Figure 6-12. Deselect the inherit from parent box and click OK.

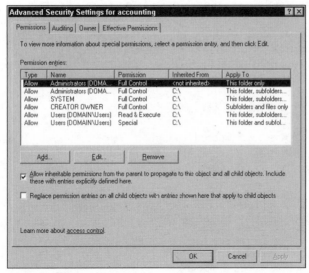

Figure 6-12: Permissions are inherited from the parent folder by default. This behavior must be disabled to set proper folder permissions.

5. When you disable inheritance, a dialog box is displayed, as shown in Figure 6-13. You have two options: You can either copy the existing inherited permissions to the object or remove them. If you remove the permissions, any existing permissions inherited from the parent object will be lost. Copying the permissions will preserve the permissions. Click Copy so that the permissions are not lost. Click OK to close the Advanced Security Settings dialog box. You can now remove the Users group from the Security tab.

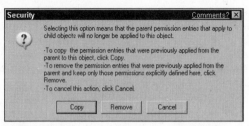

Figure 6-13: When you disable inheritance, you must decide whether to copy the inherited permissions to the object or remove the inherited permissions.

6. Click the Add button to add the Accounting group to the list. The Select Users, Computers, or Groups dialog box is displayed, as shown in Figure 6-14.

7. Enter the group name in the Enter the object names to select box and then click the Check Names button. Click OK to add the group.

8. Select the newly added group in the list.

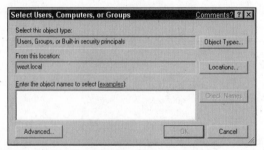

Figure 6-14: The Select Users, Computers, or Groups dialog box is used to add users or groups to the Security tab of a folder's Properties window.

9. The default permissions are Read and Execute, List, and Read. The Accounting group will need to be able to add and change files in this directory as well. Click the Allow box for the Modify permission. The Write permission is automatically added when Modify is selected. Although most of the permissions are easy to understand, the Full Control permission can be confusing. When Full Control is selected, it provides all of the permissions listed and also allows the user or group to change the permissions on the file or folder. In most cases, you do not want to assign Full Control to anyone but

administrators unless you are delegating control. Figure 6-15 shows the Security tab with the new permissions for the Accounting group. Click OK to save the changes.

Figure 6-15: The Accounting group has been granted Modify permission for the accounting folder.

Although it is only necessary in specific cases, it is possible to control permissions in a more granular fashion.

1. Click the Advanced button in the Security tab to show the Advanced Security Settings dialog box.

2. On the Permissions tab, the assigned permissions are shown. Click the Accounting group's permissions and click Edit. The Permission Entry dialog box is displayed, as shown in Figure 6-16.

   As you can see, the Modify permission granted on the Security tab of the object Properties dialog box grants almost all of the listed permissions. The exceptions are those permissions that allow the user or group to change permissions, such as Full Control, Change Permissions, and Take Ownership. The Delete Subfolders and Files permission is also not selected because it allows the deletion of subfolders and files in this object that the selected user does not have permissions to. For example, if a file existed in the Accounting folder and the Accounting group did not have delete permissions to that file, the Delete Subfolders and Files permission would allow members of that group to delete the file.

3. The final permissions-related concept is ownership. Click the Owner tab in the Advanced Security Settings dialog box. The Owner tab is shown in Figure 6-17.

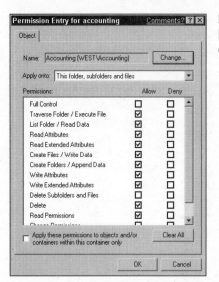

Figure 6-16: The Permission Entry dialog box is used to change permissions on an object at a more granular level.

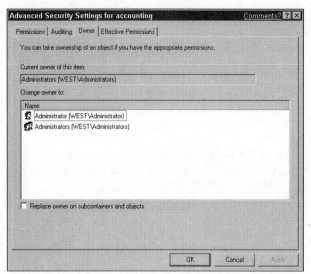

Figure 6-17: The Owner tab of the Advanced Security Settings dialog box is used to change the ownership of an object.

4. The owner of an object can change the permissions on that object even if that owner is not explicitly assigned the Full Control permission. This is useful because an administrator can take ownership of an object if permissions are

changed to make the object inaccessible. To change ownership, select from the list the user to whom you want to change ownership and then click OK. Ownership can be taken only by administrators or users who have been granted the Take Ownership permission.

Auditing

Auditing is a useful security tool. In Windows Server 2003, a large number of things can be audited. Auditing allows an event to be logged each time a specified action is taken. As file permissions were just discussed, file auditing will be addressed first.

You must first enable auditing. You can enable auditing through the local security policy for a system that is not a domain member or through a Group Policy for a domain member server. Enabling auditing through a Group Policy is covered in the next section, "Group Policies."

1. On a standalone server, click Start, select Administrative Tools, and then Local Security Policy. The Local Security Settings MMC snap-in will open.

2. Double-click Local Policies in the left pane and then click Audit Policy. The current audit policies are listed in the right pane, as shown in Figure 6-18.

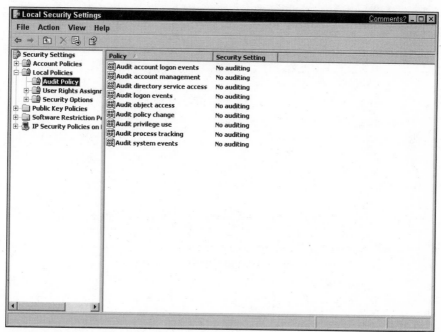

Figure 6-18: The audit policies must be modified to enable auditing.

3. For each type of auditing you want to enable, right-click and select Properties. Select Success or Failure (or both) in the Audit object access Properties dialog box to enable that type of auditing, as shown in Figure 6-19, and click OK.

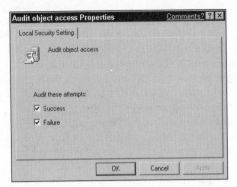

Figure 6-19: The audit policy can be enabled for success and failure.

Auditing can be configured for any file or folder.

1. To enable auditing, right-click the object, and click Properties.

2. Select the Security tab and click the Advanced button to open the Advanced Security Settings dialog box. Select the Auditing tab, as shown in Figure 6-20.

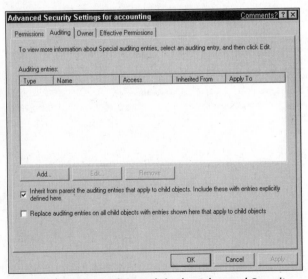

Figure 6-20: The Auditing tab in the Advanced Security Settings dialog box lists the current auditing entries, if any, and can be used to add a new entry.

3. To add an auditing entry, click the Add button.

4. You must then specify a user or group for whom auditing will be enabled from the Select User, Computer, or Group dialog box. You can select the Users group to audit for all users, or you can select a specific user or group. In this example, auditing will be enabled for the Accounting group because it is the only group with access to the object. Enter the name and click OK. The Auditing Entry dialog box is displayed, as shown in Figure 6-21.

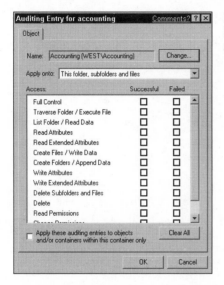

Figure 6-21: The Auditing Entry dialog box is used to audit specific events on an object.

The Auditing Entry dialog box is similar to the Permission Entry dialog box discussed in the previous section. Each auditing entry has a Successful and Failed box. Check the Successful box to log an event when the selected event is successful and vice versa. To audit when files are created, for example, check the Successful box under Create Files / Write Data. Each time a file is created successfully, an event will be logged.

Auditing can be enabled for a number of objects aside from files and folders. For a standalone server, other events, such as logon events, can also be audited. Enabling these audit policies means that the associated events will be logged to the Security Event Log.

The Audit account logon events will log an event each time a user logs on to the system. The Audit logon events policy is similar, except more information is logged. An example of a log entry from this policy is shown in Figure 6-22.

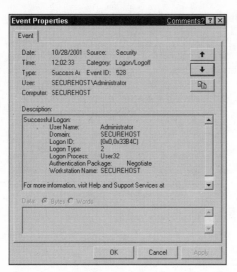

Figure 6-22: A log entry from the Audit logon events policy shows the username and workstation name from which the logon occurs, as well as more advanced information.

Group Policies

Group Policies are the most powerful tool at your disposal for customizing security in Windows Server 2003 when an Active Directory infrastructure is in place. Group Policies are set in the Active Directory Users and Computers tool and are applied to specific collections of users, groups, or computers called Organizational Units (OUs), sites, or domains and set specific security settings. Each one of these policies is known as a Group Policy Object (GPO), and the collection of GPOs makes up the Group Policy. A default GPO exists for each OU, site, or domain that is always in place and affects all objects in the OU, site, or domain. You can edit these default policies and you can also add new policies to keep a logical separation of specific policies. These policies can also be prioritized so that certain policies will override others. If your default domain GPO has the highest priority and you set a specific parameter, that parameter will be overridden in any other policy, for example.

In addition to being set in a specific OU, site, or domain, a GPO can also be linked to other OUs, sites, or domains. This is advantageous in that if you have more than one OU for organizational clarity but want to apply the same security policy to each of these OUs, you can link the GPO to each one rather than configuring a separate GPO for each OU.

Adding and removing Group Policy Objects

Group Policies are configured in the Active Directory Users and Computers tool.

1. Open the tool by opening the Start menu and selecting Administrative Tools and Active Directory Users and Groups.

2. Right-click in the left pane the domain, site, or OU for which you want to configure Group Policies and then select Properties.

3. Click the Group Policy tab in the domain Properties dialog box, as shown in Figure 6-23. The Group Policy tab shows the existing GPOs or linked GPOs for the OU, site, or domain.

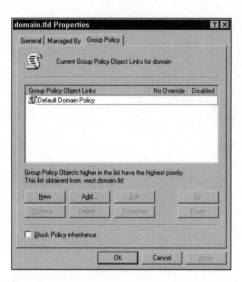

Figure 6-23: The Group Policy tab of the domain Properties dialog box is used to work with GPOs.

Creating a new GPO

Creating a new GPO is simple. In the Group Policy tab of the Properties dialog box, click the New button and the new GPO will be created. Type the name for the new GPO and press Enter. The new GPO will now be in the list.

Adding a linked GPO

Add a link to a GPO in another OU, site, or domain with the following steps:

1. Click the Add button in the Group Policy tab. The Add a Group Policy Object Link dialog box will open, as shown in Figure 6-24. Only the GPOs in domains and OUs are shown by default.

2. Click the Sites tab to show GPOs on sites or the All tab to see all GPOs in Active Directory.

3. Select the GPO to link from one of the three lists and then click OK. The linked GPO will appear in the list in the Group Policy tab.

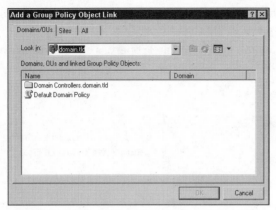

Figure 6-24: The Add a Group Policy Object Link dialog box is used to link a GPO from one domain, site, or OU to another.

Removing a GPO

To remove a GPO or link, select the GPO and then click the Delete button in the Group Policy tab. A dialog box will be displayed, as shown in Figure 6-25. The dialog box allows you to delete either the GPO link or the link and the GPO itself. Be careful not to delete a GPO if it is linked to other OUs, sites, or domains because it will be removed from all locations. In this case, you must choose to remove only the link. After you choose to remove either the link or the entire GPO, click OK and it will be deleted.

Figure 6-25: A dialog box is displayed when you click the Delete button, and you can remove either the entire GPO or just the link to the GPO.

Editing Group Policy Objects

Editing the GPOs is what allows you to set policies for the OUs, sites, or domains where the GPO is applied. The process of editing a GPO involves moving through the object tree in the Group Policy tool and changing object settings, as you will see in this section. To edit the GPO, choose Start, select the Administrative Tools menu, and open the Active Directory Users and Computers tool.

1. In the tool, right-click the domain, site, or OU that has the GPO you want to edit and then select Properties.

2. Click the Group Policy tab in the Properties dialog box.

3. Select the GPO to edit and click the Edit button. This will open the Group Policy Object Editor, as shown in Figure 6-26.

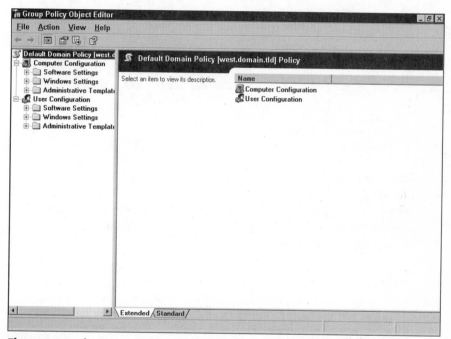

Figure 6-26: The Group Policy Object Editor is used to set the specific policies within a GPO.

The GPO Editor has two sections: Computer Configuration and User Configuration. These are simply categories to separate settings that affect computers from settings that affect users. When both users and computers are in an OU, site, or domain, Computer Configuration settings are applied to the computer objects in the OU and User Configuration settings are applied to user objects.

This chapter can't possibly cover all of the GPO Editor settings, but they are fairly self-explanatory. For an example, browse down the left pane to Computer Configuration, Windows Settings, Security Settings, Local Policies, Audit Policy, as shown in Figure 6-27.

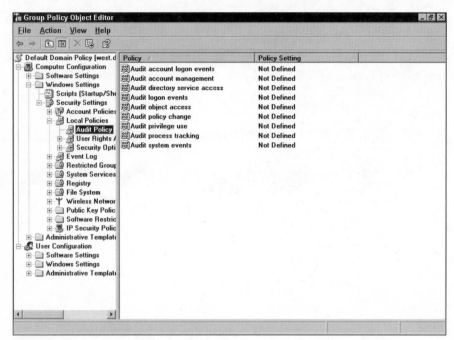

Figure 6-27: The Audit Policy section of the Computer Configuration section is used to configure local audit policies on systems.

In the "Auditing" section in this chapter, you learned how to enable auditing on a local system using the Local Security Policy snap-in. That section noted that you could use Group Policy to enable auditing for an entire domain. This is the section of the GPO responsible for that functionality and is similar to the Local Security Policy snap-in. To enable auditing of a specific type of event, double-click the event type in the right pane or right-click it and select Properties. The Properties dialog box for that policy will open, as shown in Figure 6-28. You can then enable auditing for success or failure (or both) and click OK to save the policy. The changes that you make will be reflected in the GPO Editor.

Note   Changes that you make in the GPO Editor are applied to the GPO immediately.

As an example of a User Configuration setting, navigate to User Configuration, Administrative Templates, System, and then Ctrl+Alt+Del Options, as shown in Figure 6-29. The available policy options are shown in the right pane. This particular group of settings allows you to specify what users affected by this GPO see when they press the Ctrl+Alt+Del keyboard combination on their systems. You can disable several of the options that normally appear by double-clicking the specific setting, making the change, and clicking OK.

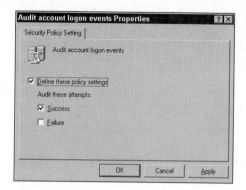

Figure 6-28: The Properties dialog box for a policy is used to enable or disable and set configuration options for the policy.

Group Policies can be used for an incredible range of administrative tasks, from locking down workstation and user account security to installing software automatically.

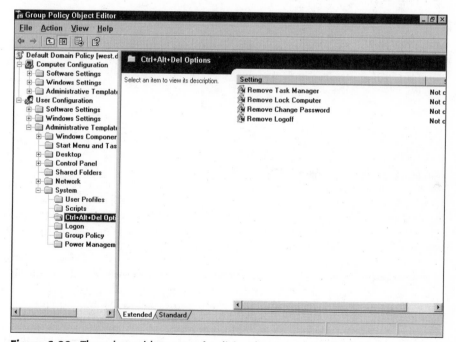

Figure 6-29: There is a wide range of policies that can be set for both users and computers in a GPO.

Group Policy Object security

Only a few security settings can be configured for a GPO, and this is only to control what can work with the GPO itself.

1. In the Active Directory Users and Computers snap-in, locate the OU, site, or domain with the GPO you want to edit, right-click it, and select Properties.

2. Click the Group Policy tab in the Properties dialog box, select the GPO to configure, and click the Properties button.

3. Click the Security tab in the GPO Properties dialog box, as shown in Figure 6-30.

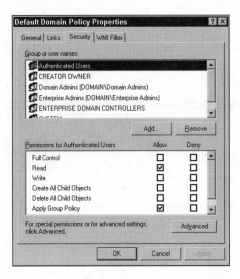

Figure 6-30: The Security tab of the GPO Properties dialog box is used to set security on the GPO itself.

The security settings follow the standard file permission type model with Read, Write, Create object, Delete object, and so on. You can use these permissions to delegate the ability to edit the GPO to users not in the Domain Admins group.

Complex permissions can be set on a GPO by clicking the Advanced tab and then setting permissions from the Advanced Security Settings dialog box, but these permissions are so granular that they are far too numerous to list and explain here. In most cases, the simple permissions will be enough for your environment.

Internet Connection Firewall

Internet Connection Firewall (ICF) is not something that will be used often in a Microsoft Windows Server 2003 implementation because most environments will have a proper firewall in place. It does, however, have some purpose in small networks.

External firewalls are used when you want to protect an entire network from attacks. ICF, however, is useful when you have a small network, most likely only a single server attached to a DSL or cable Internet connection.

 Cross-Reference External firewalls are discussed in depth beginning in Chapter 16.

In such a small implementation, a firewall is sometimes not financially viable (although small firewall products are now appearing in the $300 to $500 range). In this case, the server would sit on the Internet unprotected from attack. This is where ICF comes into play.

ICF is similar to the other personal firewall products on the market, except that it is integrated into Windows. It is a fully stateful firewall (see Chapter 16 for an explanation of stateful firewalls) that protects all traffic on a given network connection.

In working with ICF, you must first identify which network connection on your system you want to protect (almost always the connection to the Internet). If you have only one Internet connection, this is simple. Right-click My Network Places and select Properties. The Network Connections window will open, as shown in Figure 6-31.

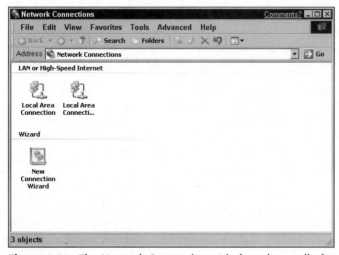

Figure 6-31: The Network Connections window shows all of the network connections on your system.

Each network connection on your system is shown in the Network Connections window, including LAN connections, VPNs, and dial-up connections. The example system has two network interfaces; the first one is connected to the Internet. This is the connection for which we will enable ICF. Right-click the connection for which you want to enable ICF and select Properties. Click the Advanced tab, as shown in Figure 6-32.

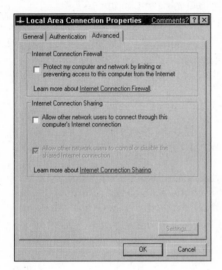

Figure 6-32: The Advanced tab of a network connection's Properties dialog box is used to enable and configure ICF and Internet Connection Sharing (ICS).

Enable ICF by selecting the ICF check box. After ICF is enabled, no inbound connections are allowed on that network connection. This is ideal for a home system or a workstation, but if this is a server attached to the Internet, you might want to run a Web or mail server on it.

ICF has the capability to allow incoming connections to specific services. If you were running a Web server on the system, you would want to allow incoming HTTP traffic. To enable services, click the Settings button on the Advanced tab of the network connection's Properties dialog box. The Advanced Settings dialog box will open, as shown in Figure 6-33.

A list of available services is shown in the Services tab. Checking the box for each service allows it in through ICF. In the case of a Web server, you would check the box for Web Server (HTTP). When you check a box, you are required to specify the system name or IP address of the computer where the service is running. This will be the local system's name.

The list of services available is somewhat limited, and you might have another service for which you want to allow access, such as a Microsoft SQL Server. You can add your own services to the list.

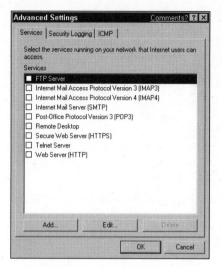

Figure 6-33: The Services tab of the Advanced Settings dialog box is used to allow incoming connections when ICF is enabled.

1. Click the Add button to open the Service Settings dialog box, as shown in Figure 6-34.

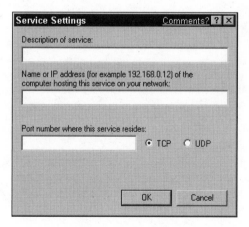

Figure 6-34: The Service Settings dialog box is used to add or edit services for ICF.

2. Provide a description for the service.

3. Specify on which system the service resides in the Name or IP Address box. Unless ICS is enabled, this will always be the name of the local machine. You can also allow connections to other systems when ICS is enabled.

4. Specify the incoming port number for the service that is being added. Microsoft SQL Server operates on port 1433 using TCP. Figure 6-35 shows the completed Service Settings dialog box.

5. Click OK to save the service.

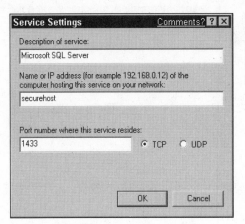

Figure 6-35: The Service Settings dialog box has been completed to allow incoming connections to a Microsoft SQL Server on the local system.

Figure 6-36 shows the configured Services tab of the Advanced Settings dialog box. Incoming traffic to the local Web server and Microsoft SQL Server will be allowed and all other traffic will be denied.

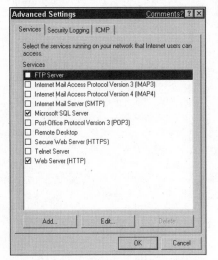

Figure 6-36: The Services tab of the Advanced Settings dialog box has been used to allow incoming Web and SQL server traffic.

The Advanced Settings dialog box can be used to configure other ICF features as well. ICF has the capability to log unsuccessful incoming and successful outgoing connections. Click the Security Logging tab of the Advanced Settings dialog box, as shown in Figure 6-37.

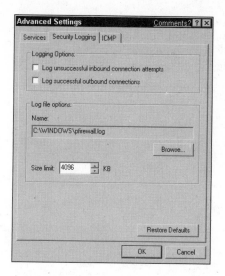

Figure 6-37: The Security Logging tab of the Advanced Settings dialog box is used to enable connection logging in ICF.

Selecting either of the two Logging options will enable that type of logging. The Log unsuccessful inbound connection attempts option logs each blocked attempt from an external user to access a service on your system. Connections to blocked services are not logged. The Log successful outbound connections option logs every outbound connection from this system to the ICF log.

The Security Logging tab's Log file options section allows you to configure the log file to which the data will be logged and configure the maximum size of the log. The oldest events in the log file will be overwritten when it reaches its maximum size. The logging options will generate a large amount of data, especially on a heavily used system, when the Log successful outbound connections option is enabled.

The final tab in the Advanced Settings dialog box is the ICMP tab, shown in Figure 6-38. ICMP is a low-overhead protocol used for TCP/IP stack management. The Ping command is an implementation of ICMP requests and ICMP echoes.

When ICF is enabled in its default state, other users on the Internet cannot use the Ping command to check whether your system is up or not. This occurs because all incoming packets are blocked by default, including ICMP echo requests. To enable other users to ping the system, select the Allow incoming echo request box in the ICMP tab.

A number of other less common ICMP messages are listed in the ICMP tab. The incoming requests are fairly uncommon requests for information, such as subnet mask and default router. You will rarely be required to enable these requests, especially on a small network or a single system.

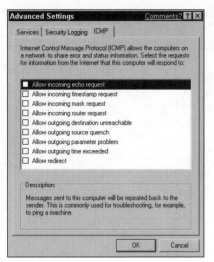

Figure 6-38: The ICMP tab of the Advanced Settings dialog box is used to allow ICMP packets in and out of the systems protected by ICF.

The outgoing requests are also rarely required. Unless you are doing routing on your local network, they do not need to be enabled. This is especially true on a single system.

The final ICMP option is to allow ICMP redirect. ICMP redirect packets are used when the routing table on a remote router changes. ICMP redirects can, however, be used to poison your system's routing table and for denial of service (DoS) and should not be allowed into your network or system through ICF.

After you have configured ICF for your system, click OK to close the Advanced Settings dialog box. Click OK to close the network connection's Properties dialog box to enable ICF.

Summary

This chapter tackled the issue of securing your Windows Server 2003. It explained how, through hardware configuration, proper operating system installation, setting file permissions, configuring auditing, and setting policies, you can ensure the most secure system possible in your environment. However, never forget to take potential security gaps, such as the danger of using a FAT file system for a disk partition on a production Windows Server 2003, into account.

✦   ✦   ✦

Securing Applications

A great number of applications run on Windows Server
2003. Everything from mail servers to database servers
to Web application servers is available. Any time an application is available to any user, trusted or untrusted, security is a
major issue. Chapter 1 discussed internal and external threats
and explained why even local users can be a security threat;
however, many applications are Internet applications that
exchange or serve data to clients on the public network, and
the Internet provides a larger group of potential attackers.

Securing systems is covered in earlier chapters. Securing the
system from attacks will stop attacks against the operating
system software, but will not stop attacks against applications
running on the system.

Securing Web and FTP Servers

Web and FTP servers are common applications on Windows
Server 2003. Many Internet service providers (ISPs) and Web
hosting companies provide hosting on Microsoft Windows-
based servers. Windows-based Web servers have an advantage over other platforms because they natively support ASP
and ActiveX, among other languages. Other platforms do,
however, have their own advantages.

A Web server seems like a basic application. To Internet
clients, a Web server seems to only serve HTML content. With
the advent of the following, however, Web servers are more
complex than they appear:

 ✦ Server-side processing

 ✦ Innumerable scripting languages

✦ Database connectivity

✦ Other dynamic content

FTP servers have problems of their own. An FTP server's purpose is simply to send and receive files using the FTP protocol. The problems with FTP occur when Access Control Lists (ACLs) are configured incorrectly or there are security vulnerabilities in the FTP server itself.

Web and FTP servers should always be on standalone servers and not domain member servers if they are accessible from untrusted networks. As discussed briefly in Chapter 2, a domain member compromise can lead to the compromise of any and all other systems in the domain because of the inherent trust between domain members. Intranet Web servers and internal FTP servers are commonly installed on domain members because it eliminates the need to maintain a separate user database for users wanting to access those services.

Securing Web servers

By far, the most common Web server running on Windows Server 2003 is Microsoft Internet Information Services (IIS). Windows Server 2003 comes with IIS, as does Windows 2000 Server and Windows NT 4.0 Server. Other Web servers running on the Windows platform are rare, so the discussion here focuses mainly on IIS.

IIS is a full-featured Web server. Some Web servers are modular and some are stripped-down, basic Web servers, but IIS has most of its functionality built in. Features such as ASP are native to IIS. IIS also has the capability to use external modules, such as Perl and PHP.

Much of the security of a system running IIS relates to the Web applications running on that system. Secure scripting techniques are beyond the scope of this book, but keep in mind that regardless of what attempts you make to secure your server, an insecure application can lead to the compromise of the entire system.

Patches and fixes

The most important step to securing a Web server with IIS is to always keep up to date on patches and fixes. Many of the common vulnerabilities in IIS have fixes released and are left open for weeks or months before they are exploited.

For example, the Code Red worm used a vulnerability in the Microsoft Index Server and the default behavior for IIS with .ida files to infect a huge number of Internet sites. The vulnerability used by Code Red to attack these servers and propagate itself was repaired in a patch released by Microsoft literally months before.

This leads to a huge gap in security. Either system administrators are unaware of these patches, or they are too apathetic to look for or apply them. The skills necessary to find the most recent patches are not commonly taught in courses that system administrators take, nor are they frequently discussed around the office water cooler.

If you are concerned with security, keeping your Web server patched with the latest patches and fixes is very important. Doing so will prevent a large percentage of the attacks you will encounter in running a Web site. You can usually find these patches by subscribing to the Microsoft security bulletins mailing list and browsing the Microsoft security Web site. Information about these resources is listed in Appendix B.

Default sites

Other problems with IIS security are the default Web site and the administration Web site. The default Web site and HTML administration site should be removed for maximum security, as vulnerabilities have been found in the sample files installed in the default Web site. In addition, a compromise in the administration Web site can result in a compromise of the entire Web server.

Extension mapping

As previously stated, IIS is a full-featured Web site. It subscribes to the "on by default" school of thought when it comes to features. This is excellent thinking for a Web server that is included with every copy of Windows, because even inexperienced administrators can get just about any type of scripting running on an IIS server. From a security standpoint, however, this is the wrong approach to take. It's the opposite approach to minimization (discussed in Chapter 3), and opens a number of potential vulnerabilities. One of these features in IIS is the use of extension mappings that map file extensions to specific programs or actions.

A number of these extensions are vulnerable to attack. The key to securing the Web server is to remove all mappings that you don't need.

1. To view the existing mappings, open the IIS snap-in.

2. Right-click the Web site for which to configure the extensions in the left pane and then select Properties.

3. Select the Home Directory tab, and click the Configuration button.

4. The Application Configuration dialog box is shown in Figure 7-1. None of the mappings are required for basic operation of the Web server; however, as many IIS installations use ASP scripts, you may want to leave the .ASA and .ASP extensions in place. Determine what other extensions are needed and leave those in place. This is also the location where you can add new ISAPI extensions.

   To remove unneeded extensions, select the extension to remove and then click the Remove button. Click OK to save the changes to the Application Configuration dialog box. Click OK to close the site Properties dialog box.

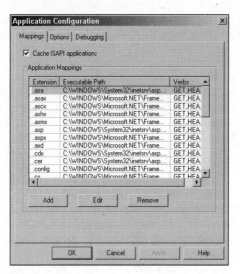

Figure 7-1: The Application Configuration dialog box is used to configure extension mappings for a Web site.

On a related note, you can also disable all applications on a specific Web site if none are required. Open the site Properties dialog box, and click the Home Directory tab. Changing the Execute Permissions setting to None means no applications can be launched and only static content can be displayed. This is a good idea if you only use static content because it prevents many types of attacks on your site.

ODBC

Microsoft Windows has a set of features used for connecting to databases called Open Database Connectivity (ODBC). The ODBC drivers can be used to connect to any database for which a driver is installed, and the client side interface is always consistent.

ODBC is often used to interface Web-based scripts to databases. One of the problems is that an inherent feature of ODBC is the capability to pass operating system commands in database calls.

You can disable this dangerous ODBC functionality by making a change in the system's Registry. Change the Registry entry, `HKEY_LOCAL_MACHINE\Software\Microsoft\Jet\4.0\engines\SandboxMode` to a value of 3. The default value is 2.

Isolating content

Directory traversal attacks were discussed in Chapter 2. A directory traversal attack can traverse directories, but cannot traverse disk partitions. As a directory traversal attack relies on the ability to move through a Web site's directory structure and locate files that can be used to compromise the system, isolating the Web site directories from the system directories can avoid these attacks.

The key to isolating content is having the Web content on a different disk partition from the operating system files or any other important files that could lead to a system compromise. This partition can be on the same disk as any other partition or on a separate disk.

For example, most Windows Server 2003 systems store operating system files in the directory C:\WINDOWS\. The IIS wwwroot directory should be on a logical drive other than C:.

Permissions and content restrictions

An important IIS feature is its use of the IUSR_machinename and IWAM_machinename accounts. Anonymous users accessing Web sites on an IIS server use the IUSR_machinename credential. Web applications using a global .asa (an ASP object definition file) use the IWAM_machinename credential. Employing these user accounts, you can customize the security of files on the system.

These permissions essentially have two similar roles: to restrict content within the site itself, and to restrict anonymous Web users from accessing any other files on the server.

By default, anonymous users have permission to access only the Web site files. This is the key to security. It is important that no files on the server have permissions assigned to the Everyone group or the IUSR_machinename or IWAM_machinename accounts.

These permissions' other use is to control access to files in the Web site. Most password-protected Web sites are protected at the script level, but many intranet sites and some other sites use native password authentication. You will recognize such authentication when your browser launches a password dialog box, as shown in Figure 7-2.

Figure 7-2: When you do not have permissions to access a Web object by default, you are prompted for a user name and password.

Configuring permissions on objects can become complex. Essentially, when you create a new object or folder and inheritance is enabled (as is the default), the object will inherit the permissions of its parent folder. You must open the Properties dialog box for the object and select the Security tab, as shown in Figure 7-3, to configure permissions.

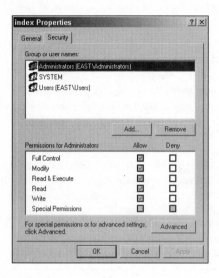

Figure 7-3: The Security tab of the object's Properties dialog box is used to set permissions.

To disable permission inheritance for the object so you can ensure that the permissions you set are the ones that will be in effect, take the following steps:

1. Click the Advance button and deselect the Inherit from the parent box. You will be prompted as to what to do with the current inherited permissions.

2. You can choose to either leave the inherited permissions in place by clicking Copy, or remove the inherited permissions by clicking Remove.

3. Click OK to close the Advanced Security Setting dialog box. If only the inherited permissions are present on the object and you remove them, everyone will be denied access to the object and you will be prompted as such. Only the object's owner will be able to set permissions.

4. You can now set the permissions on the object. Click the Add button to add a user for whom to configure permissions. Enter the user name or group to add and click OK. If there is more than one match in the user database for the name you entered, you will be able to select the one you want from a list.

Now that users have been added to the list, they can be assigned permissions. For a Web site, the site administrator will have write permissions, but most users will only have read permissions, or read and execute permissions for directories containing scripts. For anonymous users to have access to the site, the IUSR_machinename account must be granted access.

There is more to IIS authentication than simply setting permissions, though. You can also configure how the authentication process operates.

1. Open the Internet Information Services snap-in.

2. Right-click the Web site to configure and then select Properties.

3. Click the Directory Security tab, and click the Edit button under Anonymous access and authentication control.

The Authentication Methods dialog box is shown in Figure 7-4. There are two sections in this dialog box. The first configures anonymous access to the site. By default, anonymous access using the IUSR_machinename account is enabled. Files in the site directories must be configured with the read permission for the IUSR_machinename account for them to be accessible. Disabling anonymous access from the Authentication Methods dialog box is effective for the entire site. If you want some objects in a site to be accessible anonymously and others to be accessible to only specific users, this setting must be enabled and permissions are used to set security.

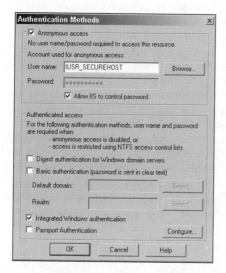

Figure 7-4: The Authentication Methods dialog box is used to configure how anonymous and other users access the site.

The other section of the Authentication Methods dialog box is used to configure how users other than anonymous users access the site. By default, only Integrated Windows authentication is enabled. This method uses Kerberos if supported by the server, and falls back to Windows NT/LAN Manager (NTLM) challenge/response and is relatively safe. The disadvantage to Integrated Windows authentication is that it is only supported in Internet Explorer, and not in other browsers.

Digest authentication creates a one-way hash of the authentication information and sends this to the server. The server creates a one-way hash of the known authentication information and compares the two. If the two hashes match, the user is authentic. Digest authentication has a number of advantages over Integrated authentication. Digest authentication is an HTTP 1.1 standard and is supported in more (though not all) browsers. It can also pass through firewalls and proxy servers because the authentication credentials are passed in the same method as with Basic authentication, although hashed.

Note   There is an infinitesimally small chance that the same hash could be generated by different plaintexts.

Basic authentication is insecure. The user name and password are passed to the server in plain text over HTTP. The major advantage to basic authentication is that almost all browsers support it. However, you should avoid using it because it discloses passwords in plain text to anyone monitoring network traffic.

Finally, IIS now supports Passport authentication natively. Configure Passport by clicking the Configure button in the Authentication Methods dialog box. Previously, it was necessary to code Passport authentication into scripts. Passport authentication uses the Microsoft Passport service to authenticate users. Passport is marketed as a single authentication point for Internet users. Their information is stored in a central directory so that it does not need to be entered at each site. Passport is obviously not a good choice for intranets and internal users, but can be a viable option for sites that authenticate external users. Passport can provide an alternative to maintaining a user database through scripts and database connections.

Passport has two main features: Single Sign In (SSI) and Express Purchase (EP). Passport has a number of advantages for e-commerce sites. The user's shipping and credit card information can be stored in a central location (the Passport service), and it will be available for any site on the Internet with these features. Microsoft hosts the Passport service, so you do not have to maintain database servers for user information. Theoretically, you can use Passport and a third-party fulfillment service, and eliminate the database server portion of an e-commerce architecture altogether.

Using Passport also has disadvantages. The most obvious is that you lose control of your user database. You can still control access as you would normally, but the database is off-site. Also, if any point in your link to the Passport service fails, including the service itself, you have no method of authenticating users.

IP address restrictions can be configured on a Web site. These restrictions control who can access a site based on source IP address. To configure these restrictions, right-click the desired Web site in the MMC snap-in and then select Properties. Click the Directory Security tab, and click the Edit button under IP address and domain name restrictions.

Figure 7-5 shows the IP Address and Domain Name Restrictions dialog box. As you can see, all computers are granted access by default. With this setting, adding systems to the list will block their address. You may have an abusive user or something similar and want to block a system or set of systems. Click the Add button and then enter one of the following:

✦ A single IP address

✦ A starting and ending address for a range of IP addresses

✦ A domain name to block

Blocking by domain name is not a good idea on sites with any amount of load because each connection will require a DNS lookup, which will have a negative effect on performance.

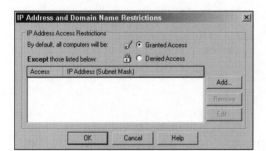

Figure 7-5: The IP Address and Domain Name Restrictions dialog box is used to control which computers can access a site.

You can deny all access by default by selecting the Denied Access option. Add the computers to the list by IP address, IP range, or domain name, for which to grant access. This is a useful feature for intranet sites, so that only internal computers can access the site, or even for departmental sites, so that only computers in the specific department have access.

IIS log files

IIS log files are useful security tools. Through analysis of these files, you can see attacks attempted against your Web server regardless of their success or failure. By default, these log files are located in C:\WINDOWS\system32\LogFiles\ <servicename>. Normally, for IIS Web server logs, <servicename> is W3SVCn, where n is the instance number of the Web site.

The log files contain detailed information regarding each of the following:

✦ Specific HTTP request (every GET, PUT, and so on)

✦ Time and date

✦ Source IP

✦ Method (GET, PUT, and so on)

✦ Uniform Resource Identifier (URI)

✦ HTTP status code

✦ TCP port

✦ Username

✦ Destination IP

✦ User agent

The key to analyzing these files is looking for unusual patterns of traffic or unusual URIs. For example, a directory traversal attack would show a URI similar to "../../../../../CMD.EXE." You may see a series of such entries as an attacker attempts to determine where the target file is located. You can block the source IP address or file an abuse report with the respective ISP. You also need to make sure that your server is not vulnerable to the attack in question (per this chapter's earlier section on patches and fixes).

You can use the log files to locate other information, as well. Many traffic analysis programs, such as WebTrends or LiveStats, are simply log file analyzers with Web reporting front ends. These programs analyze your log files and provide statistics as to which objects are accessed most often and from what locations. The amount of information that can be derived from the IIS logs is fairly extensive.

Logging in IIS is also configurable. Open the IIS snap-in, right-click the desired site, and click the Web site tab, as shown in Figure 7-6. Logging is enabled by default using the W3C (World Wide Web Consortium) Extended Log File Format. As an accepted standard, this log file is readable by many log analyzers. You can also select the Microsoft IIS Log File Format or the NCSA Common Log File Format. A fourth option, ODBC logging, will write log information to a database specified by clicking the Properties button. You need to specify the ODBC DSN, table name, and user name and password for the database.

The Properties button is used to configure the logging behavior. The Logging Properties dialog box is different depending on which log file type you have selected (IIS and NCSA formats are uncommon and will not be covered). Clicking the Properties button with the W3C format selected displays the Extended Logging Properties dialog box, as shown in Figure 7-7.

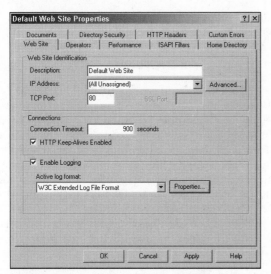

Figure 7-6: The Web Site tab of the site Properties dialog box is used to configure logging.

The General Properties tab is used to configure the behavior of the log file itself. By default, a new log file is created daily. You can also choose to create new log files hourly, weekly, or monthly. The two additional options are Unlimited file size, which never creates a new log file, and When file size reaches n, which creates a new log file each time the log reaches the specified threshold size. For sites with very high traffic, you might choose the hourly or maximum file size options so that the log files don't become too large and unwieldy.

Figure 7-7: The Extended Logging Properties dialog box is used to set the logging behavior for the W3C log file format.

The Use local time for file naming and rollover option causes the system to create new files based on local time rather than the default, which is GMT. GMT is used by default only with the W3C log file format; other formats always use local time.

You can also specify the directory into which log files are written. The default is shown, but they can be placed in any location. If the server has a large amount of traffic, you might want to put the log files in another partition for a number of reasons. Having the logs on another physical drive or array (and a separate controller too, preferably) reduces the performance impact on the system drives when a large amount of log activity is occurring. Also, if the log files grow so large that they consume all of the available disk space, having them on a drive other than the system drive will not affect the system. If the system drive becomes full, the system will become unstable and could crash. The Log file name entry under the Log file directory displays what the log file name actually looks like when it is written. This is based on both the service instance for the directory and the log time period for the actual file name.

Click the Extended Properties tab in the Extended Logging Properties dialog box to configure extended options, as shown in Figure 7-8. This tab sets which fields are written to the log files. The default fields, as previously discussed, should normally be sufficient, but you may want to add more detail. You will most likely not want to remove the Date and Time fields, but you may want to add and remove the extended options. A number of useful options are not enabled by default, such as Referrer, which can indicate other sites linking to yours without permission, and Bytes Sent, Bytes Received, and Time Taken, which can indicate the traffic level on your server.

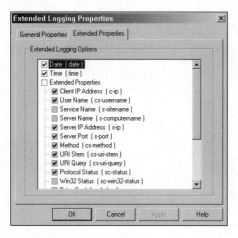

Figure 7-8: The Extended Properties tab is used to set what fields are logged to the log file.

Securing FTP servers

Securing FTP servers is similar to securing Web servers. This section focuses on IIS, but other FTP servers are available for Windows. These are sometimes implemented in the quest for better security, but are not usually the best solution. Many of the principles presented here can be applied to other FTP servers as well.

Keeping up to date on patches and fixes is very important with FTP servers. FTP servers are notorious for directory traversal vulnerabilities and buffer overflows.

In addition, isolating content is also important with FTP servers. In the event a directory traversal vulnerability is discovered and exploited on your server, isolating content can limit the damage an attacker can do. Content should be stored on a separate partition for this reason. Another reason to keep FTP data on another partition is a reason that is surprisingly common in real-world situations. Normally, anonymous users do not have write access to an FTP server. Occasionally, intentionally or not, anonymous users are granted write permissions on the server. This is when software pirates move in. When they discover this site with write access enabled, they will often use it as a distribution point. This usually entails uploading large amounts of data until the drive is full. A full system drive leads to system crashes. If the content is isolated and the drive becomes full, the effects are minimized.

The IIS default FTP site is fairly secure. Anonymous access is enabled, but write access is disabled for the entire site, and anonymous users don't have write permissions.

Setting FTP site security settings is virtually identical to Web site settings. Open the IIS snap-in, right-click the FTP site, and select Properties. Logging is configured on the FTP Site tab. Anonymous access can be enabled and disabled on the Security Accounts tab and the anonymous username (IUSR_machinename by default) can be changed. IP address and domain name restrictions are configured from the Directory Security tab.

The only real difference with an IIS FTP site is in the Home Directory tab, as shown in Figure 7-9. By default, Read and Log visits are enabled. This allows users to have read access and site access is logged. You must select the Write option if you want to allow write access to the site. Then set permissions as you would for a Web site. By default, the IUSR_machinename is a member of the Domain Users group, which has permissions on many folders. If you simply enable the Write permission on the FTP site without ensuring that the permissions are set correctly, you could inadvertently enable anonymous write access.

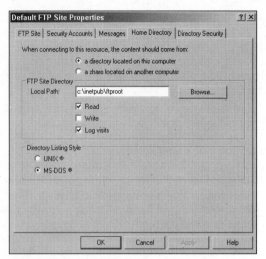

Figure 7-9: The Home Directory tab of the FTP site Properties dialog box is used to configure access for the entire site.

Securing Mail Servers

Mail servers are inherently insecure. With the services they provide, they must accept plaintext data over an unprotected SMTP or POP3 port. This is similar to the requirement with a Web server that plaintext data is received on the HTTP port.

Attacks can be launched against the server through these ports. Attacks, such as buffer overflows, can be easily sent over a mail port, and the system can be compromised. Using a firewall with an application filter or stateful inspection can help to avoid some attacks, but they cannot be relied upon for 100 percent of your security.

Making a mail server secure

Securing a mail server is fairly difficult. You can't change many things on a mail server without changing the entire behavior of how the mail process works.

The first step is to ensure that your mail application is kept up to date with the latest patches and fixes. This is a recurring theme throughout this chapter and the entire book. When security vulnerabilities are found, the application vendor will typically release a patch to repair the application. If you don't apply these patches, the vulnerabilities will still exist in your system and will probably become well known by attackers. Attackers will then go through all servers running that particular application looking for the vulnerability to exploit, and your server will be on that list.

Aside from that, not a lot can be done to secure a mail server. Standard SMTP and POP3 mail transactions are done in plain text. Anyone with access to a link over which you are sending or receiving mail can view the messages using a sniffing program.

One step you can take to secure mail is using encryption over these links. Some Mail User Agents (MUAs) support SSL encryption for SMTP and POP3 connections. Many mail servers also support SSL encryption. If both your Mail Transfer Agent (MTA) and MUA support encryption, you can eliminate plain text message transfers.

Cross-Reference   See Chapter 9 for more information about using SSL for mail.

Many mail servers also support the same restrictions as described for Web servers above. For example, Microsoft Exchange supports IP address and domain name restrictions. These can be used to restrict who can connect to the server. This is useful to restrict connections to only a given set of users or to block abusive users.

Most (if not all) mail servers also have logging capabilities. Mail server logs are useful for finding abusive users attacking your server or using it to send spam. Reviewing your logs is an important part of maintaining security on a mail server.

Another point of security on a mail server is an anti-virus solution. E-mail worms, both destructive and benign, are rampant on the Internet. The problem is not as severe as some make it, but it is fairly prevalent.

Many third-party e-mail virus scanners exist on the market. Some integrate with the MTA, and some act as a gateway to filter mail before it reaches the MTA. In any case, try to filter viruses before they reach your network. This removes the responsibility for controlling viruses (by not opening unknown attachments and so on) from your users.

Controlling spam on your servers

Spam controls are often implemented at a corporate level to prevent spam from entering the network. It is sometimes also an optional feature at the service provider level. These controls limit the junk e-mail that users or customers have to deal with.

Spam control is almost always done using a filter. An array of filtering products is available. Some MTAs and even some MUAs, such as Outlook, incorporate spam filters.

Spam filters normally inspect both the headers and body of an e-mail for certain characteristics, and matching messages are either discarded or sent to a holding area for sorting. Messages are held in case the filter mistakenly identifies one or more legitimate messages as spam. A person can be assigned to browse the quarantined mail for misdirected items. This prevents the loss of important items.

Spam is usually blocked on one of two criteria: sender or body content. Known spam items often originate from the same locations or have the same content. Blocking by sender is often difficult. Spammers will use dial-up accounts that have dynamically assigned IP addresses. Blocking messages from a single IP address will not help because the IP address is changed at each dial-up. Blocking an entire block of IP addresses may restrict content from legitimate users. IP addresses can also be spoofed in the e-mail, although that is a more difficult task.

The remaining option is blocking by envelope sender (from address). This header is never the actual sender of the spam's e-mail address, but it is often the same spoofed address every time the spammer sends mail. Blocking by envelope sender is somewhat effective, but problems occur when the spammer spoofs a legitimate e-mail address. For example, I can easily send an e-mail and set the From address to anything I desire. I can set it to the address of another user I know of (maliciously or otherwise). If a spam filter blocks that address, not only can I not send my spam, but the legitimate user cannot send mail through the filter either. Many legitimate users could be unaware of what's going on.

The other spam blocking technique is blocking the actual message body content. For example, today I received two spam messages from different senders; however, both messages had identical content. If I had set a spam filter on the first message, I wouldn't have received the second, and I wouldn't receive any more in the future. This can be done at a mail gateway level to block spam to an entire organization.

Securing DNS Servers

A number of DNS servers exist. The most common is the Berkeley Internet Naming Daemon (BIND), which is usually run on a Unix platform. Windows Server 2003 includes its own DNS server, as well. As the Windows-based DNS server is not very robust and administration is difficult to automate, it has not been accepted into the major market for DNS servers, ISPs, and Web hosting facilities. However, the Microsoft Windows DNS server is commonly used is to enable Active Directory.

The major problem with DNS security is that an attacker can potentially change the DNS record for a given site and make it point to any location they want. This is known as *poisoning the record*.

Regardless of which DNS server you are using, some basic tenets of security are valid. The basic two principles are limit zone transfers and limit DNS updates.

Zone transfers are used when a master/slave relationship is set up between two DNS servers. The master server maintains the DNS zone record. Any changes to the zone are done on the master server. The slave server then requests a zone transfer from the master on a fixed schedule. The entire zone is transferred to the slave server where it is kept to serve requests.

The master/slave relationship is different from DNS caching. A caching DNS server caches only the specific record requested by a client. A slave server stores the entire zone. Caching is automatic while a slave zone must be configured manually.

A client, malicious or otherwise, can only request DNS records for names or addresses that he knows. If he wants to look up the address for `www.microsoft.com`, he requests the www record from the DNS server responsible for the microsoft.com domain.

If an attacker wanted to see every record for microsoft.com, however, he could request a zone transfer. Without proper security, the DNS server would send the entire zone to the attacker. The attacker would then know exactly which systems were in the microsoft.com network and what their addresses were. This is an example of an information leak vulnerability, as discussed in Chapter 2.

Zone transfers are normally limited based on IP address. You should know which servers are operating as slave servers to your master DNS servers. Only these systems will be allowed to perform zone transfer operations. This is more difficult in an ISP environment where there are a large number of DNS zones and slave servers may be located in a number of locations, but vigilance here is just as important. The method for implementing this restriction varies based on the DNS server vendor.

The other major DNS security problem is zone poisoning. This occurs in two ways. The first and less common method is through dynamic updates. Dynamic DNS updates are required with Windows Server domains, but are normally not used. Dynamic updates should be disabled on any publicly accessible DNS server. If dynamic updates are enabled, an attacker can spoof an update and point a record to whichever server he chooses.

The second method of zone poisoning is poisoning the DNS cache. This attack is much harder to prevent, and is virtually impossible to prevent if you are not the master server for the zone. The problem occurs when a record is changed for a particular DNS zone by an attacker. This change is then propagated through any DNS cache servers requesting the record. By the time the record is fixed, the cache servers that have already cached the record will not refresh the record until the cache expires. The cache can be poisoned by either attacking the master DNS server for the zone directly, or spoofing that server so that when cache servers request the record, they make the request to the spoofed server rather than the actual master server.

Securing Other Applications

Aside from the two major Internet applications, Web and mail, there are many other applications. Each has its own security considerations. Database servers, for example, require customized security on a per-database and per-table level, as well as application security.

A large number of applications exist on the market, and each has its own security provisions. Some general information on security considerations for other applications is provided here.

Security considerations for other applications

Database servers, human resource information system (HRIS) packages, accounting products, and supply chain management applications are just a few of the applications available, and each requires extensive security.

Many application vendors maintain security mailing lists to which notifications are sent when new patches are released. If not, checking the vendor Web site on a regular basis to see which updates are available is prudent. These security updates should be installed as soon as possible, first on a non-production system to check functionality, and then on the productions system.

There are essentially two types of applications, those that integrate into Microsoft Windows for authentication, and those that do not. For those applications that do integrate into the Windows security model, user and group maintenance is simpler. Users in the Windows user database can be assigned access to the application. Microsoft SQL Server works in this way. Other applications maintain their own user database. This makes administration somewhat more complex, as there is more than one user database to maintain.

Inside applications, there is often a distribution of permissions across different parts of the application. For example, databases often have permissions set per-database and per-table, and accounting packages have different permissions for the payroll component and the AR component. These permission settings are important to consider when ensuring the application stays secure. Ensure that users only have access to the absolute minimum possible. Sticking to this rule will avoid users inadvertently having access to data that they shouldn't.

In addition to the basic security considerations that apply to all applications, certain applications have specific needs, as well. Databases, for example, can contain sensitive data that should be stored in an encrypted form. Other applications may also have encryption requirements.

Overall, the key to securing applications is to become familiar with each application through any available documentation and through using and administering the software. After you are familiar with it, you will be better equipped to improve its security. Specific documentation for security on a particular application might be available. There are, for example, a couple of books written entirely on the subject of security for the Oracle database.

Securing multi-tier applications

Multi-tier applications are common in many environments. Many e-commerce applications and enterprise-class applications are multi-tiered, with at least a front-end Web server and a back-end database server, and sometimes servers running middleware applications.

A number of security considerations exist for a multi-tier architecture, including two main problems. The first problem is a familiar one by now; the servers on each tier of the architecture are insecure. All of the servers should be made as secure as possible.

To ensure the security of the back-end and middle-tier servers, these should be isolated from the public network. Only the front-end servers should ever be accessible. This often means isolating the other servers on private network segments, or making sure firewall policies to those systems are restrictive. It should be impossible for the middle and back-end servers to be contacted from an untrusted system.

Finally, the method in which data is passed from the front end through the other tiers should be secure. This can mean a lot of things. The application itself should be secure so that it cannot be used to poll arbitrary data from the back end by untrusted users. Data should also be moved through the tiers in an encrypted form if it is sensitive, such as credit card information.

Multi-tier applications have a completely different set of requirements when it comes to security. Due to the method in which data processing is separated across a number of servers, you cannot approach security as you would for a normal application that runs on a single, isolated server. Security in a multi-tier application must be considered from the beginning of development right through implementation and maintenance.

Summary

After securing your systems (hardware and operating system software), the next logical step to ensuring that your data is safe from attackers is to shore up the applications running on your systems.

This chapter discusses the importance of and means to secure your Web servers, FTP servers, mail servers, and DNS, including using patches and fixes, removing default sites, and removing extension mappings to reduce application vulnerabilities.

✦   ✦   ✦

Authentication and Encryption

Encrypting Your Data

Cryptography is an incredibly complex subject. To fully understand the entire field, one needs a firm basis in mathematics, as well as a firm grasp of computer science. Fortunately, this extensive knowledge is not necessary to understand most of how cryptographic algorithms and protocols are implemented. You can leave the design of the specific formulas to the experts.

Note   If you're interested in learning more about cryptography, Wiley & Sons' *Applied Cryptography*, written by Bruce Schneier, is the absolute best reference for those without a firm footing in math. It begins with a walkthrough of different cryptographic methods, then explores different algorithms and protocols in detail, and then discusses specific implementations.

There are a number of reasons to use encryption for your data. You may need to send important documents to colleagues over e-mail. Perhaps you travel with a laptop containing sensitive data and are concerned about theft. You might simply want to send a love letter to your husband or wife on company time (not that I condone such actions). These are all valid reasons to use data encryption.

Cryptography is all around us without us even knowing it. Many types of signals, such as digital satellite TV and police radio communications, are encrypted. You can even buy encrypting telephones, although the party you're calling has to have the same type of phone and the proper codes to decipher the encrypted signals. As you'll see later in this chapter, distributing cryptographic keys (also referred to as key distribution) with absolute security is one of the more difficult problems facing cryptographers.

Introduction to Cryptography

Cryptography is the science of enciphering (encrypting) a plain text message into unreadable ciphertext. There is evidence that cryptography has been around for many years. Throughout history a need has existed for messages to be sent that cannot be read by an eavesdropper. An eavesdropper is considered to have full access to the encrypted message. As long as cryptography has existed, the complementary art of cryptanalysis has also existed. Cryptanalysis is the practice of deciphering encrypted ciphertext.

Stories abound about the struggle between cryptographers and cryptanalysts, most in times of war. The most famous, however, is the breaking of the German Enigma encryption device at Bletchley Park in England. (Bletchley Park is now a museum for the code-breaking activities during World War II). The German Enigma machine is an example of a closed system. It was never exposed to public scrutiny, and those involved believed it to be unbreakable. The belief was a fallacy because when the allied code breakers received an Enigma from a captured U-boat, they exploited weaknesses in the design to break any ciphertext generated by the machine.

Cryptography has many uses above and beyond the simple encryption of messages but they all fall back on the same basic encryption operation. Cryptographic protocols exist for all of the following:

✦ Secure elections

✦ Anonymous message passing

✦ Coin flipping

✦ Bit commitment (an example of bit commitment is when a magician makes his guess as to which card will be drawn from a deck and places it in a sealed envelope)

✦ Even playing poker over a distance without a player being able to cheat

The list could go on, but every one of these protocols is based on the ability to encrypt a message and sign a message using cryptography.

The most secure (barring a few exceptions) encryption systems today are open systems. The algorithms are widely available for inspection by anyone, including potential cryptanalysts. These algorithms are secure, not through obscurity but rather through peer review and open testing by the community. Many of these algorithms have no known weaknesses, and can only be deciphered with the key (the key is the mathematical algorithm used to encrypt the message) or by using a brute force attack (testing every possible key). In many cases (especially when using large keys), brute force attacks would take many years — or many lifetimes.

The origins of cryptography are far back in history. Originally, however, cryptography was based on substitution and transposition ciphers. A *substitution cipher* is when each letter in the plain text message is replaced based on a key to create the ciphertext. The simplest example of a substitution cipher is the ROT13 algorithm. ROT13 is short for Rotate 13 positions, and each letter in the plain text message is replaced with the letter 13 positions away in the alphabet. The letter A is replaced with the letter N, for example. ROT13 is especially simple because putting the ciphertext message through ROT13 again results in the original plain text. It is easy to visualize ROT13 as the alphabet written around the outside of a circle. To find a letter's replacement you would locate the letter directly opposite on the circle. Some substitution ciphers use a simple method of replacing one character with another, but some are more complex. These complex ciphers replace blocks of letters or have multiple keys based on letter position. Many substitution ciphers have been invented and almost all of them are extremely simple to break using computers.

Transposition ciphers do not replace the letters in the plain text message; the letters are instead rearranged. The most basic transposition cipher is a columnar transposition cipher. The plain text message is written across the page a certain number of letters wide. Reading down each column of the page then generates the ciphertext. To decrypt the message, the recipient must know how many letters wide the original page was. He can then write out the message vertically to obtain the plain text. Substitution and transposition ciphers are sometimes combined to create a more complex algorithm that is more difficult to break.

One-time pads

One encryption system is unbreakable. This system is known as a one-time pad. You create a one-time pad by randomly choosing data and marking it on a piece of paper (or on digital media). Two copies of the pad are made; one is issued to the sender and one to the receiver of the message. The sender uses the one-time pad to encrypt his message and then destroys the plain text message and his copy of the one-time pad. The one-time pad must have at least as many characters as the message because each character in the message is encrypted using one character on the pad, usually by adding them modulo 26 (modulo 26 explanation momentarily). The receiver then decrypts the message using her copy of the one-time pad and then destroys her copy of the one-time pad so it is never reused. This system is unbreakable because the one-time pad is randomly generated, so the ciphertext could decipher into any possible message. Modulo 26 addition (simplified) is a method of adding alphabetical characters to create ciphertext. The integer values of two letters are added (a=1, z=26), and if the result is greater than 26, 26 is subtracted. For example, adding A and B would equal C, as A=1 and B=2. Adding M to Q, however, results in 30 (M=13, Q=17). 26 is then subtracted from 30 resulting in 4=D.

One-time pad encryption may be strong, but its implementation is difficult. Similar to many other crypto systems, its difficulty lies in key distribution. Somehow you need to get the pad (or pads) to the recipient without having them stolen en route. This is even more difficult in a situation where a one-time pad is used to encrypt data on a computer. The pad would need to be sent over the same lines of communication as the message if the recipient did not already have it. The traditional key distribution method for a one-time pad is for each party to receive a pad while physically together before they separate and begin to send messages. A possible solution to the distribution of the pads is by encrypting them using a public key algorithm and then placing them on a CD-ROM or tape and sending them by some physical carrier to the recipient. This is not a secure method, but it is possible depending on the lifespan of the data being encrypted.

Symmetric key encryption

Symmetric key encryption is simply when the same key that is used to encrypt the data is also used to decrypt it. An example of a symmetric algorithm is 3DES. When the two parties exchange data encrypted using a symmetric algorithm, the data is very secure. A number of specific implementations of symmetric encryption are nearly impossible to break if the attacker has only the ciphertext. The problem here of course is key distribution.

Key distribution is a common problem in cryptography. You need some way of getting the key you want to use to the recipient of your encrypted message. If an attacker can steal that key during this process, he can decrypt all messages sent using that key.

Symmetric key encryption is one of the simpler forms of cryptography. The key is some random value that, combined with the plain text and fed through a given algorithm, creates the ciphertext. The ciphertext's recipient, also having the key, can put the whole thing back through the algorithm to obtain the plain text.

The key to symmetric key encryption (no pun intended), other than key distribution, which is not unique to symmetric key encryption, is the strength of the algorithm. A weak algorithm is vulnerable to a number of attacks, such as known plain text attacks (where both the encrypted and decrypted messages are known) and even ciphertext-only attacks (only the encrypted text is known). Symmetric algorithms that have withstood the test of time and peer review are the preferred algorithms to use rather than newer, less thoroughly tested algorithms.

Public key encryption

To overcome the problems with key distribution, there is another cryptographic protocol called public key encryption. Public key encryption was developed fairly recently, by Whitfield Diffie and Martin Hellman in 1976.

Public key encryption uses a pair of keys: one public and one private. The public key can be distributed freely. It is extremely difficult to generate the private key with only the public key. Using the public key you can encrypt data that only the holder of the associated private key can decrypt.

Public key cryptography relies on a *one-way function*, a mathematical function that is easy to calculate in one direction, but nearly impossible to calculate in the reverse direction. Cryptography uses a special type of one-way function called a *trapdoor one-way function.* A trapdoor one-way function contains some piece of data that makes it easy to compute in reverse. In public key cryptography, the public key is that data that makes the reverse direction of the function (decryption) easy.

Public key encryption is useful because the public key can be freely distributed. Anyone can encrypt data to you using your public key, and you can always decrypt it. None of the key distribution problems of other cryptographic protocols exist. This is not to say that public key cryptography is perfect; it has its own shortcomings. Public key cryptography is slow and vulnerable to chosen-plain text cryptanalysis.

With these shortcomings, public key cryptography is often used in conjunction with symmetric cryptography. Public key cryptography solves the key distribution problems inherent with symmetric cryptography, and symmetric cryptography solves the speed downfall of public key cryptography.

Such a hybrid cryptography system is seen in the Secure Shell (SSH) protocol for secure remote shell access, among others. Public and private keys are first generated. The public key is then distributed to any recipient with whom you want to communicate. When the communication is initiated, the recipient generates a session key, encrypts it using your public key, and sends it to you. You then decrypt the session key using your private key and use the session key for a symmetric algorithm. In this case, the key distribution is handled by public key cryptography and a symmetric algorithm handles the communications. The session keys are also often regenerated at given intervals and resynchronized using the public key algorithm so that if the session key is discovered, only the data encrypted during the time that session key was in use is compromised.

Key escrow

Key escrow has been a hot topic often discussed under the guise of law enforcement. Strong cryptography, which uses many digits to encrypt information providing a very high level of privacy, has long been a thorn in the side of governments and law enforcement agencies, especially in times of crisis such as World War II and terrorist attacks against the United States over the last several years.

In each of these situations, it is known or believed that the adversaries used strong encryption on their communications so that they could not be read in transit. Strong encryption allows these adversaries to communicate without the threat of their messages being decrypted before they become irrelevant.

Strong encryption is not simply a tool used by fascists and terrorists, however. The allied side also used strong encryption during WW II, and it is still used by government and law enforcement organizations. A number of civilian uses for strong encryption also exist, including the communication of private documents.

Because of the use of strong encryption by "bad guys," there has been some backlash against the authors and distributors of strong encryption tools, such as PGP, which is discussed later in this chapter. Some people call for an outright ban on strong encryption, and others call for key escrow, (which is explained shortly). The export of strong encryption was banned by the United States Commerce Department for some time. This ban simply resulted in the development of strong encryption software (a legitimate industry) in other countries.

An obvious hypothesis is often used to counter the call for a ban on strong encryption. Strong encryption technology has the capability to allow those living in countries with oppressive governments to communicate with the outside world with less fear of reprisal. The other argument against the outright ban on strong encryption is that the development of strong encryption algorithms and their implementations is a process that can be done by one or a few well-educated people. Any ban on strong encryption would not stop its use, but only drive it underground. Criminals (who would be the target of a ban) would most likely not be affected by it.

Key escrow is another answer to the problems with strong encryption and the power it allows criminals. Key escrow is a method of embedding a second private key into a public key algorithm. This second key can be used to decrypt messages in the same way as the original private key. The second private key, however, is held in escrow by a government or law enforcement agency. This agency that holds the key in escrow can then decrypt any message encrypted using a protocol with key escrow built in.

Key escrow has a number of difficulties in its implementation. The implementation would most likely be similar to that of wiretap privileges; a court order would be necessary to use the escrowed key to decrypt messages. Possibilities for misusing the escrowed keys are plentiful, and the escrow key's security is also a potential weak point. The other uncertainty is which body would be responsible for the escrow. An escrow held within the United States could also cause international diplomacy problems.

At this time, there is no good answer to the problems presented by strong encryption. An outright ban would never work, and key escrow faces problems with both implementation and acceptance.

Key escrow was legitimately proposed by the U.S. government some time ago with the Clipper Chip, a hardware encryption device using an algorithm called SkipJack. Under the guise of national security, SkipJack has not been made available for scrutiny by independent parties. As has been discussed earlier in this chapter, the most secure algorithms are those that are open to evaluation by anyone. A good encryption algorithm is not vulnerable through simple inspection. Security cannot be attained through obscurity.

The lack of public analysis is only the first disadvantage of a closed controlled key escrow-based system. Because it has many shortcomings, many big players in the cryptography field have expressed their opposition to such a system that would be the only allowed crypto system in the United States. The Clipper Chip proposal has since faded away, but a similar proposal may come back with recent terrorist attacks as justification despite the invasion privacy that it entails.

Cryptographic signatures

You can also use cryptography to sign documents. Create a simple signature using public key cryptography by encrypting the document you want to sign with your private key. The recipient, who has your public key, can use that key to decrypt the document. As long as the recipient can be sure of the validity of your public key, he can be sure that you signed the document.

Messages with this type of signature can be decrypted and read by anyone with your public key, but a simple solution exists to this problem. If you first sign the document by encrypting it with your private key, encrypt the document with the recipient's public key. The recipient must first decrypt the document with his private key and then verify the signature with your public key.

For large documents, using public key cryptography to sign the entire document is slow. In practice, the document is normally hashed using a one-way hash first (similar to a one-way function) and then the hash is signed. The hash is far shorter than the actual document, but is still long enough that the probability of it not being unique is miniscule. A hash is simply a function that creates a number based on the actual text of the document. A 128-bit hash would have a 2 in 128 chance of having the same value for two different documents. Longer hashes are more unique. MD5 is a one-way hashing function, as is the UNIX crypt function.

Steganography

Not so much a branch of cryptography as it is an art form, *steganography* refers to the practice of embedding secret messages into innocuous messages or other documents. Originally, steganographers wrote messages so that certain letters would combine to form the hidden message. The recipient only had to know which letters to remove to reassemble the secret text.

Steganography is still surprisingly common, even with the invention of unbreakable encryption schemes. With encryption, an eavesdropper knows that you sent a message, even if he cannot read it. With steganography, there is no evidence a message was even sent. There are now ways to hide a message written in miniscule holes in a piece of paper so that the message is only readable through a microscope. You'd need to know which part of the paper to look at first though. Invisible ink also counts as a type of steganography.

Another type of steganography that is getting quite a bit of media coverage lately is embedding messages in digital images. You can change certain data bits in an image to encode a message and then put that image in a place on the Internet with thousands or millions of other similar images. The recipient would know which image to download and have the right information to get the message back out of the image. A number of software programs do this automatically.

Windows Server 2003 Encrypting File System

Windows Server 2003 includes an Encrypting File System (EFS). EFS allows you to encrypt files on an NT File System (NTFS) partition automatically. EFS is based on the CryptoAPI architecture built into Windows Server 2003. No administration is required to use EFS by default. EFS only encrypts files on disk; when files are sent over the network, they are decrypted first. EFS is not a replacement for network encryption protocols such as IPSec or SSL.

**Cross-
Reference**   CryptoAPI is discussed in detail in Chapter 5.

What is EFS?

EFS uses a hybrid encryption system. Files are encrypted using a randomly generated session key called a File Encryption Key (FEK) and a symmetric algorithm (3DES or DESX). The FEK for each file is encrypted using the user's public key and a public key algorithm (RSA or RSA Enhanced). If a user wants to access an encrypted file, the system decrypts the FEK using his private key, and then decrypts the file using that FEK. This is all done transparently at the file system level. Key pairs and certificates are generated automatically for the user if they do not already exist.

EFS is designed for security in all aspects. EFS runs in kernel mode memory, which is not accessible by user processes, and also runs in the non-paged memory pool so that encryption keys are never written to the page file. This ensures that users cannot write programs to steal the FEKs, although they could write a kernel-level device driver for the attack. EFS also ensures that any temporary files created from encrypted files are also encrypted so the data cannot be read. That EFS protects temporary files is a great advantage over similar products.

EFS is also designed for data recovery and sharing. It is possible, by design, for a file's FEK to be encrypted using a number of public keys so that a number of users can access the encrypted file. The data recovery portion of EFS allows the decryption of encrypted data by a user or group known as *recovery agents*.

All files encrypted with EFS have their FEKs encrypted using the recovery agents' public keys and placed in a special field called the Data Recovery Field. When the data is to be recovered, the FEK is decrypted by a recovery agent and used to decrypt the file. This is essentially a method of key escrow where the recovery agents have access to all encrypted files in a domain. For systems that are not in a domain, the Administrator account is used as the recovery agent.

EFS is made up of a number of components. The EFS driver resides between the NTFS and the Kernel I/O manager. Data flowing from the I/O manager to NTFS through the EFS driver is encrypted if the encryption attribute on that file is set.

Data flowing from NTFS to the I/O manager is decrypted if it is encrypted and the appropriate keys match. The EFS driver is the component that makes EFS transparent to the user.

The EFS driver also communicates with the EFS service. The EFS service is integrated with the security subsystem and CryptoAPI to manage keys. The EFS service handles FEK encryption of the FEK and communication with the user interface.

Using EFS

EFS-protected files are encrypted at the file-system level. Regardless of what an attacker does, such as reinstall the operating system, the protected files are only accessible to the user with the appropriate private key and certificate. In addition, files cannot be both compressed and encrypted. Enabling encryption will disable compression.

Follow these steps to encrypt a file:

1. Locate the file you want to encrypt.

2. Right-click the file and then select Properties.

3. Click the Advanced button in the General tab, as shown in Figure 8-1.

Figure 8-1: Click Advanced in the General tab of the file properties window to access the EFS setting.

4. Select the Encrypt contents to secure data check box, as shown in Figure 8-2, and click OK.

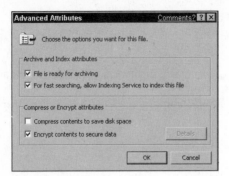

Figure 8-2: Select the Encrypt contents to secure data check box to enable EFS.

5. Click OK to save the file properties.

This is the basic method to encrypt a file. The file contents are encrypted and decrypted on the fly as you work with the file. To turn off decryption on the file, simply follow the previous directions and deselect the Encrypt contents to secure data check box.

Clicking the Details button shown in Figure 8-2 allows you to configure the users that are allowed to transparently access the contents of the encrypted file. It also lists the Data Recovery Agents for the file.

Entire folders can also be encrypted. When encryption is set on a folder, all new files created in that folder will be encrypted.

Command line encryption

EFS provides the cipher.exe command line utility to enable and disable encryption on a file or folder. The cipher utility also shows the status of the current directory and files contained within, as shown in Figure 8-3.

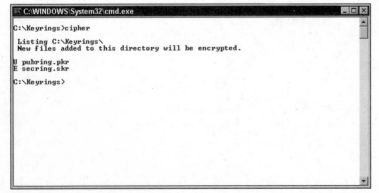

Figure 8-3: The cipher.exe utility can be used to view the encryption attributes of a directory and the files within.

Cipher can be used with the /E switch to set encryption and the /D switch to remove encryption. By default, cipher works only on directories. To work with specific files, you must use the /A switch. Figure 8-4 shows cipher being used to remove the encryption attribute for a file.

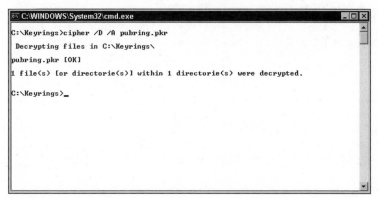

Figure 8-4: The cipher.exe utility can be used to set and remove the encryption attribute from files and folders.

The cipher.exe utility has many more uses than just changing the encryption attribute on files and folders though. By running the command cipher /K, a new file encryption key is created for the current user. Figure 8-5 shows the generation of a new FEK.

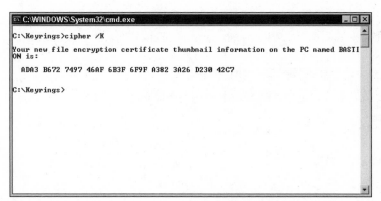

Figure 8-5: The cipher /K command is used to create a new FEK for the current user.

The cipher command can also be used to update the FEK and public key for the current user for all encrypted files by specifying cipher /U /N. Cipher has one other use. It can wipe the data from all unused portions of the disk. By typing `cipher /W:<path>`, cipher will remove all data from unused portions of the volume on which `<path>` resides. An expert attacker can recover data on unused areas of the disk that has been moved or deleted (and, therefore, removed from the file index). The `cipher /W` command makes this type of attack impossible.

Configuring encrypted file recovery agents

Files encrypted with EFS can be forcefully recovered by anyone who is designated as a recovery agent. You will want to choose those recovery agents carefully, as they will be able to decrypt any file.

The EFS Recovery Policy is an important part of a good EFS architecture. It allows FEKs to be recovered and users' files to be decrypted. You should manage recovery agents thoroughly, and keeping the recovery agents' certificates either on a secure system or exporting them and keeping them on a disk in a secure location is recommended. When recovery is required, the certificates can be imported. Recovery should only be done on a secure machine to keep the decrypted files safe.

Adding recovery agents is a complex process. You must have a certificate authority (CA) installed. You should first create a new group.

For more information on installing a Certificate Authority, refer to Chapter 13.

1. From the Start menu, choose Administrative Tools ➪ Active Directory Users ➪ Computers.

2. Double-click your domain in the left pane; then right-click Users and select New ➪ Group.

3. Type a name for the group, as shown in Figure 8-6, and then click OK to add the group.

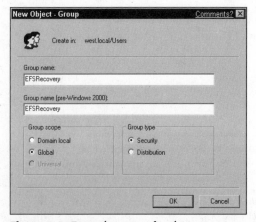

Figure 8-6: Enter the name for the new group and then click OK.

Now that you have a group, you can add specific users to it.

1. Locate the newly created group in the right pane, right-click, and select Properties.

2. Click the Members tab.

3. Click the Add button to open the Select Users, Contacts, or Computers dialog box.

4. Enter the username you want to add in the Enter the object names to select box and then click Check Names. Figure 8-7 shows the dialog box with a name that has been checked. Click OK to add the user.

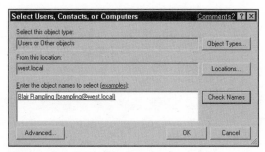

Figure 8-7: Enter the username to add to the group.

5. Figure 8-8 shows the Members tab of the group Properties dialog box with the user added. Click OK.

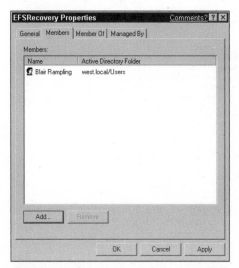

Figure 8-8: The user has been successfully added to the group.

The next step is to assign Enroll permission to this group on the EFS File Recovery template.

1. From the Start menu, click Administrative Tools ⇨ Active Directory Sites and Services.

2. From the View menu, select Show Services Node. The Services container will appear under Sites.

3. Double-click Services in the left pane. Click Public Key Services and then select Certificate Templates, as shown in Figure 8-9.

4. Right-click EFS Recovery in the right pane and then click Properties.

5. Click the Security tab.

6. Click Add to open the Select Users, Computers, or Groups dialog box, enter the group name created earlier, and click Check Names. Figure 8-10 shows the new group selected. Click OK to continue.

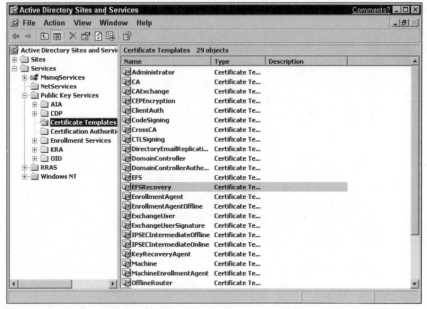

Figure 8-9: Active Directory Sites and Services is used to assign the Enroll permission to the new group.

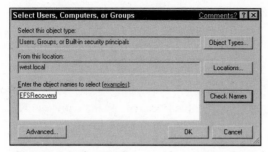

Figure 8-10: The newly created group is selected to add to the security list.

7. Select the newly added group from the list and then click the Allow box for the Enroll permission, as shown in Figure 8-11.

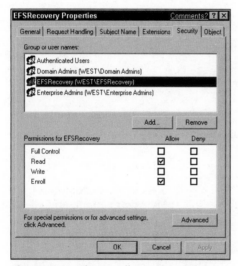

Figure 8-11: The Enroll permission has been granted to the new group.

8. Remove the Enroll permission from any other groups or users that will not be EFS Recovery Agents

9. Click OK to save the new permissions. Close the Active Directory Sites and Services tool.

Each group member must now request a certificate.

1. The group member must log on to the domain.

2. Select Run from the Start menu, type **mmc**, and click OK.

3. From the File menu, select Add/Remove Snap-in.

4. Click Add and then select Certificates from the list, as shown in Figure 8-12. Click Add.

Figure 8-12: Choose Certificates from the list of available snap-ins.

5. The next dialog box prompts you to choose which account certificates will be managed. Accept the default setting of My user account, and click Finish.

6. Click Close in the Add Standalone Snap-in dialog box.

7. The Add/Remove Snap-in dialog box should now contain the Certificates snap-in for the current user, as shown in Figure 8-13. Click OK to add the snap-in.

8. Double-click Certificates in the left pane, right-click Personal, select All Tasks, and Request New Certificate.

9. Click Next on the opening dialog box of the Certificate Request Wizard.

10. Select EFS Recovery Agent from the list of Certificate types, as shown in Figure 8-14. Click Next.

Figure 8-13: The Certificates snap-in has been chosen to add to MMC.

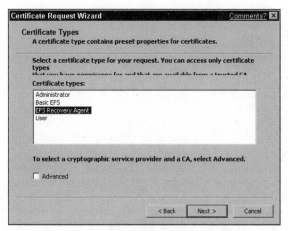

Figure 8-14: Select the EFS Recovery Certificate.

11. Assign a name and description to the certificate so that you can identify it, as shown in Figure 8-15, and click Next.

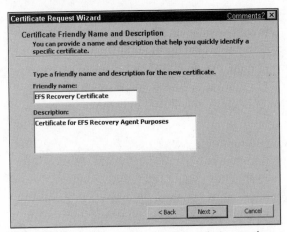

Figure 8-15: Assign a name and description to the certificate for future reference.

12. A summary of the information given is shown, as in Figure 8-16. Click Finish to request the certificate.

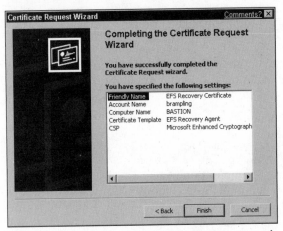

Figure 8-16: A summary of the information entered is shown before the request is submitted.

13. You will be prompted if the certificate request is successful. Double-click Personal in the left pane and then click Certificates. Your newly issued certificate should appear in the right pane, as shown in Figure 8-17.

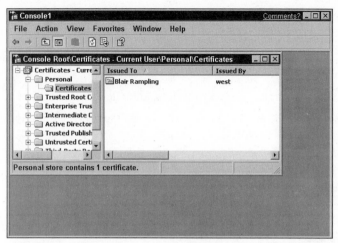

Figure 8-17: The newly issued certificate should be displayed in the list of personal certificates.

14. Right-click the certificate in the right pane and then select Open. Verify the details of the certificate, as shown in Figure 8-18.

Figure 8-18: Verify the details of the new certificate.

15. Click OK to close the Certificate details; then close the MMC window.

The next step is to enable the recovery policy and add the certificates. You must be logged in as a domain administrator to perform these steps.

1. From the Start menu, select Administrative Tools ➪ Active Directory Users ➪ Computers.

2. Right-click the domain, select Properties, and click the Group Policy tab.

3. Select the Default Domain Policy, as shown in Figure 8-19, and click Edit to open the Group Policy editor.

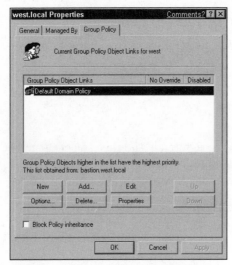

Figure 8-19: Select the Group Policy Object to edit then click the Edit button.

4. Expand Computer Configuration, Windows Settings, Security Settings, and click Public Key Policies.

5. Right-click the Encrypting File System container and then select Add Data Recovery Agent. By default, the local administrator is automatically designated as a recovery agent. Performing this allows you to designate other users as recovery agents. Click Next.

6. Select the Recovery Agents. If certificates are published in Active Directory, you can use the Browse Directory button and add user accounts. If certificates are not stored in Active Directory, use the Browse Folders button to locate the certificates. Click Next.

7. Click Finish after you've reviewed the summary.

At this point, the user or users that you designated as recovery agents will be listed within the Encrypting File System container.

Encrypted file recovery

To recover a file, any recovery agent can simply remove the encryption attribute or open the file if in a domain.

If you have a standalone system, the EFS Recovery process is different. The local administrator must first export the recovery key and make a backup. If no backup is made before a failure or data loss, the encrypted files cannot be recovered.

The command is cipher /R:<filename>, as shown in Figure 8-20.

Figure 8-20: The recovery key and certificate must be exported and saved if encrypted files are to be recovered in the future.

It is important that the two files generated by the cipher /R command are kept safe and the password is not lost. These three things are necessary to recover encrypted files.

Imagine that the system has suffered a failure, and the encrypted files need to be recovered on another system. The original recovery agent key and certificate are different on this system so the local administrator cannot recover the files. You now need the backed up key and certificate and the associated password.

1. Browse to the location containing the saved PFX and CER files.

2. Right-click the PFX file and select Install PFX.

3. The Certificate Import Wizard will open. Click Next to continue.

4. You will be prompted for the file to import, as shown in Figure 8-21. Click Next to accept the default (the file you originally selected).

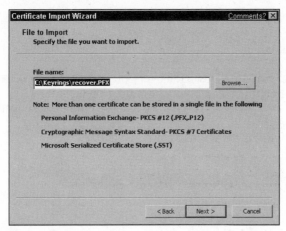

Figure 8-21: You are prompted to specify the certificate file to import.

5. Enter the password that you specified when you originally created the files, as shown in Figure 8-22. You do not need to check the Enable private key protection box; otherwise, you will be prompted for a password every time the certificate is used. If you select the Mark this key as exportable box, you will be able to export the key again at a later time.

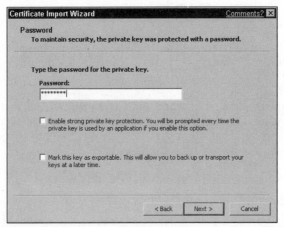

Figure 8-22: You must enter the password that was used when the certificate files were originally created.

6. You are now prompted for the store in which to place the certificate. Select Place all certificates in the following store and then click Browse.

7. Select the Personal store from the list, as shown in Figure 8-23, and click OK.

Figure 8-23: Select the Personal store from the list of certificate stores.

8. Figure 8-24 shows the certificate store set to personal. Click Next to continue.

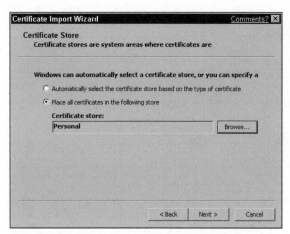

Figure 8-24: The certificate will be imported into the personal store.

9. A summary will be displayed. Verify the information, as shown in Figure 8-25, and click Finish to import the certificate.

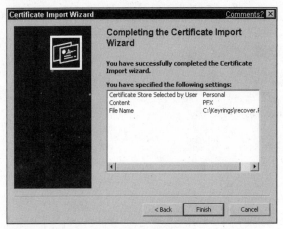

Figure 8-25: The summary shows which certificate is being imported into which store.

10. You will be prompted if the import was successful, as shown in Figure 8-26. Click OK.

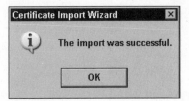

Figure 8-26: You are prompted as to the status of the import when it is complete.

You should now be able to open the encrypted files restored from the failed system, and disable the encryption attribute for those files.

Third-Party Encryption Software

A number of third-party encryption packages are available. The most common third-party encryption package is Pretty Good Privacy (PGP) originally written by Phil Zimmerman and now distributed by Network Associates. There is both a freeware and commercial version of the software; if it's for personal use you can use the freeware version.

In its most basic form, PGP encrypts text; however, many additional features have been added to PGP over time. Through the use of plug-ins for e-mail client software, PGP can encrypt, sign, and decrypt e-mail messages on the fly.

PGP can use both public key and symmetric algorithms for encryption. Several industry standard algorithms are supported, such as 3DES and RSA. Normally, files or e-mail messages are encrypted using the recipient's public key and your public key so that both can be used to later open the encrypted text.

When PGP is integrated with an e-mail client, which is done by default during the installation, it is simple to use. During the installation, you are asked if you have existing PGP *keyrings* (contact points used for referrals), or if you are a new user, as shown in Figure 8-27.

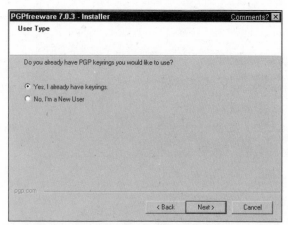

Figure 8-27: When installing PGP, you are asked if you have existing keyrings or are a new user.

For this example, assume that you don't have any existing keyrings.

1. Select No, I'm a New User and then click Next.

2. Specify the installation directory and then click Next.

3. Select the components you require to install, as shown in Figure 8-28. Click Next.

4. Review your selections, and click Next to begin the installation.

5. After PGP has installed, the Key Generation Wizard starts, as shown in Figure 8-29. Click the Expert button to begin the key generation process. The Expert mode allows more control over the key pair parameters.

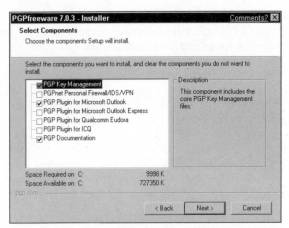

Figure 8-28: Select the PGP components you require.

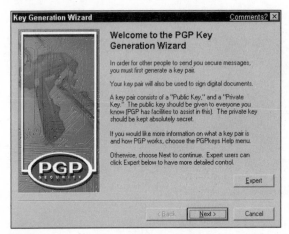

Figure 8-29: Click the Expert button to generate keys in expert mode; otherwise, click Next.

6. Enter your name and e-mail address. The e-mail address is linked to the key so that e-mails to you can be automatically encrypted using your public key. You also need to select the key type and the key length. A key length of 2048 is adequate for normal communications, but you can step down to 1024 for more speed and less security, or use a longer key for more security. You can also set a key expiration. Making your key expire is a good idea as it is more

secure to generate a new key every so often in case your key pair is cracked or your private key is lost without your knowledge. Keys are often set to never expire. You will need to create a new key after the current one expires. Figure 8-30 shows the Key Parameter Selection dialog box.

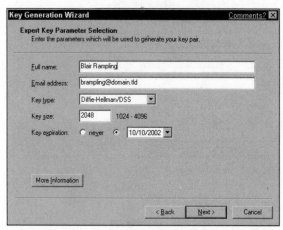

Figure 8-30: The key parameters can be configured in expert mode.

7. Figure 8-31 shows the Passphrase Assignment dialog box. The passphrase you enter here will become part of your private key and be used every time you decrypt or sign a message. Encrypting a message does not require the passphrase because only the recipient's public key is needed for encryption. The Passphrase Quality bar reflects the difficulty with which the key pair could be cracked. More spaces, punctuation marks, and special characters as well as a mix of numbers and letters dictate how secure the passphrase is. It is not vital to make the Passphrase Quality bar reach its maximum level. If your communications warrant an extremely high amount of security, a longer, more difficult passphrase is recommended. For communications with less value or a shorter lifetime, a less secure passphrase is acceptable. After you have entered your preferred passphrase, click Next to continue.

8. The key pair is finally created, as shown in Figure 8-32. Click Next to continue.

9. Now that the key pair has been created, you can add it to your keyring. Click Finish to do this. The keyrings are simply files that contain all of your public and private keys. The public keys are held in a file called pubring.pkr and the private keys in secring.pkr. You may have a large number of public keys if you do a lot of communication using PGP.

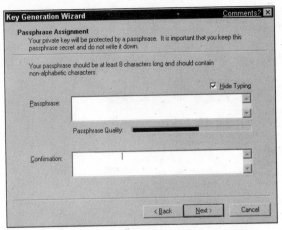

Figure 8-31: The passphrase is required any time your private key is used, which is for signing and decrypting messages.

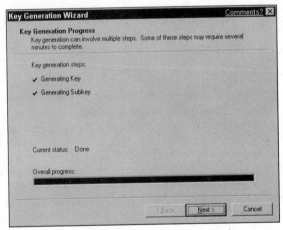

Figure 8-32: The key pair has been created.

Now that PGP is installed and you've generated keys, you can begin to use it. First, you can encrypt a file.

1. Locate the file to encrypt, right-click, and select PGP ⇨ Encrypt & Sign.

2. Figure 8-33 shows the Key Selection Dialog dialog box. Select which keys will be able to decrypt the file. They are automatically placed in the Recipients field so that you can always decrypt what you encrypt. You can drag any public keys from the keyring to the recipient's field below; then click OK.

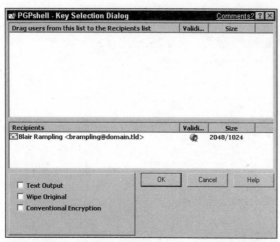

Figure 8-33: The PGP Key Selection Dialog dialog box is used to select which public keys will be used to encrypt the file.

3. As you are also signing the file, you are prompted for your passphrase, as shown in Figure 8-34. If you were encrypting only, the passphrase would not be needed because the private key is not used. Enter the passphrase and then click OK.

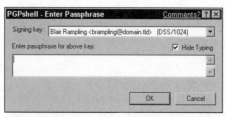

Figure 8-34: Enter your passphrase to complete the Encrypt & Sign operation.

Figure 8-35 shows the encrypted file. Notice that the original file still exists. If you want to keep only the encrypted file, you should right-click the original file, select PGP, and select Wipe. This will cause the file to be deleted in a safe manner. The file will be deleted normally, and all traces of it will be wiped from the disk. You will be left with only the encrypted version.

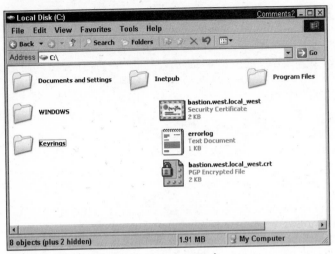

Figure 8-35: The file has been encrypted.

Sending an encrypted e-mail is just as easy. When you create a new message in Outlook, for example, select Encrypt on send or Sign on send from the PGP menu. If you choose to encrypt, when you send the message, PGP will try to match the recipients' e-mail addresses with public keys in your keyring and automatically add those to the recipients in the PGP Key Selection Dialog dialog box. If those keys are not found, PGP will search the public key databases for a match. If a match is still not found, you will be presented with the PGP Key Selection Dialog dialog box and an error and be asked which public keys to use for the encryption. If a recipient does not have a public key in the Key Selection Dialog dialog box when the message is sent, he will not be able to read it. Finally, if you selected to sign the message, you will be prompted for your passphrase.

When reading PGP messages, as encrypted messages come up in the preview pane, you are prompted for your passphrase by default. If you enter it successfully, you can view the message. Signed messages are also processed automatically in the preview pane. By default, messages are not automatically decrypted when you open them to read, forward, or reply. If you enable the Automatically decrypt/verify when opening messages feature in the PGP options dialog box (Options from the PGP menu in Outlook), you will be prompted for your passphrase and messages will be decrypted automatically.

Summary

This chapter focused on encrypting data in Windows Server 2003. The chapter began by defining cryptography and how it is used to secure information. The three different encryption systems discussed were one-time pads, symmetric key encryption, and public key encryption. A discussion of the controversies surrounding Key Escrow was also included.

You then read about the Encrypting File System (EFS) in Windows Server 2003. EFS allows files on an NTFS partition to be encrypted. Files are encrypted and decrypted using a File Encryption Key (FEK), and the entire process is transparent to the user. Files can be encrypted through Windows Explorer or by using the cipher command.

Encrypting File Recovery Agents are an important part of implementing EFS. These are the users that are able to recover FEKs and files that have been encrypted by other users. The EFS Recovery Policy determines who is able to decrypt users' files. By default, the administrator is designated as the file recovery agent. You can assign additional users this role by editing the EFS Recovery Policy.

The chapter ended with a look at third-party encryption software that can be used as an alternative to EFS. The most common encryption software is called Pretty Good Privacy (PGP) and is distributed by Network Associates. PGP's main purpose is to encrypt text; however, many plug-ins are available that enhance its functionality.

✦   ✦   ✦

Securing Web Pages and E-mail Using SSL and TLS

Web pages and e-mail are normally transmitted in plain text over the Internet. In addition, there is almost no control over the path that your traffic will take. It travels through numerous routers controlled by many different parties, and the path may change often, as the Internet can dynamically change routing around problems.

Any point through which this traffic travels is a potential problem. Simple packet sniffing programs, such as snoop, included with Sun Solaris, tcpdump on Unix platforms, or Network Monitor or windump for Windows, can be used to view raw data traveling over the local network. In addition, the dsniff group of programs can be used to sniff specific information, such as smtp mail using mailsnarf. Even mail passwords can be grabbed if the traffic crosses the attacker's network.

Network traffic is sniffed by placing the local system's network adapter in promiscuous mode. When in this mode, the network adapter listens for all traffic on the local subnet instead of only traffic destined for the network itself. The limitation of this, however, is that only traffic on the local network can be captured. There are other methods of performing packet captures, such as using the management and logging facilities built into routers, but these are somewhat less common.

A number of solutions exist to the problem of traffic sniffing and session hijacking. Encrypting the data being transferred makes stealing the information very difficult. It is not a fool-proof solution, but it is a vast improvement over plain text.

Even with encrypted data, attacks are possible, although an attacker can't sniff data in real time. An attack against encrypted data begins with recording the encrypted flow of traffic. The attacker now has as much time as he likes to break the encryption. Most encryption systems are vulnerable to attack given enough time and resources through brute force attacks. Some are also vulnerable to other attacks that break the encryption much faster because of inherent holes in the algorithm. The only unbreakable encryption system is a one-time pad, as discussed in Chapter 8, but it is not feasible to use such an algorithm for encrypting traffic flows.

A brute force attack on your data will take significant time and resources as long as a large enough key is used for encryption. Given that, there is a trade-off to be made for the attacker. Is it truly worth weeks, months, or even years to decrypt the traffic? This is what makes encrypting your data worthwhile. An attacker is unlikely to waste his time breaking your encryption. If your data is less important, you can use a smaller key, which makes a brute force attack easier but the encryption and decryption process faster. The more important the security of your data, the larger the key you will want to use, although this slows the protocol down.

One of the major developments necessitating the implementation of encryption of data across the Internet has been e-commerce. For customers to be able (and comfortable) to give you their private information, such as credit cards, you must be able to prove to them that the information will not fall into the wrong hands.

Secure Sockets Layer (SSL) and Transport Layer Security (TLS) are methods of encrypting HTTP traffic for just this reason. Using certificates, the identity of the host can be verified and traffic to that host can be encrypted. This way, information such as credit card numbers cannot be sniffed. SSL literally enables e-commerce to function.

Just as HTTP traffic is sent in plain text across the Internet, so is SMTP traffic. SMTP traffic is often more private because it contains the e-mail messages that you are sending to other parties. SMTP traffic is sniffed just as easily as any other kind of traffic.

There are two solutions to the problem of plain text SMTP. The first solution (discussed in Chapter 8) is encrypting your messages using PGP or another encryption method. PGP is the ideal solution because mail is encrypted through the entire path to the recipient. The recipient is the only one who can decrypt the message. The major disadvantage to using encryption methods like PGP is that the recipient must have the software and be able to use the software (which can be confusing for a less skilled user). You must also have the recipient's public key, but that can often be retrieved from a central key repository.

E-mail can also be secured using SSL and TLS. If both the client and server support the feature, SMTP traffic can be encrypted, obstructing traffic-sniffing attacks. The advantage of this method over client-based encryption systems is that no extra steps are required beyond those for sending a regular e-mail, and the recipient does not need special software. Additionally, no key exchange is required. The disadvantage is that if any of the SMTP links between the sender and the recipient are unencrypted, the message is vulnerable at those points.

There are other problems with the security of mail and Web traffic from the use of plain text. One of the most common is POP3 passwords, which are sent in clear text (synonym for plain text). A solution to this problem, called APOP, is also available. APOP is a method of encrypting user names and passwords for POP3 accounts.

Introduction to SSL and TLS

SSL and TLS are essentially versions of the same certificate-based encryption system, although TLS is not backward compatible with SSL. The original widely implemented version of SSL is SSLv2. (SSLv1 was never adopted.) SSLv2 was mainly developed by Netscape and was implemented beginning in Netscape Navigator 1.1. SSLv2 was not well implemented, however, so Microsoft developed a protocol called Private Communications Technology (PCT). PCT was backward compatible with SSLv2. Netscape then developed SSLv3, a complete rewrite that was also backward compatible with SSLv2. The lack of an encryption protocol standard resulted in a process that was not very clear.

Due to the lack of a clear standard for encryption protocols, the Internet Engineering Task Force (IETF) decided to develop a standard to function across all platforms. TLS was developed in that process, which is similar to SSLv3 yet not backward compatible because of some small changes to increase security. TLS is still not widely implemented even though it is several years old.

SSL is used to encrypt TCP sessions. SSL will not work with transport layer protocols such as UDP, which are not reliable. SSL operates by providing a layer between the application protocol, such as HTTP, and the transport protocol, TCP. Normally, a plain text HTTP request would be placed in a TCP packet and sent to the remote host. SSL provides an encrypted channel over which the HTTP request is sent. SSL provides both encryption and prevention against an attacker tampering with data in transit.

An SSL connection has two phases: the handshake and data transfer. The handshake phase verifies the identity of the server and performs key exchange. After the server is authenticated and keys are exchanged, those keys are used to encrypt the data transfer phase of the connection. The data transfer phase occurs similarly to a normal TCP session where data is split into pieces that fit into the message transfer agent (MTA) of the lower-level protocols, except the payloads are encrypted.

The SSL handshake is similar to most cryptographic protocols.

1. The client initiates the connection by sending a list of supported cryptographic algorithms (or ciphers) and a random number to the server.

2. The server then replies with the following: its certificate, its selection of cipher from those supported by the client, and its own random number. The certificate contains the server's public key as well as features that verify the identity of the server.

3. The client must use the certificate to authenticate the server. In this step, the client also generates another random number, encrypts it using the public key contained in the certificate, and sends it to the server.

   This value is called the `pre_master_secret` and is used later for key generation. This value is the seed used for creating the encryption keys for the data transfer and must stay secure. Key exchange represents one of the biggest difficulties in encryption.

4. The client and server now share each other's random values as well as the `pre_random_secret` value. They each generate encryption keys and message authentication codes (MACs) from these values using a known key derivation function (KDF). The MACs are then exchanged and compared. If the MACs match, the key generation and the handshake phase were successful. If not, there was either an error or evidence of a man-in-the-middle attack.

The client and server now have encryption keys that can be used for symmetrically encrypting the actual data. The SSL Record Protocol performs data transfer.

1. The record protocol splits up the data into smaller fragments (similar to TCP) and calculates a hash of the fragment, referred to as the MAC. The *hash* is a number generated from a string of text used to ensure that a message was not tampered with while being transferred.

2. The MAC and fragment are encrypted using the encryption keys created in the handshake phase, and a header is added. The entire package is called a record.

3. A record header is added to the record containing the SSL version, the record length, and a content type. For records containing data, the content type is `application_data`.

4. The record is then encapsulated in the TCP packet and transmitted.

5. When the server receives the packet, it decapsulates the record out of the TCP packet, inspects the header, and decrypts the data.

6. The MAC is generated for the data and compared to the MAC contained in the encrypted record, again to minimize the risk of a man-in-the-middle attack. If the MAC matches, the data is passed to the application.

SSL Performance Issues

Using SSL has one great downside, and that is in performance. SSL is highly CPU-intensive and averages, in a real-world environment, about one-fifth of the throughput of a plain text TCP session. This means that your Web server would serve five times as many pages without SSL as it would with SSL enabled. SSL can slow the server down by 2 – 100 times.

The most obvious (and cheapest) solution is to minimize where SSL is used. If a particular Web page does not require SSL, it should not be used (likewise for any other SSL-enabled application).

When SSL places a high load on your servers, it can be alleviated through a number of methods. The most basic ways are through scaling up and scaling out. *Scaling up* entails adding more or faster CPUs to the server. As SSL is CPU-intensive, adding CPU resources will allow for more load. *Scaling out* is the process of adding more servers to share the load. Scaling out is sometimes difficult and often requires special hardware for the front end of the cluster.

A more suitable method of increasing SSL efficiency is adding a (or several) dedicated SSL processing card or unit. Intel provides the e-commerce accelerator product, Nortel the iSD-SSL, and f5 the BigIP SSL accelerator outboard units, which only perform SSL operations and send plain text HTTP requests to your Web server, offsetting the load. Sun Microsystems also has an SSL accelerator card that fits inside its servers (although it is not relevant to a Windows-based environment) to offload SSL transactions. Numerous similar products are available from other vendors.

Almost all cryptographic operations are CPU-intensive. Cryptographic algorithms are nothing more than number crunchers. Keys are generated by running long strings through key generation algorithms, data is encrypted by putting it through an algorithm with the key as input, and so on. SSL, however, uses more resources on the handshake phase than the data transfer phase. Most of the load incurred in the handshake phase is from the decryption of the `pre_master_secret` value encrypted using the server's public key by the client.

One of the largest variables that affect the performance of SSL is the size of the keys used in the handshake. Using larger keys dramatically reduces the performance of the transaction but dramatically increases security. The opposite is true for smaller keys. A happy medium does exist. There comes a point where going to a larger key becomes pointless. For example, if it takes 100 years to break a 768-bit key and 1000 years to break a 1024-bit key, what difference does that make to your e-commerce site? It's doubtful that the credit cards in your encrypted transactions will be around in 100 years, so it's not much use to take a significant performance hit to increase that security.

Because the handshake is the most expensive part of an SSL transaction in terms of system resources, SSL requests transferring a lot of data are more resource-effective than those transferring small amounts of data. Also, the larger the key, the more expensive the handshake. Reducing the number of SSL handshakes pays off even more when larger keys are being used. Instead of transferring many small chunks of data over separate SSL connections, it is more effective to perform one large transfer, when possible. Take this into consideration when designing applications using SSL.

An alternative approach to the problem of expensive handshakes is session resumption, used to cache the `master_secret` key from an existing session. This key can be used for subsequent connections to the same server. This cache should only exist for a short amount of time, however, as the longer the cache time is, the more keys will be cached in the server.

Session resumption saves cost to the client because the cache of session keys will be relatively small. A client will talk to only a handful of servers, so maintaining and searching that cache is not very resource-intensive.

For a server, on the other hand, session resumption is far more expensive. The higher the traffic on the server, the larger the cache will become. Aside from the I/O resources needed to write the cache, as the cache grows, the resources needed to search the cache and retrieve a given key quickly grow. Maintaining a small cache is important on the server, and a fine balance needs to be made between the effectiveness of session resumption and its cost.

Note   Session resumption is useful in some cases, but the previous method of consolidating data transfers to as few SSL connections as possible is still the best method of improving SSL performance.

Secure HTTP with SSL

SSL was originally used for Web traffic. SSL was first built into Web browsers, but was created to be flexible enough that it can be used by any protocol. As previously discussed, there are a number of situations where you would want to implement SSL for HTTP traffic such as e-commerce and EDI, and Web-based banking.

HTTP is carried over SSL through simple encapsulation. While HTTP is normally carried over TCP, SSL provides another layer on which the HTTP data travels. Everything above SSL in the protocol stack is encrypted as SSL provides an encrypted tunnel for plaintext data. In actuality any data, not just HTTP, can be carried in this SSL tunnel if the process for the SSL handshake is implemented.

HTTP over SSL is known as HTTP Secure (HTTPS). It runs over a separate port number from HTTP, 443 by default. A standard HTTP server running on port 80 is not able to decrypt the HTTP requests on the SSL channel. Encrypted requests must be sent to a server that understands such requests. You can run an HTTPS server on any port, but the client must know to which port to connect. Default ports provide a more convenient method of connecting.

The client first makes a request using a URL beginning with `HTTPS://`. This instructs the client system to use SSL to make the connection to the server and to use port 443 unless another port is explicitly specified.

The client begins the SSL handshake with the server to establish the SSL connection. After the SSL handshake is complete and a secure tunnel has been established, the HTTP request is sent. The client receives the HTTP response, and the SSL connection is closed. No data, other than the SSL handshake, is sent by either the client or server until the SSL tunnel is established.

During the SSL handshake, the server certificate is sent to the client so the client can verify the identity of the server. This is done automatically. The client checks the common name of the server contained in the certificate against the URL to which it is connecting. If the two match, the server is understood to be authentic.

If the identity of the server does not match the information in the certificate, in most cases the user can choose to override the verification step. This is dangerous because many users do not understand the ramifications of this action if an attacker has created the server certificate and the remote site is being maliciously used to steal information.

After the SSL handshake is complete and the HTTP traffic is transferred over the SSL tunnel, the connection is closed. Either the server or the client can send `close_notify` to close the connection.

Encrypted E-mail Transmission

E-mail can be encrypted using TLS just as HTTP traffic is encrypted using SSL, although there are some problems with the implementation. Sending encrypted e-mail using third-party applications, such as PGP, was discussed in Chapter 8. Using a secure tunneling protocol, such as TLS, takes a different approach. The mail software on both ends of the connection must support this protocol for the procedure to work.

While HTTP uses a separate port for encrypted and plaintext communications, SMTP over TLS uses a practice called upgrading. A plain text connection is made, which is then upgraded to an encrypted connection (all on the same port) before data is sent.

SMTP over TLS uses an extended SMTP command called STARTTLS. When the initial connection to the server is made and the server sends the 220 response, the client sends an EHLO command to identify itself to the server. The server then responds with a list of SMTP extensions it supports. If the STARTTLS extension is supported, SMTP over TLS is possible.

To begin the TLS upgrade (assuming STARTTLS is a supported extension), the client sends the STARTTLS command. The server responds with a 220 response, which means "ready for tls," and the client begins the TLS handshake to establish a TLS tunnel. Most implementations are also backwards compatible with SSLv2 and SSLv3.

After the handshake is complete, an encrypted tunnel exists between the client and server. This is where HTTPS would send the HTTP request. Instead, the SMTP client sends another EHLO over the encrypted tunnel and then proceeds with the mail operations. When the mail transfer is complete, the connection is closed.

One major problem with SMTP over TLS is that much of the SMTP traffic carried over the Internet is relayed between several SMTP servers before it reaches its destination. The connection from one point to another point may be encrypted, but any number of the other connections may be in plaintext.

SSL Caveats

SSL is not the absolute answer to encryption needs for Internet protocols. A number of problems are inherent with SSL, most of which have workarounds.

While SSL solves the problem of TCP connection hijacking and traffic sniffing, it is susceptible to session hijacking and sniffing itself. Hijacking or sniffing an SSL session is normally useless, except in one case.

If the attacker is able to get the `master_secret` value, he can decrypt and encrypt packets in the SSL session at will. Essentially, the attacker can access all of the traffic traveling over the encrypted tunnel. Actually getting the `master_secret` is usually very difficult, but it is possible with a poorly written SSL implementation. Poor programming techniques can result in the value being stored in memory regions where it is accessible to other processes or even written to disk.

There is also a caveat to session resumption (discussed earlier in this chapter). Although it is normally eliminated in most SSL implementations, using a truncation attack against a poorly written implementation without proper error handling is possible.

Normally, when a connection is complete, one side sends `close_notify` to instruct the other side to end the connection. The session can be cached for the purpose of session resumption. A truncation attack occurs when an attacker sends a TCP FIN packet to one end of the connection, then uses session resumption to hijack the connection. For this reason, session resumption is usually only allowed when a `close_notify` has been sent.

Network obstacles can also cause SSL to be unable to properly function. Two of these problems occur with proxies and virtual hosts. Proxies require special implementations to support HTTPS traffic. Normally, a proxy server accepts an HTTP request from a client, establishes its own connection to the destination server, retrieves the data, and returns the data to the client.

HTTPS does not function over proxies for this reason. The proxy server cannot accept the request because the connection needs to be made directly to the remote server using SSL.

Using the proxy Connect method avoids this problem. Using Connect, a TCP session, rather than the application protocol (such as HTTP), is proxied. The proxy server accepts the TCP packets from the client and passes them unaltered to the server. This allows SSL packets to traverse the proxy. This causes its own set of problems because a client could use the Connect method to pass any traffic through the proxy server, but it is a requirement for SSL to function.

Virtual hosts also cause a problem with HTTPS. When using virtual hosts, the Web server inspects the host header in the HTTP request to properly route the request to the correct virtual server on a system.

There is no workaround for this problem with virtual hosts. To use SSL, each host must have its own IP address. Multiple addresses can be assigned to a single interface, but each site must have a unique address. Sites that do not use SSL can still use virtual hosts.

Using SSL with Microsoft IIS

Microsoft's Web server, included with Internet Information Services (IIS), supports SSL secured Web sites. There are a number of steps to creating a secure site with IIS.

To use SSL, you first need a server certificate. The most common way of obtaining one is through a Certificate Authority (CA), such as Verisign or Thwate. The process is relatively easy but does cost money. To obtain a certificate, create a certificate request and send it to the CA. The CA will then send you the certificate.

1. Create the site that will be secured.

2. After the site has been created, right-click the site in the left pane of the IIS snap-in, select Properties, and click the Directory Security tab, as shown in Figure 9-1.

3. Click the Server Certificate button to launch the Web Server Certificate Wizard. Click Next to proceed past the wizard's introductory page.

4. Figure 9-2 shows the first step in the wizard. You must choose how to assign a certificate to the site. Assuming this is a new secure site, ensure that the default option of Create a new certificate is selected and click Next.

5. You can select whether to create the request and send it later, or to send the request immediately (see Figure 9-3). The option to immediately send the request is only available if there is a CA online locally. Accept the default option to create the request and send it later; then click Next.

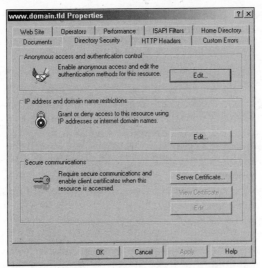

Figure 9-1: The Directory Security tab of the site Properties dialog box is used to create a new certificate request.

6. Give the certificate a name, as shown in Figure 9-4. The best name for the certificate is the same name as the site (its DNS name). You can also select the key length for the certificate. The key length is determined based on the CA you want to use. For example, Verisign accepts 512, 768, and 1024-bit keys for normal certificates, and only 1024-bit keys for certain certificates. 1024 is the recommended value unless your CA requires something different.

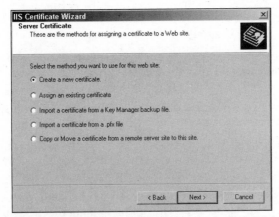

Figure 9-2: You must select the method with which to assign a certificate to the site.

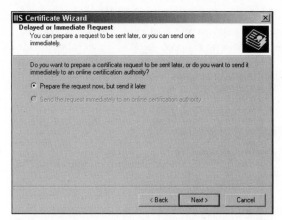

Figure 9-3: You can create the request and send it immediately or later.

7. From this step in the wizard, you can also choose to make this a Server Gated Cryptography (SGC) certificate and select an option that allows you to select the Cryptographic Service Provider (CSP) for the certificate. An SGC certificate is a special type of certificate that allows export versions of Internet Explorer and other browsers with 40-bit security to use 128-bit security for certain sites, such as financial institutions. It is unlikely you will need to create an SGC certificate.

The option to select the CSP allows you to change the CSP used to generate the certificate. By default, the CSP is set to the Microsoft SChannel Cryptographic Provider. If you have another CSP installed, such as a hardware device or other software CSP, you can select this box and then select the CSP from the list in the next step. If you don't use a third-party CSP, do not select this option, and the default CSP will be used. Click Next to continue.

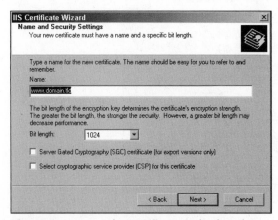

Figure 9-4: Name the certificate and select the key length.

8. The next step, as shown in Figure 9-5, requires you to specify an organization name and organizational unit for the certificate. The organization name should be the same as the name on your certificate of incorporation, as the CA commonly uses this document for verification of your corporate identity. The organizational unit should be your department or some other identifying information. Click Next to continue.

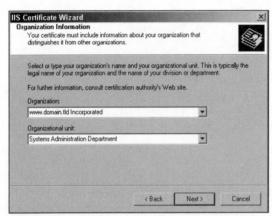

Figure 9-5: Enter the name of your organization and department.

9. Enter the common name for your site, as shown in Figure 9-6. As discussed earlier in this chapter, clients use the common name you enter here to verify the identity of your server. The common name should be the same as the DNS name of your site. Click Next to continue.

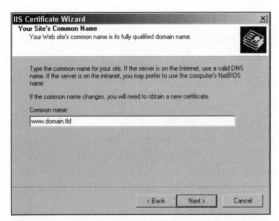

Figure 9-6: Specify the common name for your site. This must match the DNS name of the site for Internet sites.

10. Figure 9-7 shows the next step in the wizard. Specify your locale information. The CA uses this information and it is embedded into your certificate. Select your country, and specify your state or province and city. Click Next.

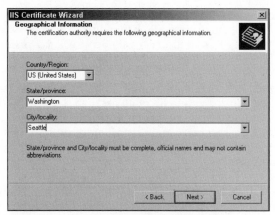

Figure 9-7: You must specify your locale as identifying information for the new certificate.

11. Specify a file in which to save the certificate request, as shown in Figure 9-8. This file will be sent to the CA for generation of the actual certificate. Click Next to continue and a summary of the information you specified is displayed. If this information is correct, click Next and the request will be generated.

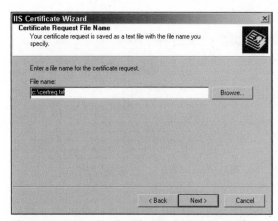

Figure 9-8: Specify the file in which to save the certificate request.

Caution Ensure that the information in your certificate request is accurate. Mistakes in the request can cause the actual certificate to contain invalid information, which will cause clients to be unable to verify your identity. In most cases, you cannot get a new certificate without paying the fee again.

12. When the certificate request has been created, another summary page is shown. The key part of this page is the Click here link, which takes you to a list of third-party CAs able to grant a server certificate. Click Finish to close the wizard.

Now that you have generated the certificate request, you can send that request to a CA. Normally, the process requires you to fill out a form on the CA's Web site, provide a credit card for payment, and also fax certain identifying documents to the CA. These documents often include your certificate of incorporation, business license, or partnership documents. Sometimes you can simply provide your DUNS number for identification purposes.

After this process has been done according to the CA's instructions, the actual certificate will be sent to you via e-mail (usually in a few days). You now need to install the certificate.

1. Right-click the site in the IIS snap-in and then select Properties. Select the Directory Security tab, and click the Server Certificate button. Click Next to proceed past the introduction.

2. This time, IIS knows that there is a pending certificate request. As shown in Figure 9-9, you can choose to process the request and install the new certificate or delete the request. Accept the default setting of Process the pending request and install the certificate and click Next.

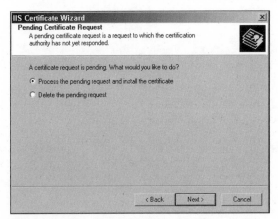

Figure 9-9: You can process the pending certificate request or delete the request and start the process again.

3. Specify the path to the actual certificate returned from the CA, as shown in Figure 9-10, and click Next.

4. A summary of the certificate information will be shown. Verify the information and click Next to continue. The certificate is installed and another summary is displayed. Click Finish to close the wizard.

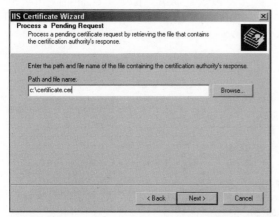

Figure 9-10: Specify the path to the certificate sent to you from the CA.

Your site is now capable of accepting SSL connections. By default, SSL connections are accepted on port 443. You can change this port by editing the Web Site tab of the site's Properties dialog box. When this port is changed, however, users will not be able to access the site as usual by typing `https://www.domain.tld`. They will need to specify the port number as well, as in `https://www.domain.tld:port`.

Encrypting SMTP Traffic in Windows Server

Windows Server and more specifically, IIS, contains its own SMTP server. This SMTP server is also used when Microsoft Exchange is installed. This SMTP server has the capability to receive e-mail from clients using SSL encryption.

If you are running Microsoft Exchange 2000, open the Exchange System Manager snap-in. In the left pane, expand Servers, the name of your server, Protocols, and SMTP. Right-click Default SMTP Virtual Server and then select Properties.

If you are not running Microsoft Exchange, do the following:

1. Open the IIS snap-in. The Default SMTP Virtual Server, if it is installed, will be located in the left pane under the server name. Right-click it, and select Properties.

2. In the Default SMTP Virtual Server Properties dialog box, click the Access tab, as shown in Figure 9-11. The Access tab is used to configure how other systems interact with the SMTP server. You will need to add a certificate to the SMTP server.

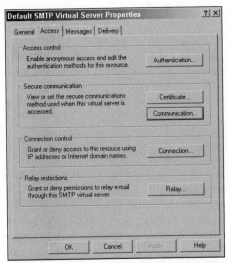

Figure 9-11: The Access tab of the Default SMTP Virtual Server Properties dialog box is used to configure how other systems can communicate with the SMTP server.

3. Click the Certificate button in the Access tab. The Web Server Certificate Wizard is launched. Click Next to continue past the introduction. You need to decide how to assign a certificate to the SMTP server. This process is the same as the process used to assign a certificate to a Web site in the previous section. You can assign an existing certificate to the SMTP server. For example, if you have a certificate with the common name of domain.tld for a Web site and mail to the SMTP server is addressed to domain.tld, that certificate can be assigned to the server by selecting the Assign an existing certificate option, clicking Next, and selecting the certificate from the list. The alternative is to follow the steps in the previous section for requesting a new certificate.

4. After a certificate has been installed, clients can connect to the SMTP server using SSL. Client configuration will be addressed later. There are two settings available for configuring the behavior of the SSL connection. Click the Communication button in the Access tab of the Default SMTP Virtual Server Properties dialog box. The Security dialog box is displayed.

5. You can select the Require secure channel box to require every connection to the SMTP server to use SSL. When this option is selected, you can also select the Require 128-bit encryption option. This causes the server to only accept 128-bit connections, and 40-bit export clients will not be able to connect.

The client must also be configured to use SSL to connect to the SMTP server. This example configures Microsoft Outlook 2000 to use SSL for its SMTP connection.

1. Open Outlook. If Outlook is configured in Internet only mode, select Accounts from the Tools menu, select the account to configure (normally the default account is used to send mail through SMTP), and click Properties.

2. If Outlook is configured for Corporate or Workgroup use, select Services from the Tools menu, select the Internet E-mail account to configure, and click Properties.

3. Click the Advanced tab of the account Properties dialog box, as shown in Figure 9-12. SSL is enabled for the connection to the SMTP Server by selecting This server requires a secure connection (SSL) under the Outgoing Mail server, as shown.

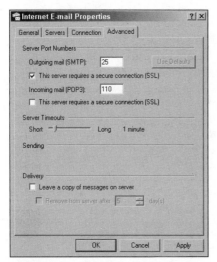

Figure 9-12: Select the check box to configure the connection to the SMTP server to use SSL.

Summary

The focus of this chapter was on securing Web pages and e-mail using SSL and TLS. With the Internet becoming more and more popular, security concerns have also increased. SSL and TLS are two methods that can be used to encrypt HTTP and SMTP traffic.

SSL is used to encrypt TCP sessions. The process is twofold and consists of a handshake phase to verify the identity of the server and perform key exchange. The keys are then used to encrypt the data. Although SSL addresses many security problems, it is highly CPU-intensive.

SSL was originally used to encrypt HTTP traffic. HTTP over SSL is known as HTTPS or HTTP Secure and runs by default over port 443. SMTP traffic can be encrypted using TLS. SMTP over TLS works by establishing a plain text connection and then upgrading it to an encrypted connection.

The chapter closed by looking at how to implement SSL secure Web sites using Microsoft Internet Information Services and how to secure SMTP traffic in Windows Server.

✦   ✦   ✦

Windows Server 2003 Authentication

Authentication is one of the major cornerstones of the software architecture of any secure application. Authentication is the first element presented to the user of a given multi-user operating system or application. Many different authentication methods are available to software developers, and many have been tried and proven vulnerable to attack over the years.

The most basic authentication method is a system with an embedded password, and any user with that password has full access to the system. From here, authentication grows to user lists with hashed or encrypted passwords and to external authentication systems such as smart cards and biometrics.

Authentication has two key functions. It must provide a method of identifying a user at initial logon, and it must provide a way to identify the user to the internal systems in the operating system, such as file systems, for access control purposes.

The Authentication Process

The actual authentication process consists of verifying a user's credentials (user name and password) against a user database; however, there is more to the authentication process in Windows. After a user is authenticated, the user must be provided access to resources.

During an interactive logon (a user is logging on at a system console), authentication is handled by the Winlogon process. The Winlogon process uses a component known as the Graphical Identification and Authentication (GINA). When you press Ctrl+Alt+Delete and the logon dialog box is displayed, you are looking at the GINA.

The Ctrl+Alt+Delete keystroke is called the Secure Attention Sequence (SAS). This is in place to thwart keystroke loggers and other Trojan horse programs used to capture login information by posing as the GINA. Using the Ctrl+Alt+Delete sequence interrupts any user programs running, and renders Trojan horse programs inoperable. The SAS is integrated into the GINA. A non-standard GINA may have a different SAS.

1. After the username and password information is provided to the GINA, that information is passed to the Local Security Authority (LSA) through a local procedure call (LPC).

2. The LSA then passes that information to a process called the Security Support Provider Interface (SSPI).

3. The SSPI sends the credentials to the default Security Service Provider (SSP), which is Kerberos in Windows Server 2003.

4. Kerberos checks the logon target in the credentials. If it is the same as the local computer name, or no KDC is available for that target, the Kerberos SSP returns an error that no logon servers are available and the SSPI then moves on to the next SSP. If the Kerberos SSP successfully authenticates the provided credentials, it returns a ticket granting ticket (TGT) to the LSA. The TGT is used by the LSA to get other service tickets. The service tickets confirm the user's identity so the user does not have to re-authenticate when accessing other network services.

5. If the Kerberos authentication cannot locate a valid server, the SSPI moves to the next SSP. In Windows Server 2003, the next SSP is NT LAN Manager (NTLM).

6. The SSPI passes the credentials to the MSV1_0 process. For local logins, the MSV1_0 process references the Security Accounts Manager (SAM) database directly. The process is also the same if the logon attempt is to a domain and the local system is a domain controller.

All local logins use NTLM for authentication using the MSV1_0 process. NTLM does not cause a security problem in this case, as credentials are not transmitted over the network.

After the credentials have been processed and the proper authentication passed back from the SSP to the LSA, the LSA is free to grant resource access to the user.

Basic Authentication

Windows Server 2003 provides a basic authentication method that is quite secure by default, but some discussion of the history of Windows network authentication is warranted. In Windows NT 4.0, prior to Service Pack 4, the only authentication available was through either LanManager (LM) challenge/response (LM, supported for Windows 3.11, Windows 95, and DOS) or Windows NT challenge/response

(NTLM). When a client authenticated, it used both LM and NTLM to communicate with the server in case the server did not support NTLM.

Challenge/response works by using a hash of the password. A hash is created by putting the password through a given algorithm (the hashing algorithm). Good hashing algorithms for passwords are always one-way algorithms that can easily turn the password into the hash value, but make it nearly impossible to turn the hash into the password. The LM, NTLM, and Unix crypt function are all one-way hashes. After the client and server have the hashed password stored, the authentication process can begin, as shown in the following steps (the password hash is only stored on the server once, when it is generated).

1. The server sends a challenge, consisting of a string of random data to the client.

2. The client encrypts the challenge data using the password hash, and returns that data to the server.

3. The server uses the password hash to decrypt the data and checks the decrypted data against the original challenge.

If the decrypted data and the challenge string are the same, the user is authenticated.

The problem with Windows NT 4.0 before (and in many cases after) Windows NT Service Pack 4 (SP4) is that both the LM and NTLM responses are sent in reply to the challenge. The LM response is insecure in its design because it is not encrypted. A tool such as L0phtcrack can be used to sniff the challenge and response off of the network. Because the algorithm and the challenge and response are known, L0phtcrack can use the same algorithm and challenge to encrypt a potential password and compare the result to the response. If the result and the response match, the potential password is the correct password. L0phtcrack uses two types of attacks to generate potential passwords: a dictionary attack where each word in a dictionary file is used, and a brute force attack where all possible combinations of characters are tried. The dictionary attack is much faster and will crack any weak passwords, while the brute force attack takes much longer but will crack almost any password. Another way that LM makes it easier for L0phtcrack is that the password is hashed in two 7-byte sections (passwords are a maximum of 14 bytes). L0phtcrack can crack the first 7 bytes and the second 7 bytes of the password separately, speeding up the process.

SP4 introduced a new version of the authentication protocols, called NTLMv2. NTLMv2 uses a larger encryption key (128 bits) as well as a more advanced algorithm, Message Digest 5 (MD5), as opposed to Message Digest 4 (MD4) used by NTLM challenge/response. At this point, it seemed that SP4 was the answer to the password insecurity problems. Unfortunately, this was untrue. There are two issues with the NTLMv2 implementation. First and most important, a Registry change must be made to each system. The LMCompatibiltyLevel Registry entry must be set in the HKEY_LOCAL_MACHINE\SYSTEM\CurrentControlSet\Control\Lsa key. This DWORD entry can be set to one of five values:

✦ The default value of 0 allows normal operation with LM and NTLM; NTLMv2 is not implemented.

✦ A client setting of 1 implements NTLMv2 but will allow fallback to the older, less secure methods if NTLMv2 is not supported, and, therefore, does not increase security.

✦ A client value of 2 allows only NTLM and not LM, which helps somewhat, but NTLM is still vulnerable to all but the most basic cracking attempts.

✦ A client value of 3 sends NTLMv2 authentication only. Values of 0-3 on a domain controller will all allow the processing of LM, NTLM, and NTLMv2 responses.

✦ Settings of 4 and 5 are only for use on domain controllers. Setting 4 causes the server to refuse any LM authentication responses, and 5 causes it to refuse both LM and NTLM responses, allowing only NTLMv2 responses.

The second problem with the NTLMv2 settings is that if the domain controller setting is 4 or 5, many downlevel clients will be excluded from authenticating to the domain. Clients such as OS/2, DOS, and older versions of Windows only support LM or NTLM authentication. You need to weigh the cost of upgrading clients to newer versions against the degraded password security with LM and NTLM challenge/response.

Windows Server 2003 using Active Directory includes full support for LM and NTLM for downlevel clients, NTLMv2 for clients that support it, and the implementation of Kerberos for Windows XP and 2000 clients. In other words, in a Windows Server 2003 environment, the NTLM authentication protocol is used when one or both of the computers is running Windows NT 4.0 or earlier. For example, NTLM is used if a computer running Windows NT Workstation 4.0 is authenticating to a Windows Server 2003 domain controller.

Kerberos is discussed in detail in the Chapter 11, but it is an authentication protocol that has been around for many years and has been proven to be very secure on many platforms. Kerberos is also a challenge and response architecture, but is more secure than NTLM and NTLMv2, and can be run on a distributed architecture.

Kerberos

The Kerberos authentication protocol was developed at Massachusetts Institute of Technology (MIT) in the 1980s. Kerberos is the default authentication method used within a Windows Server 2003 or Windows 2000 Server environment. Active

Directory, Windows XP, Windows Server 2003, or Windows 2000 clients will all authenticate using Kerberos.

Cross-
Reference   Kerberos is explained in detail in Chapter 11.

Kerberos is a secure authentication protocol. It leverages the fact that it is extraordinarily difficult to determine the private key from the public key in public key cryptography. As long as the client keeps the private key secure, the authentication mechanism is secure.

Windows Server 2003 integrates Kerberos seamlessly into the authentication process, so no user intervention is required. All key generation is done automatically, and keys are stored in Active Directory. The Kerberos services are installed at the same time as Active Directory. The Windows Kerberos implementation is also compatible with the MIT Kerberos implementation on Unix, although setting up the MIT Kerberos implementation is a complex process.

Kerberos provides one major advantage over traditional Windows authentication methods in that it supports proxy and forwarding. In older authentication systems, a user could connect to a Web server, and credentials would be passed automatically from the workstation. It was not possible, however, to pass those credentials from the Web server to a back-end database server. Kerberos supports forwarding, allowing the user's credentials to be passed on to as many tiers as required.

External Authentication

A number of external authentication methods that are compatible with Windows Server 2003 are available, including the following:

✦ Smart Cards

✦ Biometrics

✦ RSA SecurID tokens

Almost all external authentication methods are more secure than password authentication, except those few that are poorly designed or implemented.

A number of advantages exist to using external authentication methods, one of the biggest being the ability to move to a two-factor authentication system. A two-factor authentication system requires two things: the external authentication device, and a password or PIN number. While this minimizes the risk of losing either a password or the device, there is still a risk of an attacker gaining both. The biggest disadvantage to external authentication is cost. Traditionally, devices such as smart card readers and biometrics have been very costly; however, devices such as fingerprint readers are now available for about 100 dollars each, so cost is less of an issue than it used to be. External authentication methods are the best bet when strong authentication security is required.

Biometrics

Biometrics refers to the use of some unique part of the body to verify the identity of a user. The most obvious unique part on the body is a fingerprint. Other characteristics used for biometrics include hand geometry and the layout of the eye (retinal scans). Biometric authentication has a number of advantages. It is nearly impossible to fake the biometric criteria, and it is also difficult to steal the authentication token. Another advantage is that a user cannot leave their authentication token at home as they can with smart cards or token-based systems. Biometric systems sometimes use a PIN as an extra identifying factor, as well.

Biometric systems are still fairly uncommon. The cost of biometric readers is falling and some portable computers even have built-in fingerprint readers. There are no real disadvantages to using a biometric system if it fits your needs.

Token-based systems

Token-based authentication systems, such as SecurID from RSA Security, have been around for quite some time. They are well established and common in a number of large organizations. These systems are one of the strongest authentication methods, but are also expensive and require a large amount of work for implementation.

The way token-based systems work is based on a one-time password. This password is generated in a number of ways on different systems. With the RSA SecurID system, each user is assigned a token that automatically generates a code. A new code is generated after a random time has elapsed, usually less than a minute or so. The user must enter this code and a PIN when logging in to the system.

The code is usually generated using a time-based algorithm. The tokens and the server both generate the valid code based on the current time and an embedded 64-bit key in the token. With SecurID, you are prompted for your user name and passcode when logging in to a system. The passcode is the combination of the PIN and code displayed on the token.

Smart cards

Smart cards have been touted as the "next big thing" in the data security arena for several years. Smart cards were supposed to integrate credit cards, bankcards, health insurance cards, driver's licenses, and more onto one card of about the same size. Smart cards have a number of security features that normal magnetic-stripe cards lack, but adoption of these has been very slow. Even today, they are only being tested in a handful of places to integrate services. The move to a "cashless society" is not happening as quickly as many futurists had expected.

A smart card is similar in size to a credit card. There are a variety of different types of smart cards, including cards with only storage capability and integrated circuit cards (ICC) with built-in circuitry. ICCs are used with Windows for authentication. Smart cards require a smart card reader. The reader provides power to the smart card for the integrated circuitry as well as a data connection to the computer.

One application where smart cards have been adopted more quickly, however, is as an external authentication device for network users. A user can simply insert their card into a reader at any workstation, automatically log in, and have their profile retrieved from the server. They are implemented for this purpose in a number of thin-client devices where there is little or no local storage. The user simply inserts the smart card, enters a PIN, and they have their entire profile available at the thin client.

Smart cards can also be used for authentication to traditional workstations. Windows Server 2003 provides built-in support for smart card authentication. Smart cards are essentially a storage device for encryption keys. In a Kerberos authentication situation, for example, the user's private key is stored on the smart card rather than on the computer. This improves security because it is not possible to steal the key. Another advantage to smart card authentication is that password maintenance is eliminated, reducing administrative overhead.

Certain administrative tasks cannot be done using smart card authentication when computer accounts are involved, including the following:

✦ Joining a computer to a domain

✦ Promoting a system to a domain controller

✦ Configuring a remote access connection

Implementing smart card authentication in Windows Server 2003

Implementing authentication using smart cards in Windows Server 2003 is a fairly complex process. You must already have a public key infrastructure (PKI) in place with certificate services. After a certificate authority (CA) is in place, you can continue.

Cross-Reference Chapter 12 explains PKI, and Chapter 13 covers the implementation of certificate services.

The first step is to set permissions on the Smart Card certificate template; then enable it.

1. Log into the CA system with an account that has administrative access to the CA.

2. Launch the Certification Authority snap-in from Administrative Tools located on the Start menu.

3. Double-click the CA in which the users will be enrolled, right-click Certificate Templates, and click Manage. The Certificate Templates snap-in is displayed, as shown in Figure 10-1.

Cross-Reference   Certificate templates are discussed in detail in Chapter 13.

Note   There are two certificate templates for smart cards, and you should decide on one or the other. The two available templates are Smartcard Logon and Smartcard User. Smartcard Logon is used when the smart card is being used for logon only. Other certificates can be created for other purposes, but a Smartcard Logon certificate is valid only for logons. The Smartcard User template is used when the smart card will be used for secure e-mail purposes as well as logons.

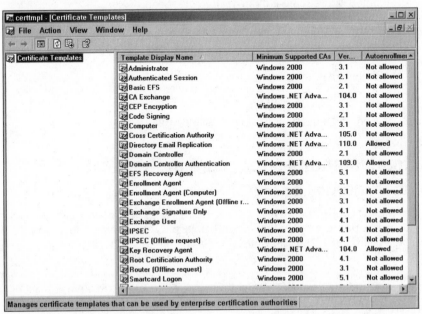

Figure 10-1: The Certificate Templates snap-in is used to manage certificate template configuration.

4. Select the template that you will use — Smartcard Logons or Smartcard User. Right-click the template and then select Properties.

5. Click the Security tab. The Security tab, shown in Figure 10-2, is used to set permissions on the template. You must ensure that the user who will be the enrollment agent has Read and Enroll permission on this template. The enrollment agent must also have Read and Enroll permissions on the Enrollment Agent template.

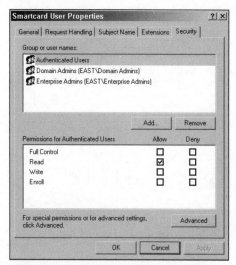

Figure 10-2: The Security tab of the template properties dialog box is used to set permissions on the certificate template.

The next step is to configure the CA to issue Enrollment Agent and smart card certificates. These templates are not enabled by default.

1. Under the CA in which the users will be enrolled in the Certification Authority snap-in, right-click Certificate Templates, select New, and select Certificate Template to Issue. Figure 10-3 shows the Enable Certificate Templates dialog box.

2. Select the Enrollment Agent template; then choose either the Smartcard Logon or Smartcard User template (hold Ctrl to select more than one template), and click OK. You can add both the Smartcard Logon and Smartcard User certificates if you want to configure different smart cards with either of these.

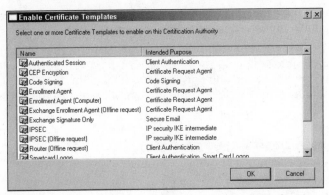

Figure 10-3: The Enable Certificate Templates dialog box is used to allow templates to be used for certificate issuance.

Figure 10-4 shows the Certification Authority snap-in with the new certificate templates added. These templates can now be used to issue certificates.

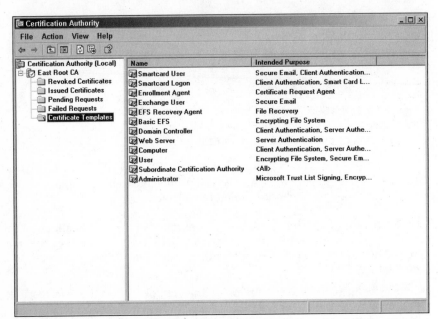

Figure 10-4: The required certificate templates have been added to the CA.

You now need to request an enrollment agent certificate for the user who will be responsible for enrolling smart cards. You can follow this process for as many users as will be enrolling smart cards, but all of these users must have Read and Enroll permissions on the Enrollment Agent certificate template, as discussed earlier in this chapter. Certificates are requested using the Certificates MMC snap-in. Open this snap-in by clicking Start, Run, typing **certmgr.msc**, and clicking OK. The Certificates snap-in is shown in Figure 10-5.

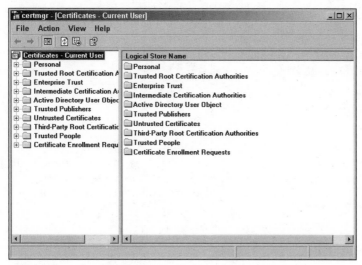

Figure 10-5: The Certificates snap-in is used to view and request certificates.

To request an Enrollment Agent certificate, take the following steps:

1. Double-click Personal in the left pane.

2. Right-click Certificates under Personal, select All Tasks, and select Request New Certificate.

3. When the Certificate Request Wizard is displayed, click Next to continue past the introduction.

4. The next step, as shown in Figure 10-6, is to select the certificate type to request. Select Enrollment Agent and then click Next to continue.

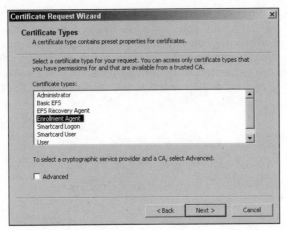

Figure 10-6: Select the certificate type to request.

The next step is optional. You can specify a friendly name and description for the certificate. This provides a simpler way of viewing the certificate in the Certificates snap-in. Click Next to continue. You can now review the settings you have chosen, and click Finish to request the certificate. If auto enrollment is supported, the certificate will be issued automatically.

You can now enroll users for smart cards. The smart card reader must be installed on the system being used for enrollment.

1. Log into that system as the user with the enrollment agent certificate.

2. Connect to the CA server using a Web browser to the address `http://<servername>/certsrv`, as shown in Figure 10-7. Remember that to use Web-based certificate enrollment, Internet Information Service (IIS) must be installed, and Active Server Pages (ASP) must be enabled.

3. Click Request a certificate.

In the next step, you can make a simple or advanced certificate request.

1. Click advanced certificate request.

2. Select what type of certificate request to make (refer to Figure 10-8).

3. Click Request a certificate for a smart card on behalf of another user by using the smart card certificate enrollment station to enroll a smart card user. Figure 10-9 shows the Smart Card Certificate Enrollment Station.

4. Select the certificate template to use — either Smartcard Logon or Smartcard User, as discussed earlier.

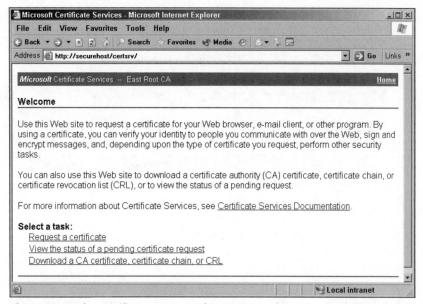

Figure 10-7: The certificate server Web page is used to request certificates and view request status.

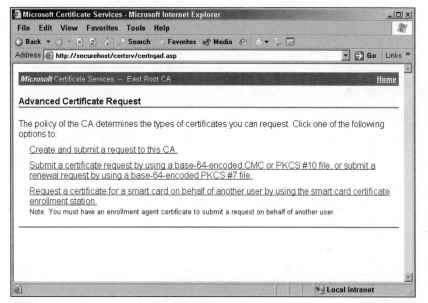

Figure 10-8: The Advanced Certificate Request page allows you to choose the type of certificate request to make.

5. Select the CA in which to enroll the user, and select the CSP to use. The CSP will depend on the smart card reader you are using. Support is included for some readers while others will require a CSP to be installed. The instructions included with the reader will dictate what is necessary.

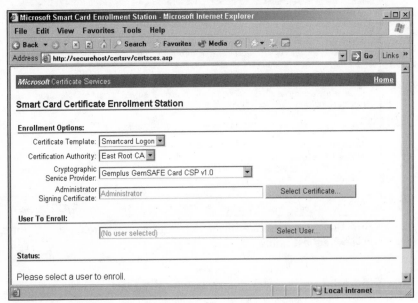

Figure 10-9: The Smart Card Certificate Enrollment Station is used to enroll users for smart cards.

6. The Administrator Signing Certificate is set to the Enrollment Agent certificate for the current user by default. You can select another Enrollment Agent certificate from the list of available certificates by clicking the Select Certificate button; then select the user to enroll by clicking the Select User button, enter the user name, and click the Check Names button in the Select User dialog box, as shown in Figure 10-10.

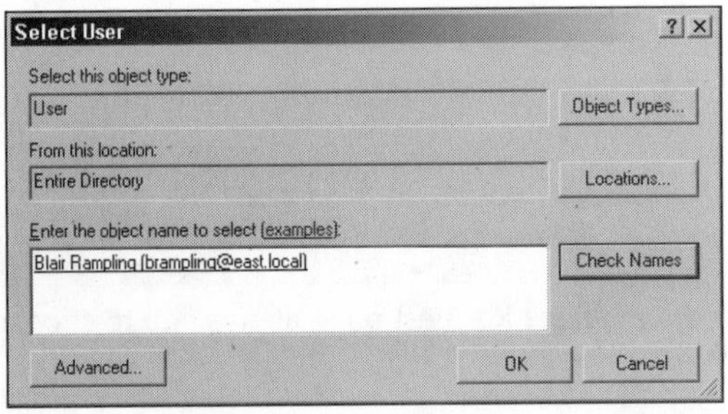

Figure 10-10: The Select User dialog box is used to specify the user to be enrolled for a smart card.

7. After you select the user, click OK in the Select User dialog box. Insert the user's smart card in the reader and then click the Enroll button. You will be prompted for the PIN of the smart card. The default PIN is different depending on the card manufacturer. You should also select the option to force the user to change the smart card PIN on first use.

The user can now use the smart card for logon. The user simply inserts the smart card into the reader and is then prompted for their PIN. The PIN is used to access the private key stored on the smart card to authenticate against the public key on the authentication server.

Summary

This chapter focused on authentication in Windows Server 2003. Authentication is the process of identifying users at logon and identifying them to other internal systems. In a Windows Server 2003 environment, the default authentication protocol is Kerberos. NTLM is still supported for those systems that do not use Kerberos.

Windows Server 2003 supports a number of different external authentication methods, including smartcards, biometrics, and RSA SecureID tokens. When implemented properly, these methods are more secure than password authentication.

This chapter also outlined how to implement smart card authentication in Windows Server 2003. The process includes configuring the Enroll permission on the appropriate certificate templates and configuring the CA to issue the certificates. A certificate request is submitted for the user responsible for enrolling smart cards. After these steps have been completed, users can be enrolled for smart card certificates.

✦　　✦　　✦

Kerberos

Kerberos, an authentication protocol designed at the Massachusetts Institute of Technology (MIT) in the 1980s, addressed many of the flaws in standard authentication systems of the time. Using public key cryptography and a ticketing system, users are authenticated and granted access to network resources.

Consider some of the problems in traditional authentication methods, many of which are local. With standalone Microsoft Windows servers or Unix systems, logons are local only. When a user authenticates, his authentication is only valid on the local system. This problem doesn't exist when using the domain model with Windows, but that configuration has the following problem.

With many distributed authentication systems, when a user logs on, his password is sent in some form over the network. Microsoft Windows has functioned in a number of ways from sending plain-text passwords, to sending encrypted passwords, to sending only a hash of the password to the domain controller. A number of problems with these methods have led to Windows passwords being easily sniffed from the network and cracked.

Kerberos addresses both of these problems, and provides a fully distributed secure authentication method. In fact, Windows Server 2003 and Windows XP use Kerberos for authentication when configured in a domain.

 Chapter 10 discussed the use of Kerberos for authentication when configured for a domain in Windows Server 2003 or Windows.

Relying heavily on cryptography, Kerberos uses public key cryptography for key distribution, and symmetric key cryptography for the actual authentication.

Kerberos Overview

Kerberos provides two services: authentication, and ticket granting. These functions can be integrated into one server, or they can be distributed. The basic method of how Kerberos works without distributed ticket granting is as follows. Most of these steps happen automatically; the only interaction with the user is when the password must be entered for their private key.

Basic Kerberos

Both the user and all services to which the user wants to connect must have public keys stored on the Kerberos authentication server (AS). These keys will be used later in the process to initiate the authentication. The service keys are randomly generated, while the user's key is generated based on a password.

1. When the user wants access to a specific service, he sends a request containing his identity and the service to which he wants access to the authentication server. The AS then takes over.

2. The AS generates a random session key that will be used with the symmetric algorithm to authenticate the user to the service. Two copies of this key are encrypted, one each with the public keys of the user and the service. These encrypted keys are both sent to the user. The message encrypted with the service's key is called the ticket.

3. The user then uses his private key to decrypt the session key encrypted with his public key by the AS. He creates a message containing a timestamp called the authenticator, encrypts it using the session key, and sends both this message and the message from the AS containing the session key encrypted with the service's public key to the service.

4. The service now decrypts the session key, and uses the session key to decrypt the timestamp. The timestamp is verified to a relative level of accuracy (a few minutes) to guard against a replay attack. After this process is complete, the user is authentic.

It is also possible for the service to authenticate to the user. In this case, the service creates a message following the previous exchange containing the timestamp from the last step and the identity of the service. It encrypts that message with the session key and then returns it to the user. The user can decrypt this message, and verify the authenticity of the service.

Figure 11-1 depicts the Kerberos authentication process.

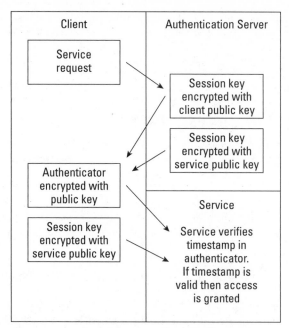

Figure 11-1: The Kerberos authentication process

Distributed Kerberos

You can add another Kerberos server to the process to enable the architecture to scale properly. In the previous example, every authentication requires work on the part of the AS. It is possible to separate the work of ticket granting and authentication.

Distributed Kerberos implementations have two servers, the AS and a ticket granting server (TGS). These can reside on separate systems or on the same system. The AS and TGS together are referred to as a Key Distribution Center (KDC).

When the two processes are distributed between two servers, a user first requests a ticket to authenticate to the TGS from the AS in the exact same method as in the previous section. In this case, the ticket created by the AS is called a ticket granting ticket (TGT). The user is authenticated to the TGS using this ticket.

After the user is authenticated to the TGS, new tickets to access services are requested from the TGS rather than the AS. The process is the same as the process for requesting tickets from the AS except that instead of the user's public key being used to encrypt the reply from the TGS, the session key created by the AS (when the TGT was granted) is used. As you may remember from Chapter 8, symmetric encryption is far faster than public key encryption, so the load on the TGS is lower than on the AS with a similar number of tickets granted.

The TGT also expires. This adds an element of security to the process because rather than the user's public key being used for each authentication, the session key from the TGT is used. This reduces the possibility of the user's key pair being compromised. As the TGT expires and is regenerated every so often, a compromise of the TGT is less damaging.

Kerberos authentication across realms

As discussed later in this chapter, Kerberos allows for the creation of realms to create logical separations in an organization. Realms are used to scale Kerberos to larger implementations. Each realm contains an AS and a TGS.

It is possible to authenticate users from one realm to services in another. The realm containing the services (B) must have a remote ticket granting server (RTGS) for users in the other realm (A). This RTGS is registered by the realm containing the users (A).

The process for cross-realm authentication will seem familiar after seeing the interaction between the AS and TGS.

1. The user is granted a TGT by the AS in realm A, and authenticated to the TGS in realm A.

2. The realm A TGS then authenticates the user to the RTGS in realm B with a TGT.

3. The RTGS is then used to grant the user access to services in realm B.

The biggest advantage to cross-realm authentication is the ability to configure a hierarchy of RTGS. For example, users in realm A may want to access services in realm C. It is not, however, necessary that realm A has a RTGS in realm C.

Realm A can have a RTGS registered in realm B, which then has a RTGS in realm C. The user authenticates to the AS in realm A, is given a TGT, uses the TGS in A to authenticate to the RTGS in B, and uses the RTGS in B to authenticate to the RTGS in C. The RTGS in C then provides tickets to services in realm C. Figure 11-2 provides an example of cross-realm authentication in a hierarchy.

This may seem like an excessive amount of work, but configuring such a hierarchy in large organizations is often necessary. Without a hierarchical layout, each realm would need to have an RTGS in every other realm. Where n is the number of realms, n(n 1) RTGS would need to be registered. This number quickly becomes excessive as the number of realms rises. Using a hierarchical model, this number can be vastly reduced.

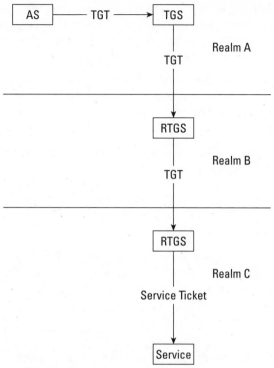

Figure 11-2: An example of cross realm authentication in a hierarchy

Advanced Kerberos ticketing

A number of tickets features go beyond the standard Kerberos authentication process. These features can be used for automation and to reduce the overhead on the Kerberos servers.

Ticket renewal

A ticket can sometimes be renewed, and there are advantages and disadvantages to doing so. Typically, TGTs are renewed because service tickets can be regenerated without user input.

Generating a TGT requires a user to enter their password. Every time a TGT expires, the user must enter their password again. This is somewhat disadvantageous because each time the password is entered, it could be sniffed using a keyboard sniffer or by "shoulder surfing."

The larger disadvantage of an expiring TGT is in automation. For example, if a TGT expires while some automated process or long batch job is running and you are away from the office, nothing will happen until you return and enter your password, at which time a new TGT and a new service ticket are generated.

Setting the RENEWABLE flag in the ticket indicates that the ticket may be renewed. In addition to an expiry time, a renewable ticket also contains a maximum renewal time value after which the ticket may no longer be renewed and a new ticket must be generated.

The advantage to expiring tickets is that they limit the amount of damage that can be done with a compromised ticket. While a compromised password may be used until the password is changed, a compromised Kerberos ticket is only valid until it expires automatically and must be renewed. The problem with ticket renewal is that it extends the amount of time in which damage may be caused by an attacker with a compromised ticket to the maximum renewal time.

As you can see, ticket renewal is a compromise either way. You can configure the maximum renewal time value as you see fit for the best compromise between security and convenience to fit your needs. You may be able to set the value to three days so that jobs will run over the weekend.

Invalid and postdated tickets

Another way to solve the problem of jobs running unattended while requiring Kerberos authentication is through the use of postdated tickets. These tickets are generated with a starting time and can only be used after that time.

Postdated tickets are normally issued with the INVALID flag and POSTDATED flag set. A postdated ticket will also have a start time value of when the ticket will become valid. When the start time has passed, the ticket can be sent to the TGS with the VALIDATE option specified. The TGS can then return the ticket without the INVALID flag. Tickets with the INVALID flag set will not be accepted for authentication.

The advantage to postdating tickets is that if a ticket is compromised before it becomes valid, it can be made permanently invalid so that the validation request is not honored.

For a client to request postdated tickets, the client must first request his TGT from the AS with the ALLOW-POSTDATE option specified. When the TGT is issued, it will have the MAY-POSTDATE flag set. This flag indicates to the TGS that postdated tickets can be issued.

Initial tickets

Initial tickets refer to any ticket generated directly by the AS. Some services may only accept tickets that are issued directly by an AS, which means that the tickets are issued in response to a password being entered rather than on cached credentials. The initial flag is used to indicate this.

The advantage to having a service require an initial ticket is that a ticket from the AS requires the user to enter a password, while a ticket from a TGS does not require a password. This increases security because a compromised TGT cannot be used to access the service. In addition to these uses of the initial flag, all tickets generated by the AS also have the flag set to indicate that they are initial tickets.

In addition to the INITIAL flag, two other flags indicate how the ticket was created. The PRE-AUTHENT and HW-AUTHENT flags are used to indicate that some form of authentication has occurred prior to the ticket request from the AS. The AS sometimes requires this, such as when smart card readers are being used.

Authentication proxying and forwarding

It may also be necessary for services to be able to use a user's authentication credentials for other purposes. This is especially true in a multi-tier environment where some middleware may have a need to access a back-end database using the credentials of the user making the request. This is possible with Kerberos using proxying and forwarding.

Proxying is configured when the PROXIABLE flag is set in a TGT. Normally, a ticket can only be generated for a specific network address that is the one specified in the TGT originally sent to the AS in the first step of a ticket request. When proxying is enabled, tickets can be generated by the TGS for addresses other than this original address.

This allows tickets to be generated so that a system can use the identity of a user to authenticate to another service. For example, the user could request a service ticket to access service B with the identity of the user but the network address of service A. The generated service ticket will contain the PROXY flag, which indicates to service B that the ticket was generated through the proxy feature. This is implemented so that service B can provide proper auditing of the ticket origin.

The restriction when using the PROXIABLE flag is that the service can't request a TGT, only a service ticket. Using the FORWARDABLE flag, however, will allow TGTs to be requested for other addresses on behalf of the user. This enables authentication by a service without the user having to enter his password if a TGT is requested for the service. In this case, the FORWARDED flag is set in the ticket generated for the service to indicate its status.

Designing a Kerberos Architecture

The design of a Kerberos architecture can go a long way to the future scalability, or lack thereof, of the implementation. For example, if your organization is distributed along fairly rigid boundaries, such as organizational units or branch offices, each may have a relatively small number of users or systems. They might, in fact, be small enough to have all of the users in a single realm.

The problem is going to occur when these sites grow to push the performance limits of a central Kerberos server. The process for migrating one Kerberos server to a number of servers is more difficult than planning for expansion and implementing a number of realms in the beginning.

With Windows Server 2003 and Active Directory, each domain is equivalent to a Kerberos realm. Each Active Directory server is a complete KDC, and with a proper AD structure, Kerberos will be handled adequately.

Architecture

A Kerberos architecture must be able to scale well as your organization grows. Predicting future growth is always difficult, but it is important to try to make a fairly accurate estimate and then double it. This is not a hard and fast rule, but you get the idea. It is always better to overestimate than underestimate. Overestimating may cost more money up front, but the amount of money spent upgrading when growth is underestimated is usually more.

You can scale Kerberos by using separate realms or by using slave servers. Again, if using Windows Server 2003 (and you probably are if you're reading this book), the Kerberos architecture is decided for you. Each Active Directory server is also a Kerberos KDC, and each domain is a Kerberos realm, although the term is rarely, if ever, used in Windows except when talking about realms external to Windows.

Each method of scaling Kerberos has its advantages; as with many concepts, simply choosing one or the other is seldom the best answer. In most cases you will use a combination of the two principles.

Realms are organizational groups similar to Windows domains. By default, all users in a realm can access all services in the realm. Users from other realms can access services in the local realm, and local users can access services in other realms through the use of RTGS.

Realms are used for a logical separation of users and services. If you have logical divisions within your organization, such as branch offices, each group will have its own realm.

As mentioned previously, each realm has a KDC. This is inherent in the design of Kerberos because there is one master KDC in each realm. As the first method of scalability, implementing realms improves performance by spreading the load of authentication over multiple KDCs.

In addition to the load being balanced across the KDCs, the administrative load is also distributed. Instead of the entire user base and the overhead that goes with it, such as key storage, being stored on one server, it is distributed across the realms.

This is advantageous for a number of reasons. A large key database on a KDC will slow the server significantly because at a certain point, search performance deteriorates faster than the rate of growth of the database.

The other reason why more realms with fewer users are advantageous is because replication to slave servers requires fewer resources. Slave KDCs are the second scalability method with Kerberos.

Slave KDCs are implemented for two reasons: redundancy and scalability. The origins of slave KDCs are in redundancy. Slave KDCs are implemented to have a server available for failover in case the master KDC fails. In an implementation with only a single master KDC, if the KDC fails, no Kerberos authentication can occur. In most cases, services that use Kerberos authentication are capable of falling back to some sort of local authentication, but this is a last resort. Normal users will not have local accounts on each system with which to access these services.

Slave servers can also be used for scaling a Kerberos implementation. Having a number of slave servers distributes the load of authentication across those systems. In addition, slave servers can be used to improve performance at remote sites. A slave server can be installed at each remote site so that authentication is done within the site, and does not have to travel over a slow network link. Password changes and other administrative tasks are still done to the master KDC across the WAN link, as is the propagation of the KDC database from the master to the slaves. Authentication traffic, which is much more common, is not passed over the link though. Database propagation can also be tuned for a good compromise between up-to-date slave servers and low network traffic.

In most cases, scalability will come from a combination of separate realms and a number of slave servers. Seldom does one or the other provide the best solution, except where the user base is small and not much growth is predicted. In that case, one realm with a master and at least one slave KDC would be adequate.

Having a master KDC with no slaves is rarely a good idea. In this case, a failure of the master would constitute a failure of the entire Kerberos architecture. For redundancy purposes, at least one slave KDC should be provided, preferably two. In most cases, more than two slaves do not provide a higher level of availability.

Note Keep in mind if you are using Active Directory, there is no master KDC. This is one of the main benefits of Active Directory; everything is on a peer level. With each domain controller acting as a KDC, therefore, there is no need to implement backups.

There are, however, instances where more than two slaves are required. This is the case if you have a number of network segments that are likely to be unable to communicate if some component fails. In most cases, realms would be implemented where there were a number of separate network segments, but not necessarily in a smaller organization. Each segment should have a slave KDC in case connectivity to the master and to other slave KDCs is lost.

The Importance of time synchronization

With Kerberos, time synchronization is vital, especially on application servers. As you recall, Kerberos uses a timestamp in the authenticator message that is verified within a certain tolerance to prevent replay attacks.

If the time on a system is off of the time on the KDC by more than the allowed tolerance, Kerberos authentication will fail. Time synchronization can be provided through a number of channels, but is most often provided through Network Time Protocol (NTP). All systems should be configured to synchronize time with a single time server or to one of a group of servers slaved to the same server to prevent time inaccuracies.

In a Windows Server 2003 implementation with Windows Server 2003, Windows XP, or Windows 2000 clients and an Active Directory based domain model, the time synchronization issue becomes far less important.

These clients have the Windows Time Service running by default. This service, unless configured otherwise, sets the system time to the domain controller. The time on the domain controller can be off and it doesn't matter. What's most important is that the clients and application servers are set relative to the Active Directory (and therefore KDC) server. This avoids the problems associated with the timestamp in the authenticator being off.

Kerberos in Windows Server 2003

Windows Server 2003 implements Kerberos version 5. Each Active Directory server acts as a KDC. Kerberos is used as the primary domain authentication protocol in Windows Server 2003.

Each Active Directory server contains a Kerberos Key Distribution Center. On a network with multiple Active Directory servers, there will be more than one KDC. Although having multiple KDCs is not normal for a Kerberos implementation, the method of storing keys and user identity information in Windows' implementations allows this. Keys are stored in Active Directory and are replicated to all Active Directory servers in the domain. This way, any KDC can service the client. By default, users are directed to the nearest KDC.

The Windows Server 2003 implementation of Kerberos is also interoperable with standard MIT Kerberos implementations. Active Directory accounts can be used for authentication to Unix servers with Kerberos and other Kerberos servers. You can also configure a trust in which users from another Kerberos realm can access services in the Windows domain.

Kerberos is installed automatically on a Windows Server 2003 when Active Directory is installed. Windows Server 2003, Windows XP, and Windows 2000 clients all use Kerberos authentication automatically. Other clients use NTLM authentication.

Kerberos Group Policy configuration

It is possible to configure the behavior of Kerberos on a Windows Server 2003 (which is an Active Directory server) through group policies.

1. Open the Active Directory Users and Computers snap-in.

2. Right-click the domain to edit, and select Properties.

3. Click the Group Policy tab, select the policy to edit, and click the Edit button.

The Group Policy snap-in will open.

Kerberos policies can be found by navigating in the left pane of the Group Policy snap-in to Computer Configuration, Windows Settings, Security Settings, Account Policies, and clicking Kerberos Policy. The Kerberos Policy settings are displayed in the right pane, as shown in Figure 11-3.

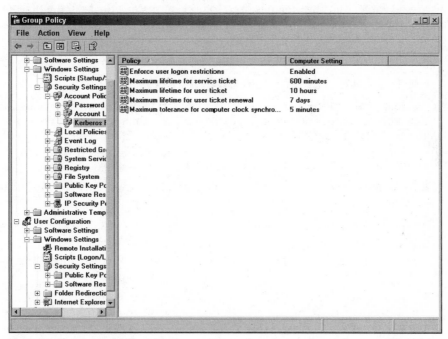

Figure 11-3: Group Policy Objects can be used to change the Kerberos settings in the domain.

A number of settings can be used to customize Kerberos behavior. All are used to set time parameters except the Enforce user logon restrictions setting. This is used to determine whether Kerberos logons have the same restrictions applied as regular Windows logons. These restrictions include logon schedules and workstation restrictions as configured for each user in their account information.

The remaining settings are for setting the Kerberos behavior during the authentication process. The maximum lifetime for service ticket and maximum lifetime for user ticket settings specify the longest amount of time for which a particular ticket is valid. All tickets will expire after the specified time unless they are explicitly specified to expire sooner. It is not possible to make a ticket expire any later than the specified maximum lifetime.

Note   In Windows Server 2003, Ticket Granting Tickets (TGS) are referred to as User Tickets.

The maximum lifetime for user ticket renewal setting specifies how long a user ticket can exist and be renewed. After the specified lifetime expires, a new ticket must be created.

Finally, the maximum tolerance for computer clock synchronization specifies the largest amount of time deviance of the timestamp in the authenticator message. As discussed earlier, the timestamp is used to prevent replay attacks. If the timestamp is different from the time on the Kerberos server by more than this value, the authentication will fail.

Windows Kerberos interoperability

As previously mentioned, Kerberos in Windows Server 2003 is interoperable with other Kerberos implementations. To enable interoperability, you must configure a realm trust between the Windows Server 2003 domain and the target realm.

1. Open the Active Directory Domains and Trusts snap-in.

2. Right-click the domain from which to create the trust in the left pane and then select Properties.

3. Click the Trusts tab, and click New Trust.

4. Click Next to continue past the introduction to the New Trust Wizard. You must first specify the name of the realm with which to create the trust relationship, as shown in Figure 11-4. Click Next to continue.

5. Specify that the trust being created is a realm trust, as shown in Figure 11-5. The New Trust Wizard can also be used to create domain trusts. Click Next to continue.

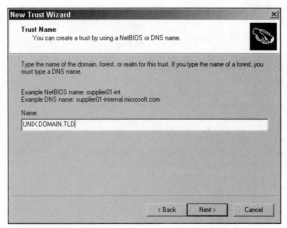

Figure 11-4: Specify the realm with which to create the trust relationship.

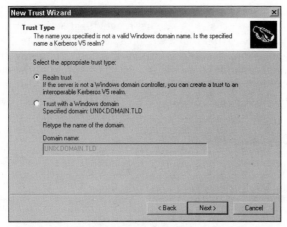

Figure 11-5: This selection indicates that you are creating a realm trust.

6. You can now specify whether this will be a transitive or nontransitive trust, as shown in Figure 11-6. Trust transitivity specifies the behavior of the trust in relation to other trusts. An example earlier in this chapter explained how a user in realm A could access services in realm C through an RTGS in realm B when realms are configured in a hierarchical model. Transitive trusts allow this to occur. With a transitive trust, the fact that realm B trusts realm A and realm C trusts realm B means that realm C also trusts realm A. A nontransitive trust would not allow that trust relationship to be transferred. Select transitive or nontransitive based on your architecture, and click Next to continue.

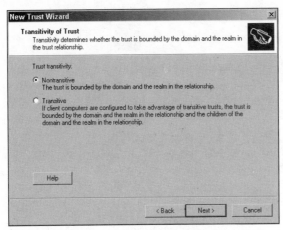

Figure 11-6: You must specify whether this trust relationship will be transitive or nontransitive.

7. Select the direction of the trust relationship, as shown in Figure 11-7. The default setting is a two-way trust. Domain users will be able to use services in the other realm and users in that realm will be able to access domain services. The other options are one-way trusts in either direction. A one-way incoming trust allows users in the Windows domain to access services in the other realm. A one-way outgoing trust allows users in the other realm to access services in the domain. After you select a direction, click Next to continue.

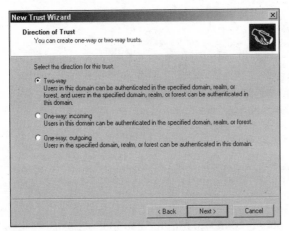

Figure 11-7: Specify a direction for the trust relationship.

8. Enter a password for the trust relationship, as shown in Figure 11-8. The password is simply used for working with the trust. In some cases, the password

must be specified in the remote domain when trusts are configured. Click Next to continue.

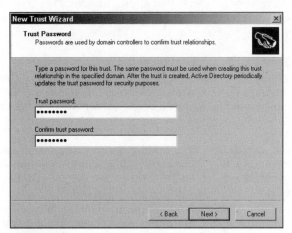

Figure 11-8: Specify a password for the trust relationship.

9. Finally, you have a chance to review your selections. Make sure the correct information has been entered and then click Next to create the trust. A summary dialog box is shown after the trust has been created. You are reminded to create the trust in the remote realm as well depending on the trust direction. Click Finish to close the wizard. Figure 11-9 shows the Trusts tab of the domain properties dialog with the new trust in place.

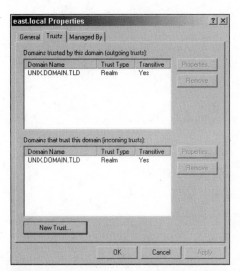

Figure 11-9: The new trust relationship has been created.

Summary

This chapter focused on the Kerberos authentication protocol. Kerberos provides a fully distributed authentication method, and is the default protocol used within a Windows Server 2003 domain.

Kerberos provides two services: authentication and ticket granting. To provide both of these services, an Authentication Server (AS) and a Ticket Granting Server (TGS) are required. The AS and TGS together are referred to as a Key Distribution Center (KDC). The two processes can run on a single server, or they can be distributed, meaning that the two processes can run on two different servers.

The chapter also looked at two different methods of scaling a Kerberos architecture: using separate realms and using slave servers. In a Windows Server 2003 domain, Kerberos is integrated with Active Directory. Each domain controller is also a KDC, so scalability is achieved by adding additional domain controllers.

In terms of configuring Kerberos in a Windows Server 2003 environment, the behavior of Kerberos can be configured through a group policy. You can also use the Active Directory Domains and Trusts snap-in to configure interoperability with other Kerberos implementations.

✦   ✦   ✦

Public Key Infrastructure Overview

Public key cryptography was discussed at some length in Chapter 8. Public key cryptography uses a key pair containing a private key known only to the key holder and a public key that is shared with other users. Anyone with the public key corresponding to your private key can encrypt messages to you and verify your digital signature on a document.

On a theoretical basis, a public key infrastructure (PKI) outlines the structure for all of the public key-based cryptographic and authentication services on your network. In most implementations, however, the PKI simply outlines the control of keys and certificates.

A third-party certificate authority (CA), such as Verisign, is a good example of part of a PKI. (Verisign is by far the largest and most well known CA.) If you have had a secure Web site before, you may be familiar with such a CA. Verisign is a trusted party that issues certificates to organizations after verifying their identity. If a user goes to a secure Web site within that organization, for example, they can be assured of the authenticity and security of that site, as long as they trust the CA that issued the certificate.

Trust is the most important factor in a PKI, and trust is, in fact, delegated through the levels of the PKI. Essentially, a PKI is a series of trust relationships between CAs that enables the use of certificates and keys across the enterprise.

PKIs are implemented for a number of reasons. The most common reason for a PKI is currently e-commerce. In a traditional face-to-face transaction, goods are exchanged for money at the time of purchase. You can easily verify the individual you are dealing with at the time of a face-to-face transaction, although if goods are being exchanged for money at the same time, the identity of the parties is not really important.

Trusting a seller becomes an issue when money is being exchanged for goods or services that are not being supplied immediately. For example, say you want to buy a new bedroom set. Unless you have a big truck, you can't take delivery of the bedroom set immediately. You pay for the items up front, and the merchant delivers them to your house.

In this example, you must have an element of trust in the merchant. It is a face-to-face transaction, but you are giving the seller money without immediately receiving anything. The seller could take your money, close up shop, and never deliver the product for which you paid. You must establish a trust relationship with the seller. You are more likely to have trust in an established company, for example, than a new furniture store or someone running a yard sale.

People establish trust in another person or company in a variety of ways. For example, people are more willing to trust a nice looking store than a store that is poorly maintained. If a company has a large existing customer base and has been in operation for a long time, such as a large chain, we are more willing to trust it than an upstart company that has not established itself as trustworthy.

In the case of the Internet, there is no way to walk into the store from which you are purchasing the merchandise to check things out. There is often no way to tell if the company is new or old, if they are operating out of a well-maintained facility or a run-down building, and so on. More importantly, there is no way to establish that the party you are dealing with is who they claim to be. If you trust a certain corporation and want to buy a product from them, you need to be able to establish that you are placing your order with that company and not someone else claiming to be that company.

This is the driving force behind the establishment of a PKI. There must be a system in place that allows you to establish trust in a company and verify their identity. The PKI can consist of a number of third-party certificate authorities (CAs) that verify the identity of the merchant and grant them a certificate. You can use the certificate during a transaction to verify the identity of the other party.

With this certificate, you can now trust the other party and verify their identity. You have not, however, simply trusted them, but passed that responsibility on to another, the CA. To trust the merchant, you must trust the CA. The key element of a PKI is the ability to delegate trust between parties.

Other than e-commerce, there are more reasons for the implementation of a PKI. As they become better understood, PKIs are being implemented on more and more networks. Windows Server includes certificate services, which provides most of what is needed for an internal PKI.

Cross-
Reference   Windows Server's Certificate Services is discussed in Chapter 13.

Having an internal PKI provides a number of advantages. It is possible to configure a number of services to use a PKI, increasing security across the entire organization. For example, the Windows Encrypting File System (EFS), as discussed in Chapter 8, uses certificates extensively. Implementing a PKI through certificate services allows you to specify recovery agents who can decrypt EFS-protected files.

This is only one example of a service enabled by a PKI. A PKI provides the infrastructure for every encrypted application on your network, as in the following examples:

✦ IP Security (IPSec) uses certificate-based encryption.

✦ Secure Shell (SSH) uses public key cryptography for authentication.

✦ Secure Sockets Layer (SSL) uses certificates for identification.

A PKI provides a central infrastructure for controlling all of the keys and certificates used on the network. It allows any service to verify the identity of any user in the PKI.

More About PKI

PKIs can be discussed in both the theoretical and the practical environment, as the practical implementations fall far short of what a PKI is capable of in theory. PKIs were conceived with the notion that all cryptography, key control, and authentication across the entire enterprise and for external clients would be handled by the PKI. In practice, most PKIs do not encompass this much functionality, and often provide only certificate services.

Most people do not understand what a PKI is. The term Public Key Infrastructure is used for everything from a simple certificate authority that generates certificates for SSL Web sites to massive software implementations costing vast sums of money.

A PKI is a system containing a number of components. The components of a PKI are certificates, the certificate authorities that manage them, and anything else responsible for the use of public key cryptography for authentication and encryption.

Essentially, a PKI provides key and certificate issuance and revocation in a central location, centralizing key management, the most difficult part of most encryption operations.

PKIs in theory

A PKI enables you to implement public key and certificate-based encryption and authentication systems across all of your systems. The PKI provides a network of trust on which secure applications can be built.

A PKI should provide the basis for the following three security elements:

✦ Authentication

✦ Integrity

✦ Confidentiality

Authentication is the verification of the identity of a party in a transaction. Integrity is the verification that data has not been altered in any way after the point at which it is signed. Confidentiality is the restriction that no party can view encrypted data in its plaintext form except those specified to do so.

The most important part of a PKI is that it implements these features in a secure manner. A user must be able to trust that the PKI will provide these services without any chance that they will be broken. (It is impossible to make any encryption system unbreakable other than one-time pads, but the point is that users need to be given a secure system; otherwise, they will lose trust in the system and it all falls apart.) For example, if you receive a message from a user and the authentication feature of the PKI at your site tells you that it is authentic, you do not know that message is authentic. You only know that the PKI thinks it is authentic. If you trust the PKI, you will assume the message is authentic. If you do not trust the PKI, you may assume that the message is not authentic.

A PKI is usually built on a hierarchical trust model. At the top of the trust model is a root CA. This CA can delegate trust to lower-level CAs for specific uses. A root CA can delegate trust to an enterprise CA for all systems and users within that enterprise. The enterprise CA for domain.tld, for example, is fully trusted to issue certificates for `host.domain.tld` and `user@domain.tld`.

As stated, there can be lower-level CAs in an enterprise as well. These CAs, delegated by the enterprise CA, can provide certificate services for specific parts of the enterprise such as subdomains. There is a huge advantage to this hierarchical model with CAs in that the load of certificate services is spread across the lower-level CAs for most operations. Higher-level CAs are only referenced for requests that cannot be answered by the lower-level CA.

PKIs in practice

In practice, a PKI usually entails a series of trust relationships between certificate authorities. Public key cryptography was discussed in Chapter 8 and public and private keys were explained, but the subject of certificates has not yet been discussed.

What is a certificate?

In public key cryptography, everyone has two keys, one public and one private. If Alice wants to send an encrypted message to Bob, she must first get his public key. The problem occurs, however, when the public key that she receives does not really belong to Bob. A third party, Eve, somewhere in the middle of the exchange, could be spying on this transaction. When Bob sends Alice his public key, Eve can intercept that key and send another key that looks like Bob's (it has Bob's name in it) but to which she actually holds the private key.

Now Alice has a public key that she thinks belongs to Bob, but was actually generated by Eve. When Alice encrypts her message using the false Bob key, Eve can simply intercept the message and read it. Bob ends up with indecipherable garbage, or nothing at all.

Key exchange is the primary problem with public key encryption. In certain implementations, a public key can be signed by a third party to verify its authenticity, but that is not a secure method because anyone could sign the key pretending to be anyone else. Ideally, the key would be sent to someone with whom you have physical contact and they would verify and sign the key.

The idea of certificates solves this problem to some extent. A certificate is, for all intents and purposes, simply a signed public key. The difference is that while other keys are signed by any third party, certificates are generated by a certificate authority.

Just like key pairs, certificates can be revoked if they become compromised or are no longer needed, and they can be set to expire. In fact, most certificates do expire and must be renewed on a regular basis (normally annually).

Certificates also have a number of uses in a networked environment. They are used to sign public keys and are therefore used for the following:

+ Encryption of e-mail
+ Encryption of files
+ SSL transactions on a Web site
+ Authentication

Chapter 8 has an example of generating a certificate for use with Microsoft Windows Encrypting File System.

A Certificate Authority

A company called Verisign was previously mentioned in this chapter. If you have ever run a secure Web server, you may be familiar with CAs such as Verisign. If a customer logged on to your secure Web site to buy your product using his credit card, he would want to verify your identity and verify the security of that information. Verisign is a trusted third party who signs your public key, and, in this case, you are using that public key for SSL sessions. The process for obtaining a certificate is this: You first use the key management system in your Web server to generate a key pair. The key pair is just like any other key pair used in public key cryptography (one public and one private key, and the private key is normally protected by a passphrase). The key also contains information about the Web site and organization for which it was generated.

The next step is to forward the public key information, identifying documentation, and payment to a CA such as Verisign. Verisign then verifies your identity and the information in your key, and generates a certificate that is returned to you. That certificate ensures the users of your secure site that a trusted third party has verified the authenticity of your public key, and it is safe to use that key to encrypt their sensitive data. As long as the user trusts the CA, they can trust your public key and your identity.

An external third-party CA such as Verisign is the most basic possible PKI. It is, however, possible to have your own CA or even multiple CAs on your own network, and it is often necessary when using encryption.

 Chapter 13 discusses the implementation of your own CA on a Windows Server system.

How the PKI works

In most cases, a PKI works as follows:

1. A user (or system) creates a key pair.

2. The user then generates a certificate request. The certificate request contains the public key and identifying information about the user, such as name, e-mail address, and so on.

3. The CA verifies the information and creates a certificate containing the information and the public key.

4. The certificate is then stored in the PKI's certificate store. This can be contained in the CA or in some other directory service such as Active Directory. The certificate is then available for use by any application requiring it.

The PKI features included with Windows Server include many of the features mentioned. Certificate Services is the core component of the Windows Server PKI because it essentially controls the operation of all other PKI components.

Windows Server also includes certificate stores where certificates reside after they are created. These certificate stores are available to PKI-enabled applications. PKI-enabled applications are another feature of the Windows Server PKI. Many applications are PKI-enabled, such as IPSec and Internet Information Server (IIS).

The other components to the Windows Server PKI are the management components. Certificate policies and templates control the issuance and revocation of certificates in response to client requests. The Certification Authority and Certificate Templates MMC snap-ins are used to manage the CAs and templates.

One of the key features of Windows Server and Windows XP is PKI auto enrollment. Auto enrollment allows keys to be generated and certificates to be granted without any input from the user.

This auto enrollment is what enables features such as EFS to operate with no user intervention. While the user simply selects a box to enable EFS, behind the scenes a key pair and certificate are created and added to the PKI if they do not already exist. This key pair is what is used to encrypt the File Encryption Key (FEK).

Designing a PKI

The requirements for a PKI differ from organization to organization. Normally, however, there are three levels to a PKI implementation. These consist of the following:

- ✦ A root certificate authority
- ✦ A certificate authority responsible for controlling certificate policy
- ✦ A certificate authority for issuing certificates

The issuing CAs are usually internal for internal uses, such as authentication, and external, trusted third parties for external uses, such as SSL-protected Web sites.

The first thing a PKI needs is policies and procedures. The certificate policy defines the rules for using the PKI. The certificate policy is a procedural document rather than a technical one. This policy defines what action to take for certificate issuance and revocation (for instance, in the event a private key is lost or compromised). In addition to the certificate policy, a certificate practice statement (CPS) explains the detailed operation of the PKI. While the certificate policy is a more general policy, the CPS defines the certificate management of the PKI in detail.

These PKI policies will define a number of variables. Some are more basic, such as acceptable key lengths, certificate lifetimes, and acceptable CSPs. Key lengths and lifetimes both contribute to security. Longer key lengths make private keys more secure against attack. The disadvantage to longer key lengths is that public key algorithms operate slower with longer keys. Having a longer key makes the theoretical time to mount a brute force attack longer and, therefore, allows a longer key lifetime. Longer key lifetimes allow more time for the key to be compromised, while shorter key lifetimes increase administrative overhead because more certificates are renewed more often.

Some policies are more difficult to define. The policy should outline how security is provided for the CA systems, both physically and logically. The security of these systems is paramount because if a CA certificate is compromised, all certificates from that CA and any subordinate CAs are also compromised. Root CAs can be secured by taking them offline. This requires a larger amount of administration because an offline root CA must be a stand-alone rather than an enterprise CA. This does not cause a problem with enrollment because the subordinate CAs are enterprise CAs, which integrate into Active Directory.

Related to this policy is another step involved with the PKI design: the layout of the trust hierarchy. You must decide if a third-party root CA will be used or if the root CA will be an internal enterprise root CA. You must also decide if the root CA will issue certificates, or if a number of subordinate CAs will be implemented.

The policies will also outline how users are authenticated when a certificate is issued. By default, users are enrolled in the CA automatically if the CA is an enterprise CA and the user is logged in using Active Directory. It is also possible to have certificate requests authenticated manually by one or more other parties so that the chances of issuing a certificate to an unauthorized user are reduced.

Enrollment and revocation processes are another important planning step. Certificates are requested either automatically or manually. It is possible to manually enroll using either a Web browser or the Certificate Request Wizard. You can also disable either of these as well as auto enrollment. You can more tightly control certificate processes by allowing only certain enrollment methods. Methods for integrating enrollment processes into custom applications also exist.

Revocation policies are important. When a certificate becomes invalid for any reason, it must be revoked. A certificate may become invalid for a number of reasons. The most drastic reason is the compromise of the key associated with a certificate, but the change of identifying information of the certificate subject could also be a cause. The policy should define how certificates are revoked and for what reasons, as well as when and where the certificate revocation list (CRL) is published.

The final planning phase is system maintenance and disaster recovery. It is important to maintain the CAs because if the CA certificates are lost, all trusts from that CA down in the hierarchy stop functioning. All certificates will need to be recreated with a replacement CA. A good backup of the CAs should always be maintained.

Summary

A Public Key Infrastructure (PKI) outlines the control of keys and certificates. The driving force behind the PKI is that it establishes a system of trust where identities can be verified. A PKI is a system of certificates and certificate authorities that binds a public key to a specific identity.

A PKI infrastructure consists of a number of components, including certificates and certificate authorities (CA). The CAs are responsible for verifying the identity of those requesting certificates. The certificates are the digital statements binding the public key to the entity. Other PKI components include certificate stores that store certificates, certificate templates, and certificate policies.

A PKI infrastructure normally consists of three levels: a root CA, an intermediate CA responsible for controlling certificate policies, and a CA for issuing the certificates. Once the CA infrastructure is defined, policies can be configured defining certificate issuance and revocation procedures. Enrollment and revocation process can also be configured.

✦   ✦   ✦

Installing and Configuring Certificate Services

A public key infrastructure (PKI) can be an important part of a security architecture. As discussed in the previous chapter, Windows Server 2003's Certificate Services plays a significant role in a PKI.

While installing Certificate Services is easy, it is actually a very complex set of services, and without a thorough understanding of how Certificate Services works, your PKI can become insecure.

Learn how Certificate Services works inside and out in your environment. Before any roll out of a Certificate Services-based PKI, you should first do a limited scope trial. This trial should involve not only technical staff, but also a selection of staff that will be using the PKI in the full roll out. This trial will reveal any design or implementation problems, and can even lead to the decision that a PKI is unnecessary. A PKI involves a large amount of maintenance and administration, and the benefits may not always outweigh the costs.

Planning for Certificate Services

Planning for an implementation of Certificate Services essentially entails deciding on the architecture of the certificate authorities (CAs). Two types of CA can be installed: enterprise or stand-alone. A stand-alone CA is the most basic type of CA that can be installed under Windows Server 2003. The purpose of a stand-alone CA is to provide Certificate Services for nonenterprise-type applications, such as stand-alone Web servers. A stand-alone CA does not require Active Directory to operate. It can issue almost all types of certificates except logon certificates. Certificate requests to a stand-alone CA are set to pending, and an administrator must verify the identity of the requestor and choose whether to issue the certificate or deny the request. Certificate templates are not used with stand-alone CAs and policies are far less important. It is much simpler to install and maintain a stand-alone CA than the enterprise version.

An enterprise CA requires Active Directory and is used as the basis for an enterprise-wide PKI for an organization. An enterprise CA can issue all types of certificates, including logon certificates. When using an enterprise CA, a user's logon credentials are used as proof of identity. Because of this, a logged-in user can have certificates generated automatically. Certificate requests are not held pending the review of an administrator.

The next step in planning is to decide how the certification hierarchy will work. CAs are further broken into root CAs and subordinate CAs. Every CA has a certificate of its own for identification. A root CA can issue any type of certificate, including certificates to other CAs and to itself. The CAs receiving certificates from the root CA are subordinate CAs. These subordinate CAs can also issue any kind of certificate, including those to subordinate CAs. You can have a certification hierarchy that is several layers deep.

Computers in an Active Directory architecture are configured to explicitly trust the enterprise root CA. Through this explicit trust of the root CA, they also inherently trust any subordinate CAs below the enterprise root CA. In most cases, you will have a root CA that only issues certificates to subordinate CAs and subordinate CAs that are responsible for all other certificate services. In a smaller environment, you will probably have no problem with only a root CA.

Note   In addition, it is possible, though expensive and quite difficult, to have a third-party CA trust your root CA. Through this process, certificates issued by your root CA and subordinate CAs will be trusted by other organizations who trust the third-party CA. The third-party CA becomes a CA that is one level higher than the enterprise root CA in the trust hierarchy.

Installing Certificate Services

This section assumes Certificate Services was not installed when Windows Server 2003 was installed. If you are installing an enterprise CA, make sure you have write permissions to Active Directory and that the system is a member of a domain (remember an Enterprise CA requires Active Directory). To install Certificate Services, follow these steps:

1. Click Start, point to Control Panel, and click Add or Remove Programs.

2. Click Add/Remote Windows Components. The Windows Components Wizard opens, as shown in Figure 13-1. (As you can see, Certificate Services is not installed.)

3. Highlight Certificate Services and click the Details button. As shown in Figure 13-2, there are two sub-components to Certificate Services: the Certificate Services CA and Certificate Services Web Enrollment Support. The Certificate Services CA is the basic CA discussed so far in this chapter. Web Enrollment Support allows users to request certificates from a Web browser and will be discussed later.

4. Click Cancel to close the Certificate Services dialog box and return to the Windows Components Wizard. Select Certificate Services and all subcomponents will be selected. When you select Certificate Services, the Microsoft Certificate Services dialog box is displayed, as shown in Figure 13-3. After you install Certificate Services, you cannot rename the computer or change its domain membership because it becomes an integral part of the CA's identity. Click Yes to continue.

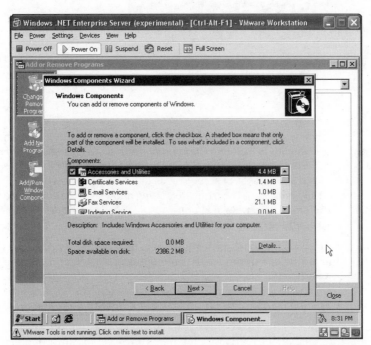

Figure 13-1: The Windows Components Wizard is used to add and remove Windows components after Windows has been installed.

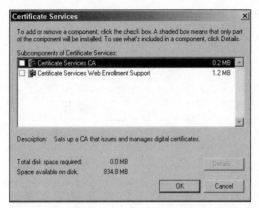

Figure 13-2: There are two subcomponents to Certificate Services.

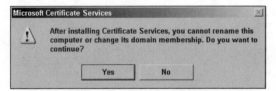

Figure 13-3: After you install Certificate Services, you cannot rename the system or change its domain membership.

5. Now that Certificate Services is selected, click Next in the Windows Components Wizard. The next step is to select the type of CA to install, as shown in Figure 13-4. In this example, an enterprise root CA will be installed. Subordinate CAs should only be installed if a root CA of some sort is in place. The Use custom settings to generate the key pair and CA certificate setting allows you to customize the CA certificate creation; otherwise, it is done automatically using default settings. Click Next to continue.

6. If you selected the Use custom settings to generate the key pair and CA certificate setting in the last step, you are now required to select the settings for the key pair, as shown in Figure 13-5. You can select the cryptographic service provider to use, the hash algorithm, and the key length. You can also decide to use an existing key or to import a key. Click Next to continue.

7. The next step is required whether you chose the Use custom settings... option or not. You must specify a common name for the CA, as shown in Figure 13-6. This common name will be used to refer to the CA and will be appended to the domain name information to create the distinguished name, as shown. You can also set the CA certificate's expiration. Five years is the default setting. Click Next to continue.

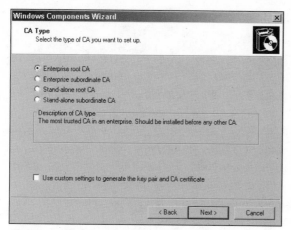

Figure 13-4: You need to select the type of CA that will be installed.

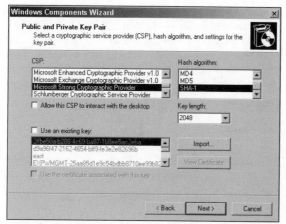

Figure 13-5: Set the custom settings for the CA key if you selected the Use custom settings... option in the previous step.

8. The key pair is now generated. Specify the certificate database location and the certificate database log location, as shown in Figure 13-7. You can also store configuration information in a shared folder. Specifying a shared folder is not normally done for an enterprise CA. Click Next to continue.

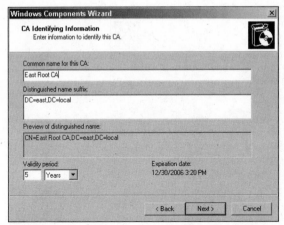

Figure 13-6: Enter a common name for the CA and, optionally, set the validity period for the CA certificate.

9. If IIS is running, you will be prompted that it will be stopped during the installation process. Click Yes to allow IIS to be stopped. You will also be prompted for the Windows Server 2003 media. Certificate services will now be installed. Click Finish when it completes to close the Windows Components Wizard.

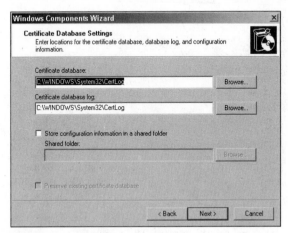

Figure 13-7: Specify the location for the certificate database and log.

You can specify an issuer policy statement for the CA. This statement is displayed when a user clicks the Issuer Statement button when viewing the CA certificate. This file must be in place before Certificate Services is installed. The file name must be CApolicy.inf, and it must be in the SystemRoot directory. The file will contain contents as follows:

```
[Version]
Signature="$Windows NT$"
[CAPolicy]
Policies=policyname
[policyname]
OID=1.0
Notice="issuer policy statement"
URL="http::://url.domain.com/policy"
```

The first two lines of the file must be exactly as shown. The policyname can be any name you want to use, as long as it is the same in both the Policies statement and the next section header. The OID is also an arbitrary value.

The Notice statement specifies a text policy statement that will be shown when the Issuer Statement button is clicked in the CA certificate. If the URL statement is used, the URL will be shown as a link in the policy statement. Any combination of Notice statement and HTTP, FTP, and LDAP URLs can be included.

Configuring the Certification Authority

Now that Certificate Services have been installed, you can begin to configure the CA.

1. Click Start, Administrative Tools submenu, and select Certification Authority. The CA snap-in will open, as shown in Figure 13-8.

2. The CAs in the enterprise are shown in the list in the left pane. Expanding the CA shows issued and revoked certificates, pending and failed requests, and certificate templates. Right-click the CA and select Properties. The CA Properties dialog box is displayed, as shown in Figure 13-9.

3. The General tab of the CA Properties dialog box shows information about the CA. The upper section shows the CA name and installed CA certificates. The lower section shows the CSP and hash algorithm used by the CA. You can select a certificate from the list and click the View Certificate button to see details about the CA certificate.

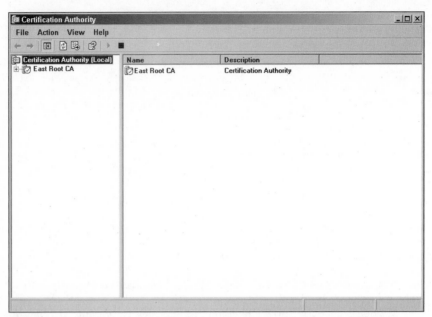

Figure 13-8: The CA snap-in is used to configure the CAs in your enterprise.

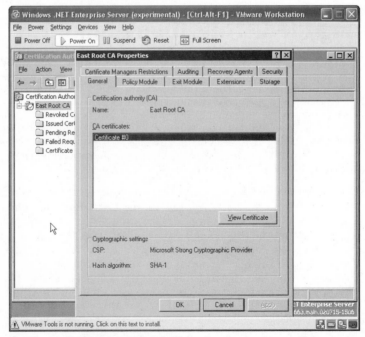

Figure 13-9: The CA Properties dialog box is used to configure settings that apply to the entire CA.

4. The Policy Module tab, shown in Figure 13-10, displays information about the CA's active policy module. The policy module is responsible for handling certificate requests when they are received by the CA. One policy module is included with Windows Server 2003, the Windows default policy module. You can also write custom policy modules and acquire third-party policy modules. The default module adds both certificate revocation list distribution points and authority information access points to issued certificates, and determines the default action taken on certificate requests.

Within the Policy Module tab, the Select button is used to select a different policy module, although there will be only one in most cases. Click the Properties button to display the Properties dialog box for the default policy module, as shown in Figure 13-11. This setting determines how certificate requests are handled by default. The default setting causes the CA to first refer to the setting in the certificate template to determine whether the request should be fulfilled or held, and if there is no setting, fulfill the request automatically. This setting can be overridden by selecting the option to set certificate status to pending. Similar to a CA in stand-alone mode, this will hold all certificate requests until approved by an administrator. This allows a more detailed check of the certificate requestor's authenticity, but leads to far more administrative overhead.

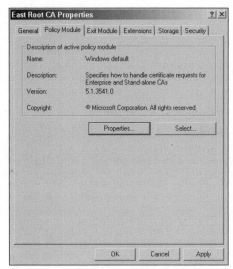

Figure 13-10: The Policy Module tab is used to configure and change the policy module for the CA.

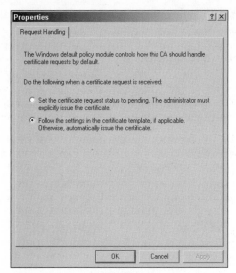

Figure 13-11: The Properties dialog box for the default policy module is used to set the default behavior of received certificate requests.

5. Use the Exit Module tab, shown in Figure 13-12, to add and remove exit modules in the CA. Exit modules are similar to policy modules, but determine what is done with a certificate after it is issued. A default exit module is included that allows publishing of certificates to both Active Directory and the file system, and publishes the Certificate Revocation List. Use the Add and Remove buttons to add or remove exit modules from the list.

Select the default exit module and then click the Properties button. The Properties dialog box for the default exit module is shown in Figure 13-13. The only setting available allows certificates to be published to the file system if configured in the certificate template. By default, this behavior is not allowed.

6. The Extensions tab is shown in Figure 13-14. By default, there are two extensions in the CA: CRL Distribution Point (CDP) and Authority Information Access (AIA). Both of these control publishing points. The CDP and AIA publishing points both publish to the file system, LDAP directory, Web site, and FTP site on the CA system. Add and remove publishing points as you require.

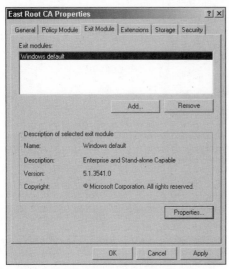

Figure 13-12: The Exit Modules tab is used to configure which exit modules are used within the CA.

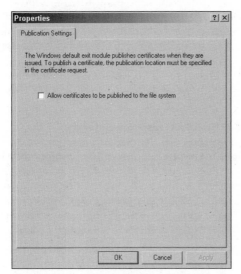

Figure 13-13: The Properties dialog box for the default exit module can be used to enable or disable the ability to publish certificates to the file system.

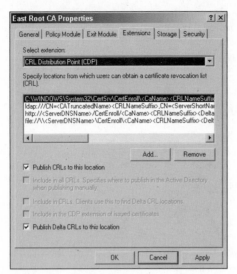

Figure 13-14: The Extensions tab is used to set publishing points for CDP and AIA.

Note

The CRL Distribution Point (CDP) is a publishing point to where the Certificate Revocation List (CRL) is published. The CRL is used to inform clients and other CAs which certificates have been revoked. The Authority Information Access (AIA) publishing point is used for clients and other CAs to retreive certificates for the CA.

7. Use the Storage tab, shown in Figure 13-15, to view the storage points for the certificate database and certificate database log. You cannot change this information with an Enterprise CA.

8. The Certificate Managers Restrictions tab shown in Figure 13-16 provides a finer granularity of control over the certificates that a certificate manager can manage (a certificate manager is any user that has been assigned the Issue and Manager Certificates permission from the Security tab). The default option selected is Do not restrict certificate managers. This means any certificate manager can manage certificates for any group, user, and computer. By selecting the Restrict certificate managers option, you can configure the specific groups, users, and computers that a certificate manager can manage.

9. The Auditing tab shown in Figure 13-17 allows you to enable auditing for Certificate Services and specify the types of events that should be audited. Keep in mind that you must enable the Audit object access setting within a group policy before events can be written to the Security log.

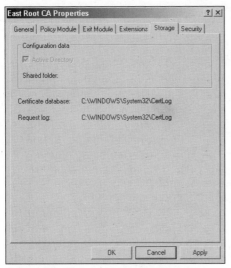

Figure 13-15: The Storage tab shows where certificates are stored.

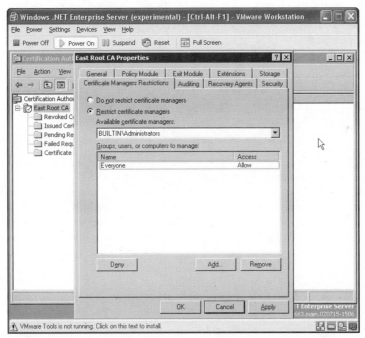

Figure 13-16: The Certificate Managers Restrictions tab is used to configure the subjects for which a certificate manager can manage certificates.

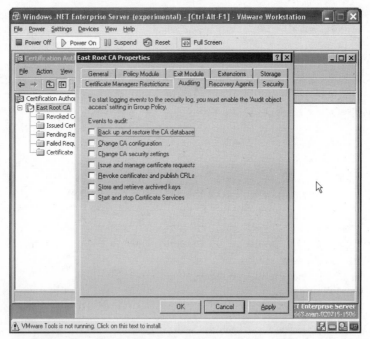

Figure 13-17: In the Auditing tab, you can enable auditing of Certificate Services.

10. The Recovery Agents tab shown in Figure 13-18 allows you to specify what happens when a certificate request includes a key archival. If you select Do not archive the key, any private key associated with a certificate's public key will not be stored by the CA. Selecting the second option means that the CA will store the private key, in which case, you must specify at least one recovery agent.

11. Use the final tab, the Security tab shown in Figure 13-19, to control access to the CA itself. From this tab, you can configure who can request certificates from the CA, who can issue and manage certificates, and who can manage the CA. When certificate requests are placed in the queue for approval, users with the Issue and Manage Certificates permission can approve those requests.

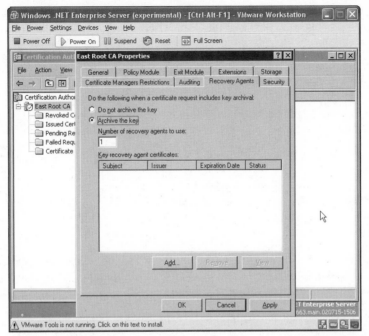

Figure 13-18: The Recovery Agents tab allows you to configuring recovery agents.

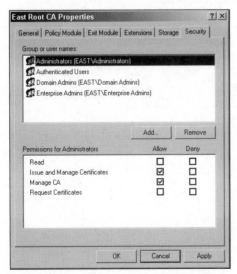

Figure 13-19: The Security tab controls which users can use and manage the CA.

Certificate templates are the most important concept in a CA. A certificate template is a set of rules that controls what happens when the CA receives a certificate request. There are many preconfigured certificate templates. Not all of these certificate templates are installed by default. You can see which certificate templates are installed by clicking Certificate Templates in the Certification Authority snap-in, as shown in Figure 13-20.

As stated, these are only the active certificate templates. You can also view all certificate templates. Either right-click the Certificate Templates container in the Certification Authority snap-in and select Manage, or click Start, Run, enter certtmpl.msc, and click OK. The Certificate Templates snap-in is shown in Figure 13-21.

Existing certificate templates are shown in the right pane. You can create a new certificate template by right-clicking an existing template and then selecting Duplicate Template. The properties dialog box for the new template is displayed so you can configure it.

You can essentially take two directions when creating certificate templates. The first option is to create a large number of specific templates, one for each type of certificates that a certificate subject will have.

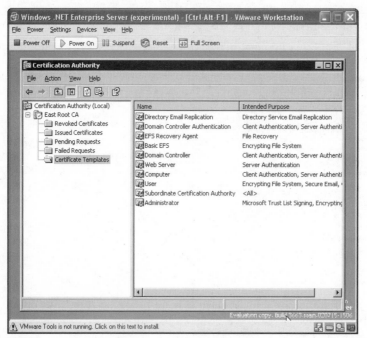

Figure 13-20: The installed certificate templates are shown in the Certification Authority snap-in.

Figure 13-21: The Certificate Templates snap-in is used to manage certificate templates.

Note
A certificate subject refers to any object that will have a certificate. Users and computers can both be certificate subjects.

The other option is to have a small number of certificate templates that assign certificates for a number of different applications. Each option has advantages and disadvantages. Having a large number of certificate templates with more specific rules allows a certificate subject to have fewer certificates for only the applications they require. As they gain more certificates, however, it becomes more difficult to manage.

Having a broader certificate template has advantages, as well. Only one certificate is issued for a number of applications. This eases the administrative burden of having a large number of separate certificates, but users end up with a number of certificates they don't use. The other disadvantage of this method is that it is more difficult to restrict certificate usage. You might want to limit certain users from requesting certain certificates, but doing so becomes impossible with this method.

A common practice is to configure certificate templates for each group of users requiring certificates for a different set of applications. For example, if certain users require e-mail encryption certificates and EFS certificates, while other users require EFS and IPSec certificates, you can create two certificate templates, one for each group. It will obviously be more complex than this for most environments though.

Creating certificate templates

To create a new certificate template, you need to copy an existing template in the Certificate Templates snap-in. Right-click an existing certificate template, and select Duplicate Template. The Properties of New Template dialog box is displayed, as shown in Figure 13-22. The General tab is displayed by default.

Give the new certificate template a name. The template name is the same as the template display name with the spaces removed by default. After the template names are set and changes are applied, the name cannot be changed. The Validity period sets the amount of time for which the certificate is valid. It cannot be set to a longer time than the CA certificate's validity time. The Renewal period sets the amount of time before the certificate is renewed. The certificate is renewed before its validity expires. When selected, the Publish certificate in Active Directory option causes the certificate to be added to Active Directory; otherwise, the certificate will only be stored in the local certificate store. If the Do not actively enroll if a duplicate certificate exists in Active Directory option is selected, it will cause all requests to first check the Active Directory for an existing duplicate certificate. If a duplicate certificate is found, the new certificate will not be automatically created.

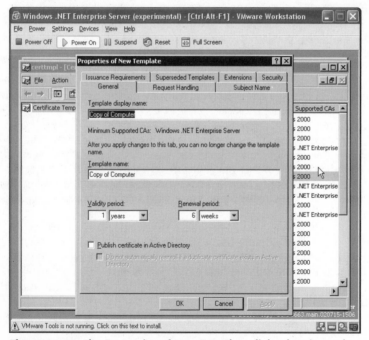

Figure 13-22: The Properties of New Template dialog box is used to configure a new certificate template, copied from an existing certificate.

Figure 13-23 shows the Request Handing tab of the Properties of New Template dialog box. This tab is used to set the behavior for certificate generation when a request that fits the template is received.

1. Set the certificate purpose to either Encryption, Signature, or Signature and Encryption.

2. Set the minimum key size for the certificate.

3. Set the acceptable CSPs for the certificate. The selected CSPs will be the only one(s) allowed for certificate creation.

If no CSPs are selected, any CSP will be allowed.

A number of options are also available in the Request Handling tab. The first option, Archive subject's encryption private key, causes the private key in the key pair associated with a generated certificate to be archived. The archived key can then be used if the original key is lost. If this option is not selected, a new key pair must be generated if the private key is lost. In this case, nothing encrypted to the old key will be able to be decrypted.

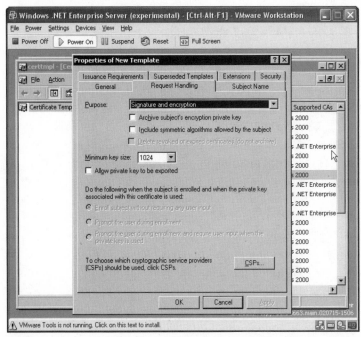

Figure 13-23: The Request Handling tab is used to configure what action is taken when a certificate request is received.

The Include symmetric algorithms allowed by the subject option sets whether or not the certificate will allow the use of symmetric algorithms supported by the subject. Allow private key to be exported specifies whether or not the private key can be exported by the subject. This can be disabled to alleviate potential security problems stemming from the exported key being compromised. Selecting Require user input for autoenrollment causes the user to be prompted for input when they are requesting a certificate through autoenrollment.

Figure 13-24 shows the Subject Name tab used to configure where the subject name information is taken from. In an enterprise CA, you can pull the subject name from the Active Directory entry for the subject who must be logged in. The Build from this Active Directory information option causes this behavior. You can also choose which name information to use for the certificate and choose to include extra information. By selecting the Supply in the request option, the subject name must be present in the certificate request. Autoenrollment cannot be used in this case, because an administrator must manually verify the subject's identity. This is the only possible behavior for a stand-alone CA.

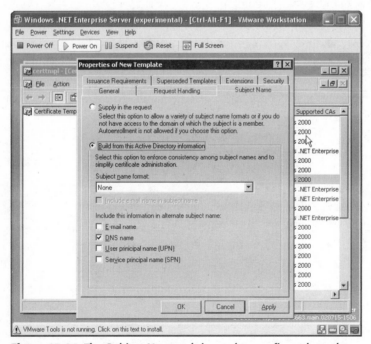

Figure 13-24: The Subject Name tab is used to configure how the subject identity information is determined.

The next tab in the Properties of New Template dialog box is Issuance Requirements, as shown in Figure 13-25. The Issuance Requirements tab is used to set the steps required before the certificate is issued. The setting with no options selected will cause the certificate to be automatically issued. Selecting the CA certificate manager approval option causes any certificate request for this template to change to pending status. Pending certificate requests need to be approved by an administrator.

The This number of authorized signatures option enables the rest of the configuration settings in the Issuance Requirements tab. This option causes the specified number of signatures to be required on a request before a certificate is issued.

The Superseded Templates tab shown in Figure 13-26 is used to set which certificates are superseded by this certificate template. Any certificate created through the templates in this list is removed when a certificate is created by this template. This feature is used when a more general certificate template should supersede a more specific one. For example, if the current certificate template created a certificate for both e-mail and EFS, a certificate template that created only an EFS certificate or only an e-mail certificate (or both) would be added to the superseded templates list.

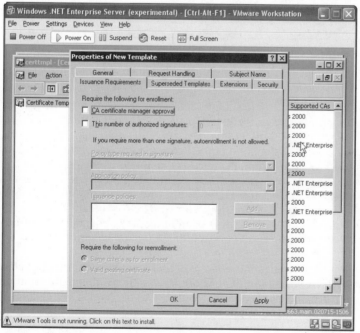

Figure 13-25: The Issuance Requirements tab is used to configure the steps required before a certificate is issued in response to a request.

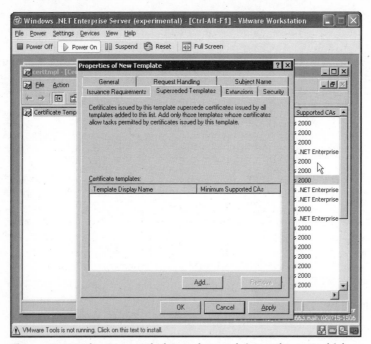

Figure 13-26: The Superseded Templates tab is used to set which certificate templates are superseded by the current template.

To add a certificate template to the superseded templates list, click the Add button, select a certificate template from the list displayed, and click OK.

Figure 13-27 shows the Extensions tab of the Properties of New Template dialog box. This tab is used to configure the extensions included in the certificate template. These extensions control the certificate template's more detailed behavior. There are extensions other than those shown but they are less common. Also, not all templates will have all of the extensions shown. The Certificate Template Information extension is not editable. It is used to display information about the template in the description box.

The Application Policies extension is used to define which application policies are included in the certificate template. The application policies define for what purpose the certificate created by the template may be used. To edit which application policies are included, select the Application Policies extension and click the Edit button. The Edit Application Policies Extension dialog box is displayed, as shown in Figure 13-28. Certificates created by the template shown can currently be used only for EFS. You can add application policies by clicking Add, selecting the policy from the list shown, and clicking OK. The policy will be added to the list of included policies. You can remove an application policy from the list by selecting it and then clicking Remove.

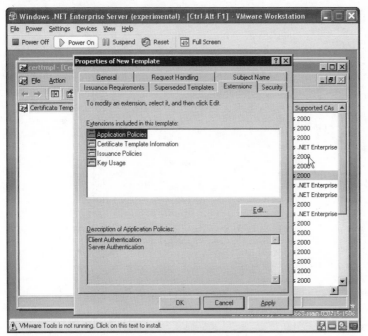

Figure 13-27: The Extensions tab is used to view and configure extensions included in the certificate template.

Note　When selected, the Make this extension critical option within extensions causes the issuance of a certificate to fail if the policies within an extension cannot be applied.

The Issuance Policies extension is used to configure issuance policies for a template. These policies define under which conditions a certificate is issued. The Key Usage extension controls the purpose for which the keys associated with a certificate may be used. You can edit the key usage policy by selecting Key Usage and then clicking Edit. The Edit Key Usage Extension dialog box is shown in Figure 13-29.

The top section of the Edit Key Usage Extension dialog box is used to configure how a key may be used for signing, if the certificate template is configured to create a signing key in the Request Handling tab. If the key is for both signing and encryption, you cannot make any changes, as shown in Figure 13-29. If the certificate is used for signing only, you can enable the following:

✦ Nonrepudiation

✦ Certificate signing

✦ CRL signing

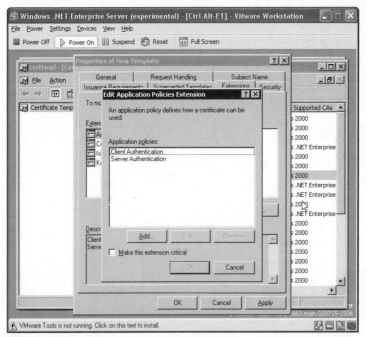

Figure 13-28: The Application Policy extension is used to configure for which applications a certificate created with a certain template may be used.

The lower part of the Edit Key Usage Extension dialog box is used to set encryption behavior for the certificate. You can select to allow plain text key exchange or only enciphered key exchange. Allowing plain text key exchange can reduce security slightly. If you choose to only allow encrypted key exchange, you can also allow the key to be used to encrypt user data.

The final tab in the Properties of New Template dialog box is the Security tab, as shown in Figure 13-30. The Security tab is used to control who has access to the certificate template. A user must be assigned at least Enroll access to request a certificate using the template. The read and write permissions control who can edit the template. The Enroll and Autoenroll permissions control who can use the template to request certificates.

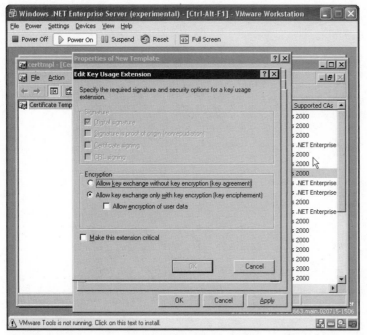

Figure 13-29: The Edit Key Usage Extension dialog box is used to configure how a key created using the certificate template may be used.

As previously discussed, a common method of issuing certificates is to determine for which applications users need certificates and configure a certificate template for each group requiring a unique set of certificates. You should now have the knowledge to create such a template.

This template will need specific customizations in the application policies and security settings to control for which applications the certificate will be valid and which users will be able to use the template.

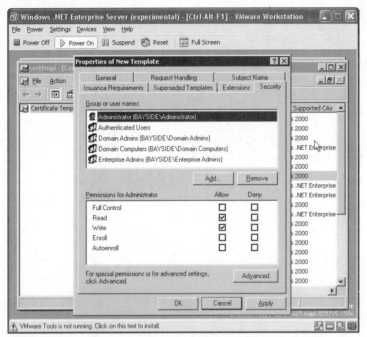

Figure 13-30: The Security tab is used to control access to the certificate template.

Enabling certificate templates

As previously shown, the Certification Authority snap-in is used to view which certificate templates are available by selecting Certificate Templates in the left pane. Only the certificate templates shown are available for enrollment. New certificate templates can be added very easily.

The templates to be added to the CA must first exist in the Certificate Templates snap-in. (See the previous section for information on creating and viewing templates.) To add a template, right-click Certificate Templates in the Certification Authority snap-in's left pane, select New, and select Certificate Template to Issue. Figure 13-31 shows the Enable Certificate Templates dialog box. Only templates that are not already enabled are shown in the list. Select the template you want to enable from the list and then click OK.

It is equally simple to remove certificate templates so they are no longer available for enrollment. Click Certificate Templates in the left pane of the Certification Authority snap-in. Select the certificate template in the right pane, right-click, and select Delete.

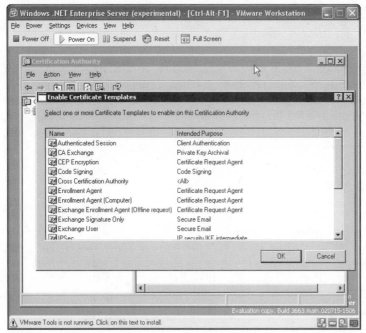

Figure 13-31: The Enable Certificate Templates dialog box is used to make certificate templates available for enrollment.

Certificate Enrollment

Certificate enrollment can be done in a number of ways. The most common enrollment method is autoenrollment. When you use an application requiring a certificate, a certificate request is automatically created and submitted to the CA. If there is no CA in use, the certificate is created locally and self-signed. If a CA is in use, the request is sent to the CA. In a stand-alone CA, the request is placed into the pending requests queue and an administrator must approve the request. With an enterprise CA, depending on the certificate policy, the request is fulfilled automatically, as the certificate subject's authenticity can be verified through Active Directory.

You can view the certificates that have been created through the Certificates MMC snap-in. Select Run from the Start menu, type **certmgr.msc**, and click OK. From the Certificates snap-in, double-click Personal and then click Certificates. The issued certificates are shown in the right pane, as shown in Figure 13-32. The certificate shown was created by the CA for file recovery.

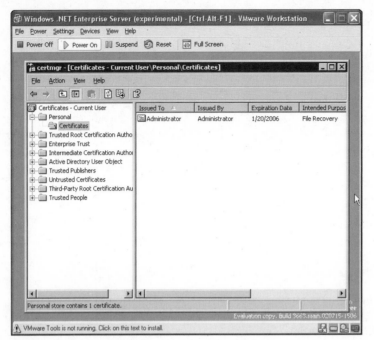

Figure 13-32: The Certificates snap-in is used to view existing certificates and can be used to request new certificates.

You can use the Certificates snap-in to request new certificates as well.

1. Right-click Certificates under Personal, select All Tasks, and select Request New Certificate. This will launch the Certificate Request Wizard.

2. Click Next to continue past the introduction.

3. The first step in the Certificate Request Wizard is to select the type of certificate to request, as shown in Figure 13-33. You can only request certificates provided by templates in the Certification Authority snap-in. Also, only templates to which you have the enroll permission are shown in the list. If you select the Advanced check box, you can choose the CSP, key length, CA, and other advanced options for the certificate.

4. If you have checked the Advanced box in the last step, you need to choose a CSP, as shown in Figure 13-34. Only CSPs configured in the certificate template are shown. In this step you can also select a key length, mark the key as exportable, and enable strong private key protection. If the key is marked as exportable, you can later export the key to make a backup. If this option is not selected, the key cannot be exported, which is more secure but less convenient if you lose your key and do not have a backup. If strong private key protection is enabled, you will be prompted every time the key is used. This is often inconvenient, but can provide increased security. Click Next to continue.

Figure 13-33: Choose the type of certificate to be requested.

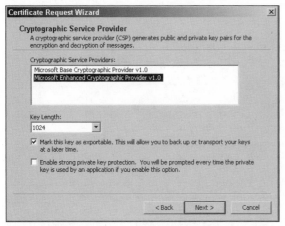

Figure 13-34: If the Advanced check box was selected in the previous step, the CSP, key length, and other options can be set for the certificate.

5. The next step, shown in Figure 13-35, is also necessary only if the Advanced option was selected in the first step. You can select the CA to which the certificate request will be sent. The default CA is shown. You can select a different CA by clicking the Browse button, selecting the CA from the list displayed, and clicking OK. The list of available CAs is retrieved from the CA list published in Active Directory. Click Next to continue.

6. The next step is the same whether the Advanced option was selected in the first step or not. You are now required to enter a friendly name and, optionally, a description for the certificate, as shown in Figure 13-36. The friendly name is used when viewing the certificate in the Certificates snap-in. Click Next to continue.

7. Review the options you have selected. If everything looks correct, click Finish to submit the certificate request. You will be notified as to the success or failure of the request. Figure 13-37 shows the new certificate in the Certificates snap-in. If autoenrollment is not available either because a stand-alone CA is in use or it has been disabled, the new certificate will not be granted until an administrator reviews the request.

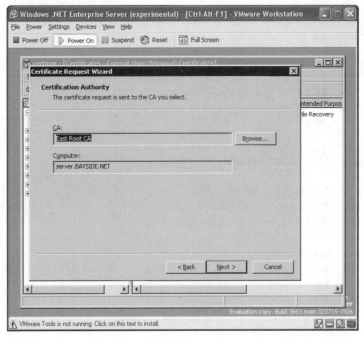

Figure 13-35: If the Advanced check box was selected in the first step, you can select the CA to which to send the certificate request.

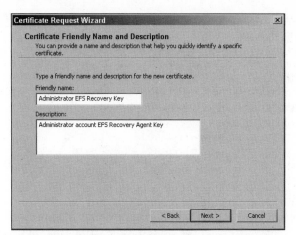

Figure 13-36: Enter a friendly name and optional description for the certificate.

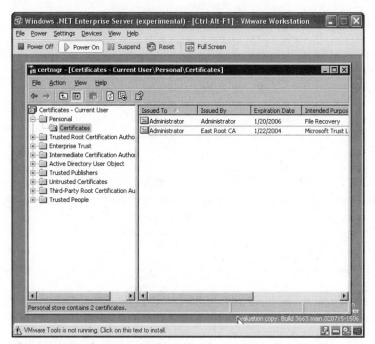

Figure 13-37: The new certificate has been granted and is shown in the Certificates snap-in.

There is another way to request certificates as well. Recall that when Certificate Services was installed earlier in the chapter, the Certificate Services Web Enrollment Support option was also installed. This option allows users to request certificates using a Web browser. Keep in mind that to use Web-based enrollment, IIS must be running. If the Certificate Services Web Enrollment support option was installed before IIS, you must run the `certutil -vroot` command (from the command line) to create the virtual roots.

1. Use a browser to open `http://machinename/certsrv`, as shown in Figure 13-38. This Web page can be used to request a new certificate, view the status of a request, or download CA certificates. Downloading CA certificates is used to configure a trust to this CA from another external CA.

2. Click the Request a certificate link to request a new certificate, as shown in Figure 13-39. There are two methods of requesting a certificate: simple and advanced. Only a User Certificate can be requested from this CA using the simple method. Select a certificate type from the list.

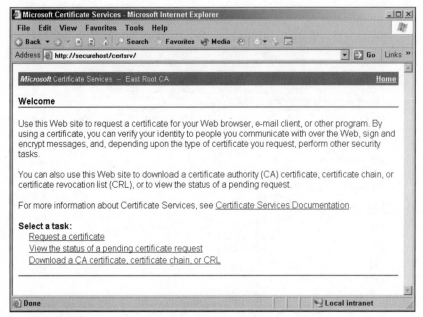

Figure 13-38: Certificate Services Web Enrollment Support is used to allow certificate requests from a Web browser.

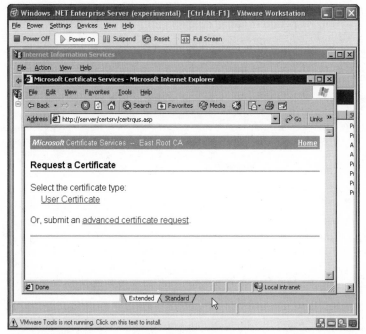

Figure 13-39: You can select a certificate type to generate from the list or submit an advanced certificate request.

3. The next step requires you to enter identifying information if any is required, as shown in Figure 13-40. This information is required if identifying information cannot be pulled from your login credentials. You will be required to provide this information if using a stand-alone CA. Clicking the More Options link displays a section where you can select a CSP and certificate request format and enable strong private key protection. This is a limited set of the advanced options available for a request. Click Submit to submit the request.

Figure 13-41 shows the results of the certificate request. This certificate was issued automatically. If autoenrollment is not possible, the request will be queued and you will need to wait for an administrator to approve the request. You can view the status of a pending request using the view status link on the root Certificate Services Web page. The issued certificate can now be installed by clicking the Install this certificate link. When you click the link, you are notified if the certificate was installed successfully.

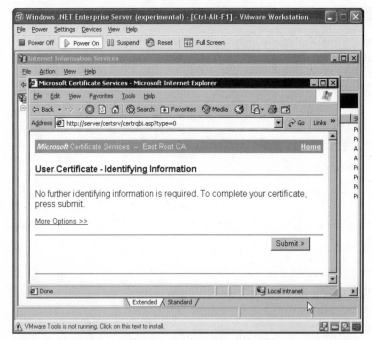

Figure 13-40: You may be required to enter identifying information depending on the configuration of your CA.

1. A certificate can also be requested using the advanced certificate request link. When you click this link, the Advanced Certificate Request page is displayed. From this page you have three options:

    • Submit a request to the CA.

    • Submit a request in a CMC or PCKS#10 file.

    • Enroll a smart card.

Cross-Reference Smart card enrollment is covered in Chapter 10.

    Click Create and then submit a request to this CA.

2. The next step in an advanced certificate request is to select a certificate template from the list for the type of certificate to create. You might be required to enter identifying information for the offline template.

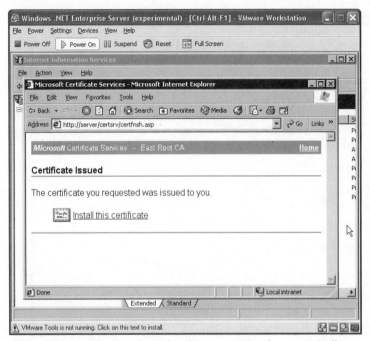

Figure 13-41: If the certificate has been generated automatically, it can now be installed.

3. Further down the page is the Key Options section, as shown in Figure 13-42. This is similar to the advanced options in the Certificate Request Wizard. You can choose whether to create a new key set or use an existing key set. If you choose to use an existing key set, you must specify its location. You can also select the CSP, key usage, and key length. By default, the CA automatically determines the key container name, but you can also manually specify a key container name by selecting that option. The Mark keys as exportable and Enable strong private key protection options are the same as in the wizard, but the Export keys to file option allows you to enter a path and have the keys exported during the certificate request process. Finally, you can choose to place the certificate in the local machine certificate store rather than in the CA store.

4. Even further down the page is the Additional Options section. This section allows you to set the request format and the hash algorithm used to sign the request. You can save the request to a file if you later want to use it again. You can also set attributes and the friendly name for the certificate. Click Submit to submit the certificate request.

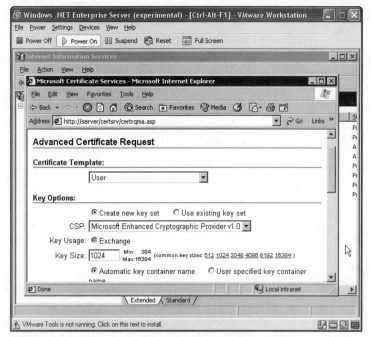

Figure 13-42: You can set advanced key options for the certificate request.

After you submit the request, the process is the same as with a simple certificate request. The certificate is either generated automatically or the request is placed in a queue for an administrator to review.

The other advanced method of submitting a certificate request is from a file.

1. From the Advanced Certificate Request page, click the Submit a certificate request by using a file link. The file may have been created through the CA Web page or through another method.

2. Specify the file name in the Saved Request box, and select the certificate template to use.

3. You can specify any additional attributes in the Attributes box at the bottom of the page. Click the Submit button to submit the request.

Again, after the request is submitted, it is either processed automatically and the certificate is returned for installation, or it is placed into the queue for review. Figure 13-43 shows the Certificates snap-in with all of the newly created certificates installed.

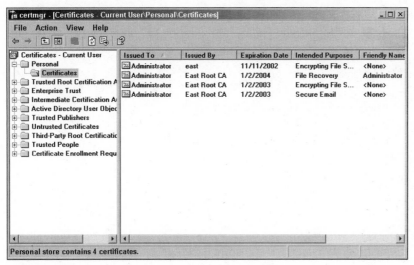

Figure 13-43: The newly created certificates have been installed and are shown in the Certificates snap-in.

Summary

The focus of this chapter was on the installation and configuration of Certificate Services in Windows Server 2003. The first step in implementing Certificate Services is to determine the type of CA to install—an enterprise CA or a stand-alone CA, keeping in mind that an enterprise CA requires Active Directory. If there is an existing root CA in place, you can add subordinate CAs to establish a hierarchy.

Certificate Services can be installed using the Add or Remove Programs applet within the Control Panel. If you plan to use Web browsers for certificate enrollment, you must install the Certificate Service Web Enrollment Support component. After the service is installed you can use the Certificate Authority snap-in to manage the service.

Default certificate templates are automatically installed with Certificate Services. You can create additional templates by making a duplicate of an existing one within the Certificate Templates snap-in. After the duplicate template has been created, you can configure its properties. It must then be added to the list of available certificate templates within the Certificate Authority snap-in.

The chapter ended by looking at certificate enrollment. Certificate enrollment can be accomplished in a number of ways, including auto enrollment, through the Certificates snap-in, or using a Web browser.

✦   ✦   ✦

L2TP and PPTP VPNs

Virtual private networks (VPNs) have existed for quite some time, but are only recently enjoying widespread implementation. You can connect a client or another network to your local network two ways. The traditional method is using a point-to-point network connection, such as a point-to-point T1 link or dial up to a Remote Access Service (RAS) system.

With the proliferation of Internet connections, both to homes and businesses, and the advancing speed of those connections, using dedicated point-to-point links when a connection to the Internet already exists is becoming less economical. Because of the architecture of the Internet, traffic can easily be routed from one network to another or from a client to the local network.

This type of connection through the Internet presents a unique problem, though. The Internet is a public place. Any data sent over the Internet is unprotected and could be read by anyone. Before network-to-network and client-to-network connections can be made over the Internet, a method of protecting that data has to be found.

The solution to this problem is a VPN. A VPN is simply an encrypted tunnel over which all data from the client (individual or network) is sent. The tunnel is impenetrable to attackers because all of the data is encrypted from end to end. VPNs use their own set of protocols for creating the tunnel and encapsulating data. Layer 2 Tunneling Protocol (L2TP) and Point-to-Point Tunneling Protocol (PPTP) are discussed in this chapter. IPSec is discussed in Chapter 15.

PPTP has existed for a fairly long time in Microsoft Windows. It is a proprietary tunneling protocol that can be used for both LAN-to-LAN and remote access VPNs. PPTP is widely supported and widely implemented. PPTP is actually an extension of Point-to-Point Protocol (PPP), commonly used for dial-up connections. PPTP works by first creating a PPP connection, then creating a PPTP control connection, and, finally, sending encrypted PPP packets over the PPTP tunnel.

PPTP has its disadvantages. Its authentication method is typically a fairly insecure password protocol, such as MS CHAP, although it can be configured to use certificates with Extensible Authentication Protocol (EAP) in Windows Server 2003. The PPTP encryption method is also fairly insecure.

L2TP is combined with IPSec to provide VPN connections. L2TP is advantageous because it uses certificates for both authentication and encryption, so it is more secure than PPTP. Disadvantages to L2TP are that it cannot operate with clients that are on a network using network address translation (NAT) due to a limitation of the Internet Key Exchange (IKE) protocol, and it is only supported by Windows Server 2003, Windows XP, and Windows 2000 systems.

Deciding to use PPTP or L2TP essentially comes down to compatibility. If you require compatibility with Windows NT 4.0 or other operating systems that do not support L2TP, use PPTP. In most other cases, L2TP is the better choice because of increased security. A Windows Server 2003-based VPN server can support both PPTP and L2TP connections simultaneously.

The examples in this chapter are based on the assumptions that the VPN server is a domain member and an enterprise root CA is installed in the domain. An enterprise root CA is required for most of the L2TP functionality in Windows Server 2003.

LAN-to-LAN VPNs

Connecting one LAN to another is a common need; for example, connecting a branch office to a main office. Connecting all of the networks in an organization can centralize services such as file sharing and e-mail services. Having fully interconnected networks is an essential requirement for many organizations.

Overview of LAN-to-LAN VPNs

You can connect two LANs with a point-to-point connection or using a VPN. A point-to-point connection is the traditional way to connect two networks, as in the past, a link such as a T1 was the only way to connect networks. These types of connections are expensive, and become more so as connection speed rises. A large number of these connections are still in place due to legacy implementations, special requirements such as reliability or excessive security, or network managers unfamiliar with VPN technology. Some sites have large networks of point-to-point connections.

Point-to-point connections do have advantages. They can be more stable than VPN connections, especially with quality of service agreements. Point-to-point connections are also sometimes seen as more secure because they do not traverse the Internet. An encrypted connection across a point-to-point connection is more secure than an equivalent encrypted VPN connection across the Internet because it is less vulnerable to eavesdropping. You should not be lulled into a false sense of security with a point-to-point connection, however, because it is still vulnerable to eavesdropping, although far less so.

While a point-to-point connection between two LANs goes directly from one site, to the telephone company, to the other site, the network connection is completely private (other than the Telco). A VPN connection works differently. A VPN connection creates an encrypted tunnel over the Internet. Each site is connected to the Internet, and the VPN protocol creates a logical tunnel between the two sites. The data can be sniffed off of the network using a packet sniffer in this case, but the VPN protocol makes the data fairly resistant to attack.

LAN-to-LAN VPNs can be implemented in a number of ways. A VPN server can be used inside the network, or the VPN can be configured in a piece of network equipment such as a firewall, router, or specific VPN device. Firewall-to-firewall VPNs are fairly common in branch office situations.

In Windows Server 2003, a LAN-to-LAN VPN is called a router-to-router VPN. Router-to-router VPNs in Windows Server 2003 are configured between two systems as routers using the Routing and Remote Access Service (RRAS).

Implementing a PPTP router-to-router VPN

Before you begin to configure a router-to-router VPN, you first need to configure the network connections on the VPN server. This system should have two network interfaces: one connected to the Internet, and the other to the internal network. You can set up a LAN-to-LAN VPN over a dial-up connection, but at least one system must be permanently connected to the Internet to receive the connection. With the proliferation of cable and asymmetric digital subscriber line (ADSL) connections, a permanent connection is within the budget of almost all small sites.

The first step to configuring a PPTP router-to-router VPN is to configure RRAS on each server. You must first add the computer accounts for each router to the RAS and Internet Authentication Service (IAS) Servers group if the systems are domain members. You must be a domain administrator to perform this step.

1. Open the Active Directory Users and Computers snap-in from the Start, Administrative Tools menu. Click the Users object in the left pane.

2. Locate and double-click the RAS and IAS Servers group in the right pane. Click the Members tab, as shown in Figure 14-1.

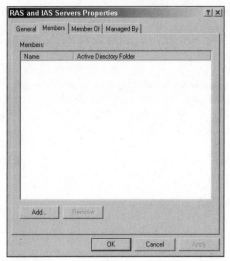

Figure 14-1: The Members tab of the RAS and IAS Servers Properties dialog box is used to view and add members to the group.

3. No computers are members of this group by default. You should add any computers that will be used for RRAS to the group. Click the Add button to open the Select Users, Contacts, Computers, or Groups dialog box, as shown in Figure 14-2.

4. By default, Computers is not in the list of object types to be searched. Click the Object Types button, select Computers, and click OK.

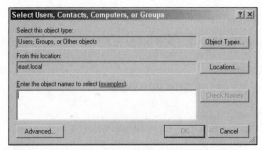

Figure 14-2: The Select Users, Contacts, Computers, or Groups dialog box is used to add members to the group.

5. Type the computer name to add to the group in the Enter the object names to select box and then click the Check Names button. The computer name you typed will be underlined if the object was successfully located in the directory. If the object cannot be found, you will be notified. If more than one object in the directory matches what you typed, you will be able to select from a list of matching objects. When you have specified the computer, click OK to close the Select Users, Contacts, Computers, or Groups dialog box.

6. The added computer will be shown in the Members list. Click OK to close the RAS and IAS Servers Properties dialog box after you have added the required members.

You must now configure RRAS. On the system that will be the VPN router, open the Routing and Remote Access snap-in from the Administrative Tools menu. RRAS must be configured using the Routing and Remote Access Setup Wizard before it can be used.

1. In the RRAS snap-in, right-click the server object in the left pane and select Configure and Enable Routing and Remote Access. The Routing and Remote Access Server Setup Wizard will launch. Click Next to continue past the introduction page.

2. The next step, shown in Figure 14-3, is to select what type of RRAS server to configure. Select the Remote access (dial-up or VPN)option and click Next to continue.

3. The next page allows you to specify whether the server will receive dial-up and/or VPN connections. Select VPN and then click Next.

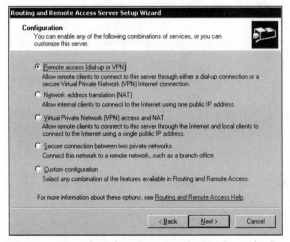

Figure 14-3: Select the RRAS server type from the list.

4. The VPN connection page appears. You can set security on a network connection. This security will ensure that only VPN connections can access the VPN server from the Internet. Select your Internet connection in the list and then click Next.

5. If you want to allow connections into the system from the Internet connection, select No and then click Next.

6. You now need to choose how IP addresses will be assigned to remote clients (refer to Figure 14-4). If you use DHCP on this server already, choose Automatically. If you choose Manual, you can specify a range of addresses that will be assigned. Choose the selection that fits your environment, and click Next. With a LAN-to-LAN VPN, you will only need a number of addresses equal to the number of VPN connections you will have. Click Next to continue.

7. If in the previous step you selected to specify the range of IP addresses, you must specify that range, as shown in Figure 14-5. No addresses are specified by default. Click the New button to display the New Address Range page. Enter the beginning and ending addresses for the range. Click OK to add the range to the list and then click Next to continue.

8. Figure 14-6 shows the next step in the wizard. You must decide whether or not to use Remote Authentication Dial-In User Service (RADIUS) for authentication of the VPN and other RAS clients. Windows Server 2003 comes with a RADIUS server called Internet Authentication Service (IAS). If you are implementing a large number of VPN connections, using a RADIUS server makes administration easier. With only a few connections, implementing IAS is a large amount of work. Click Next to continue.

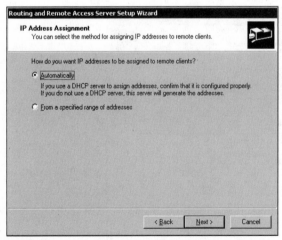

Figure 14-4: You need to select how IP addresses will be assigned to VPN clients.

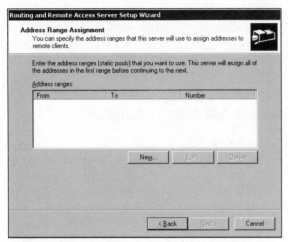

Figure 14-5: If you choose to specify a range of IP addresses manually, you must add those ranges in this step of the wizard.

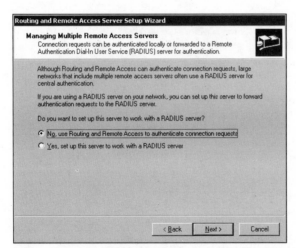

Figure 14-6: You must select whether or not to use RADIUS for authentication.

9. After you have made your selections in the wizard, the VPN server is config-ured. Click Finish to complete the wizard process. A window will appear, as shown in Figure 14-7, informing you that a DHCP relay agent must be config-ured to have Dynamic Host Configuration Protocol (DHCP) messages relayed between remote access clients and the internal DHCP server.

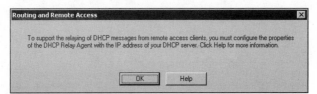

Figure 14-7: The DHCP relay agent must be configured for DHCP-related messages to be relayed between remote access clients and an internal DHCP server.

After the process is complete, RRAS is enabled. Figure 14-8 shows the RRAS snap-in after RRAS has been configured and enabled.

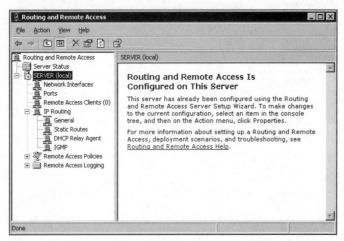

Figure 14-8: After RRAS has been enabled, its configuration settings are shown in the RRAS snap-in.

You now need to configure a demand dial interface in RRAS.

1. Right-click Network Interfaces in the left pane and select New Demand dial Interface. Click Next to continue past the introduction to the Demand Dial Interface Wizard.

2. Figure 14-9 shows the first step in the Demand Dial Interface Wizard. Specify a name for the connection and then click Next to continue.

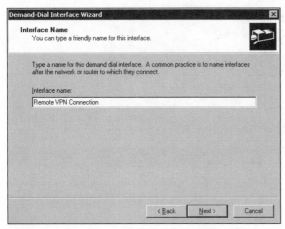

Figure 14-9: Assign a name to the new demand dial connection.

3. The next page allows you to select the type of VPN connection you want to create. Select Connect using virtual private networking (VPN), as shown in Figure 14-10 and then click Next.

4. Choose a VPN protocol for the connection, as shown in Figure 14-11. Click Next to continue.

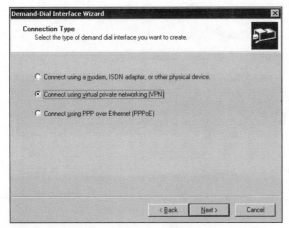

Figure 14-10: Select the type of demand dial connection.

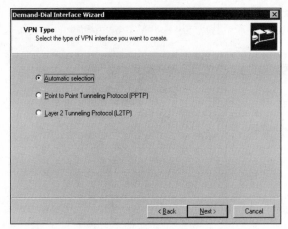

Figure 14-11: Choose the VPN protocol for this connection.

5. The next step, shown in Figure 14-12, requires you to specify the destination address for the demand dial connection. If you are using a two-way connection, specify the Internet address of the other VPN router. If you are using only a one-way connection, leave this box blank, and the system will receive connections but won't make outgoing connections. Click Next to continue.

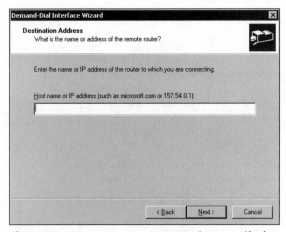

Figure 14-12: For a two way connection, specify the remote system's address. For the receiving end of a one-way connection, do not enter anything.

6. Specify which protocols are to be used over the VPN connection, as shown in Figure 14-13. Only routable protocols can be used, so only IP and IPX will be available. Any protocol you choose must be installed on the system. You can

also choose the Add a user account so a remote router can dial in option. Click Next to continue.

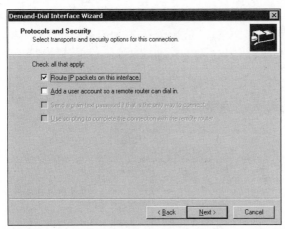

Figure 14-13: Select the protocols to be used over the VPN connection.

7. Configure a static route to the destination network, Click the Add button and type in the Destination, Network Mask, and Metric. Click OK and then click Next.

8. Figure 14-14 shows the next step if you chose the Add a user account so a remote router can dial in option. The username is automatically generated based on the demand dial interface name. Specify and confirm the password to be used and then click Next to continue.

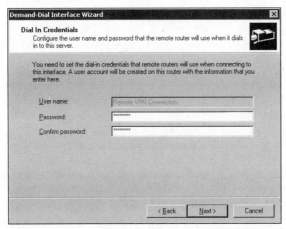

Figure 14-14: Specify the password for the demand dial user account.

9. Specify credentials for the connection to a remote VPN router, as shown in Figure 14-15. If you are using a two-way connection and specified a remote address earlier in the process, enter the username, password, and domain information for the remote VPN connection. The remote router may not have been configured yet, but you should know what credentials you will be using.

If you are using only a one-way connection and this system will be receiving the connection, specify the username and leave the rest blank because this information will not be used. Click Next to continue.

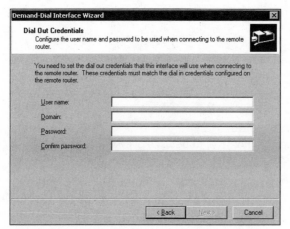

Figure 14-15: You must specify the credentials for the remote system if this system will be making an outgoing connection.

10. Click Finish to complete the Demand Dial Interface Wizard. The new demand dial interface will be shown under Network Interfaces in the RRAS snap-in. If you chose to create a user account during the process, the user account will be created, the password set, and all of the associated permissions assigned.

On the other end of the VPN connection, you should follow the same process laid out in the preceding steps. The process only varies if a one-way connection is being made. While the receiving VPN router will not have an IP address or user credentials specified in the Demand Dial Interface Wizard, the calling router will have these specified. On the calling router, you do not need to create a user account for receiving a connection in the wizard because it will never receive a connection.

After both ends of the connection have been created, you can right-click the demand dial interface on either end in a two-way connection or on the calling end in a one-way connection and select Connect. The connection should be successful.

Now the VPN connection should be able to be established between the two routers. However, if you did not specify a static route while configuring the demand dial interface, the routers do not know anything about the remote site, so they do not know what traffic to send over the VPN connection. You must specify routes for traffic to the other site.

1. In the RRAS snap-in, expand the router in the left pane, expand IP Routing in the left pane, right-click Static Routes in the left pane, and select Add New Static Route.

2. The Static Route dialog box is shown in Figure 14-16. Select the newly created demand dial interface from the Interface drop-down box.

3. Specify the network and subnet mask for the remote site. You can also set a metric for the route if you are using more than one route to the same destination. This can be used to configure back-up routes to a remote site.

4. Finally, select the Use this route to initiate demand dial connections option so that traffic reaching the router will cause it to connect to the remote router. Click OK to save the route.

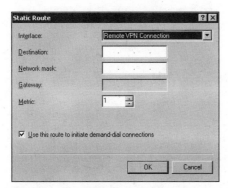

Figure 14-16: Creating a static route allows traffic to the remote site to traverse the VPN connection.

There is still a problem for systems other than the VPN router, though. If a routing protocol such as RIP or OSPF is not configured on your network and the VPN router is not configured as the default gateway of the workstations on your network, a static route must be added to the workstations to access the remote site. This is because without a specific route to the remote site network, traffic will be sent through the default gateway. If the default gateway is not the VPN router (which it probably will not be), the router that is the default gateway will not know the proper destination for the traffic. You can add a static route to the router that is the default gateway so that any traffic sent with a destination address in the remote site network is redirected to the VPN router. This is a networking design task beyond the scope of this book.

A static route is added to the workstation using the route add command. The destination network in this case is 192.168.101.0, and the gateway is the local VPN router at 192.168.103.1. The -P option makes the route *persistent*. Persistent routes are not lost upon reboot. A simple way to create the static routes is using logon scripts. You can write the script to verify the user's location (if the domain spans multiple sites) and create the static routes automatically.

Note   All of the preceding steps must be done for each site, including the VPN configuration and the routing configuration. Static routes, both in RRAS and on workstations, will point to the destination network at the remote site.

You might notice that the VPN connections configured earlier disconnect automatically after five minutes. This is because the connections are on-demand connections. You can make these connections persistent if the network connections over which the VPN is made are permanent. In the RRAS snap-in, right-click the demand dial interface created earlier and then select Properties. Click the Options tab, shown in Figure 14-17. The default setting for a connection is on-demand with a disconnection after five minutes. You can change the setting to a different amount of time or select Persistent Connection to have the connection always active. Persistent connections should be two-way and should be set as persistent on both VPN routers.

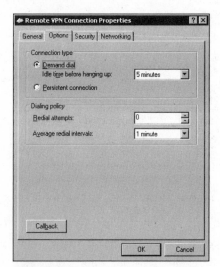

Figure 14-17: The Options tab of the demand dial interface Properties dialog box can be used to set the connection to be persistent.

After you have configured a router-to-router VPN, you can add the remote router to the domain at the main site.

Implementing an L2TP router-to-router VPN

Implementing an L2TP router-to-router VPN is similar to implementing a PPTP VPN, except there are some extra steps. First of all, you must have a Certification Authority (CA) installed on your network, as discussed in Chapter 13. Each of the VPN routers should have its internal and external interfaces configured and a CA should be in place. For an L2TP connection, you must have a computer certificate installed on the answering router and a user certificate installed on the calling router.

To create an L2TP router-to-router VPN, follow the preceding directions for creating a PPTP VPN. Rather than selecting PPTP for the VPN protocol when creating the demand dial interface, choose L2TP. Proceed through all steps to configure RRAS and the demand dial interface on each router. A certificate-based L2TP VPN should be one-way, and the router local to the CA will be the answering router. Do not enter an address for the remote router when configuring the demand dial interface on the answering router. Also, you do not need to create a user account on the calling router.

After RRAS has been configured for the VPN on each router, you can create the server certificate on the answering router. This certificate will identify the answering router to the calling router when the VPN connection is established.

1. Click Start, Run, type **mmc**, and click OK. An MMC console will open.

2. In the MMC console, click File and then select Add/Remove Snap-in to open the Add/Remove Snap-in dialog box.

3. Click the Add button in the Add/Remove Snap-in dialog box to display the Add Standalone Snap-in dialog box, as shown in Figure 14-18. Select Certificates and then click Add.

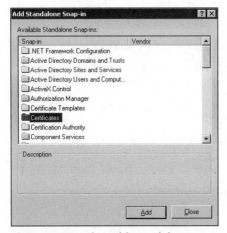

Figure 14-18: The Add Standalone Snap-in dialog box is used to select the snap-in to add to MMC.

4. When you select Certificates and click Add, you are required to select the scope of which certificates the snap-in will manage, as shown in Figure 14-19. As a computer certificate is required, select Computer Account and then click Next.

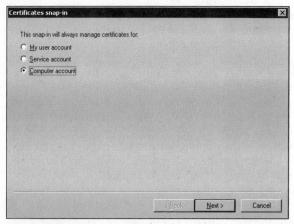

Figure 14-19: You must choose for which account to manage certificates.

5. Specify for which computer account certificates will be managed. Accept the default setting of Local Computer, and click Finish. The snap-in will be added to the list in the Add/Remove Snap-in dialog box.

6. Click Close to close the Add Standalone Snap-in dialog box and then click OK to close the Add/Remove Snap-in dialog box. The snap-in will be added to MMC.

7. Now that the snap-in is installed, double-click Certificates under Console Root.

8. Double-click Personal to expand the Personal certificates container, as shown in Figure 14-20.

9. Right-click Certificates, select All Tasks, and select Request New Certificate.

10. The Certificate Request Wizard is used to request a new certificate. Click Next to bypass the introduction page.

11. Choose the type of certificate to create, as shown in Figure 14-21. If the system is a domain controller, you will need to create a domain controller certificate. Domain controllers will have a certificate by default, but the CA does not issue it. If the system is a domain member, create a Computer certificate. Click Next to continue.

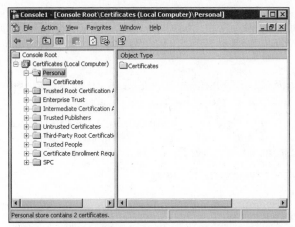

Figure 14-20: Expand Certificates and Personal to find the personal certificates container.

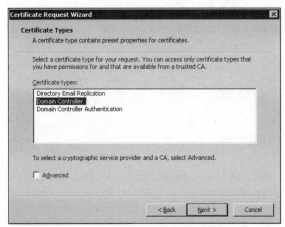

Figure 14-21: You must choose the type of certificate to request.

12. Specify a friendly name and a description for the certificate. This step is optional, but it allows you to more easily identify the certificate later. If you choose to give the certificate a friendly name or description, enter it and then click Next to continue.

Review the selections you have made, and click Finish to request the certificate. You will be informed as to whether the request was successful or not. The certificate will be added to the list of certificates in the MMC snap-in.

The next step requires you to create a user certificate for the user account that will be used for the demand dial interface. Before the certificate can be requested, however, you must enable the Router certificate template on the CA. Certificate templates are discussed at length in Chapter 13.

1. Log on to the CA as a user with rights to administer the CA. Select Certification Authority from the Administrative Tools menu to launch the CA snap-in.

2. Double-click the CA in the left pane to expand, right-click Certificate Templates, select New, and select Certificate Template to Issue. The list of disabled templates, as shown as in Figure 14-22, is displayed.

3. Select Router (Offline request), and click OK.

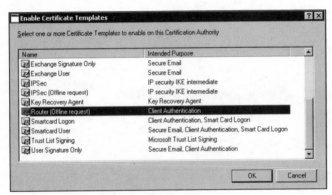

Figure 14-22: Select the Router certificate template so that Router certificates can be issued.

4. The Router (Offline request) template will be added to the list of certificate templates in the right pane of the CA snap-in. You can now close the CA snap-in. To request the certificate, log on to the calling router as an administrative user. Open Internet Explorer and then connect to the CA Web Enrollment page, typically `http://machinename/certsrv` where machinename is the CA server's name. You may need to provide logon credentials to access this Web page; log in as a user with rights to request certificates in the domain in which the CA is located.

5. From the first page of the Web Enrollment Web site, click Request a Certificate.

6. You are then asked what type of certificate to request. Click Advanced certificate request.

7. On the next page, click Create and submit a request to this CA. You can now choose the certificate type to request and set certificate options.

8. Choose Router (Offline request) for the certificate type and then enter the username that will be used to make the connection in the Name box.

9. Figure 14-23 shows the bottom of the certificate request page. Select the Use local machine store option so that the certificate is stored locally rather than in the CA, and click Submit.

10. The certificate request will be generated and the certificate should be issued automatically. Click Install this certificate to add the new certificate to the local certificate store.

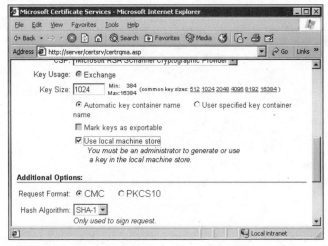

Figure 14-23: Select the Use local machine store option; then click the Submit button.

Now the computer certificate exists on the answering router and the user certificate exists on the calling router. The user certificate must be associated with the user on the answering router so that authentication can occur when the connection is made.

1. On the calling router (on which you should have just created the Router certificate), open the certificates snap-in for the local computer account. Open the Personal certificate container. The newly created certificate should be in the list in the right pane.

2. Make sure that you are selecting the correct certificate by checking that the Issued To field contains the name of the account for the VPN, as specified during the certificate request process, and that the Intended Purposes field contains Client Authentication. Right-click that certificate, select All Tasks, and select Export. The certificate export wizard will be used to export the certificate but not the associated private keys. Click Next to continue past the introduction page.

3. The next step requires you to choose whether or not to export the private key. Choose No, and click Next to continue.

4. You must now select the format of the exported certificate, as shown in Figure 14-24. Accept the default setting of DER Encoded Binary X.509, and click Next to continue.

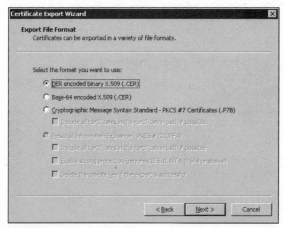

Figure 14-24: Choose the format for the exported certificate.

5. The exported file should be saved to the local hard drive or to a floppy disk. Specify a filename and location for the certificate, as shown in Figure 14-25. You will need to get the certificate file to the other VPN router so you may want to save it to a disk and send the disk to the other site. Do not specify an extension for the file because it will be appended automatically. Click Next to continue.

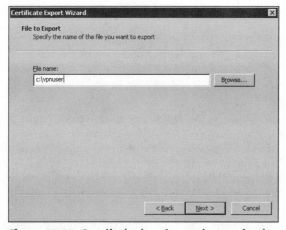

Figure 14-25: Specify the location and name for the certificate file.

6. Review the selections you have made and then click Finish to export the certificate.

The certificate file you created now must be moved to the other site so that it can be associated with the user account for VPN connections.

1. Open the Active Directory Users and Computers snap-in for the domain containing the answering VPN router.

2. Select Advanced Features from the View menu.

3. Locate the user created during the configuration of the demand dial interface in the Users container in Active Directory Users and Computers. Right-click that user, and select Name Mappings. The X.509 Certificates tab of the Security Identity Mapping dialog box is shown in Figure 14-26.

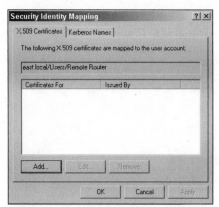

Figure 14-26: The Security Identity Mapping dialog box is used to associate certificates with user accounts.

4. Click the Add button in the Security Identity Mapping dialog box, select the certificate exported from the calling VPN router, and click Open.

5. A summary of the certificate information is shown as in Figure 14-27. Verify that the information is correct and then click OK. The certificate will be added to the user account. Click OK to close the Security Identity Mapping dialog box. You can also close the Active Directory Users and Computers snap-in.

Now all of the certificates have been installed for the L2TP connection but RRAS needs to be configured.

1. On the answering router, open the RRAS snap-in. Right-click the server name for the answering router, and select Properties.

2. Select the Security tab in the Properties dialog box, and click the Authentication Methods button.

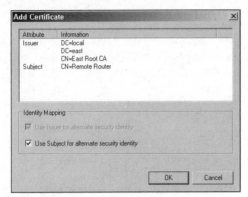

Figure 14-27: Verify that the information contained in the certificate is correct and then click OK to associate it with the user account.

3. In the Authentication Methods dialog box, shown in Figure 14-28, ensure that the Extensible authentication protocol option is selected and then click OK. Click OK again to close the Properties dialog box.

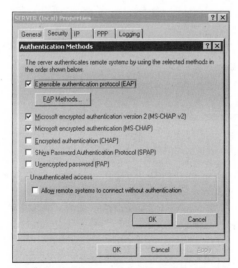

Figure 14-28: Ensure that the EAP option is selected in the Authentication Methods dialog box for the RRAS server.

4. One more configuration change must be made on the answering server. Under the server name in the left pane, click Remote Access Policies. Only one remote access policy is defined by default, and it will be displayed in the right pane. Right-click the policy and then select Properties.

5. Click the Edit Profile button in the Properties dialog box and select the Authentication tab.

6. In the Authentication tab, as shown in Figure 14-29, select the EAP methods button. From the Select EAP Providers window, click the Add button. From the list, select Smart Card or other Certificate, and click OK.

7. From the Select EAP Providers window, click the Edit button. The Smart Card or other Certificate Properties dialog box shown in Figure 14-30 appears. It is used to configure the computer certificate that will be used during the authentication process. There may be more than one certificate in the list with the same name. Make sure you choose the certificate that has the name of the answering VPN router and that was issued by the enterprise root CA, as shown. If you select a certificate that was self generated (if the system is a domain controller, for example) the VPN connection will not authenticate.

8. Click OK to close the Smart Card or other Certificate Properties dialog box, click OK to close the Edit Dial-in Profile dialog box, and click OK to close the profile Properties dialog box.

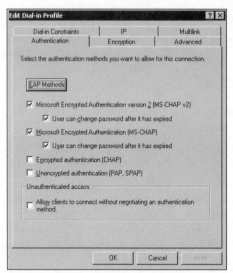

Figure 14-29: Select the EAP methods button in the Authentication tab of the Edit Dial-in Profile dialog box, and choose Smart Card or other Certificate.

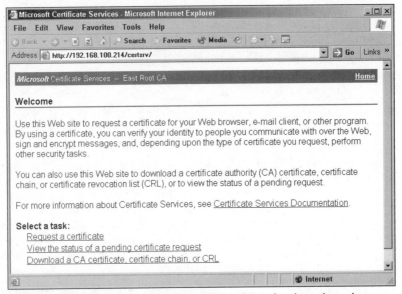

Figure 14-30: Select the computer certificate from the drop-down box that was issued by the enterprise root CA.

The answering VPN router is now properly configured. There are a few steps to take on the calling router to configure proper authentication. On the calling router, you must make the enterprise root CA used by the answering router a trusted root CA. Open Internet Explorer on the calling router and return to the certificate services Web Enrollment Web site for the CA. This time, rather than request a certificate, you will download the CA certificate.

1. From the Certificate Services Web page, shown in Figure 14-31, click Download a CA certificate, certificate chain, or CRL.

2. As you want to trust certificates issued by the CA, click install this CA certificate chain. You will be notified when the certificate chain is installed. You can now close Internet Explorer.

3. Verify that the CA is now a trusted root CA on the calling VPN router. Open the Certificates snap-in for the local computer account, as previously explained. Expand Trusted Root Certification Authorities in the left pane and then click Certificates. The root CA added in the previous steps should be displayed in the list in the right pane, as shown in Figure 14-32.

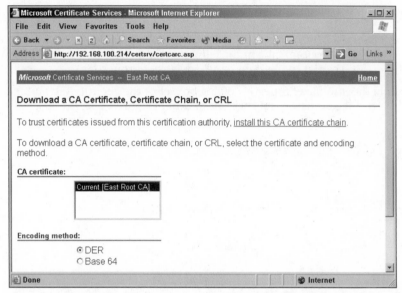

Figure 14-31: The Certificate Services Web page for the CA used by the answering VPN router can be used to make that CA a trusted root CA for the calling router.

Figure 14-32: The CA for the answering router is now a trusted root CA for the calling router.

You can now configure RRAS to use certificate authentication.

1. Open the RRAS snap-in on the calling VPN router. Select Network Interfaces under the router name in the left pane, right-click the demand dial interface created earlier in the right pane, and select Properties.

2. In the interface Properties dialog box, click the Security tab and then select Advanced (custom settings), as shown in Figure 14-33.

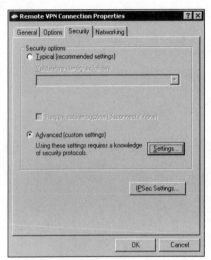

Figure 14-33: Select Advanced in the Security tab of the demand dial interface Properties dialog box.

3. Click the Settings button. Figure 14-34 shows the Advanced Security Settings dialog box. In this window, select Use Extensible Authentication Protocol (EAP), and select Smart Card or other Certificate from the drop-down box. This configures the calling connection to also use EAP with a certificate.

4. After selecting EAP in the Advanced Security Settings dialog box, click the Properties button. In the Smart Card or other Certificate Properties dialog box, shown in Figure 14-35, ensure that Validate server certificate is selected.

5. Choose the enterprise root CA for the answering router from the list of trusted root CAs. This CA will only be in the list if you followed the earlier step of making that CA a trusted root CA for the local system. You can select the Connect only if server name ends with option and specify the DNS suffix for the answering server, but that selection can make it more difficult to get authentication functioning. Click OK to close this dialog box and the others that are open. The changes will now be saved to the demand dial interface.

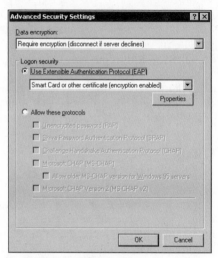

Figure 14-34: Select EAP in the Advanced Security Settings dialog box and select Smart Card or other Certificate from the drop-down box.

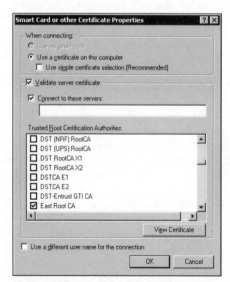

Figure 14-35: Select the root CA in which issued the computer certificate to the answering router from the drop-down box.

There is one final step to configuring the VPN connection. Right-click the demand dial interface, and select Set Credentials. Select the user certificate created earlier from the drop-down box. This certificate is the one that was exported and attached to the user account for the connection. Click OK after you have made your selection.

You should now be able to right-click the demand dial interface, select Connect, and the connection should be established successfully. You still need to configure routing, as discussed at the end of the PPTP VPN section before the connection is useful.

Remote Access VPNs

VPN connections are not only useful for connecting one network to another, but also for providing individuals with remote access to your network. The traditional method of providing a modem pool for users to dial in is becoming outdated with the advent of broadband Internet connections to the home over cable and ADSL. A user who is used to having high-speed Internet access of up to 1.5Mbps will not want to use a 56kbps dial-up connection to the corporate network.

VPNs provide a method of allowing users to utilize their high-speed Internet connections to access the corporate network. The corporate network will need enough bandwidth to support the number of users who will be connecting via VPNs, as well. A VPN provides a secure tunnel for data between the user's computer and the internal corporate network without exposing that network to attack from the Internet.

Implementing a PPTP remote access VPN

The configuration of an answering VPN router for a remote access VPN is identical to that of a router-to-router VPN. Refer to the earlier section in this chapter, "Implementing a PPTP Router-to-Router VPN," for the steps to configuring the answering router. Perform only the steps involved in configuring RRAS. You do not need to configure a demand dial interface to enable remote access VPNs.

Configuring a remote access VPN is actually a simple process. After you have configured RRAS as a VPN server, you simply need to configure the VPN client. One of the key changes you must make is to enable dial-in access for each account that will have permission to connect.

1. Open Active Directory Users and Computers in the domain containing the VPN server.

2. Right-click a user to enable and then select Properties.

3. In the Dial-in tab for the user, change the Remote Access Permission to Allow Access, as shown in Figure 14-36, and click OK to save the changes. This will allow that user to dial in.

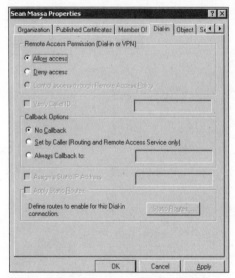

Figure 14-36: A user must have the Remote Access Permission set to Allow Access to be able to connect via a VPN connection.

Another option exists for the Remote Access Permission that is only available if you are running your domain in native mode. It is not available in mixed mode. Selecting the Control access through Remote Access Policy option will grant or deny a user access based on the policies defined in RRAS rather than explicitly in the account properties. By default, no policies are defined that can take advantage of this setting.

Now that the user account has been assigned dial-in access, you can proceed to configure the VPN client. The example used here is for a Windows Server 2003 client, but the process is similar for Windows XP clients. For other operating systems, refer to the proper documentation for the exact procedure.

1. Right-click My Network Places on the desktop, and select Properties. This action will open the Network Connections folder.

2. Double-click New Connection Wizard and then click Next to continue past the introduction.

3. Choose the connection type, as shown in Figure 14-37. Select Connect to the network at my workplace, and click Next to continue.

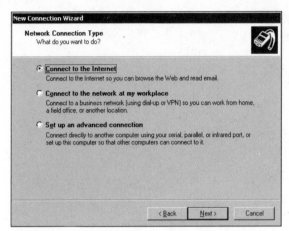

Figure 14-37: Select the type of network connection to create.

4. Select whether to use a dial-up or VPN connection, as shown in Figure 14-38. Select Virtual Private Network connection, and click Next to continue.

5. Assign a name to the connection, as shown in Figure 14-39. This name should describe the connection so it is easy to identify in the Network Connections folder. Click Next to continue.

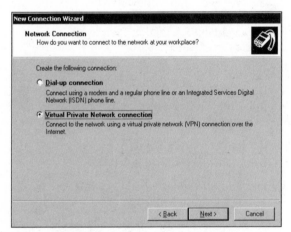

Figure 14-38: You can use a dial-up or VPN connection to connect to the corporate network.

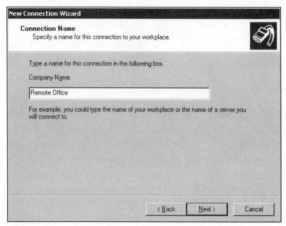

Figure 14-39: Assign a name to the connection so it is easier to identify.

6. Specify whether to have Windows automatically dial the initial connection to the Internet or public network before establishing the virtual connection, as shown in Figure 14-40. Click Next.

7. Specify the address for the remote VPN server, as shown in Figure 14-41. This will be the address to which the VPN client connects, and should be the external IP address of the VPN server configured earlier. Click Next to continue.

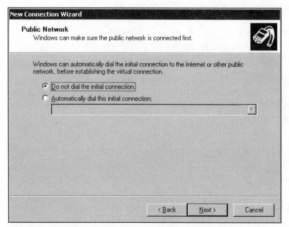

Figure 14-40: Configure Windows to automatically dial the initial connection to the Internet or public network.

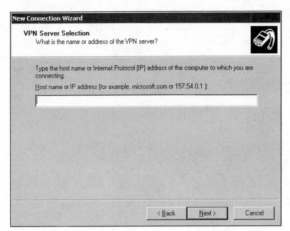

Figure 14-41: Specify the address of the VPN server to which to connect.

8. Specify whether the connection you are creating will be available to all users or just yourself, as shown in Figure 14-42. If the computer is a shared system and you want anyone to have access to the connection, you can make selection in this step. If the computer is not shared with other users or you do not want other users accessing the connection, select My use only. Click Next to continue.

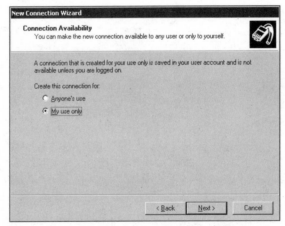

Figure 14-42: You can make the connection available to all users of the computer or just yourself.

9. After you have completed these steps, the connection is completed. In the final page of the wizard, you can select the option to have a shortcut to the connection placed on the desktop. Click Finish to complete the wizard.

The Connect dialog box is displayed, as shown in Figure 14-43. This is a good time to test the newly created VPN connection. Enter the username and password for the connection, and click the Connect button. You can also choose to save the password for either yourself only or all users on the computer.

Figure 14-43: The Connect dialog box is used to connect to the newly created VPN.

The VPN should connect with no problem. When the connection is active, an icon appears in the taskbar. You can click this icon to view details about the connection.

Implementing L2TP remote access VPNs

Implementing an L2TP VPN is similar to implementing other VPN types. As with PPTP Remote Access VPNs, you must first configure RRAS on the VPN server. Follow the directions in the "Implementing PPTP Router-to-Router VPNs" section of this chapter for the RRAS configuration only. Stop before you configure a demand dial interface because that is unnecessary in this case.

As with an L2TP router-to-router VPN, the server should have a computer certificate. Follow the directions in the "Implementing L2TP router-to-router VPNs" section for creating a computer certificate. After the computer certificate is created, you can configure RRAS to accept EAP authentication.

1. In the RRAS snap-in, right-click the server name and then select Properties.

2. Click the Security tab, and click the Authentication Methods button.

3. In the Authentication Methods dialog box, select Extensible Authentication Protocol and then click OK.

4. Click OK to close the server Properties dialog box.

You must next configure the remote access policy to accept EAP.

1. In the RRAS snap-in, select Remote Access Policies in the left pane under the server name.

2. Right-click the policy in the right pane, and select Properties.

3. Click the Edit Profile button.

4. In the Edit Dial-in Profile dialog box, click the Authentication tab, select EAP Methods, click Add, and select Smart Card or other Certificate from the drop-down box. Click OK and then click the Edit button.

5. In the Smart Card or other Certificate Properties dialog box, select the computer certificate created earlier, making sure to select the certificate residing in the enterprise root CA. Click OK to close the windows.

You are now almost ready to configure the VPN client. Only two steps remain to configure certificates for the connection first.

1. Open Internet Explorer in the client and go to the Certificate Services Web site for the CA in which the VPN server resides.

2. Click Download a CA certificate, certificate chain, or CRL.

3. Click install this CA certificate chain.

This will make the CA a trusted root CA for the client system, and allow the client to ensure the VPN server is authentic.

Now you must create a user certificate.

1. Make sure you are authenticated to the CA as the user with whom you will log on to the VPN. When you connect to the CA Web site, enter the domain logon credentials for that user.

2. Click Request a certificate and then click User Certificate.

3. You are notified that no more information is needed (because you are logged on as the domain user). Click the Submit button to request the certificate. The certificate should be issued automatically.

4. Click Install this certificate to install it into the local certificate store.

You are now ready to configure the VPN client. Follow the instructions for creating a VPN connection in the "Implementing PPTP Remote Access VPNs" section of this chapter to do the basic client configuration. You should now have a VPN connection in the Network Connections folder accessed by right-clicking My Network Places on the desktop, and selecting Properties.

1. Right-click the VPN connection, and select Properties.

2. Click the Networking tab and then select L2TP IPSec VPN from the Type of VPN drop-down box, as shown in Figure 14-44. The Automatic setting will often default to PPTP depending on the environment.

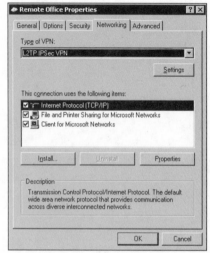

Figure 14-44: Select L2TP for the VPN type so PPTP is not used inadvertently.

3. Click the Security tab in the connection Properties dialog box.

4. In the Security tab, shown in Figure 14-45, select Advanced (custom settings), and click the Settings button.

5. In the Advanced Security Settings dialog box shown in Figure 14-46, select Use Extensible Authentication Protocol (EAP), and select Smart Card or other Certificate from the drop-down box. Click the Properties button.

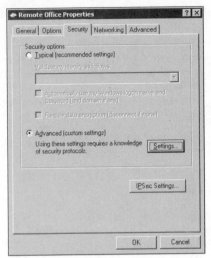

Figure 14-45: Select Advanced (custom settings) in the Security tab of the connection Properties dialog box to use a certificate for authentication.

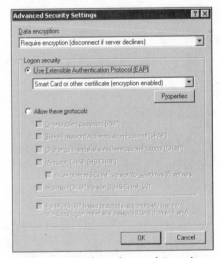

Figure 14-46: The Advanced Security Settings dialog box must be used to specify EAP authentication.

6. The Smart Card and other Certificates dialog box, shown in Figure 14-47, must be used to set what is used for authentication. A smart card can be used for authentication if it has been configured and a smart card reader is present by simply selecting Use my smart card. (See Chapter 10 for details on smart card authentication.) For this example, a certificate is used rather than a smart card. Select Use a certificate on this computer. Ensure that Validate server certificate is selected. Do not select Connect only if server name ends with, but select the CA established as a trusted root CA earlier from the drop-down box.

7. Click OK to save the settings in the three dialog boxes.

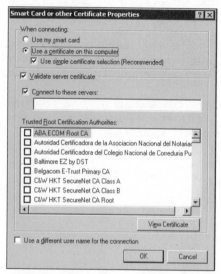

Figure 14-47: The Smart Card and other Certificates dialog box is used to configure the specifics of the EAP authentication.

Now that the configuration changes have been made, you should be able to double-click the VPN connection and it should connect automatically. You are not required to enter a username or password because the username is taken from the certificate, and the certificate is also used for authentication. Unlike with a user certificate for a router-to-router VPN, the user certificate created here is automatically assigned to the appropriate user account.

Summary

The focus of this chapter was on L2TP and PPTP VPNs. VPNs are quickly replacing the traditional dial-up method of connecting a client or network to your local network. A VPN is simply an encrypted tunnel over which all data is sent. VPNs use the Layer 2 Tunneling Protocol (L2TP) and the Point-to-Point Tunneling Protocol (PPTP) for creating the tunnel and encapsulating data.

PPTP is an extension to the Point-to-Point Protocol. With a PPTP VPN, a PPP connection is first created followed by a PPTP control connection. Encrypted PPP packets are sent over the PPTP tunnel. PPTP's main disadvantages are its authentication method and its relatively insecure encryption method.

L2TP is used in conjunction with IPSec. The advantage of using L2TP over PPTP is that it uses certificates for authentication and encryption. The main disadvantages are that pre-Windows 2000 clients do not support it and it cannot work with NAT.

One of the ways in which LANs can be interconnected is through the use of a LAN-to-LAN VPN. The remaining portions of the chapter provided step-by-step details on how to create and configure PPTP and L2TP router-to-router VPNs in Windows Server 2003.

✦   ✦   ✦

IPSec

IP Security (IPSec) is a protocol designed for tunneling IP data in an encrypted form over a network connection. IPSec also provides computer authentication so that each party in a connection can be sure of the authenticity of the other party.

IPSec attempts to provide-end-to-end security so that data is fully encrypted and secure from the source to the destination. At no point in transit is the data decrypted; decryption occurs only when it reaches its final destination. IPSec has been criticized for its excessive complexity leading to potential vulnerabilities due to administrative oversights, among other things. However, IPSec remains the best protocol currently available and supported for the functions that it performs. While IPSec is overly complex, Point-to-Point Tunneling Protocol (PPTP), which has similar functionality, is overly simplistic and insecure.

IPSec in Windows Server 2003 is used as the basis for Layer 2 Tunneling Protocol (L2TP) virtual private networks (VPNs). In addition, it can be used independently for securing IP network connections.

What is IPSec?

IPSec is a superset of two protocols and can operate in two modes. The two IPSec protocols are Authentication Header (AH) and Encapsulating Security Payload (ESP). AH is used only for authentication, integrity, and replay protection. It does not encrypt data. ESP, on the other hand, provides encryption as well as authentication, integrity, and anti-replay.

As stated, IPSec can operate in one of two modes, transport mode or tunnel mode. Transport mode secures only the IP packet payload, while tunnel mode secures the entire IP packet. Transport mode works by appending the AH or ESP header to the original IP packet header and securing the payload. Tunnel mode works by securing the original IP packet, including headers, and encapsulating the secured packet in another IP packet.

IPSec uses a protocol called Internet Key Exchange (IKE) before data is transmitted. IKE establishes the parameters of the IPSec connection. These parameters are collectively called a security association (SA). IKE occurs in two phases. The first phase is called main mode negotiation and comprises the establishment of an authenticated connection.

1. The two parties first negotiate the encryption and hash algorithms, the authentication method, and the Diffie-Hellman (DH) group to be used for key material.

2. The IKE process exchanges the public values used by the DH algorithm.

3. The DH algorithm is used to generate the master key. The master key is the key used for encryption through the remainder of the IKE process.

4. The last step in the first phase is authentication. The master key generated during the key exchange process is used to authenticate the two parties in the transaction.

The first phase of the IKE process is basically in place to secure the second phase of the process. The second phase, or quick mode negotiation, is used to establish the actual connection security. In the second phase, the computers negotiate the IPSec protocol (AH or ESP), and the encryption and hash algorithms. The session key is also refreshed so that the same key from the first phase of IKE is not reused. The final step is to submit all of the negotiated information and keys to the IPSec driver. A value called the security parameters index (SPI) is also sent. The SPI is a unique arbitrary value used to differentiate one SA from another. When a system has a number of IPSec connections, it will have a number of different SAs, one for each connection.

The keys generated by the IKE process do expire in time. This expiry (expire time) reduces the amount of damage that can be done if the session or master key is compromised. In fact, when the keys expire, the entire SA is renegotiated. You can, however, regenerate the session key by simply running through phase two of the IKE process and using phase one's cached results. This is done because phase one is far slower than phase two.

In addition to normal IPSec, which operates at Layer 3 in the ISO network model, IPSec is also an integral part of L2TP. IPSec provides the authentication and encryption functions while L2TP provides the Layer 2 tunneling function. IPSec can be used for tunneling in Windows Server 2003, but L2TP should be used in all cases where it is supported.

Configuring IPSec

IPSec is configured through two places in Windows Server 2003. It can be configured locally for the local computer only, or it can be configured in a group policy. To configure IPSec for the local computer, follow these steps:

1. Open MMC by clicking Start, Run, typing **mmc**, and clicking OK.

2. In the MMC console, select Add/Remove Snap-in from the File menu.

3. Click the Add button in the Add/Remove Snap-in dialog box. Figure 15-1 shows the Add Standalone Snap-in dialog box. This dialog box is used to add snap-ins to the MMC console.

4. Select the IP Security Policy Management snap-in and then click Add.

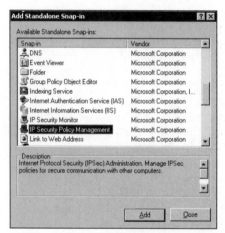

Figure 15-1: The Add Standalone Snap-in dialog box is used to add snap-ins to MMC.

5. When you select the IP Security Policy Management snap-in and click Add, you must then specify the scope that the snap-in will manage, as shown in Figure 15-2. You can manage the IPSec policies for the local computer or another computer or the local domain or a foreign domain. Select the scope for the snap-in, and click Finish.

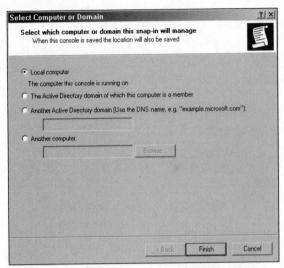

Figure 15-2: When adding the IP Security Policy Management snap-in, you must select the scope for which the policy will be managed.

6. Click Close to close the Add Standalone Snap-in dialog box. The snap-in you selected will now be displayed in the Add/Remove Snap-ins dialog box, as shown in Figure 15-3. Click OK to add the snap-in.

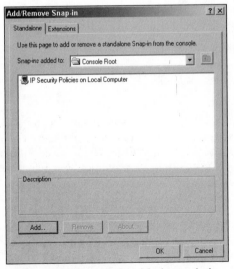

Figure 15-3: The newly added snap-in is shown in the list.

You can now work with the IP Security Policy Management snap-in for the local computer. You can also edit IPSec policies through group policies. This allows you to apply the IPSec policies to specific groups of users or computers or the entire domain, depending on how your group policies are configured. To edit IPSec policies through a group policy, take the following steps:

1. Open the Active Directory Users and Computers snap-in from the Start, Administrative Tools menu.

2. Right-click the domain for which the policy will be configured and then select Properties.

3. Click the Group Policy tab in the domain Properties dialog box, as shown in Figure 15-4.

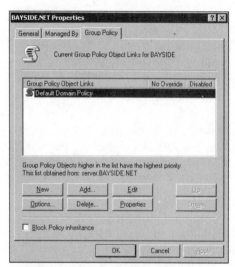

Figure 15-4: The Group Policy tab of a domain's Properties dialog box is used to configure policies for the domain.

4. In the Group Policy tab you will find at least one policy, the default domain policy created when Active Directory is installed. This policy applies to the entire domain. There may be other policies in your environment as well. Select the policy you want to edit, and click the Edit button. This will open the Group Policy snap-in.

5. Within the Group Policy snap-in, expand Windows Settings and then Security Settings under Computer Configuration, and select IP Security Policies on Active Directory, as shown in Figure 15-5.

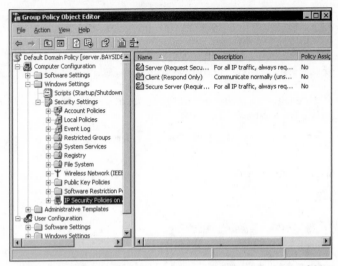

Figure 15-5: The IP Security Policies on Active Directory object in the Group Policy snap-in is used to configure IPSec for the group policy object.

After you open either the Group Policy snap-in or the IP Security Policy Management snap-in, you can add or edit IPSec policies. As you can see in Figure 15-5, three default IPSec policies are unassigned. The three predefined policies are Client (Respond Only), Server (Request Security), and Secure Server (Require Security).

If you are going to implement IPSec across your network, you will most likely want to configure most systems, such as workstations, with the Client (Respond Only) policy. Connections made using this policy do not use IPSec by default. They do, however, use IPSec if the remote machine requests an IPSec connection. Two computers configured to use this policy will not use IPSec to communicate.

For some server security with backward compatibility, you can use the Server (Request Security) policy. Computers using this policy request an IPSec connection with the remote system but allow unsecured communications if the remote system does not respond. With this policy, IPSec is used if the remote computer is using any of the predefined IPSec policies (Client, Server, or Secure Server), and IPSec is used if the remote system is not using an IPSec policy or does not support IPSec.

For systems for which security is important, the Secure Server policy can be used. The Secure Server policy requires the remote system to use IPSec or the connection is terminated. Remote systems using any of the predefined IPSec policies will communicate successfully using IPSec but systems not using an IPSec policy or systems not supporting IPSec will not communicate with this system at all.

As you can see, there is a lot to take into account when implementing IPSec. The Secure Server policy should only be used if all systems in the network are configured to use at least the Client policy and support IPSec. Configuring the entire domain to use the Client policy is not worthwhile because no systems will ever request communications using IPSec. Assigning these policies to specific computers is done through either a group policy object (GPO) specific to the computers using the policy, or through configuration directly on the local computer.

In addition to the predefined IPSec policies, you can create custom policies. Custom policies can be used to configure IPSec rules for traffic on the network in granular detail. The first step to configuring a custom policy is to create the policy itself. You can then configure rules for the policy, including filter lists. To create a new policy, take these steps:

1. Right-click IP Security Policies for Active Directory or IP Security Policies for Local Computer (depending on the scope of the snap-in you are using) and then select Create IP Security Policy.

2. The IP Security Policy Wizard is used to create a new policy. Click Next to continue past the wizard's introductory page.

3. Assign a name and, optionally, a description to the policy, as shown in Figure 15-6. Click Next to continue.

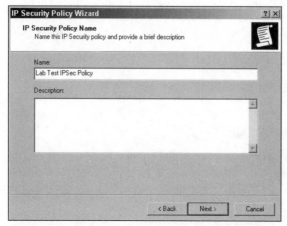

Figure 15-6: When creating a new IPSec policy you must first assign a name and optionally, a description.

4. Decide whether or not to activate the default response rule for this policy, as shown in Figure 15-7. The default response rule is used when a system requests an IPSec connection from the local computer to which the policy applies. If the default response rule is in place and no other rules apply, a default IPSec connection will be made. If no other rules apply and the default response rule is not in place, the connection will fail if it cannot fall back to an unsecured connection. Unless you have a specific reason to disable the default response rule, it should be enabled. Click Next to continue.

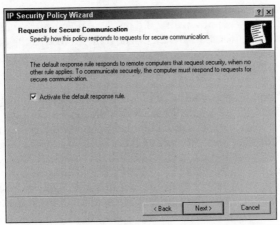

Figure 15-7: The default response rule is used in the case that no other rules match a request.

5. Figure 15-8 shows the final wizard step, which is only displayed if the default response rule was enabled in the previous step. You must set the authentication method for the default response rule. By default, the authentication method is Kerberos through Active Directory. You can also choose to use another certificate for authentication, or use a preshared key. Click Next to continue.

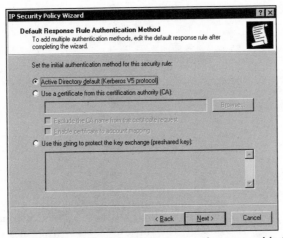

Figure 15-8: If the default response rule was enabled, you must specify the authentication method to be used with that rule.

6. The IP Security Policy Wizard is now complete. By default, the Properties dialog box for the policy opens automatically so you can further configure the policy after you close the wizard. You can deselect the Edit properties option to disable this behavior, but further configuration is necessary to have the policy do anything useful. Click Finish to close the wizard.

After you close the wizard, the Properties dialog box for the new policy will be displayed if the Edit properties option was not deselected. The Rules tab of the Properties dialog box, shown in Figure 15-9, is used to configure the policy rules. By default, the only rule in a policy is the default response rule, if that option was selected in the IP Security Policy Wizard. With only the default response rule in place, the policy is the equivalent to the Client (Respond Only) rule. To activate other functionality in the policy, you must create a new rule. When the Use Add Wizard option is selected in the Rules tab (as is the default), the Security Rule Wizard is used to add a new rule. If the option is not selected, the rule is created and you are taken to the Properties dialog box for the new rule.

1. With the Use Add Wizard option selected, click the Add button to create a new rule. Click Next to continue past the introduction page.

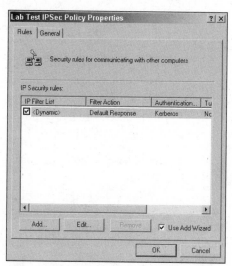

Figure 15-9: The Rules tab of the policy Properties dialog box is used to work with rules for the policy.

2. The first step in the Security Rule Wizard is the configuration of an IPSec tunnel, as shown in Figure 15-10. If you need to make a tunneled connection with a system that does not support L2TP, IPSec can be used to create a tunnel. This setting will determine if IPSec runs in tunnel mode or transport mode. In this case, select This rule does not specify a tunnel and then click Next.

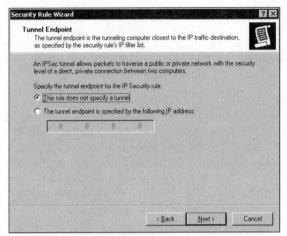

Figure 15-10: You need to decide if this rule specifies an IPSec tunnel and, if so, specify an endpoint.

Note

When creating a tunnel, two rules are required. One rule is for outgoing traffic and the tunnel endpoint will be the remote IPSec system. The other rule is for incoming traffic and the tunnel endpoint will be an IP address on the local system. Rules for tunnels must have filters which specify what traffic is sent or received over the tunnel. An IPSec Layer 3 tunnel is only used as an advanced server to server or router to router tunnel.

3. Figure 15-11 shows the next step in defining a policy rule. Specify what type of traffic the rule applies to: All network connections, Local area network (LAN), or Remote access. A rule applied to the LAN will only apply to traffic to and from the physical network interfaces on the system. A Remote Access rule will only apply to traffic on dial-up and VPN links. The default option selected is All network connections. Click Next to continue.

4. The step shown in Figure 15-12 requires you to select an IP filter for the traffic. This filter will specify what traffic is affected by this rule. There are two predefined filters: one that filters all IP traffic, and one filtering all ICMP traffic. You can also define your own IP filters. That process is explained later in this chapter. Select a filter and then click Next to continue.

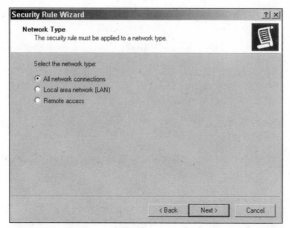

Figure 15-11: Select the type of connection to which the rule will apply.

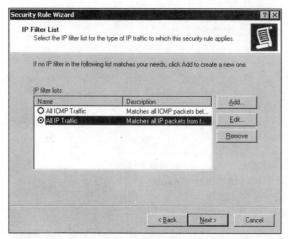

Figure 15-12: You must specify an IP Filter that will be used to determine to what traffic this rule applies.

5. Figure 15-13 shows the next step, which determines what action is taken by the rule. There are three predefined actions:

- Permit — The Permit action will use IPSec if the remote system requests it.

- Request Security — The Request Security will request IPSec and it will be used if the remote system supports it. If not, the connection will fall back to normal (non-IPSec) communications.

- Require Security — Require Security will request IPSec and will not allow communications with the remote system if IPSec is not supported.

In addition, you can define custom actions as discussed later. Choose an action and then click Next to continue.

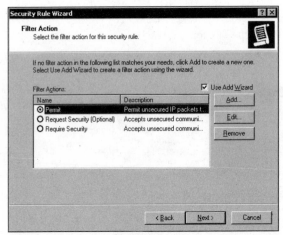

Figure 15-13: You must also specify an action to be taken when traffic matches the filter for a rule.

6. Click Finish to close the Security Rule Wizard. If the Edit properties option is selected, the properties window for the new rule appears. If you deselect this option, the rule will now appear in the list of rules in the policy Properties dialog box.

As previously stated, you can define custom IP Filter Lists and custom actions. These filter lists and actions are valid for any policy in the current scope (that is, the local computer or Active Directory). To define a custom filter list, edit a rule and then click the IP Filter List tab, as shown in Figure 15-14. Create a new filter by clicking the Add button.

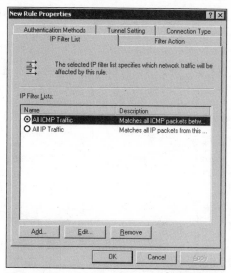

Figure 15-14: The IP Filter List tab of the Edit Rule Properties dialog box is used to select a filter or create a custom filter.

The IP Filter List dialog box shown in Figure 15-15 is used to create a custom filter.

1. Assign a name to the filter. Optionally, you can also add a description. After you have done that, you can begin to configure specific filters. Make sure the Use Add Wizard box is checked and then click the Add button to add a filter.

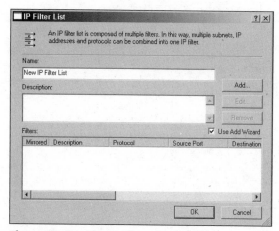

Figure 15-15: The IP Filter List dialog box is used to configure custom filter sets for rules.

2. The IP Filter Wizard has three steps. Click Next to bypass the introduction.

3. As shown in Figure 15-16, type in a description or name for the new filter. You can select the Mirrored option at the bottom of the window to specify a filter in each direction. This option causes the filter to match both the specified source and destination address and the mirror of those addresses.

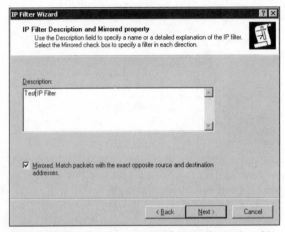

Figure 15-16: The first step in the IP Filter Wizard is to assign a description or name to the filter.

4. Specify a source IP address. As shown in Figure 15-17, from the drop-down box, you can specify any of the following:

   • Your IP address

   • Any address

   • A specific address

   • A specific DNS name

   • An entire IP subnet

   • DNS Servers

   • WINS Servers

   • DHCP server

   • Default Gateway

   Make a selection from the list, specify any other required information, and click Next to continue.

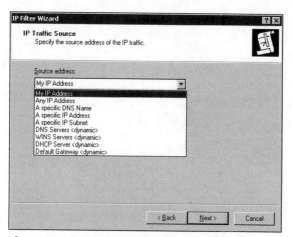

Figure 15-17: Configuring the source IP address

5. Set the destination address for the filter. This process is identical to the previous step where you set the source address. Remember that if you don't want to filter based on source or destination address, select Any IP Address from the list; however, the source and destination addresses cannot be the same. You can also filter based on the protocol and port number. Figure 15-18 shows that you can select a protocol type from the list. You can also select Any if you do not want to filter based on a protocol.

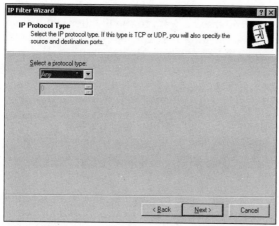

Figure 15-18: You can filter traffic based on the Layer 3 protocol.

If you do choose to filter based on a protocol and select either TCP or UDP, you can also filter based on the TCP or UDP port, as shown in Figure 15-19. As you can see, the filtering capability for IPSec is granular, and you can configure IPSec to be required for certain applications, for example.

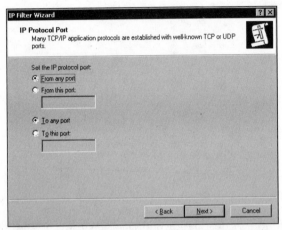

Figure 15-19: If you choose to filter based on TCP or UDP, you can also specify the ports on which to filter.

6. You can now click Finish to close the IP Filter Wizard. The new filter will appear in the list.

After you have added all of the filters you want to the IP Filter List dialog box and given it a name, click OK to save the filter list. The list will appear in the IP Filter Lists tab of the Edit Rule Properties dialog box. You can now use that filter list to filter traffic for a rule.

You can configure custom actions for a rule as well.

1. From the properties dialog box for the rule, click the Filter Action tab, ensure the Use Add Wizard option is selected, and click the Add button.

2. The Filter Action Wizard is used to create a new action. Click Next to bypass the introduction page.

3. Assign a name to the new action and, optionally, specify a description. Click Next to continue.

4. Specify a general action (permit, deny, or negotiate security), as shown in Figure 15-20. Permit and deny are obvious and affect all traffic. This is essentially a packet filtering option. Select Negotiate Security and then click Next.

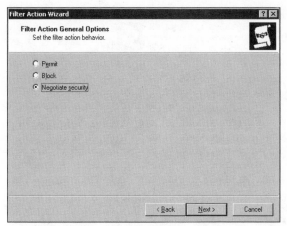

Figure 15-20: When configuring an action, you can
expressly permit or deny all traffic or negotiate IP security.

5. Specify what is to be done when communicating with systems that do not support IPSec, as shown in Figure 15-21. These systems may either not support
IPSec at all or may not have it enabled. You can either choose not to communicate with these systems at all, or fall back to unsecured communication. For
strict security, choose not to communicate with them at all.

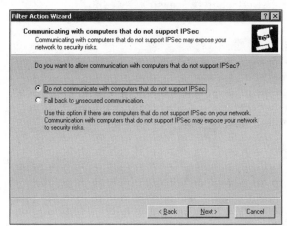

Figure 15-21: You must decide what to do when a
remote system does not support IPSec.

6. Figure 15-22 shows the next step in the wizard where you can decide what
type of security to provide, integrity and encryption or encryption only. This
determines whether the AH or ESP protocol is used. You can also select
Custom and then click the Settings button to set a custom configuration.

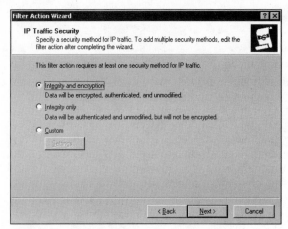

Figure 15-22: You can specify encryption and authentication or authentication only for the action or specify custom settings.

7. If you select Custom and click the Settings button, the Custom Security Method Settings dialog box is displayed, as shown in Figure 15-23. You can specify whether to use AH or ESP and select the algorithms for each. In this dialog box you can also specify a custom session key expiration based on bytes transferred or time elapsed. If a session key expiration is not specified, the session key is renewed when the master key expires.

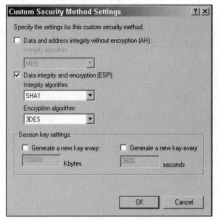

Figure 15-23: If you choose to use a custom security method, you can configure the algorithms and session key expiration.

8. Click Finish to close the Filter Action Wizard. The new filter action will appear in the list of filter actions for the policy. Select the action and then click the Edit button. The Security Methods tab of the filter action Properties dialog box is shown in Figure 15-24. A few settings cannot be set in the wizard.

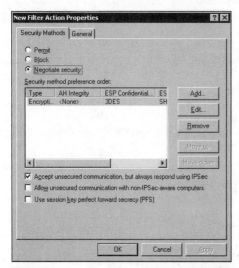

Figure 15-24: The Security Methods tab of the action Properties dialog box is used to configure security for the IPSec connection.

The Security Methods tab contains three options:

- Accept unsecured communication, but always respond using IPSec — This option, when enabled, will allow unsecured incoming connections to the local system but will only allow IPSec connections when the response is sent to the remote system. This is a useful option in that you can configure a server with this option and clients with the Client (Respond Only) IPSec policy and all communications with client computers will be IPSec-secured except the initial connection.

- Allow unsecured communication with non-IPSec-aware computer — This option allows fallback to normal IP communication if the remote system does not support IPSec. This option is configurable from the wizard, as previously shown.

- Session key perfect forward secrecy (PFS) — This option causes new keying material to be used when the session key is refreshed. Only one session key will be created with the same keying material. If the same keying material is used to create a number of session keys (this option is disabled), certain cryptographic attacks are possible on the session key. That is a very small risk, but if you are extremely security conscious you can enable this option with a small performance loss.

You can also specify more than one security method in the Security Methods tab by clicking the Add button and configuring another method. You can arrange the order in which these methods are used with the Move Up and Move Down buttons.

In addition to configuring rules, an IPSec policy has a number of other options that can be configured.

Open the policy Properties dialog box (right-click the policy and select Properties) and click the General tab, as shown in Figure 15-25. The Check for policy changes every x minutes option is used to specify how often the IPSec Policy Agent checks for policy updates in Active Directory.

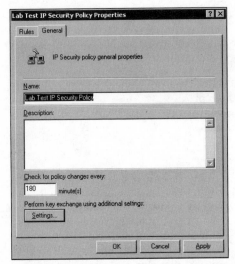

Figure 15-25: The General tab of the policy Properties dialog box can be used to set the policy update time and advanced IKE settings.

In the policy Properties dialog box's General tab, click the Settings button. The Key Exchange Settings dialog box, shown in Figure 15-26, is used to set the IKE properties for the policy. The Master key perfect forward secrecy PFS option causes the master key to require new keying material every time it is regenerated. Again, if this setting is disabled, the master key is slightly more vulnerable to cryptanalysis. The dialog box can also be used to specify the master key's expiry in minutes or sessions. A single master key is used to generate a number of session keys.

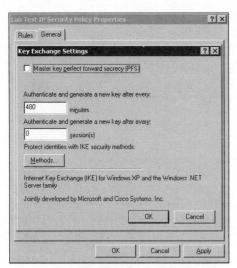

Figure 15-26: The Key Exchange Settings dialog box can be used to configure advanced IKE settings.

By clicking the Methods button in the Key Exchange Settings dialog box, you can configure the valid IKE protocols, as shown in Figure 15-27. This is a very advanced task but you can add, remove, and edit the protocols that are used for phase one of the IKE process and change the order in which the allowed methods are attempted.

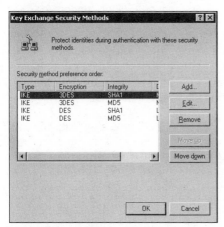

Figure 15-27: The Key Exchange Security Methods dialog box is used to customize the algorithms used for IKE.

As you can see, you can configure IPSec in a number of very different ways. Using rules and policies, you can configure two systems to communicate with each other using a preshared key, with other systems using Kerberos and Active Directory, and other systems using certificates. Rules provide a very granular way of filtering traffic and taking specific actions on that traffic. Security can be configured between specific systems only (such as between a database and application server), or enterprise wide for all systems.

IPSec Hardware

IPSec, being encryption, is generally math intensive. Computer processors are just big number crunchers, so it makes sense that math-intensive processes would not cause a problem. Encryption uses a different type of math than a general purpose CPU is built for, however, and this puts quite a load on a traditional CPU. A system running many encryption operations, such as a VPN server, could have an enormous CPU load just from the encryption and decryption operations.

For a quite some time now, cryptographers and cryptanalysts have been using encryption-specific processors. These processors are optimized for the type of number crunching required for encryption. In fact, one of the most powerful unclassified cryptanalysis machines ever built was made up of a large number of processors made specifically for the type of cryptanalysis being done, all operating in parallel. This system was far faster than an equivalent number of general purpose CPUs running in parallel and was used to crack DES.

Note   The system of cryptanalysis-specific processors working in parallel, called Deep Crack, was built by the Electronic Frontier Foundation (EFF) for under $250,000.

A number of hardware devices are built specifically for IPSec processing, as well. Offloading this processing to a hardware device both frees up CPU cycles for other purposes, and is more efficient due to the external processors' task-specific design. Intel and 3com both have network adapters with IPSec acceleration built in. A number of additional IPSec acceleration options are available.

Another direction can be taken in offloading the IPSec processing from the CPU. Companies that have integrated IPSec processing, such as Cisco, make a number of hardware-based VPN devices. Rather than offloading IPSec processing from the server, the entire VPN connection process is offloaded to a specific piece of hardware.

Summary

The focus of this chapter was on implementing IP Security. IPSec is a security protocol designed to provide end-to-end security so data transferred between computers is encrypted and secure. IPSec consists of two protocols. Authentication Header (AH) provides authentication, integrity, and replay protection. Encapsulation Security Payload (ESP) provides encryption, authentication, integrity, and replay protection.

IPSec can operate in one of two modes: transport mode or tunnel mode. In transport mode, only the IP packet payload in secured. In tunnel mode, the entire IP payload, including the header, is secured.

IPSec can be configured locally or through a group policy. By default, there are three IPSec policies, none of which are assigned. Assigning the Client (Respond Only) policy means that computers will not use IPSec unless requested to do so. The Server (Request Security) policy configures the computer to request secured communications but will also allow unsecured communications. The Server (Require Security) policy requires secure communications or the connection is terminated. Additional IPSec policies can be configured.

The chapter also looked at configuring IPSec. Using policies and rules, you can configure how two computers communicate using a pre-shared key, using Kerberos, and using certificates. Rules enable you to filter traffic and define the actions to take on that traffic.

✦   ✦   ✦

Microsoft Internet Security and Acceleration Server

ISA Server Overview

With Internet Security and Acceleration (ISA) Server, Microsoft has provided a full-featured firewall and caching server, offering products that have traditionally required purchase from a third-party vendor, and often as separate packages. The closest product that Microsoft has produced in the past is Proxy Server 2.0, which is actually quite different.

Proxy Server was a way of having a single egress point for all users to access the Internet. This allowed for content and access control as well as simple caching of content. When users are surfing the Web, for example, data is cached so that if another user accesses the same Web site they are provided the cached version instead of making another request for the information. This content caching is an easy way of providing a savings in bandwidth because when Proxy Server was released, bandwidth was expensive and scarce. Many Proxy Servers use a modem to connect to the Internet and share the connection between multiple computers.

Bandwidth has become cheap and plentiful since the release of Proxy Server 2.0. xDSL and other broadband connections are common, and connection sharing has been integrated into Windows, making Proxy Server unnecessary. It has since been phased out in favor of ISA Server. ISA Server also has similar content caching capabilities but it expands on the simplistic nature of Proxy Server.

ISA Server is a firewall as well as a content cache capable of both forward and reverse caching.

ISA Server is installed on a Windows Server 2003 or Windows 2000 Server. The hardware required depends on the load that the system will handle, but should include at least two network interfaces — one for the internal and one for the external networks if it will be used as a firewall. If it is strictly for caching, one network adapter can be used but it is not uncommon to see caching servers with multiple interfaces, depending on their configuration.

An Overview of Firewalls

A firewall is a host that controls the flow of traffic in and out of your private network (refer to Figure 16-1). The firewall is located at the ingress and egress points on the network, as discussed in Chapter 2. Its job is to inspect the packets passing through its network interfaces, and either allow or deny the traffic. Most firewalls also include support for virtual private networks (VPNs) and other features.

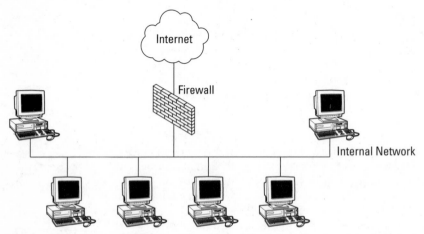

Figure 16-1: A firewall resides on the edge of the internal network and controls incoming and outgoing traffic.

It is vitally important to have a firewall on a network that is connected to any untrusted network, including the Internet. Chapter 2 outlines the ingress and egress points for traffic on the network. There must be a firewall at each ingress or egress point, although on many networks one firewall serves as both the ingress and egress point. By filtering traffic at these points, you can control what type of traffic is allowed to reach specific machines and limit that traffic to avoid potential security attacks. In most cases, the firewall is the outermost layer of network security.

Firewalls come in hardware or software configurations, with advantages and disadvantages to both. Hardware firewalls include the following:

✦ Cisco PIX

✦ Netscreen

✦ SonicWALL

✦ WatchGurard Firebox

Hardware firewalls have dedicated hardware and software developed specifically for the purpose of security. Most are available in different sizes with different throughput rates and numbers of interfaces. The main advantages to hardware firewalls are that they are often able to flow more traffic than a software firewall, require less administration for both the initial setup and day-to-day use, and they are completely independent from the operating system. The main disadvantage to hardware firewalls is cost.

Software firewalls include products such as the following:

✦ Microsoft ISA Server

✦ Checkpoint Firewall-1

✦ Axent Raptor

These firewalls are installed on standard hardware running an operating system such as Microsoft Windows or UNIX. These systems need at least two network interfaces — one for the internal network, and one for the external network. Software firewalls are advantageous because they run on hardware and software with which you are already familiar, and are usually cheaper than hardware firewalls. They provide organizations with a cost effective and efficient way of implementing a firewall solution. The major disadvantage is that they usually cannot handle as much traffic as a dedicated hardware firewall.

Some hybrid firewalls are also available. These systems are dedicated hardware systems running modified versions of standard software firewalls.

The operation of any firewall depends on the capability of the software to inspect the incoming and outgoing packets. Each packet is subjected to a set of rules to determine if it is allowed or denied. The most basic type of firewall is a packet filter that looks at the source and destination ports and addresses of the packet to determine its disposition.

Firewalls are a vital part of network and system security, but they are certainly not a complete security solution. As is stressed many times in this book, you can only achieve security by implementing security functions on multiple levels.

Both hardware and software firewalls are vulnerable to compromise. The worst possible attack on a firewall is one that results in the firewall becoming open to the flow of any packets in and out of the trusted network, allowing the attack on a system that is normally protected. A number of exploits for various firewalls involve buffer overflows, malformed packets, and other attacks that can disable a firewall or compromise its user interface. The behavior of an attacked firewall ranges from all traffic being blocked (the firewall crashes) to full access being granted to the attacker. Full access allows the attacker to change the firewall rules and gain access to the internal network.

Hardware firewalls are provided with some sort of user interface, such as telnet, an internal Web server, or any combination of these and other access methods. If these user interfaces are allowed to be accessed from the untrusted side of the firewall (which is often optional), they are open to attack. A user interface open to untrusted users may be vulnerable to buffer overflows, even if it is secured with a username and password. The best defense against such an attack is to limit access to these user interfaces with access lists based on IP addresses and to block all access from the untrusted side of the network. Even if access is required from the untrusted network, there are more secure ways of providing it, such as through a secure host on the internal network. This host can be secured through a strong encryption protocol such as SSH. Users must first connect through the firewall to the SSH accessible host using their encryption keys and then connect from that host to the firewall. Access to this host should also be limited by an access control list at the firewall to a specific set of IP addresses, although this is not always possible. Using such a configuration will also avoid passwords being sniffed on the network. If the firewall provides built-in SSH access, this can also be employed directly from the untrusted side of the network, although the SSH host may also be vulnerable to buffer overflows and other exploits.

The second type of common vulnerability in a hardware firewall is a denial of service (DoS) attack. Network devices are designed to accept packets formed according to the corresponding standards for a given protocol, normally documented in IEEE RFCs. When packets are sent to the device that are not formed in accordance with the standards (malformed packets), the device must have some method of handling them. Although most malformed packets are dealt with appropriately on most devices (usually discarded), some devices do not have proper handling for certain types of bad packets. A malformed packet to which a firewall is vulnerable can cause unpredictable results. Malformed packet exploits can cause a number of results, most often a denial of service by crashing the device.

Software firewalls are vulnerable to many of the same attacks as hardware firewalls, as well as to attacks on their base operating systems. This is a vulnerability specific to software firewalls as hardware firewalls have an operating system that is both built in to the device and designed for security. This is one of the largest downsides to using a software-based firewall; however, if the operating system is configured securely, this risk is greatly reduced. By attacking the operating system using common exploits, the attacker can cause the same results as an attack on the firewall software. Operating system attacks are more common than firewall hardware attacks because there are more security researchers and hackers with operating system knowledge.

By attacking a vulnerability in the software-based firewall's operating system, the attacker could cause any of the following:

✦ A denial of service

✦ A leak of information

✦ A change in the firewall's behavior

✦ A full compromise of the system

To combat these potential security problems, you need to fully secure the operating system and audit the firewall often.

Stateful and non-stateful inspection

The most basic type of firewall, as previously discussed, is a simple packet filter. It inspects the source and destination ports and addresses of each packet, and allows or denies the packet based on a set of rules configured by the administrator. This is known as *non-stateful inspection*. This is a fast and efficient type of firewall, but leaves specific ports and addresses wide open to attack as configured in the ruleset.

Packet filters only inspect the layer 3 (IP) and layer 4 (TCP, UDP, ICMP, and so on) headers of a packet. The source and destination addresses and ports are determined, but the filter does not inspect the other packet headers or the payload. A packet filter is not aware of the type of data traveling in the packet.

Most modern firewalls perform stateful packet inspection. Stateful packet inspection checks more of the packet header than just the source and destination addresses and ports. Stateful inspection tracks each flow of packets to ensure that it is valid. Most TCP flows form an incoming connection to an application such as Web or FTP, and the application opens a path back to the client to return data, normally on a non-privileged port higher than 1024. A stateful inspection firewall tracks the incoming connection such as a packet filter, but also inspects the return path created by the application. It is examined for inconsistencies such as changes in port numbers or IP addresses from the incoming connection. By watching for these changes, the stateful inspection firewall can avoid session hijacking and other attacks.

There is also a type of firewall that is more advanced than just stateful inspection. Some firewalls provide application filtering or proxying. Application filtering controls the entire flow of packets to and from an application to ensure that the packets are valid and the session is allowed. While stateful inspection examines the packet header, application filtering inspects the entire packet, header and payload. This level of application filtering is fairly slow, but provides more security than other less thorough inspection methods.

Firewall scalability

Due to the inspection of each packet, the loads on the processor of a firewall can become quite heavy. To meet the increasing demands being placed on firewalls, most vendors develop firewall solutions that are scalable to some point. Firewall scalability is addressed in a number of ways. Software firewalls can be moved to more powerful systems, while hardware firewalls must be upgraded to more powerful models. This is known as *scaling up*.

Scaling out is the practice of adding more systems, as opposed to adding capacity to existing systems. You can utilize an array of firewalls in several ways depending on the type of firewall you are using. Microsoft ISA Server allows you to use the network load-balancing feature of Windows to balance between multiple firewalls. After you reach a certain point, however, you may find it more effective to employ a proper firewall load-balancing device. For example, devices such as the Radware FireProof and the Cisco CSS series content switches are dedicated switches. They are fully intelligent and can balance between a number of firewalls based on several metrics. They read load data from the firewalls, and send traffic to the fastest or least-loaded firewall.

The key in both cases is to know the performance statistics of your firewall. Keep a record of CPU and memory utilization as well as traffic levels. As those levels rise and you have more history in your logs, you can begin to predict when you will need to scale your firewalls. By following basic performance monitoring practices, you can proactively address firewall load before it becomes a problem and users begin to notice slow network performance and even outages.

Intrusion Detection Systems

Intrusion Detection Systems (IDSs) are systems that are put in place to detect attacks on the network. A true IDS is meant to only listen on a network and to be undetectable, although many implementations of IDSs are not this strict. A number of IDSs are available, including the following:

✦ Network Flight Recorder (NFR)

✦ ISS RealSecure (on which the IDS capabilities in Microsoft ISA Server are based)

✦ The Cisco Intrusion Detection System (formerly NetRanger)

Many firewall products including personal firewalls also implement some type of intrusion detection system. In addition to detecting attacks, IDSs provide for forensics when an attack has occurred. By analyzing the logs, you can determine where the security vulnerabilities exist in the network. They can also provide evidence for prosecution in some cases.

A strict IDS is configured so that it can listen only on the target network. Cutting the data-send wires on its network cable or creating a custom cable without those connections sometimes accomplishes this. This creates a system that is fully capable of receiving data from the network but completely incapable of sending data. This makes it totally impossible for an attacker to learn of the existence of the IDS logically. It is still possible for an attacker to learn of the IDS physically, so they are often hidden. The reason for making an IDS physically undetectable is in case of an attacker from inside your organization. Ideally, the existence of the IDS is known by as few people as possible in the organization.

After the IDS is in place listening on the target network (it must be connected to a switch port which mirrors all traffic if you have a switched network), there must be some method of getting the data out of the IDS. For an IDS that is blackened (not visible to the target network), the data is retrieved using an out of band (OOB) connection such as a modem or private network. IDSs that are not so strict can have their data sent over the monitored network. In some cases, the data is sent to a secure log host to which data can be written but not erased. A secure log host is used so that the attacker, if they were to locate the IDS or log host, cannot delete the evidence they have left.

An IDS works through two methods. The first is by comparing the network traffic it is monitoring to the patterns of known attacks stored in the IDS. The second is through a predictive mechanism that looks for potential attacks for which it does not yet have patterns. By looking at different traffic flows, the IDS can determine which are potential attacks and send an alert so that the appropriate action can be taken.

Most full IDSs use a system of sensors with a central management point. Sensors are often placed on each network segment and their data is collected by the central management system. The management system is responsible for reporting and alerting while the sensors are responsible for detection. The sensors can be integrated into existing systems or separate units. See Figure 16-2.

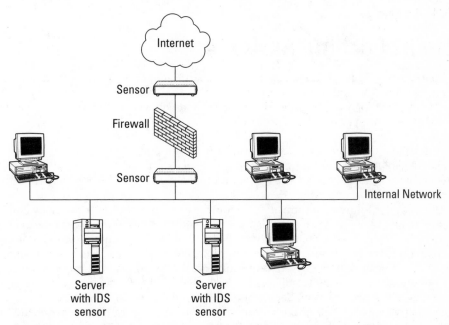

Figure 16-2: A full intrusion detection suite uses sensors at various points in the network.

There are a number of implementations of IDSs. The most common is when the IDS is integrated into a firewall product. Many firewalls have some IDS capability built in. When attacks are detected, an event is added to the log and, depending on the configuration, an alert is sent via e-mail or another channel.

Although many organizations do not implement them, full IDS suites provide the best security. Full IDS systems are often quite expensive and are not seen as a necessity because a less powerful IDS is included with many firewalls. After one serious attack, however, the necessity of a full IDS often becomes clear. Full IDSs are also large and difficult to implement and maintain, especially on larger networks with many components.

One major downfall to IDSs is that they are prone to false alarms. Sometimes legitimate traffic flows will trigger an alert in an IDS, leaving the administrator to deal with a non-existent situation. It is possible to reduce the occurrence of false alarms, but this often decreases the IDS's sensitivity to actual attacks. If you notice an exceptionally large number of specific false alarms (compared to the number of attacks), it may pay to reduce the IDS sensitivity to that type of attack. In the case of just a few false alarms, leaving the system alone is best. It is important, however, to always be vigilant with every alert from the IDS because one of the alerts you choose to ignore could be a major compromise of your network. False alarms are common if your IDS is configured to alert on port scans, as these are extremely common on the Internet from both institutions and attackers. Port scans could be an indication of a pending attack, but many are simply scans of massive blocks of addresses.

Content Caching Systems

Content caching is a transparent method of storing data on a fast system at a convenient point on your network. Content caching can reduce bandwidth usage when configured in forward caching configuration and can ease the load on Web servers when configured as a reverse proxy cache.

With ISA Server, Microsoft has provided a full content-caching solution. A content-caching solution is used for a number of reasons. Content caching is used to store content on a fast server for the acceleration of a given service, normally HTTP.

Although it is an oversimplification, a content caching solution is normally configured in one of two ways, either forward or reverse. Forward caching is the caching of content requested by users on your internal network. Caching this data locally can reduce the bandwidth usage on your Internet connection. Caching can also decrease response time for Web requests, especially when the Internet connection is slow, unreliable, or heavily utilized. For forward caching, the caching server is configured as a Web proxy server. Each workstation on the network is configured to use the caching server as a Web proxy server, and all Web page requests are then made to the cache instead of the actual site. If the content is available in the cache, it is served directly to the client avoiding any connection to the Internet (see Figure 16-3). If the content is not available, the cache retrieves it from the Internet, serves it to the client, and caches it pending the next request. Content that is not cacheable, such as dynamic content, is always retrieved by the caching server and served to the client.

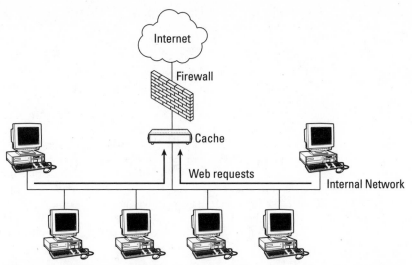

Figure 16-3: Forward caching is used to accelerate internal users' Web access and to reduce bandwidth usage.

Reverse caching is used to reduce the load on your Web servers. As show in Figure 16-4, the caching server is placed between the Web server and the egress point. Clients connect directly to the caching server instead of the Web server and it does one of several things:

✦ If the requested data is cached in the caching server, it is served directly from the cache.

✦ If the data is cacheable and not stored in the caching server, the caching server requests the data from the Web server, serves it to the client, and caches the data for the next request.

✦ Data that is not cacheable such as dynamic content is requested from the Web server and served to the client.

Eventually, cached content becomes *stale*. Web sites are often changed on a regular basis and after this occurs, the cached content and the actual content no longer match. Caching servers implement algorithms to avoid caching stale content. The server can specify the cache time in the HTTP response, but often the caching server must determine the optimal caching time itself. This amount of time is commonly determined as a factor of the amount of time since a given object was last modified. If an object has not been modified for a long time, it is cached for a longer period (it is assumed to be changed less often). Objects modified recently are cached for a shorter period to ensure they do not become stale.

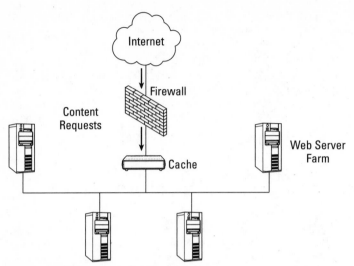

Figure 16-4: Reverse caching eases the load on internal Web servers and accelerates client access.

Software-based content caching

There are a number of software-based content-caching systems including the following:

- ✦ Microsoft ISA Server
- ✦ Inktomi
- ✦ Squid

Software-based content-caching systems are installed on existing hardware and standard operating systems, similar to software-based firewalls. Software-based caching systems have the capability to be expanded with common hardware and are often more flexible than hardware-based solutions. For example, you can add more standard disks to your caching server if you need more space, or upgrade the Central Processing Unit (CPU) if the unit is slow.

Hardware-based content caching

There are also a number of dedicated hardware caching devices, including the following:

- ✦ Cisco Cache Engine
- ✦ F5 Edge-FX Cache
- ✦ Network Appliance NetCache

These systems have dedicated hardware platforms and operating systems that are developed specifically for the application. These systems are much faster than software-based systems but require specific hardware for expansion and are not as scalable as a software system that uses commodity hardware or can be moved to a more powerful server. Upgrading the disk space on a hardware-caching device is more difficult than on a software-based system. You are often required to purchase disks and external disk units from the hardware vendor, and sometimes they are not upgradeable at all. They are also typically more expensive than software systems. Hardware caches are normally managed like networking products such as switches and routers.

Caching server scalability

Caching servers scale similarly to firewalls. Most caching servers can be configured in arrays. Some caching solutions have this functionality built in, but others require an external unit to provide this feature. Systems such as the Cisco CSS series of application switches and the Radware Cache Server Director (CSD) are external devices for load balancing caching servers.

An array of caching servers presents an inefficiency though. When a user connects through one server in the array, the content is cached on that unit. If the user then connected to another server in the array to access the same content, it would be cached on that server also. Eventually, each caching server would have cached the same data. A better idea would be to cache content on only one caching server and direct requests for that content to the respective unit in the array. This is possible through a number of methods, most of which are vendor specific. The next section discusses these methods.

Caching methods and protocols

There are a number of methods of configuring a caching server in addition to having it directly in line between the client and server. For example, Cisco's Web Cache Communication Protocol (WCCP) allows the caching server (which must support WCCP) to reside almost anywhere.

In addition, as discussed in the last section, an array of caching servers should have some method of directing requests for cached items to a specific server so that the content is not cached on a number of different servers. Microsoft's Cache Array Routing Protocol (CARP) is an example of such a solution.

Web Cache Communication Protocol

Cisco's Web Cache Communication Protocol (WCCP) is used when Cisco routers, or other routers that support WCCP and WCCP-aware caching devices are used together. WCCP is used by the devices to transparently redirect certain requests to the caching device or array of devices. WCCP delegates the traffic redirection decisions to the routers, and the caching devices only handle cacheable traffic.

Using WCCP, clients do not have to make any changes to their configuration because the redirections are done transparently. This avoids having to specify the caching server as a Web proxy server in the Web browser settings for forward caching or specify the cache server as the Web host for reverse proxy caching.

Cache Array Routing Protocol

Microsoft's Cache Array Routing Protocol (CARP) is a protocol used to distribute traffic among an array of caching servers. Servers are listed in an Array Membership List stored in Active Directory, and clients that support CARP are configured to retrieve a configuration script from any member of the array.

The configuration script retrieved by the client contains the array membership list and a hashing algorithm. The hashing algorithm is used to determine what content is stored on each member of the array. The algorithm uses a combination of a hash of the URL requested, a hash of each server's hostname, and a load factor assigned to each server to determine the preferred server for that particular content. By using this hashing algorithm, the same piece of content does not need to be kept on each server in the array, as requests will come to the preferred server first. If the preferred server for that content is not available, the second most preferred server (based on the hashing algorithm) is used.

To use CARP, you must be running ISA Server Enterprise Edition (as it is required to implement an array of caching servers). Also, each ISA Server within the array must be a member of the same Active Directory domain.

ISA Server Features

Microsoft ISA Server is a full-featured software-based firewall and content-caching solution. With one Microsoft Windows 2003 Server or Windows 2000 Server, you can have a firewall and content cache without the expenditure of purchasing more than one server and software solution or costly hardware-based systems.

ISA Server enables you to have both firewall and caching solutions on a single server. Such a layout is advantageous because it reduces initial cost and administrative overhead. Providing both services on a single box means only one system is added into the network layout at the edge of the trusted network, and you do not need to determine the optimum location for the caching device.

After the network traffic reaches a certain threshold (based on the performance of the firewall/caching server's hardware configuration), this solution becomes a bottleneck in the network layout. By separating the firewall from the caching server, more resources can be given to each to improve performance.

Windows Server integration

ISA Server integrates with Windows 2003 Server or Windows 2000 Server. The integration utilizes the Windows Server security, directory, bandwidth control, and VPN features and adds the firewall and caching services included with ISA Server to create a complete security and acceleration solution.

ISA Server includes management tools that allow for the configuration of policies for all of its features. All of the features of ISA Server are configured through a Microsoft Management Console (MMC) snap-in.

ISA Server supports all Windows authentication methods, such as NTLM and Kerberos. This integration allows ISA Server to authenticate clients for particular traffic.

Requirements

ISA Server requires Windows 2003 Server or Windows 2000 Server on a system with at least the following specifications:

✦ 300MHz CPU

✦ 256MB RAM

✦ 20MB hard drive space

✦ One NTFS formatted volume

✦ One network interface for caching, two for firewalls

These specifications should provide for up to 500 users in a forward-caching configuration with 2 to 4 GB of disk space allocated for caching, or 100 hits per second in a reverse caching configuration. As traffic increases, the hardware requirements also increase. With any more than 1,000 users or 250 hits per second, the ISA Server firewall and acceleration components should be separated onto individual systems.

As with all servers accessible to the Internet, ISA Server should be installed as a standalone system and not added to a domain. This increases the security of the other servers should the system be compromised. The exception to this rule is ISA Server Enterprise Edition if the system will be a server in an array. Because array information is stored within Active Directory, array members must be part of a Windows 2000 or Windows 2003 domain.

Firewall features

Microsoft ISA Server provides a wide variety of security features, from basic filtering to advanced intrusion detection and application filters.

Microsoft ISA Server's firewall filtering is designed in layers. At the first layer is a packet filter, followed by a circuit filter and application filter.

System hardening

One of ISA Server's most interesting features is automated system hardening. This process uses the system policy objects to enable security features built into the operating system and also disable a number of services that are not necessary for an ISA Server. This reduces the profile of the system to a potential attacker, as there are not nearly as many points to attack.

As shown in Figure 16-5, System hardening is performed through the ISA Server Security Configuration Wizard. There are three levels of system hardening available:

✦ **Secure**—The default level of hardening is Secure. The Secure setting is used when there are other applications running on the system. This ensures that required services are not disabled but is less secure than the other modes.

✦ **Limited Services**—Limited Services is used for ISA Servers that are running in integrated mode with both firewall and acceleration services. This is more secure than the Secure setting, and will disable any applications running on the system but still allow the acceleration service to operate.

✦ **Dedicated**—The most secure mode is Dedicated. This will disable all applications and unnecessary services (including the ISA acceleration service) and only the firewall portion of ISA Server will be able to operate.

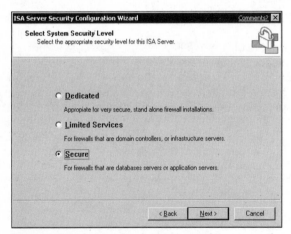

Figure 16-5: System hardening is used to secure the computer on which the firewall resides.

Intrusion detection

An IDS is built in to ISA Server based on the technology developed by Internet Security Systems (ISS). ISS produces a product called RealSecure, a well-known IDS with a good reputation. Intrusion detection compares incoming packets to stored profiles to detect attacks. When attacks are detected, an event is generated and an alert is triggered. Intrusion alerts can send e-mail messages, run external programs (paging software, for example), or start or stop services.

ISA Server's IDS operates at both the packet filter and application filter levels. The packet filter is capable of detecting a number of DoS attacks, such as WinNuke and Ping of Death, as well as detecting port scans including stealth scans.

Intrusion detection at layer 7 through the application filter can detect some DNS and POP attacks. DNS attacks, such as zone transfer attempts and buffer overflows, are detected. Other detection filters can be added using the API in the ISA Server SDK.

Server publishing

Administration of inbound traffic is made simpler by the use of server publishing. ISA Server allows you to publish the services of a server residing behind the firewall through a simple process. Instead of having to open ports or configure application filters, services are published using a wizard and the steps are automated. Server publishing is similar to protocol rules in reverse. Protocol rules provide a method for internal clients to make outbound connections using a specific protocol (enforced by ISA Server monitoring the transferred packets) while Server publishing provides a method for external clients to connect inbound to a specific server using a specific protocol.

Server publishing is accomplished by specifying the internal IP address of the server and the external IP address to which clients will connect. ISA Server creates a SecureNAT connection between the two, and clients can connect to the service while the threat of an attack is reduced.

Rule types

Flexibility is one of the features that make a firewall solution stand out above all the rest. One of the important features of ISA Server is the flexibility it offers administrators. Using rules, administrators can control the users, computers, and applications that are allowed access to the Internet and to the internal network. ISA Server supports a number of different rules, used for controlling different aspects of Internet access. When ISA Server receives a request, whether it's an inbound request or outbound request, the configured rules are processed to see whether the request is granted or denied.

ISA Server has a variety of different rule types, such as the following:

✦ **Application filters** — Application filters are proxies for specific types of data. While packet filters only inspect layer 3 (IP) and layer 4 (TCP) data and protocol rules can determine the type of protocol in the packet, an application filter is fully layer-7 aware and has access to the packet payload. Application filters can be used to block data in a more granular fashion than other filters. E-mail attachments can be stripped, specific Web content can be filtered, and FTP access can be restricted. Custom application filters can also be written.

✦ **Packet filter** — Packet filters, as previously discussed, allow or deny specific types of traffic through the firewall. Packet filter rules deny by default. For outgoing traffic, stateful inspection is used.

✦ **Routing rules** — Routing rules are used to redirect traffic through the ISA Server. Routing rules can be used to redirect specific types of traffic to caching servers or to specific network connections.

✦ **Bandwidth rules** — Bandwidth rules are used to set the priority of network traffic. These rules use the quality of service (QoS) feature of Windows 2003 Server or Windows 2000 Server to prioritize traffic.

✦ **Protocol rules** — Protocol rules allow or deny traffic based on the protocol of the communications. While packet filters operate on IP Address and TCP (or UDP) ports, protocol rules can operate on the specific protocol by reading more of the packet. Protocol rules can detect a protocol running on a non-native port.

✦ **Site rules and content rules** — Site rules and content rules are used to control access to particular sites or particular content. You may want to block file extensions such as .MP3 to save network bandwidth. Content can be blocked by file extension or MIME type, and sites are blocked based on destination sets.

Firewall policies

ISA Server's firewall uses policies for access control. By default, all traffic is denied. Access policies are defined for each type of traffic to allow. Rules can also be configured to deny traffic explicitly and these deny rules take precedence over allow rules.

Defining access policies can get unruly. ISA Server's policies make the administration of rules easier. Policies hide the actual rules, addresses, and other information so the overall set of policies is more readable facilitating understanding the behavior of packets flowing through the firewall. Unlike many other firewalls, policies can be applied to specific users and groups in an Active Directory structure or Windows NT 4.0 domain.

Basic policy elements include client and destination address sets that contain groups of addresses and protocol definitions. These address sets are used to define groups of systems for incoming and outgoing access control. Protocol definitions contain port numbers and behaviors for protocols. By defining a protocol definition, that protocol can be allowed or denied access (although ISA Server denies by default).

Some more advanced policy elements can be configured. Bandwidth priorities that affect the routing priority of different types of traffic can be defined. Traffic that is more sensitive to latency, such as teleconferencing, can be given a higher priority than less sensitive data, such as HTTP and FTP traffic. Schedules are used to control when rules are in effect. For example, access can be disabled at night or bandwidth priorities can be changed during business hours. Content groups are used for controlling the content to which certain users have access. Both file extensions and MIME types can define content groups.

Rule priority

ISA Server has two types of processing rules: ordered and unordered. The following are all unordered rule sets:

- ✦ Packet filters
- ✦ Protocol rules
- ✦ Site rules
- ✦ Content rules

In an unordered rule set, the first rules to be processed are deny rules. Traffic that is explicitly denied is discarded. If traffic is not explicitly denied by a deny rule, it is processed using the allow rules. If the traffic fits an allow rule, it is allowed in or out through the firewall. Finally, any traffic not explicitly denied or allowed by rules is implicitly denied and discarded.

Routing rules and bandwidth rules are ordered rule sets. These rules are processed in the order in which they appear within the ISA Management console. For example, if a certain type of traffic matches an allow rule near the top of the list and a deny rule lower in the list, it is allowed. This is the opposite behavior to unordered rules in which deny rules take precedence. If the deny rule was before the allow rule in the list, the traffic would be denied. In each ordered rule set, the last rule in the list is the default rule. In most cases, the default rule sets the behavior of any traffic not matching an explicitly defined rule in the list. You can usually configure the action taken by a default rule.

Rules in ISA Server are processed in a specific order, based on whether the traffic is incoming or outgoing. Outgoing traffic is processed as follows:

1. Bandwidth rules
2. Protocol rules
3. Site rules and content rules
4. Routing rules
5. Packet filters

Incoming traffic is processed using a different set of rules in a different specific order:

1. Packet filters
2. Routing rules
3. Bandwidth rules

Protocol rules, site rules, and content rules are not necessary for incoming traffic because they are only relevant to internal users. For example, an administrator blocking incoming requests for a specific file extension is not a common occurrence.

HTTP Redirector

The HTTP Redirector has the capability to redirect HTTP requests coming through the firewall and route them to the Web proxy service. Three options exist for redirected HTTP requests:

✦ By default, requests are routed to the Web proxy service for processing by Web publishing rules and routing rules.

✦ Requests can be sent directly to the requested Web server and bypass any rules in place for caching (reverse caching will not occur).

✦ Requests can be rejected outright, unless they are made directly to the Web proxy service so that no unwanted HTTP traffic passes through the firewall.

Acceleration service features

In addition to a complete firewall solution, ISA Server provides a full-featured Web caching server. A caching server can reduce network bandwidth when configured for forward caching and reduce Web server load and increase the speed of page loads when configured for reverse caching. Studies have shown that on average, 35 to 50 percent of all data can be served from the caching servers. ISA Server also includes a RAM caching feature where the content that is accessed the most is kept in RAM instead of on disk so it is retrieved much quicker.

ISA Server's Web caching feature operates as a Web proxy service. A Web proxy service accepts requests from clients then makes the request to the Web server and forwards the data back to the client. A proxy server can provide a number of advantages, including a single "choke point" for content control and blocking and increased security by allowing firewall rules that are stricter, as all outgoing requests go through a single point.

Forward caching

ISA Server can be configured to provide full forward caching services for Web and FTP to accelerate client access to the Internet and reduce bandwidth usage. Certain content, as determined by the cache configuration, is cached in the server as clients access it. To ensure that information is kept current and eventually removed from the cache, cached objects are assigned a Time to Live (TTL) value. The TTL defines how long an object within the cache remains current. One an object is retrieved from the Internet, its placed in the cache where it is assigned a TTL value. If another client requests the same object before the TTL expires, it is served directly from the cache. After the TTL expires, the object is discarded and cached again the next time it is accessed.

Multiple types of Web content (HTTP) can be cached. In most cases, all static content, such as HTML pages, images, and video files are cached. Dynamic content is typically not cached because it is often different for each request. A number of options are available for customizing what content is cached. Objects can be restricted to a maximum size, as well as specifying whether or not to cache objects that are invalid (HTTP response codes other than 200), dynamic, or have an unspecified last modification time (which makes it difficult to calculate a valid TTL).

As previously discussed, objects can have an explicitly specified TTL; otherwise, the TTL is calculated dynamically by the server based on the object's last modification time. The method by which the TTL is calculated is configurable from in ISA Server. The three settings are as follows:

- **Frequently** — causes objects to expire immediately.

- **Normally** — sets the TTL to 20 percent of the time since the last modified time with a minimum and maximum of 15 minutes and 1 day, respectively.

- **Less frequently** — sets the TTL to 40 percent of the time since the last modified time with a minimum of 30 minutes and maximum of 2 days.

There is also a fourth option that allows you to manually set custom values for the percentage, minimum, and maximum.

For FTP caching, the TTL is not calculated automatically and there is no way for an explicit TTL to be specified on the server. TTL for FTP objects must be set manually.

Reverse caching

Reverse caching can be used to ease the load on your Web servers as well as increase the speed of page loads for clients. A reverse-caching solution places the caching server between the Web server and the clients (the Internet, in most cases). Requests are made to the caching server and objects are served from either the cache or the Web server. Static objects that are cacheable, such as images and HTML pages, and exist in the cache are served directly from the caching server to the client. Cacheable items that are not in the cache are requested by the caching server, cached, and served to the client. Non-cacheable items, such as dynamic content, are always requested from the Web server by the caching server and served to the client.

Web publishing rules

ISA Server uses the Web Proxy Service for reverse caching. Web publishing rules are used for mapping IP addresses on the caching server to Web servers behind the cache. Web publishing rules consist of a destination set and an action. The destination set specifies the external IP address to which the rule responds and allows you to set a path. The path allows you to redirect requests for specific content to different Web servers. You may want to have an image server and redirect the /images directory for purely static content as well as having a scripts server to host dynamic content to which you would redirect the /cgi-bin directory. These would be in addition to the server that would host all other types of content for that site.

The action in the Web publishing rule allows you to perform a number of actions. The default action is to discard requests, but you will want to change that action to redirect requests. As shown in Figure 16-6, the simplest redirection is to specify a single IP address or computer name that points to the Web site on the internal Web server. You can also choose to pass the original host header to the Web server, which you will need to do if you are using host headers for the Web site. If this is not selected, the address or name specified for the redirection will be passed as the host header. Finally, you can perform port redirection using the Web publishing rule action. By specifying different TCP ports for HTTP, Secure Sockets Layer (SSL), and FTP, you can direct the requests to Web and FTP servers residing on non-standard ports. It is also possible to use this feature to redirect Web requests to a certain destination set to an FTP server so the contents of the FTP site are displayed in the remote Web browser.

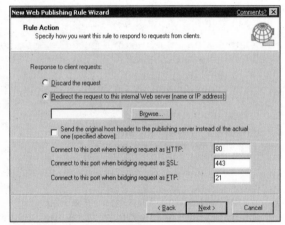

Figure 16-6: Web publishing rule actions are used to control the behavior of incoming requests when using reverse caching.

Routing rules

Routing rules are similar to Web publishing rules, but serve a different purpose. Routing rules, which are applied after Web publishing rules, can be used to redirect requests. These rules are used to redirect requests to upstream ISA Servers or other Web servers.

Active caching

Used with the ISA Server configured for forward caching, active caching allows content on the caching server to be refreshed automatically. Normally, when content becomes stale (it's TTL expires), it is dropped from the cache and then cached again the next time it is requested. With active caching enabled, the content can be refreshed before the TTL expires.

Content is designated for active caching automatically as long as active caching is enabled. If content is requested more than once within a specified period, it is added to the active caching list. The period is determined by a value that can be adjusted within ISA Server. As shown in Figure 16-7, this setting can be set to one of the following:

✦ Frequently (3)

✦ Normally (2)

✦ Less frequently (1)

The value assigned to each setting is multiplied by the TTL setting to determine the period within which the content must be requested twice to be added to (or remain on) the active caching list. For example, assume the active caching is set to Normally. If a given object's TTL is 1 minute, the object would be added to the active caching list if it were requested more than once within 2 minutes. If it is accessed twice within 2 minutes and added to the active caching list and not accessed again within 2 minutes (2*TTL), it will be removed from the list.

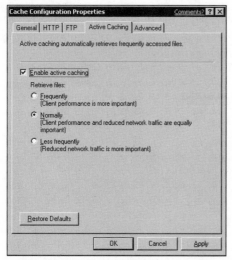

Figure 16-7: Active caching can be enabled to refresh automatically if it is requested more than once in a period defined by the active caching setting.

Items on the active caching list are refreshed automatically with a frequency based on the load of the server. If the server load is low, content is refreshed after half of the TTL has passed. The amount of time before content is refreshed increases as server load increases. A heavily loaded server will refresh active caching with almost the entire TTL passed.

Scheduled content download

The Scheduled Content Download feature is similar to active caching, but is more suitable to larger amounts of content, such as entire sites, and content that is scheduled for download is not removed from the cache like other cached data. Scheduled content download is also used in a forward caching configuration. Scheduled content download allows an administrator to schedule when ISA Server should pre-fetch items and store them in the cache. For example, ISA Server can cache popular Web sites during times when the network is slow, such as during evening hours. The information is then readily available from the cache when users begin their workday.

Scheduled content downloads are configured by specifying the following:

✦ The content to be downloaded is configured by specifying the base URL of the content.

✦ The amount to download can be configured by specifying the depth on the site to download (that is, how many links deep) or can be restricted to the domain of the base site (no content outside of that domain will be retrieved).

✦ The TTL setting (see Figure 16-8) specified will override the actual TTL of the content being downloaded. This will cause the downloaded content to remain cached for a set period of time.

✦ The schedule specifies when the download occurs.

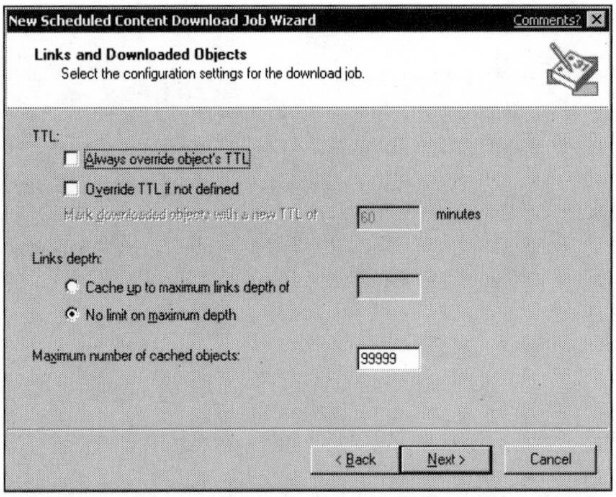

Figure 16-8: Scheduled content downloads are configured to retrieve specific content at certain times, and can change the TTL so that the content is not removed from the cache.

Scheduled content download is useful for sites that are accessed very heavily from within an organization, such as an intranet site hosted at another office. The site can be scheduled to download nightly when traffic is low, and the TTL can be set to keep the content cached until the next scheduled download.

When content is downloaded using scheduled content download, all data contained within the base URL is downloaded, and the download process follows links to retrieve that data as well. You can restrict the link depth to which the service will download, and you can also set the maximum number of individual objects to download. Dynamic content is not downloaded by default, but that option can be enabled.

SSL bridging

As mentioned in Chapter 9, SSL connections take a heavy toll on a Web server. Using SSL bridging in ISA Server has several advantages. SSL bridging is simply the ability of the ISA Server to encrypt and decrypt SSL sessions. SSL bridging is used for both forward and reverse caching.

Using SSL bridging is useful for a couple of scenarios. With an ISA Server configured for forward caching, SSL connections are usually made using SSL tunneling where the SSL connection is sent through the caching server and firewall without being inspected (as it is encrypted). Using SSL bridging, you can cache content from a secure Web site. The client makes a secure request to the ISA Server (as the client is configured for forward caching). The ISA Server decrypts the request to determine if the content is cached. If the content is cached, it is encrypted and returned to the client. If not, an encrypted request is sent to the Web server. The ISA Server decrypts the response, caches and encrypts the data, and sends it to the client.

SSL bridging is also useful for reverse caching. ISA Server can be used to take the load of processing SSL encryption and decryption off of a Web server. Clients make encrypted requests to the ISA Server, which decrypts the request and checks to see if the requested data is cached. If so, the data is encrypted and returned to the client. If not, an unencrypted HTTP request is sent to the Web server and the content is cached. The data is then encrypted and returned to the client. Because the connection from the ISA Server to the Web server is somewhat secure (it should be behind the firewall), the connection usually does not need to be encrypted.

Caching server arrays

ISA Server arrays (using CARP as discussed earlier in this chapter) allow caching to be spread across a number of servers. The caching servers in an array are load balanced and redundant, as more requests are sent to better-performing servers. If a server fails, requests are automatically directed to the next best server. Adding and removing servers in an array has no effect on the function of the array, and all load balancing is adjusted seamlessly. An array improves scalability because more servers can be added when the load on the existing array members becomes too high.

ISA Server Enterprise Edition is required to use the array features of ISA Server. The ISA Servers in the array also need to be part of a Windows 2003 or Windows 2000 domain using Active Directory. When using an array, configuration information is stored in Active Directory after the ISA Server schema is installed in the directory. All configuration information is shared between the array members automatically as it is stored in the central location.

When an array is implemented, clients using CARP will automatically direct requests to the most suitable array member. Clients that do not support CARP make their request to the array and the array member that receives the request will redirect it to the most suitable server.

Summary

Firewalls are used to control the inbound and outbound flow of traffic to a private network. Firewalls can be implemented in the form of hardware-based and/or software-based solutions. Although hardware solutions usually offer higher performance, it is often at a higher cost. Software-based firewalls provide a cost-effective solution.

Firewalls can perform non-stateful or stateful inspection. Those firewalls performing stateful inspections offer more security because they inspect more of the packet than non-stateful firewalls. Firewalls that perform application filtering offer the most security and flexibility.

Microsoft's ISA Server offers a firewall and caching solution without the need for purchasing specialized hardware. While it integrates with the security features of the Windows Server operating system, it also introduces many other security features — from basic filtering to advanced intrusion detection and application filtering.

✦   ✦   ✦

Installing and Configuring a Firewall

Microsoft Internet Security and Acceleration (ISA) Server comes in two versions. The Standard Edition contains the basic firewall and caching services. Enterprise Edition adds the array features, as discussed in the previous chapter.

The installation procedures for ISA Server Standard Edition and Enterprise Edition are similar. There are only a few key differences if you want to use the ISA Servers in an array configuration. For the ISA server to join an array, it must be a member of a domain, and the Active Directory schema must be modified. If this is not done, the ISA Server Enterprise Edition can still be installed as a standalone system.

Installing Microsoft ISA Server

The actual ISA Server installation process is the same for both the Enterprise and Standard Editions. Before you can install the Enterprise Edition, however, you must first perform a schema update. The examples that follow use the Enterprise Edition.

Installing the Active Directory schema update

The schema update only needs to be installed if you are planning to use ISA Server Enterprise Edition in an array configuration. You can install Enterprise Edition in standalone mode if you do not want to add the server to an array.

When you first insert the ISA Server media, the setup dialog box is automatically launched, as shown in Figure 17-1. You should first read the release notes; then click Run ISA Server Enterprise Initialization to continue.

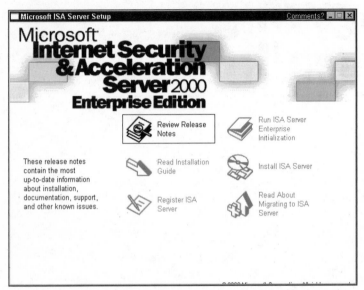

Figure 17-1: The ISA Server setup dialog is launched automatically when the media is inserted.

The schema installation is a simple one-step process, but once installed the schema cannot be removed from the Active Directory database. You are asked if you want to continue with the process (refer to Figure 17-2). Click Yes to update the schema.

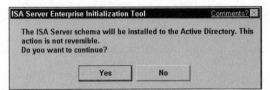

Figure 17-2: Click Yes to begin updating the AD schema.

After clicking Yes, you can configure the behavior for ISA Server policies, as shown in Figure 17-3. You can configure policies at the Enterprise level, array level, or a combination of both. Enterprise level policies apply to all arrays and allow administrators to maintain centralized control. For decentralized administration, array administrators can be permitted to configure their own policies.

By default, the specified policy is applied to all arrays. If you select Use array policy only, each array must have its own policy defined.

When Use this enterprise policy is selected, the Allow array-level access policy rules that restrict enterprise policy box is not selected by default. In this configuration, array policies cannot be created. Select the box to further restrict the enterprise policy by creating array policies. This allows you to delegate the administration of array policies to others. For example, create a single enterprise policy with general settings applying to all arrays. Array administrators can then apply further restrictions through array-level policies as needed.

Select the Allow publishing rules check box to allow those with access to configure the array policies to create publishing rules and publish internal servers. The default setting does not allow server publishing at the array policy level.

Finally, the Force packet filtering on the array setting, by default, does not allow an array administrator to disable packet filtering. Deselecting this check box allows array policy administrators to disable packet filtering. If an array administrator disables filtering, you could have security problems because doing so opens a hole in the network where packets can pass without inspection. Click OK to continue.

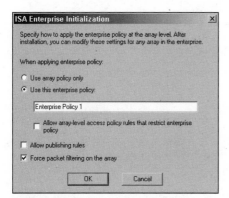

Figure 17-3: You can configure the policy behavior for the ISA Server schema modifications.

During the installation of the ISA Server schema, the installation progress is displayed, as shown in Figure 17-4.

You are notified when the schema update is complete, as shown in Figure 17-5. Click OK to finish the installation.

After the Active Directory schema is updated for an Enterprise Edition installation, you can continue with the ISA Server installation.

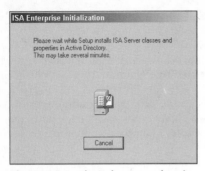

Figure 17-4: The schema update is in progress.

Figure 17-5: You are notified when the schema update is complete.

Installing ISA Server

Click Install ISA Server in the Microsoft ISA Server setup dialog box, as previously shown in Figure 17-1. The ISA Server setup process will begin.

1. Click Continue on the introductory setup dialog box.

2. Enter your CD key and then click OK.

3. Click OK to continue when your Product ID is displayed. You must now accept the license agreement.

4. Figure 17-6 shows the next step in the ISA Server setup. You can select the installation type.

   • Typical Installation installs the most common ISA Server components.

   • Custom Installation allows you to select each component you want to install.

   • Full Installation installs all ISA Server components.

   You can also configure the target folder for the ISA Server installation. Click Custom Installation to see the available components.

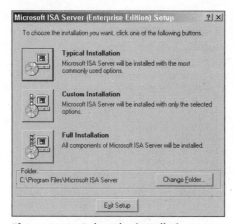

Figure 17-6: Select the installation type and target directory for ISA Server.

5. The available components are shown in Figure 17-7. The ISA Services component is the minimum required to install ISA Server. Select Add-in services and click Change Option to view the individual components.

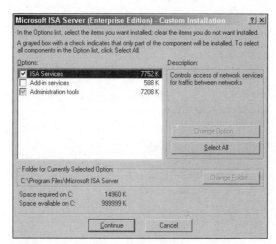

Figure 17-7: Select which ISA Server components to install.

6. Two Add-in services are available for ISA Server, as shown in Figure 17-8. The H.323 Gatekeeper is used to proxy H.323 videoconferencing calls, such as Microsoft NetMeeting. The Message Screener service allows the filtering of content in SMTP messages passing through the ISA Server.

The Message Screener service provides functionality traditionally provided by a third-party application. SMTP content filtering is used in many organizations to filter spam, inappropriate content, and certain attachments. Select the Add-in services you want, and click OK to return to the Custom Installation dialog box. Select Administration tools and click Change Option to see the available components.

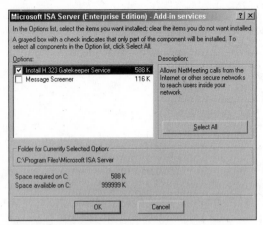

Figure 17-8: There are two Add-in services available for ISA Server.

7. The Administration tools are shown in Figure 17-9. The ISA Management component is installed by default, and is required to administer ISA Server. The H.323 Gatekeeper Administration Tool is used to administer the H.323 Gatekeeper service previously discussed.

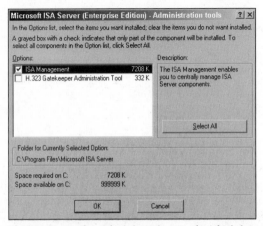

Figure 17-9: The Administration Tools administer ISA Server components.

You can also install just the ISA Management component of ISA Server on a different machine, such as a workstation, and use it to manage a remote ISA Server. Select the Administration Tools you want and then click OK.

8. Click Continue in the Custom Installation dialog box to begin installing ISA Server.

9. If you are installing ISA Server Enterprise Edition, you will be prompted to choose whether or not to install ISA Server as an array member, as shown in Figure 17-10. Click Yes to configure ISA Server as an array member. Click No to configure ISA Server as a standalone system.

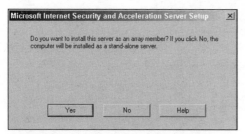

Figure 17-10: In an Enterprise Edition installation, you will be presented with a dialog box from which you can choose to make the ISA Server an array member or a standalone server.

10. If you choose Yes, you are prompted to provide a name for the ISA Server array. After you provide the array name, you are required to set the ISA Server enterprise policy configuration, as shown in Figure 17-11. These settings override the configuration set during the AD schema update and the options are identical.

11. The next step is the same for both Standard and Enterprise Edition, although the two previous steps do not exist in Standard Edition. As discussed in Chapter 16, ISA Server has three modes in which it can be installed, as shown in Figure 17-12.

ISA Server contains two major functions: a firewall and a caching server. This is reflected in the available modes.

- Firewall mode configures ISA Server as a firewall only.

- Cache mode configures the acceleration server features of ISA Server only.

- Integrated mode configures the server with both firewall and caching features enabled.

Select your desired mode and then click Continue.

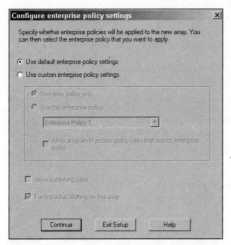

Figure 17-11: When joining an array in Enterprise Edition, you can use either the default enterprise policy settings or a custom set.

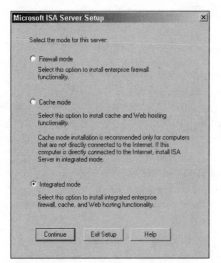

Figure 17-12: ISA Server can be installed in one of three modes.

12. If IIS is installed on the same physical server as ISA Server and it has a Web site configured on port 80 or 8080, IIS will stop and you will be notified, as shown in Figure 17-13. ISA Server requires these ports and you need to change your Web sites to different ports. The sites can be published on the original ports using ISA Server after configuration is complete.

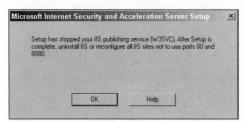

Figure 17-13: IIS stops if there are services running on port 80 or 8080.

13. If you selected Cache mode or Integrated mode you must specify where the cache will reside on the hard disks in your system, as shown in Figure 17-14. You can select the drive on which the cache will reside and the maximum cache size. Keep in mind that the cache can only reside on an NT File System (NTFS) partition. The cache can also span multiple drives if you select each drive and set a maximum cache size greater than zero. (Setting the maximum cache size to zero on a drive causes that drive not to be used for caching.) The basic formula to use when calculating the size of the cache is 100MB + 0.5MB per user.

Figure 17-14: The cache is placed on the disks you specify and the maximum size can be configured.

You will want the cache to reside on a drive (or drives) other than your system drive so performance is not degraded. Ideally, the cache will reside on a fast volume such as a RAID-1 set to speed up read and write operations because caching is highly disk intensive. The caching disks should also be on a separate channel from the system disks to isolate the I/O. Click OK to continue.

14. If the ISA Server is being installed in Firewall mode or Integrated mode, you must set the internal IP address space, as shown in Figure 17-15. This address space allows the ISA Server to separate internal requests from external requests. Enter your address range and then click Add.

15. Using the Construct Table button, you can add the private IP address ranges and the address ranges found in the Windows 2003 and Windows 2000 routing table for a specific internal network adapter to the ISA Server's Local Address Table. The Local Address Table determines which IP addresses are internal and which are external. Click OK to continue.

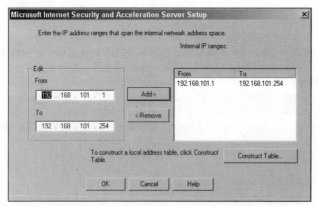

Figure 17-15: The Local Address Table is used by the ISA Server to identify which addresses are local to your network.

After the previously outlined steps have been completed, and setup copies the necessary files, ISA Server is installed. At this point a dialog box appears, as shown in Figure 17-16. You can launch the Getting Started Wizard to walk you through the steps of configuring ISA Server. This is discussed in the following section. If you do not want to start the Getting Started Wizard now, deselect the check box and then click OK. The wizard can be started at a later time.

Figure 17-16: You can start the Getting Started Wizard after setup is complete, or you can run it at a later time.

If you install ISA Server on Windows 2003, three error messages will appear at the end of the setup process informing you of the following:

✦ ISA Server is not supported by this version of Windows.

✦ ISA Server drivers have not been loaded.

✦ One or more services have failed to start.

The reason for this is that ISA Server can only run on Windows 2003 if service pack 1 for ISA Server is installed. After SP1 is installed, ISA Server will function correctly.

Firewall Configuration

Now that ISA Server has been successfully installed, you can begin its configuration. Configuration for the ISA Server firewall features is discussed here, and caching server configuration is discussed in Chapter 18.

Note   A server configured in Integrated mode will involve the steps in both this chapter and Chapter 18.

Open the ISA Server Administration tool. From the Start menu, select All Programs, Microsoft ISA Server, and ISA Management. The ISA Management MMC snap-in will open.

You will find all configuration settings in ISA Server by navigating the tree in the right pane to Servers and Arrays and then the server name.

Essentially, a few separate objects are configured in ISA Server. Filters are configured first. Filters are defined to limit what traffic rules are applied to. *Rules* are the actual objects that control the flow of traffic through the server. Routing rules are a special type of rule. Rather than allowing or denying traffic, routing rules send that traffic to another location.

These objects are discussed later in the chapter, but first a walkthrough of the ISA Server Getting Started Wizard is provided.

Getting Started Wizard

The easiest way to configure ISA Server for the first time is with the Getting Started Wizard. The first time you start ISA Management, the Getting Started Wizard opens automatically. The options configured in these steps are discussed in more detail later in the chapter.

1. To open the Getting Started Wizard manually, click the root of the tree in the left pane and then click the Welcome tab at the bottom of the right pane, as shown in Figure 17-17. Click Getting Started Wizard in the right pane. Even if you close the ISA Management MMC snap-in, it will open to the same part of the wizard the next time it is opened.

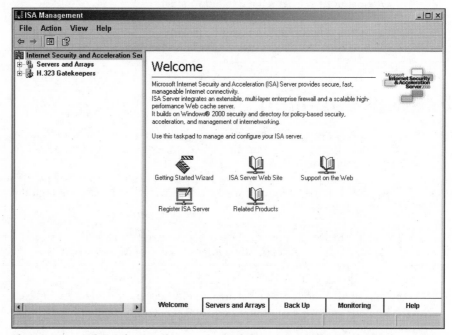

Figure 17-17: After selecting the root in the left pane and clicking the Welcome tab in the right pane, you can launch the Getting Started Wizard.

2. The Welcome dialog box of the Getting Started Wizard is shown in Figure 17-18 (the pane has been resized for convenience). A list of tasks that the wizard will complete is shown. Click Next to begin the first task.

3. Click the Select policy elements icon to continue, as shown in Figure 17-19.

4. Figure 17-20 shows the Select Policy Elements dialog box that is used to select the policy elements to be used in rules. By default, all of the policy elements can be used, but you can restrict each one by deselecting the appropriate box. Click OK after you have made your selections, and click Next to continue to the next page of the Getting Started Wizard.

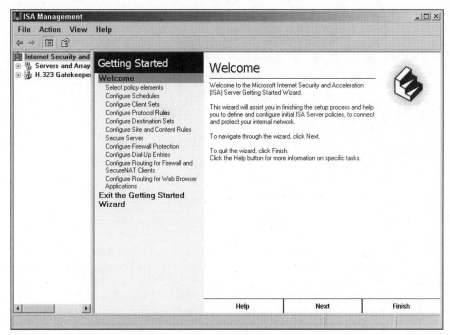

Figure 17-18: The Getting Started Wizard is the simplest way to initially configure ISA Server.

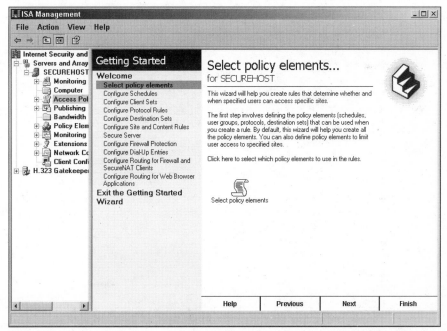

Figure 17-19: The first step in the Getting Started wizard is to select policy elements.

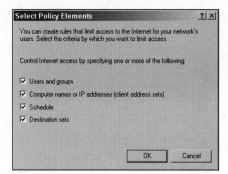

Figure 17-20: You can choose which
policies are available to use as restrictions
in rules.

5. Configuring schedules for the server is next, as shown in Figure 17-21. Use
these schedules to define when rules are applicable. For example, you may
want to define three different schedules: one for working hours, one for
evening hours, and one for weekends. By default, two schedules are defined:
weekends and work hours. The schedules you create in this step can be used
in rules created later. If you want to define a new schedule now, click the
Create a Schedule icon.

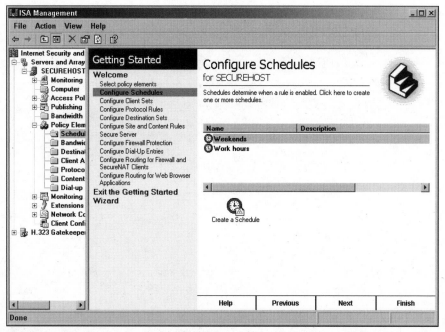

Figure 17-21: The Configure Schedules step of the Getting Started Wizard is used to
define schedules to be used later in rules.

6. The New schedule dialog box is shown in Figure 17-22. A name and a description should be provided for the schedule so that it can be referenced later when creating rules. Select blocks of time from the calendar by clicking to select an individual block or clicking and dragging to select a group of blocks. You can then change the status of those blocks from active to inactive or vice versa by using the Active and Inactive selectors.

Click OK to save the schedule. You don't have to create a schedule with all active or all inactive times. Not using a schedule in a rule means it will always be active, and not creating a rule at all has the same effect as a schedule with all inactive times. After you've configured the schedule, click OK and then Next to continue.

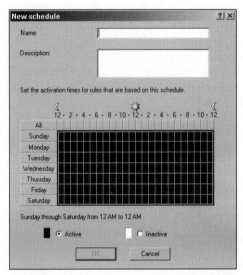

Figure 17-22: You can create new schedules by specifying a name and description and setting the active and inactive times in the calendar.

7. The next step is to create client sets (as shown in Figure 17-23) that will be used in rules later. Client sets are similar to schedules, except they restrict rules by client systems rather than by time. For example, a client set can be created for use in a rule that restricts access to a particular group of users. No client sets are defined by default. If you know the client sets that you require for rules, define them now by clicking the Create a Client Set icon.

8. The Client Set dialog box is shown in Figure 17-24. Set a name and description for the set. To add set members, click Add.

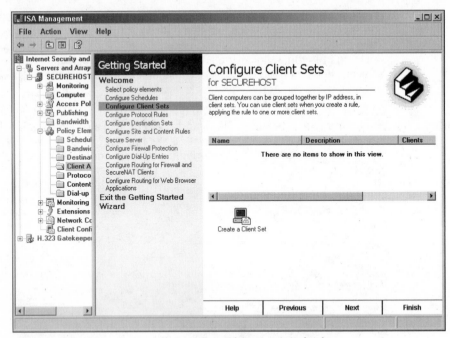

Figure 17-23: Client sets can be configured for use in rules later.

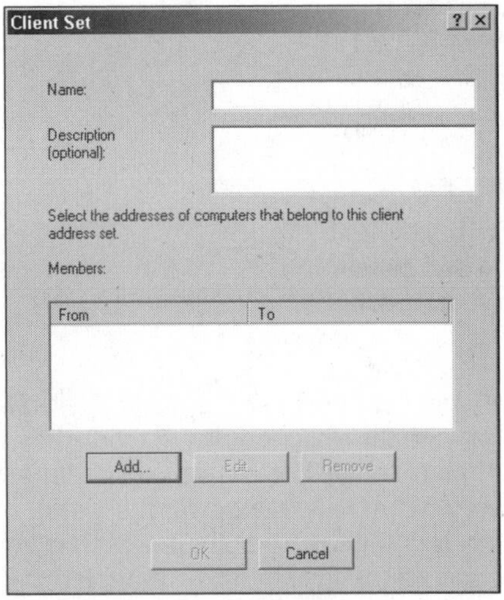

Figure 17-24: The Client Set dialog box
is used to define the systems in a client set.

9. The Add/Edit IP Addresses dialog box is shown in Figure 17-25. Specify a range of IP addresses or, for a single system, specify the same address in both the From and To box for the IP range. Click OK to add the IP address or range. Click OK to save the Client Set. Click Next to continue.

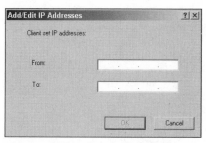

Figure 17-25: Clients are added to a set by IP range or individually.

10. You can now define protocol rules. Protocol rules use the schedules and client sets defined in the previous steps. Protocol rules control outgoing traffic through the firewall. They define which protocols internal clients can use to access the Internet.

There are two options for adding a protocol rule using the wizard. Using Create a Protocol Rule for Internet Access creates a rule that allows clients typical Internet access. Click the Create a Protocol Rule for Internet Access icon to open the New Protocol Rule Wizard. Enter a name for the protocol rule, as shown in Figure 17-26. Click Next to continue.

Figure 17-26: Enter a name for the new protocol rule.

11. Select the protocols to use with the rule. As the Create a Protocol Rule for Internet Access option was used for this rule, a number of protocols are selected by default, as shown in Figure 17-27. Only the selected protocols are shown by default. Click Next to accept the defaults. (More details on protocol rules are provided later in the chapter.)

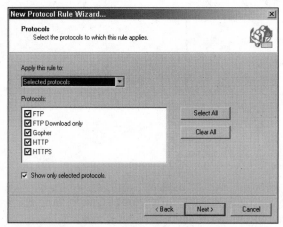

Figure 17-27: The selected protocols are allowed by this rule.

12. You can now set a schedule for the rule. Because this is a standard Internet access rule, you will most likely want to use the rule shown in Figure 17-28. If you want to limit access to work hours, however, you can use the default Work Week schedule, or use a schedule you defined earlier in the Getting Started Wizard. Click Next to continue.

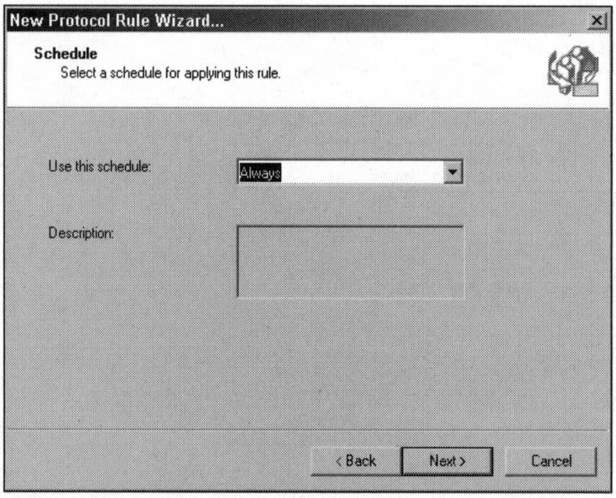

Figure 17-28: You can set a schedule for when the rule will be active.

13. You can also restrict the rule based on client sets. Again, as a default rule to allow Internet access is being created, you most likely want to allow all clients access, as shown in Figure 17-29. You can also restrict the rule based on user or group membership. Click Next to continue.

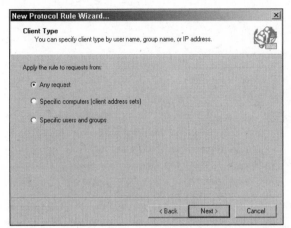

Figure 17-29: Rules can be restricted based on client sets as defined earlier or user and group membership.

14. Finally, a summary of the rule is displayed, as shown in Figure 17-30. When you click Finish, the rule is created. Click Next to continue to the next step in the Getting Started Wizard.

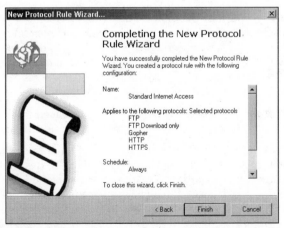

Figure 17-30: A summary of the rule being created is shown for review.

The next step is to create destination sets. Destination sets are similar to client sets except instead of being used to group local systems, they are used for creating sets of hosts on the external network. Destination sets are most commonly used in site and content rules. No destination sets are defined by default.

1. To define a new destination set, click the Create a Destination Set icon. The New Destination Set dialog box will open, as shown in Figure 17-31.

2. Enter a name and description for the destination set, and click the Add button to add IP Addresses or systems to the set.

Figure 17-31: Destination sets are created in the same manner as Client Sets.

3. Figure 17-32 shows the Add/Edit Destination dialog box. This is the point where destination sets differ from client sets. Destination sets can contain either IP addresses or names. By entering a system name in the Destination text box, you can specify a set member based on the system's fully qualified domain name (FQDN), such as `www.domain.tld`. You can specify entire domains using the * wildcard symbol, such as `*.domain.tld`.

4. Specify an address in the From box to add set members based on IP address. Add an address in the To box to specify an entire range of addresses.

5. Use the Path text box in the Add/Edit Destination dialog box to specify a certain path on the target system (or systems) to add to the destination set. Specify either an entire directory using a wildcard or a specific file to make that file or directory part of the set. Click OK to save the destination address. Click OK to save the destination set. Click Next to proceed to the next step in the Getting Started Wizard.

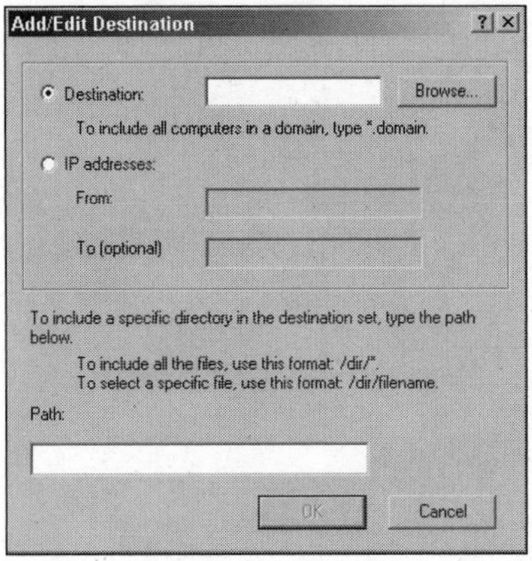

Figure 17-32: Destinations can be added based on IP address or system name.

Site and Content rules are the next Getting Started Wizard step. These rules control access to specific external locations. While a protocol rule allows an entire protocol or set of protocols access to the entire Internet, a Site and Content rule can allow or deny access to specific content. For example, a protocol rule may grant FTP access, while a Site and Content rule can control which FTP sites users have access to.

By default, rule, Allow rule, is created. This rule allows access to any content. New rules are created to deny specific content, or you can remove the Allow rule and create a deny rule to deny all content by default. To create a new Site and Content rule, do the following:

1. Click the Create a Site and Content Rule icon. The specifics of Site and Content Rules are discussed later in the chapter. Click Next to proceed.

2. This Getting Started Wizard step is different from the previous ones. No rules or filters are created. As discussed in Chapter 16, ISA Server includes a feature that automatically secures the server on which ISA Server is running. The Secure Server step in the wizard performs that process. Click the Secure Your ISA Server Computer to begin, as shown in Figure 17-33. (See the section later in the chapter for details on the ISA Server Security Configuration Wizard.) Click Next to continue.

3. You can configure packet filtering and intrusion detection on ISA Server. Click the Configure Packet Filtering and Intrusion Detection icon to set up these features. Packet filtering is enabled by default, as shown in Figure 17-34.

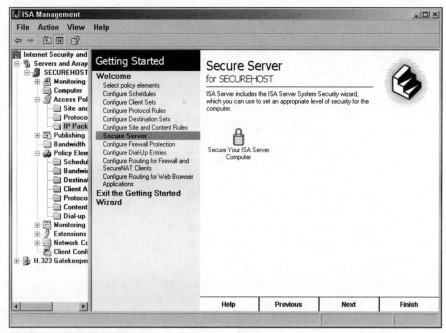

Figure 17-33: The Secure Server step is used to secure the system on which ISA Server is running.

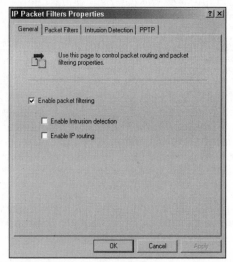

Figure 17-34: Packet filtering is enabled by default but can be disabled manually.

4. In most cases, you do not want to disable packet filtering on your ISA Server. Without packet filtering, ISA Server's Vital Packet Inspection feature is disabled, and all traffic flows freely in and out of the system. Some packet filtering options can be defined though. Click the Packet Filters tab, as shown in Figure 17-35.

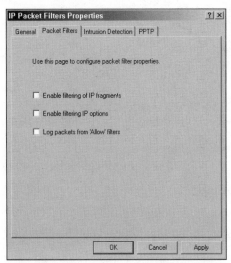

Figure 17-35: The Packet Filters tab of the IP Packet Filters Properties dialog box is used to configure specific packet filtering options.

5. Three options are available for packet filtering, all of which are disabled by default. Fragmented IP packets are packets that are not sent all at once but rather in multiple parts, requiring the ISA server to reassemble them. Fragmented IP packets are often used in Internet attacks and can sometimes cause problems on hosts that cannot properly process them. Enabling filtering of IP fragments ensures that these fragmented packets will be discarded, preventing these problems. Enable filtering of IP options cause any IP packets with IP options defined in the header to be discarded. Occasionally, packets with options can cause security problems. The final packet filtering option enables the logging of packets filtered through an allow rule. Normally, only packets filtered with a deny rule are logged.

6. You can enable intrusion detection at this point. ISA Server's intrusion detection features were discussed in Chapter 16. Simply select the Enable Intrusion Detection box to turn this feature on. After Intrusion Detection is enabled, you must set the Intrusion Detection options. Click the Intrusion Detection tab, as shown in Figure 17-36.

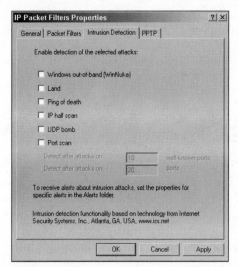

Figure 17-36: After Intrusion Detection is enabled, you must select the Intrusion Detection options.

7. The Intrusion Detection options specify the attacks against which ISA Server will protect. Selecting the appropriate boxes enables detection of all of the attacks. The Port scan option also has two extra configuration options. Both of the numerical settings specify how many ports must be scanned from one host before an attack is reported. By default, attacks are logged after scans on ten well-known ports (0 to 1024) or 20 of any port (0 to 65535). Click OK to close the IP Packet Filters Properties dialog box. Click Next to continue.

8. You can now configure dial-up entries for the ISA Server. Dial-up entries are used for two purposes. It is possible, though rare, to configure ISA Server to use a dial-up connection for the external connection to the Internet in a dial-on-demand configuration. The second use for a dial-up connection is as a backup Internet connection in case the main link fails. Click Next to continue.

9. You can configure the server to route traffic to an upstream firewall. Click the Configure Firewall Routing icon to open the Network Configuration Properties dialog box, as shown in Figure 17-37.

   By default, all traffic is routed over the primary external connection. Selecting the Chain to this computer option and specifying the upstream system directs all traffic there. This upstream server must be an ISA Server or Microsoft Proxy Server 2.0. You can also specify a user account for authentication to the upstream system. Click OK to save the changes and then click Next to continue to the last step.

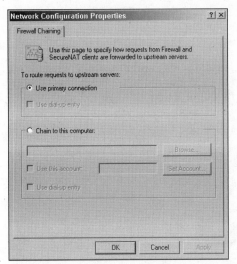

Figure 17-37: ISA Server can be configured to route traffic to an upstream firewall or proxy.

10. The final step in the Getting Started Wizard allows you to configure a routing rule for Web traffic. A default rule exists, which directs all Web traffic to the destination server. You can, however, redirect Web traffic to other locations. Changing the default rule or adding a new rule can direct specific traffic to an upstream server or to another Web server. You can also use these rules for SSL bridging. (These rules are discussed in detail later in the chapter.) Click Next to go to the exit dialog box for the Getting Started Wizard.

11. The Exit the Getting Started Wizard page contains the Register ISA Server icon. Click this icon to register your ISA Server software with Microsoft. Click Finish to complete the Getting Started Wizard.

The Getting Started Wizard is now complete. You should have a functional ISA Server installation. The remainder of this chapter discusses the individual components, such as filters, rules, and routing.

Filters

Filters control when rules are effective. A number of filters are available in ISA Server, including the following:

- ✦ Schedules
- ✦ Client Sets
- ✦ Destination Sets
- ✦ Protocol Definitions
- ✦ Content Groups

Each of these can be used to filter certain types of rules.

Schedules

Schedules filter rules based on the time of day and day of the week. A schedule contains 24 one-hour blocks of time for each day of the week, as shown in Figure 17-38. Each block can be set as active (black) or inactive (white). Active times specify when a rule will be in effect; inactive times specify when a rule will not be in effect.

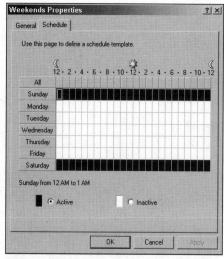

Figure 17-38: Schedules contain blocks of time that can be used to set when a rule is active or inactive.

The two default schedules are Weekends and Work Hours. The Weekends schedule is active from 12:00 A.M. Saturday morning to 12:00 A.M. Monday morning. Work Hours is active from 9:00 A.M. to 5:00 P.M. on weekdays.

You will most likely want to define your own schedules for filtering rules. Under Policy Elements in the left pane, click Schedules. The currently defined schedules are shown in the left pane. To create a new schedule, click Create a Schedule. Alternatively, you can select a schedule from the list and click Configure a Schedule to edit an existing schedule.

Creating a schedule is done through the New Schedule dialog box.

1. Enter a name and description for the new schedule, as shown in Figure 17-39.

2. You can now configure the times when this schedule is active and inactive. By default, the New Schedule dialog box sets all time blocks to active. Select individual time blocks by clicking or select groups of blocks by clicking and dragging. When you select a block or a group of blocks, click the Inactive

radio button to set them to inactive or the Active button to set them to active. Even if you select a group of blocks that contains some active and some inactive times, clicking either Active or Inactive will set the entire group to that status.

3. The modified schedule is shown in Figure 17-40. Click OK to save the schedule. It will appear in the list of defined schedules.

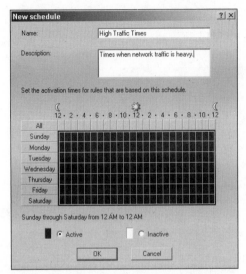

Figure 17-39: The New Schedule dialog box is used to configure a new schedule.

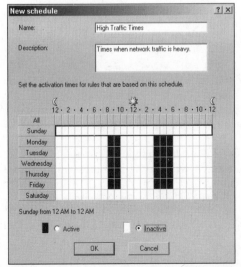

Figure 17-40: The schedule has been modified to select the proper active and inactive times.

Client sets

Client sets define groups of systems on the internal network. These sets are available in most rule types to filter which internal systems have a particular type of access. Client sets are found by selecting Client Address Sets under Policy Elements in the left pane. By default, no client sets are created. You can create a new client set by clicking Create a Client Set.

1. Enter a name for the set and, optionally, a description, as shown in Figure 17-41. Click the Add button to add client systems to the set.

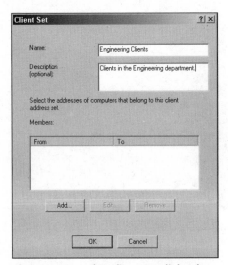

Figure 17-41: The Client Set dialog box requires a name for the set and, optionally, a description. The Add button is used to add clients.

2. The Add/Edit IP Addresses dialog box is used to add clients, as shown in Figure 17-42. IP addresses identify client systems. You can add a range of IP addresses, or you can choose a single address by typing the same address in the From and To boxes. Click OK to add the addresses.

Tip

Some dialog boxes used to enter IP address ranges allow you to enter a single IP address in the From box and click OK, while others require you to enter the same address in the From and To boxes, such as this example. Dialog boxes that function with the From box only will usually have (optional) under To.

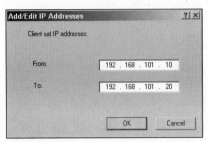

Figure 17-42: IP Addresses are added to the set by entering the range of addresses or a single address in both the From and To boxes.

Add as many addresses as you want. The value of separating systems by department or group and assigning a subnet or specific range of IP addresses becomes clear here. If one department has a specific IP address range, it can be added as a group rather than adding a number of individual addresses, as would be the case if addresses were assigned out of a central pool.

 3. Click OK to save the client set. The client set will be added to the list of available client sets.

Destination sets

Destination sets are similar to client sets. The principle is identical. A destination set contains a set of systems used as the basis for filtering a rule. In the case of destination sets, however, the systems are on the external network, which, in most cases, is the Internet.

Destination sets are found in the left pane by selecting Destination Sets under Policy Elements. The list of existing destination sets is displayed in the right pane. No destination sets are created by default in ISA Server. To create a destination set, click Create a Destination Set. The New Destination Set dialog box is almost identical to the New Client Set dialog box. The difference is seen when adding systems to the set.

 1. Enter a name and, optionally, a description, and click the Add button to add destinations to the set.

 2. The Add/Edit Destination dialog box is shown in Figure 17-43. You can define destinations by IP address in a similar method to client sets, but you can also define them by Domain Name System (DNS) name. When Destination is selected, type the system or domain's DNS name in the box, as shown. Add individual systems by typing their FQDN. Specify entire domains using a wildcard (*). For example, a single system would be www.domain.tld, but the entire domain is designated as *.domain.tld.

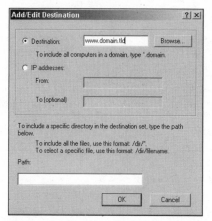

Figure 17-43: The Add/Edit Destination dialog box is used to add destinations to a set based on IP address or DNS name.

3. The Add/Edit Destination dialog box also provides an option to specify a path with the destination. In the example shown, the entire server, `www.domain.tld`, is added to the set. Using the Path option, you can add a specific file or directory to the set. For example, to add `www.domain.tld/cgi-bin/` to the set, enter `/cgi-bin/*` in the Path box.

4. Click OK to add the destination.

As with client sets, you can add any number to a destination set. To add more destinations, click the Add button and enter the information for the next destination. After you have added all of the destinations for the set, click OK to save. The new destination set will appear in the list.

Bandwidth priorities

Bandwidth priorities, found by clicking Bandwidth Priorities under Policy Elements, are used with bandwidth rules. The Bandwidth Priorities tell ISA Server which connections are better and which one should be predominantly used. The bandwidth rule (discussed later in this chapter) associates a bandwidth priority filter with specific traffic.

By default, a bandwidth priority filter is created with priorities of 100 for both inbound and outbound traffic. Bandwidth priorities can be assigned values between 1 and 200. Higher numbers are considered better connections and favored over lower numbers. For example, if an ISA Server has two connections, a T1 and a dial-up connection, the T1 should be given a higher bandwidth priority than the modem connection. Because the T1 will obviously have more bandwidth, it should be the favored connection.

1. Right-click Bandwidth Priorities in the left pane and select New, Bandwidth Priority.

2. The New Bandwidth Priority dialog box is shown in Figure 17-44. As with most filters, you must enter a name and, optionally, enter a description.

3. Set an outbound and inbound bandwidth metric. Keep in mind that the default metric is 100 for each. Click OK to save the new bandwidth priority.

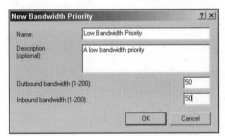

Figure 17-44: The New Bandwidth Priority dialog box is used to specify a name for the new priority and the outbound and inbound bandwidth priorities.

Protocol definitions

Protocol definitions specify the particular ports and session protocols used by application protocols. These are commonly used in rules to allow or deny certain types of traffic. Click Protocol Definitions under Policy Elements in the left pane to see the configured protocols. Most standard protocols, such as HTTP and FTP, are defined by default. In fact, a large number of protocols are defined.

You may at some time find a protocol you need to pass through the firewall using a rule that is not yet defined. You can create new protocol definitions by clicking Create a Protocol Definition.

1. The New Protocol Definition Wizard is used to define protocols. Enter a name for the new protocol definition, as shown in Figure 17-45, and click Next.

2. Specify the port number, session protocol (TCP or UDP), and the direction of the connection, either outbound or inbound, as shown in Figure 17-46. This information is available either in the documentation for the software for which you are creating the definition or from the vendor of that software. Click Next to continue.

3. You can now define secondary connections. Secondary connections occur after the initial connection is made. These may be connections that come back from the server to which you are connecting or more connections from the protocol on other ports. To use secondary connections, select Yes and then click New to add a connection.

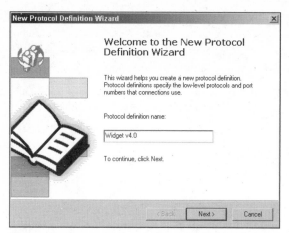

Figure 17-45: A name must be provided for the new protocol definition.

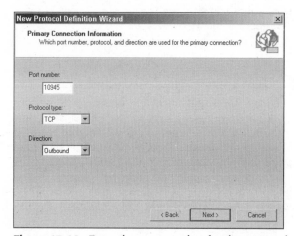

Figure 17-46: Enter the port number for the protocol, and select the session protocol and direction for the connection.

4. The New/Edit Secondary Connection dialog box, shown in Figure 17-47, is used to add these connections. Enter the range of ports (or individual port) used by the secondary connection, the protocol type and the direction, and click OK.

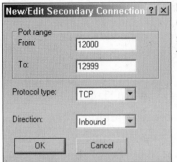

Figure 17-47: The New/Edit Secondary Connection dialog box is used to define secondary connections, which occur following the initial protocol connection.

5. The newly created secondary connection is shown in the wizard in Figure 17-48. Click Next to continue.

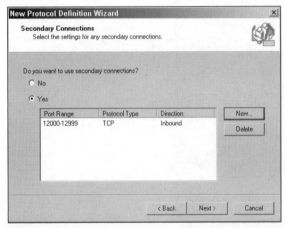

Figure 17-48: The secondary connection has been added to the list in the wizard.

6. Review the summary of the protocol definition you are creating. After you verify the information provided, click Finish to add the protocol to the list of protocol definitions.

Content groups

Content groups are similar to protocol definitions in that they define what type of traffic a rule functions for. Content groups, however, function at a higher level and allow you to control the particular types of content users have access to. Click Content Groups under Policy Elements to work with these groups.

Content groups are groups of MIME types or file extensions. They are used with Site and Content Rules to restrict what type of HTTP and FTP traffic can pass through the ISA Server. A number of content groups are defined by default, but you may need to add your own.

1. Right-click Content Groups in the left pane and select New, Content Group. The New Content Group dialog box is shown in Figure 17-49.

2. Enter a name and description for the content group.

3. Select MIME type or file extension from the Available Types drop-down box and then click the Add button to add it to the list of selected types.

4. Select as many different types as you want, making sure to click the Add button after each selection. Click OK to save the new content group.

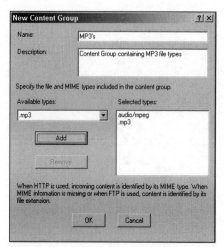

Figure 17-49: The New Content Group dialog box is used to create a group containing the selected MIME types or file extensions.

Rules

Rules control the actual flow of traffic through your server based on filters and other criteria. Rules are used for a number of purposes but the primary reason is for allowing and denying traffic passing through the server.

Protocol rules

Protocol rules are probably the first type of rule you will encounter in ISA Server. By default, ISA Server does not allow any traffic through, inbound or outbound. To allow clients access to the external network, you must define a protocol rule.

A generic protocol rule was discussed in the "ISA Server Getting Started Wizard" section in this chapter. You may, however, want to allow access for another type of traffic to a group of users. You can find protocol rules under Access Policy in the left pane of the ISA Management snap-in. Click the Create a Protocol Rule icon in the right pane to create a new rule.

1. In the New Protocol Rule Wizard is to specify a name for the rule. Enter a name and then click Next.

2. Decide if this is an Allow or Deny rule. An Allow rule is used to allow certain types of traffic; all traffic is denied by default. A Deny rule can deny traffic to a subset of an allow rule. For example, a Deny rule is useful if you want everyone but a certain client set to have a specific type of access. The Allow rule for everyone is created, and then a Deny rule for a specific group is created. This is opposed to creating an Allow rule for each group that you want to grant access and no rule for the denied group. Click Next to continue.

3. Specify to which protocol definitions the rule applies, as shown in Figure 17-50. All traffic is defined by default, but select Selected Protocols from the drop-down box to see the protocol list. Select the protocols to allow from the list, and click Next.

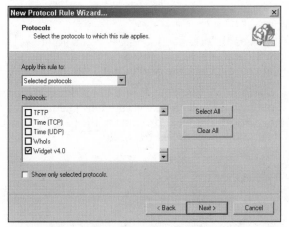

Figure 17-50: Select the protocol definitions to which this rule will apply.

4. You can now assign a schedule to this rule. The schedule will control when the rule is active or inactive. This can be a useful feature if you want to block a certain type of traffic at certain times of the day. Select the schedule from the drop-down box. By default, the rule is always in effect. Click Next to continue.

5. You can assign client sets to the rule. By default, the rule is in effect for all clients. The rule can be applied to specific client sets, as defined earlier, or for specific users and groups. This allows the rule to apply to a user no matter

which system they are logged in to. In this case, the rule will be applied to the client set created earlier. Select the client type, as shown in Figure 17-51, and click Next.

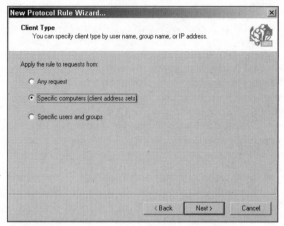

Figure 17-51: Select which client types to which the rule will apply.

6. If you selected Specific computers (client address sets), you have a chance to add client sets. Likewise, if you selected Specific users and groups, you can add user and group accounts. Click the Add button.

7. The Add Client Sets dialog box is shown in Figure 17-52. Select the desired client set, and click the Add button. You can also create new client sets at this point if the client set you need does not exist by clicking the New button. Click OK to add the client sets and then click Next to continue.

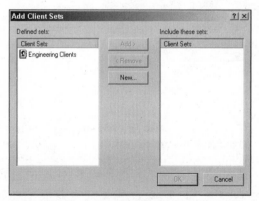

Figure 17-52: Select the client sets to be added to the rule.

8. Review the summary of the rule creation. Check the configuration settings, and click Finish to add the protocol rule.

Site and Content rules

Site and Content rules are similar to protocol rules except that instead of allowing or denying access based on protocol and client sets, they do so based on content and destination sets. After ISA Server is installed, a Site and Content rule must be configured (along with a protocol rule) before clients have access to the Internet. Click Site and Content Rules under Access Policy in the left pane, and click Create a Site and Content Rule to add a new rule.

1. In the New Site and Content Rule Wizard, specify a name, and click Next to continue.

2. Specify whether this is an Allow or Deny rule, as shown in Figure 17-53. You can also redirect denied HTTP traffic to a specified site. For example, you could redirect the request to a site that outlines your policies and procedures for Internet access. Click Next to continue.

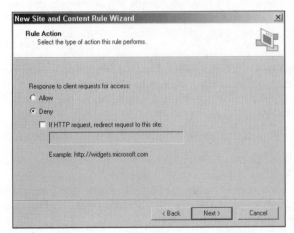

Figure 17-53: You must specify whether this is an Allow or Deny rule.

3. You can now restrict the rule based on destination sets. The rule applies to all destinations by default, but you can select a number of options from the drop-down box. All internal destinations and All external destinations will apply the rule to destinations inside and outside the firewall, respectively. Specified destination set and All destinations except selected set allow you to select a destination set from the Name drop-down box, as shown in Figure 17-54. Click Next to continue.

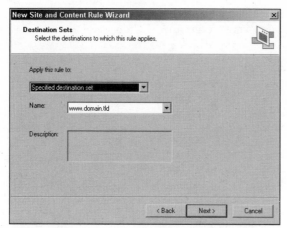

Figure 17-54: You can restrict the rule based on destination sets created earlier.

4. As with protocol rules, you can select a schedule from the drop-down box. You may want to restrict certain access to specific destinations at certain times. The rule applies at all times by default. Click Next to continue.

5. You can also restrict site and content rules based on client sets or user and group memberships in a method identical to that of protocol sets. This can restrict or allow certain clients from access to certain destinations. To filter the rule based on client sets or users and groups, follow the same procedure as for protocol rules.

6. Review the settings you have chosen, and click Finish to save the rule.

Web publishing rules

While protocol and Site and Content Rules are for allowing traffic out through the firewall, server and Web publishing rules are for allowing traffic in. Web publishing rules are specifically for publishing Web content.

Click Web Publishing Rules under Publishing in the left pane. Click Create a Web Publishing Rule in the right pane to begin.

1. In the New Web Publishing Rule Wizard, assign a name to the rule. Click Next to continue.

2. Use the destination set to set the path that is being published. For example, if you want to publish a site at `www.domain.tld`, the destination set would contain that address. Select Specified destination set from the drop-down box and then select the destination set from the Name drop-down box. Click Next to continue.

3. Filter the rule using a client set. This allows you to set different rules for different clients on the external network. You will most likely leave this set to Any request so that all requests for the published site obey the same rule. Click Next to continue.

4. Set the behavior of the rule. By default, a Web publishing rule is created that denies all incoming Web traffic. As shown in Figure 17-55, change the setting to Redirect the request to this internal Web server (name or IP address) and specify the internal Web server by name or IP address. You can also select Send the original host header to the publishing server instead of the actual one (specified above) to retain the host header generated by the client browser. If you are using host headers to separate Web sites on a server, this setting must be enabled. You can also configure bridging at this point. Bridging allows you to redirect the request to a different port on the internal server. By default, the standard ports are used. Click Next to continue.

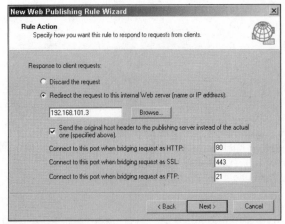

Figure 17-55: You must configure the behavior of the Web publishing rule to redirect to the server being published.

5. Review the settings specified in the wizard. After verifying the settings, click Finish to create the rule.

The published Web server should now be accessible from the outside.

Server Publishing rules

Server Publishing rules are similar to Web publishing rules except they can be used for any protocol, not just Web protocols. Click Server Publishing Rules under Publishing in the left pane. To create a new rule, click Publish a Server in the right pane.

1. Enter a name for the Server Publishing Rule and then click Next.

2. Specify the internal and external addresses for the published server, as shown in Figure 17-56. The internal address is the address on which the service to be published resides. The external address is the address to which remote users will connect to reach the published service. This external address must be assigned to the external network interface on the server. If you add an address to the interface, you must restart the ISA Server service for the change to take effect. Click Next to continue.

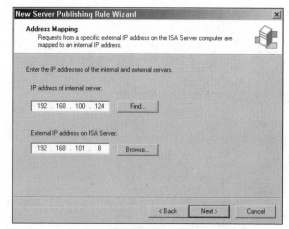

Figure 17-56: You need to specify the internal IP address of the server to be published and the external address to which users will connect.

3. Choose the protocol for the published server from the drop-down box, as shown in Figure 17-57. The number of protocols that can be used to publish a server is more limited than the number of protocols available for a protocol rule because the protocols must be able to handle a forwarded inbound connection. Select the protocol, and click Next. (Note that publishing a mail server is covered in the next section.)

4. You can now select a client set if you want to filter the rule based on the origin of the connection. Any request is allowed by default, but by selecting the Specific computers option, you can specify a client set.

5. Review the selected options, and click Finish to save the rule.

Connections to the published IP address should now be forwarded securely to the internal server.

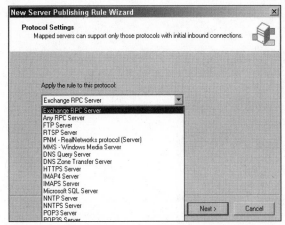

Figure 17-57: Select the protocol to use for the published server.

Mail Server Security Wizard

When publishing a mail server, use the Mail Server Security Wizard rather than a regular Server Publishing rule. This wizard creates the appropriate rules for an entire mail server, including SMTP and POP3, among others.

1. Under Publishing in the left pane, right click Server Publishing Rules and select Secure Mail Server. Click Next to continue past the introductory screen of the Mail Server Security Wizard.

2. Select the mail protocols that will be published, as shown in Figure 17-58. By selecting the Apply content filtering check box under Incoming SMTP, incoming mail will be filtered using the content filter built into ISA Server. Click Next to continue.

3. Enter the external IP address of the ISA Server that will be used to publish the services. As with a Server Publishing rule, the address must be associated with the external network interface on the server. Click Next to continue.

4. Specify the internal IP address of the mail server. Enter the address or select the On the local host radio button if the mail server is running on the same system as ISA Server. Click Next to continue.

5. Review the summary of the settings you have chosen, and click Finish to create the rules. A number of rules are created; the exact number is based on the number of protocols that will be supported.

Mail should now pass through the ISA Server unimpeded.

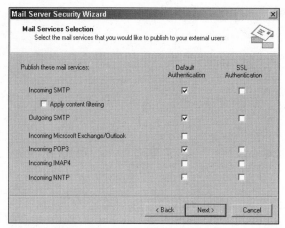

Figure 17-58: Select the mail protocols to be published.

IP packet filters

IP packet filters, located in the left pane under Access Policy, are an advanced type of filter. During the Getting Started Wizard you had an opportunity to configure Packet Filtering and Intrusion Detection. This is the location where the packet filtering rules are created.

You can create custom packet filters by clicking the Create a Packet Filter icon.

1. Enter a name for the new packet filter in the New IP Packet Filter Wizard and then click Next.

2. Select whether this filter will allow or deny packets, and click Next.

3. Choose whether to use a custom filter or select from a list of predefined filters, as shown in Figure 17-59. The predefined filters can filter a range of protocol types, such as Identd (a protocol that is commonly blocked at firewalls). Choose Custom to create a custom filter, and click Next to continue.

4. Define the filter settings. You first select an IP protocol, TCP, UDP, or ICMP. You can also select Any to use any protocol, or Custom to specify a different IP protocol number. Also, select a direction for the connection. You can filter inbound or outbound connections, or both. Depending on the protocol you select, you can also set port numbers. For example, you can set TCP port numbers by selecting Fixed port from the drop-down box and entering a port in the Port number box. The default setting is All ports and you can also select Dynamic for the Local port if the port is chosen dynamically by the protocol. Figure 17-60 shows an example of filter settings. Click Next to continue.

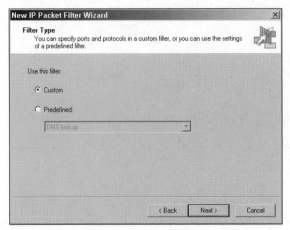

Figure 17-59: Choose to use either a custom or predefined filter.

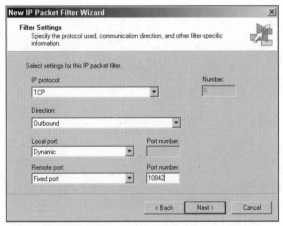

Figure 17-60: An example of a custom set of filter settings

5. Select the IP addresses for which the filter is effective. By default, the filter is effective for all IP addresses on the server's external interface, as shown in Figure 17-61. You can also specify a particular address on the external interface or an address for another computer on the perimeter network. Click Next.

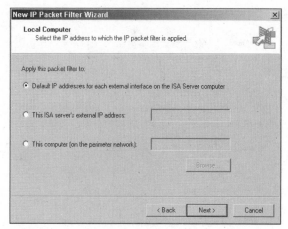

Figure 17-61: The packet filter can be effective for all addresses on the server's external interface or for a specific address only.

6. Select the remote system to which you will apply the filter. By default, the filter applies to all remote systems. Selecting Only this remote computer and entering an IP address in the box means the filter will only be effective for communications with that system. Click Next.

7. Review the settings, and click Finish to create the rule.

Traffic control

ISA Server also provides a set of rules for traffic control or quality of service (QoS). Click Bandwidth Rules in the left pane of ISA Management. A default rule is created automatically when ISA Server is installed with the Default Bandwidth Priority. The default bandwidth priority, as discussed earlier, is 100 for both incoming and outgoing traffic.

You may want to reduce or increase the amount of bandwidth allocated for specific content such as streaming media or MP3 files. To create a new rule, right-click Bandwidth Rules and select New, Rule.

1. Give the new rule a name, and click Next to continue.

2. You can restrict the bandwidth rule based on protocol. All protocols are included by default, but a specific protocol can be used. You may want to restrict certain instant messaging (IM) protocols or other unimportant protocols. To set a protocol restriction, select Selected Protocols or All IP traffic except selected, and select the protocols from the list. Click Next to continue.

3. You can assign a schedule to the Bandwidth rule. Bandwidth rules are the ultimate use for schedules. Scheduling bandwidth restrictions allows important traffic to have high priority during work hours and less important traffic, such as remote backups or synchronizations, higher priority during off hours. By default, the rule is always effective, but you can select a schedule from the drop-down box. Click Next to continue.

4. You can choose a client set or users and groups to restrict the Bandwidth rule. You can use this function to limit or expand the amount of bandwidth that certain clients have access to. Click Next to continue to the next step,

5. You can specify destination sets for the rule. This allows you to restrict the rule based on the external destination of traffic. You may want to have higher bandwidth priorities for traffic to a remote site, for example. Select the destination set option from the drop-down menu, and click Next. The rule will apply to all destinations by default.

6. You can now restrict the rule based on content groups. All content groups are included by default. Selecting content groups from the list, as shown in Figure 17-62, will restrict the rule to only those content groups. This allows you to restrict the bandwidth for certain files, such as MP3s, as in the content groups example earlier in the chapter. Click Next to continue.

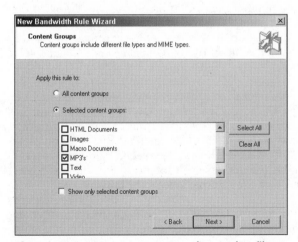

Figure 17-62: Content groups can be used to filter Bandwidth rules.

7. Set the bandwidth priority for the rule. The default setting is to use the default priority. Selecting Custom and selecting the bandwidth priority, as shown in Figure 17-63, will use that priority for the rule. The priority must be defined, as discussed earlier in the chapter. Click Next.

8. Review the Bandwidth rule settings before clicking Finish to save the rule.

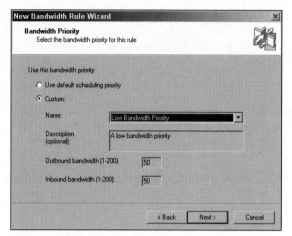

Figure 17-63: Select the bandwidth priority to use with this Bandwidth rule.

Application filters

ISA Server also contains a number of application filters. Click Application Filters under Extensions in the left pane. Figure 17-64 shows the application filters in the right pane. Most of the application filters are enabled automatically and have no options. You should explore the filters by right-clicking each one and selecting properties.

One of the filters that is configurable is the Streaming Media filter. Right-click the filter, and select Properties. Click the Live Stream Splitting tab. This tab, as shown in Figure 17-65, allows you to configure stream splitting. Stream splitting allows you to split a media stream between a number of streaming media servers, each of which rebroadcasts the stream. This splits the load between a number of servers. Load balancing streaming media servers has traditionally been a difficult task. The streaming servers must be on the internal side of the firewall.

Another useful application filter is the SMTP filter. Right-click the filter, and click Properties. The SMTP filter can be configured based on a number of factors, including keywords.

1. Click the Keyword tab and then click Add to add a Keyword rule.

2. The Mail Keyword Rule dialog box is shown in Figure 17-66. Enter the keyword and then select the keyword location in the message header, body, or both.

3. You must also select the action to be taken when the keyword is matched. You can delete the message, hold it, or forward it to another address. Click OK to save the Keyword rule.

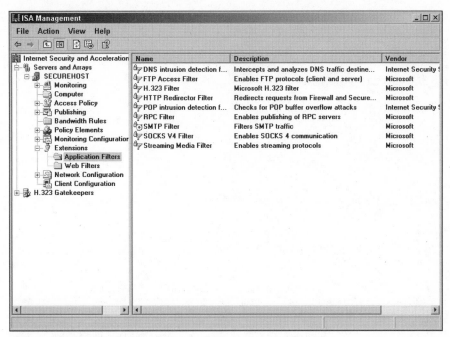

Figure 17-64: ISA Server includes a number of application filters.

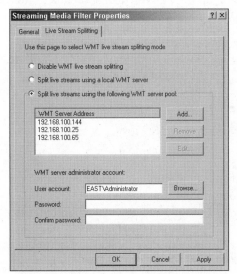

Figure 17-65: ISA Server allows you to perform stream splitting on streaming media.

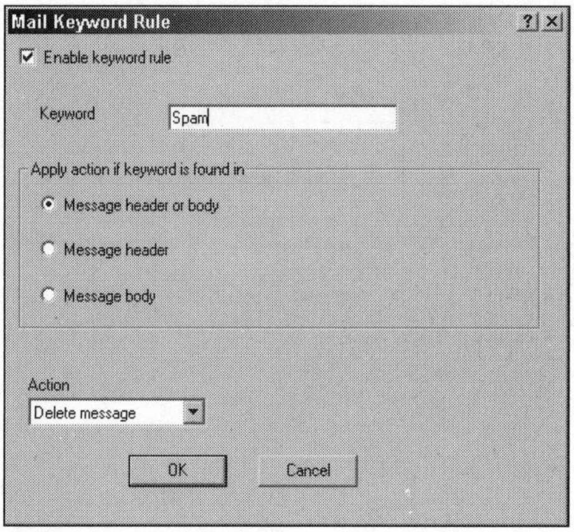

Figure 17-66: You can create a Keyword rule to perform an action on messages containing a certain keyword.

Under the Users/Domains tab you can cause messages to be rejected based on either sender or domain. Using the sender or domain rejection can stop spam from occurring from known senders.

The Attachments tab is used to handle messages with certain attachment types. Click the Add button on the Attachments tab to open the Mail Attachment Rule dialog box, as shown in Figure 17-67. An attachment rule can be applied to attachments with certain properties (a specific name, a particular extension, or a maximum size). Many sites block large or dangerous attachments, such as .EXE or .VBS files. You must also set the action to be taken when the specified attachment is found. You can delete, hold, or forward the message with the attachment.

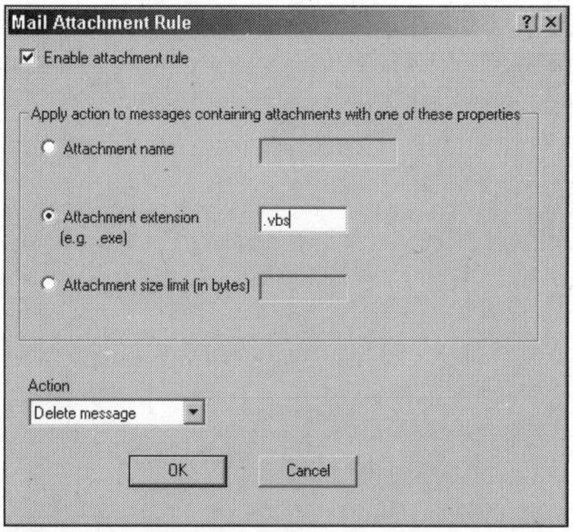

Figure 17-67: Attachment rules can handle messages with attachments with a certain name, file extension, or maximum size.

Finally, the SMTP Commands tab, as shown in Figure 17-68, is used to enable or disable specific SMTP commands and limit their maximum length. You can add a command not listed using the Add button, or disable or set the maximum length of a listed command using the Edit button. Click OK to save the SMTP Filter properties.

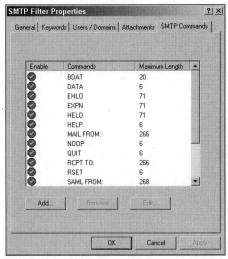

Figure 17-68: The SMTP Commands tab

Summary

Microsoft ISA Server 2000 is available in two different editions: the standard edition, and the Enterprise Edition. The Standard Edition does not support array configurations. Before installing ISA Server Enterprise Edition, you must run the Enterprise Initialization to update the Active Directory schema. ISA Server can be installed in three modes: Caching, Firewall, and Integrated. Integrated mode includes both the firewall and caching components. After ISA Server is installed on Windows 2003, SP1 must be installed for ISA Server to function correctly.

The Getting Started Wizard simplifies the process of configuring ISA Server and walks you through the process of configuring policy elements. A policy consists of various rules that determine the type of access users have to the Internet. You can apply policies at the Enterprise level only, the array level only, or as a combination of both. When an Enterprise policy is configured, array-level policies can be configured to apply further restrictions. After ISA Server is installed, at least one protocol rule and a Site and Content rule must be configured before users can access the Internet.

✦   ✦   ✦

Configuring the Acceleration Service

✦   ✦   ✦   ✦

In This Chapter

Setting caching
configurations

Analyzing traffic and
reporting findings

✦   ✦   ✦   ✦

Microsoft ISA Server's caching component provides
a complete caching service with both forward and
reverse caching functionality. The acceleration features of
ISA Server were discussed in detail in Chapter 16.

Chapter 17 outlined the process for installing ISA Server,
including both the firewall and caching components. This
chapter assumes in its examples that ISA Server is installed
in caching mode, just as the previous chapter assumed ISA
Server was installed in firewall mode.

The caching and firewall components have been separated
into two chapters for the purpose of readability. If you have
installed ISA Server in integrated mode, however, the features
in both Chapter 17 and this chapter will exist, and the Getting
Started Wizard will have both caching and firewall configuration steps.

Caching Configuration

With ISA Server installed in cache mode, you will notice a
number of differences from firewall mode. Access control
is limited to only FTP and HTTP protocols, and Server
Publishing Rules are gone; only Web Publishing Rules exist.
The reason for these changes is that when in cache mode, ISA
Server can only handle HTTP and FTP traffic.

ISA Server caches all traffic, incoming and outgoing, as long as that traffic type has caching enabled in the cache policy. Regardless of how traffic passes through the server, through rules or through the Web Proxy service, the content is cached.

The methods described in the Forward Caching and Reverse Caching sections in this chapter are only for when you have an ISA Server installation that is configured in caching mode. A number of methods exist for allowing traffic through an ISA Server firewall, and if the server is configured in integrated mode, cacheable traffic will be cached automatically.

Cache policy and size

The cache policy and size control how the caching portion of ISA Server behaves. The cache size controls the amount of disk space that can be used and the location of the cache.

The cache policy is used to set the caching behavior of traffic passing through the server. You can enable and disable caching of certain types of traffic and configure other options such as active caching.

Cache size and location

During installation of ISA Server in cache or integrated mode, you have the opportunity to set the cache size. As discussed in Chapter 17, the cache should reside on its own drive or array, and the cache disks should be fast for high caching performance. The cache should not reside on the same drive as the system files because this will degrade the performance of the operating system. Also, the cache can only reside on an NTFS formatted drive. For optimal performance, make sure the cache is large enough as per the number of clients. As already mention in Chapter 17, the general formula to follow when configuring the size of the cache is 100MB + 0.5MB per user.

You can change the size and location of the cache at any time. Click Cache Configuration under the server name in the left pane of ISA Management, as shown in Figure 18-1. From here, you can see the cache configuration in the right pane and make changes.

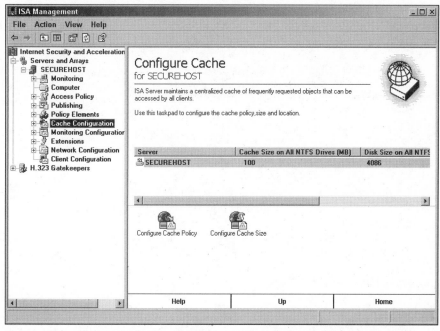

Figure 18-1: Clicking Cache Configuration on the left shows the cache size and location on the right.

To change the cache size or location, follow these steps:

1. Click the Configure Cache Size icon to open the Properties dialog box shown in Figure 18-2. As you can see, the system drive is being used for caching and the cache size is only 100MB.

2. Remove the cache from the system drive. Select the drive and then enter a value of zero in the Maximum cache size box. Click Set to make the change. You can now select the disk on which the cache will reside.

3. Enter the size of cache you want, and click Set. In this example, the E: drive is a dedicated caching volume. The entire drive will be used for caching, as shown in Figure 18-3.

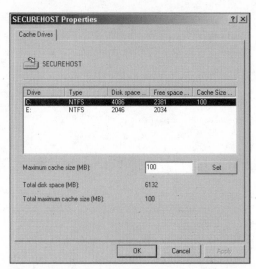

Figure 18-2: The cache is currently on the system drive, and is 100MB.

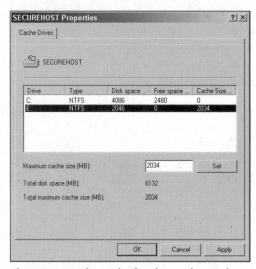

Figure 18-3: The cache has been changed to another drive and expanded.

Note

The 2034MB cache size shown in Figure 18-3 is large enough for 3,868 users, according to the formula provided earlier in this chapter. These settings are for a very large number of users.

4. Click OK in the Properties dialog box to save the changes you have made to the caching drives, and restart the Web Proxy service so the change will take effect. Figure 18-4 shows a dialog box where you can either restart the service or save the changes without restarting the service. If you choose not to restart the service, the changes will not take effect until the service is restarted manually or after a reboot.

Figure 18-4: The Web Proxy service must be restarted before changes to the cache size or location take effect.

Cache policy

Now that you've reconfigured the cache drives, you can configure the cache policies. The cache policies determine the behavior of the ISA Server cache. The cache policy basically consists of a number of different settings configured for the cache. Some of the settings included in a cache policy include an HTTP expiration policy, an FTP expiration policy, active caching, as well as several other advanced options. Keep in mind when you are configuring cache policies that they are configured at the array or server level. In other words, a global cache policy cannot be created to apply to all arrays.

To configure a cache policy, follow these steps:

1. Click the Configure Cache Policy icon to open the Cache Configuration Properties dialog box.

2. Click the HTTP tab, as shown in Figure 18-5. HTTP caching is enabled by default.

3. You can disable HTTP caching by deselecting the Enable HTTP caching check box. You can also set the update frequency or "freshness" behavior of objects in the cache.

Cross-Reference   The detailed calculation of freshness is discussed in Chapter 16.

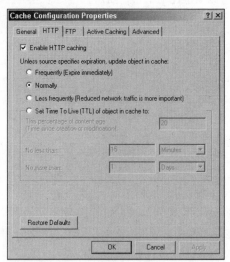

Figure 18-5: The HTTP tab of the Cache Configuration Properties dialog box is used to configure the HTTP caching features of ISA Server.

Objects with an explicitly specified expiration will always use that data to control update frequency. For objects without an explicit TTL (Time to Live), the TTL is calculated based on the object's last modified time. With the default setting of Normally, the object will expire in 20 percent of the time since the last modified time with a maximum of one day and a minimum of 15 minutes. Changing this setting to Frequently causes objects to expire immediately. Less frequently causes the object to expire in 40 percent of the time since the last modified time with a maximum of two days and minimum of 30 minutes.

You can also set the value manually. The values shown in the boxes are the default values for the Normally setting. You can set the percentage of the time since the last modified time as well as the minimum and maximum cache times. Setting too large a value will cause content to become stale, while smaller values increase network traffic and decrease the effectiveness of caching.

Clicking the FTP tab allows you to configure the FTP caching settings, as shown in Figure 18-6. As with HTTP caching, you can enable or disable FTP caching. The only other configuration option is the TTL value for all FTP content. FTP does not have the capability of retuning last modified times or explicit TTL values like HTTP, so the TTL value must be statically set. The default value is 1440 minutes, which is 24 hours. If you find FTP content becoming stale in your cache, you should lower this value. Raising the value can help to reduce network traffic, but the tradeoff in content becoming stale is probably not worth it.

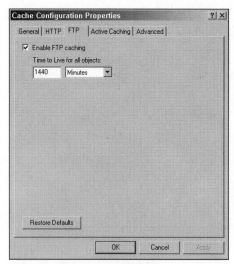

Figure 18-6: The FTP tab of the Cache Configuration Properties dialog box is used to enable FTP caching and set the TTL value for cached FTP content.

The Active Caching tab allows you to configure ISA Server's Active Caching feature, as discussed in Chapter 16. In brief, while data in the static cache is removed after the TTL expires and re-cached on the next request for that object, active caching refreshes the content before the TTL expires so that the content is always in the cache.

Active caching is disabled by default. Select the Enable active caching check box, as shown in Figure 18-7, to turn on the feature. The default active caching setting is Normally. This causes active caching to add objects to the active caching list if they are accessed more than once within (2*TTL). A setting of Frequently sets this value to (3*TTL), and Less frequently sets the value to (1*TTL). Objects on the caching list are removed if they are not accessed within these times. Object refresh intervals on the active caching list vary with the load on the server from (.5*TTL) to almost TTL on heavily loaded servers.

If network performance is an issue, you may want to select the Less frequently option which sets active caching to a minimum. If objects frequently requested by users should be regularly refreshed, select the Frequently option; keep in mind that doing so will result in an increase in traffic. The Normally option is basically a balance between the two.

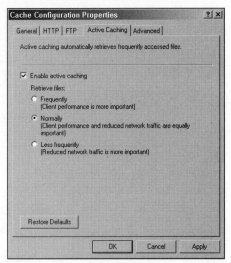

Figure 18-7: Active caching can be enabled and configured from the Cache Configuration Properties dialog box's Active Caching tab.

The Advanced tab, shown in Figure 18-8, is used to configure advanced caching settings. The first setting allows you to restrict caching to objects smaller than a specified size. This helps to keep the overall cache size down if you have limited disk space, but large objects can show some of the greatest bandwidth improvements through caching so the limit is disabled by default.

The next two settings are enabled by default. Objects without a specified last modification time are cached by default using a static TTL. This can cause problems with stale content. If you find you are having problems with these objects becoming stale, you can disable this option. In addition, all objects are cached by default including those returning HTTP status codes other than 200 (success). Even replies such as 404 (page not found) are cached. This option can also be disabled so only successful replies are cached.

The Cache dynamic content option will cause objects with question marks in their URL to be cached although this is not done by default. Dynamic content is generated when a user must input information to have the results returned, such as using a search engine to search for specific Web content. Dynamic content is typically user specific therefore it is not typically cached. The maximum size of URLs cached in memory restricts the length of a URL that can be cached in RAM. This restricts excessively large URLs from taking up RAM.

The next configuration option is the behavior of the caching server if the cached object expires and is not available and cannot be refreshed. By default, the expired object is returned from the cache if less than 50 percent of the TTL has passed but no more than 60 minutes. These values can be adjusted to whatever you feel is appropriate. Increasing these values will allow unavailable content to remain available to caching clients for longer, but it will become increasingly stale.

Finally, the Percentage of free memory used for caching value option controls how much space the RAM cache takes up. ISA Server keeps the most commonly accessed content cached in RAM for fast access rather than on disk. If the RAM cache is full, this value (50 percent of free memory) will show as utilized in the Windows Task Manager. Reducing this value has no effect on memory used for other programs on the system because ISA Server uses only free memory for the RAM cache. If other software is utilizing all of the system memory, no RAM caching will occur.

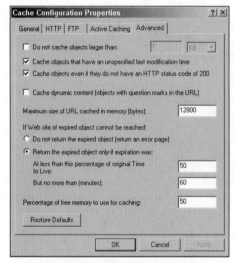

Figure 18-8: The Advanced tab of the Cache Configuration Properties dialog box is used to configure advanced caching settings and special restrictions.

Scheduled content download

Scheduled content download, as discussed in Chapter 16, allows you to download content into the ISA Server cache on a set schedule. This process enables you to synchronize content that does not change much on a schedule when network traffic is low. For example, it is useful for synchronizing Intranet sites daily at branch offices.

To configure a Scheduled Content Download job, do the following:

1. Right-click Scheduled Content Download under Cache Configuration in the left pane, point to New, and select Job.

2. Enter a name for the job and then click Next to continue.

3. Set the time and date for the job or first job in the set in the case of a recurring job. Click Next.

4. Set the frequency for the recurrence of the job, as shown in the New Schedules Content Download Job Wizard in Figure 18-9. By default, the job is run only once. You can also choose to run the job daily or on certain days of the week. Click Next.

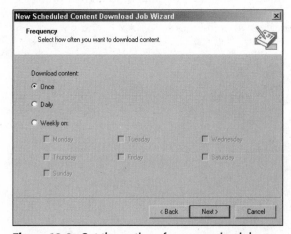

Figure 18-9: Set the options for a recurring job.

5. Specify the content to be downloaded, as shown in Figure 18-10. Enter the location containing the content to be downloaded in the box. You can specify any location that is cacheable by ISA Server. All content in the specified directory, and any links below that location are downloaded.

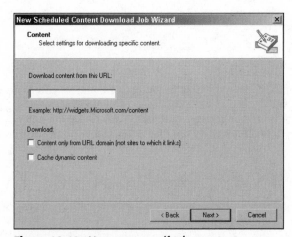

Figure 18-10: You must specify the content to be downloaded.

Two options are available for the specified content to download. By default, all links in the specified content location are followed and the content is downloaded. Selecting the Content only from URL domain option means that links to URLs other than the specified URL will not be copied. By default, dynamic content is not downloaded. You must select the Cache dynamic content option to download this content. Dynamic content should not be downloaded unless there is a specific reason, such as large amounts of bandwidth being consumed by this content. Even in such cases, it is often not possible to cache dynamic content because the content must be generated for each request.

Figure 18-11 shows the next step in the wizard. You must configure TTL options, link depth, and the maximum number of cached objects. The TTL options allow you to explicitly specify a downloaded object's TTL. If you download an intranet site once per day, for example, and the TTL is less than one day, the site will be removed from the cache before it is downloaded again on the schedule. If the TTL is short, the site will be downloaded a number of times negating the idea of the scheduled download.

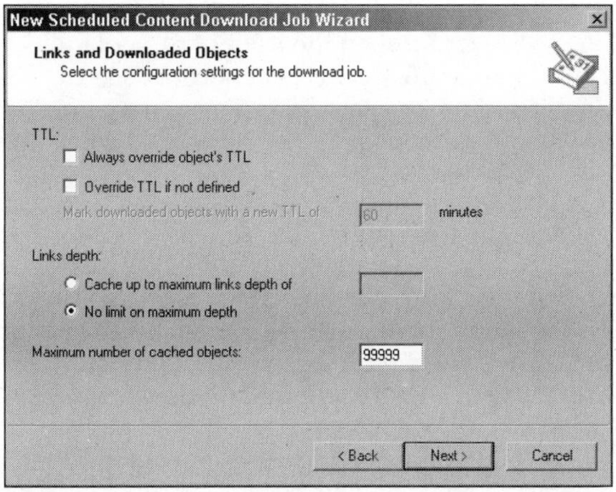

Figure 18-11: You can configure TTL and Link depth options as well as the maximum number of cached objects.

Two options exist for configuring the TTL. The first option, Always override object's TTL, will set the TTL of all downloaded objects to the value specified in the "Mark downloaded objects with a new TTL of" box. The Override TTL if not defined option will only set the TTL of an object to the specified TTL if that object has no explicitly specified TTL value.

The Links depth option controls how many levels of links will be followed during the download. By default, all links will be followed with no maximum depth. On a standard intranet site without external links, this option is fine. If the site being downloaded has external links, however, the number of downloaded objects could become extremely large because links could be followed to external sites and carry on as long as there are new links. This is only the case if the Content only from URL domain option is not selected in the previous step. To limit the link depth, select the Cache up to a maximum links depth of option and then enter the number of levels of links to be followed.

The final option is the Maximum number of cached objects. By default, a maximum of 99,999 objects are cached during the download process. Setting this limit can control the size of downloaded content in the event that you are downloading content from external sites and not limiting links depth. You can also lower this limit if your content download from an internal site is too large due to a substantial number of files on the site. Click Next to continue.

You can now review the selected options for the Scheduled Content Download Job. Click Finish to save the job. At the specified time, the content should be downloaded automatically from the source into the cache.

Forward caching

Forward caching is configured in ISA Server through the use of Protocol Rules or the Web Proxy service. As explained in Chapter 16, forward caching is used to cache content for internal users transferring HTTP or FTP traffic. This reduces network bandwidth on the outside of the caching server, and increases speed when accessing cached content.

Cache only configuration

The default behavior in which forward caching works is effective when the caching server is not also the firewall. Each Web browser must be configured to use the caching server as a proxy server. By default, the server is configured to listen on port 8080 for all internal IP addresses with which it is configured.

To enable clients to use forward caching, simply configure each Web browser to use the ISA Server as a proxy server using the port on which the ISA Server is configured to listen. By default, this port is 8080, but it is possible to change both the port number and interfaces on which the server listens.

To view or change the listener options, right-click the server or array in the left pane of ISA Management, select Properties, and select the Outgoing Web Requests tab, as shown in Figure 18-12.

By default, ISA Server listens on all internal IP addresses. The default TCP port for connections is 8080, and the server is set to use integrated authentication for requests.

You can change all of these settings. By default, all internal IP addresses are configured the same. You can set specific configuration for individual addresses by selecting the "Configure listeners individually per IP address" option and then using the Add button to add each IP on which to listen.

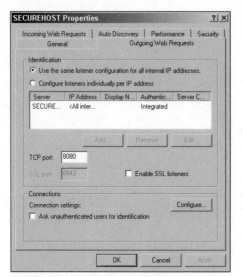

Figure 18-12: The Outgoing Web Requests tab of the server or array Properties dialog box is used to configure the ISA Server Web Proxy.

Using the Add/Edit Listeners dialog box, first select the server on which the IP address resides from the drop-down box. Next, select the IP address on which to listen from the IP Address box. You can also enter an optional display name for the listener and specify a server certificate to use for the Web Proxy server to authenticate to clients. This allows clients to verify the identity of the server. Figure 18-13 shows the configuration for a listener in the Add/Edit Listeners dialog box.

You now need to configure the authentication methods allowed for clients before you add the listener. You can select any number of authentication methods, but if none are selected, rules requiring authentication will not work. Client authentication is used when users or groups are specified as filters in rules and when the Ask unauthenticated users for identification option is selected in the Incoming Web Requests and Outgoing Web Requests tabs. In most cases, the default setting of integrated authentication is fine. This causes clients to be authenticated based on their local or domain login credentials and passwords are not transmitted over the network.

The Basic and Digest authentication methods allow ISA Server to authenticate users against a domain as well. The basic method transfers passwords in plain text over the network. The digest method can be used only with Windows 2000 or Windows 2003 domains, and uses an encrypted password transfer to authenticate. With these options, you can select the domain against which users will be authenticated. Finally, you can choose to use Client Certificates for authentication, but this method is only effective when a Secure Sockets Layer (SSL) channel is being used. Click OK to add the listener.

Figure 18-13: The Add/Edit Listeners dialog box can be used to add an IP address on which the server listens for Web requests.

Changing the TCP port on which the server listens will change the port for all listeners. Normally, the default setting of 8080 is fine unless you have another service running on that port.

You can also set the server to listen for SSL requests by selecting the Enable SSL listeners box. This will cause ISA Server to listen on the specified IP addresses and on the specified TCP port, 8443 by default. If this is enabled, the server must have server certificates for each address on which it is listening. The client must also be configured to use port 8443 for the HTTPS proxy. This configuration allows the client to connect securely to the proxy server.

Two more options exist for outgoing Web requests. Click the Configure button under connections to open the Connection Settings dialog box, as shown in Figure 18-14. By default, an unlimited number of connections are allowed to the ISA Server. You can limit the number of allowed connections (if traffic is too high, for example) by selecting the Maximum option and specifying the maximum number of connections in the respective box. You can also specify the connection timeout, which is 120 seconds by default. If there is no communication on a connection in this time, the connection will be closed.

Ask unauthenticated users for identification is the final option. By default, anyone can use the proxy for outgoing Web connections. Selecting this option causes those users who do not have an authentication token to be prompted for authentication information. If they cannot authenticate, they are denied access to the server. Click OK to save the listener.

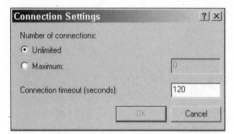

Figure 18-14: The Connection Settings dialog box is used to set the maximum number of allowed connections and the connection timeout.

Firewall and cache configuration

In a firewall configuration, protocol rules are used to provide access to the external network for internal users. Protocol rules are also used for forward caching when the caching server is also being used as a firewall.

To configure a protocol rule, do the following:

1. Click Protocol Rules under Access Policy in the left pane of ISA Management and then click the Create a Protocol Rule for Internet Access icon in the right pane. Using this icon rather than the Create a Protocol Rule icon will create a rule using all of the Internet protocols (HTTP, FTP, and so on) as opposed to having to choose each protocol manually.

2. Enter a name for the new protocol rule in the New Protocol Rule Wizard and then click Next. The standard Internet protocols are selected by default, as shown in Figure 18-15.

3. You can add protocols to the protocol rule by deselecting the Show only selected protocols box and selecting the protocols to add from the list. This will provide access to these protocols through this rule, but only HTTP and FTP traffic are cached regardless of these settings. Click Next to continue.

As this rule is being configured for caching, you probably won't need to restrict the outgoing traffic; however, if your server is in integrated mode, you may need to restrict client access using the rule. Normally you can accept the default settings for simple caching.

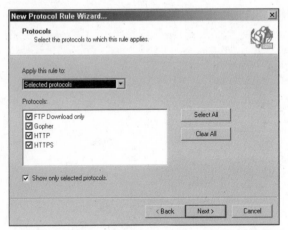

Figure 18-15: The default Web protocols are selected automatically. You can add protocols to the rule, but they will not be cached.

The next portion of the New Protocol Rule Wizard allows you to configure a schedule as to when the rule is in effect and to what the rule applies.

1. Select the schedule from the drop-down box, or accept the default setting of Always (the rule is always active) and then click Next.

2. You can apply restrictions through the rule based on client sets or users and groups. This allows you to configure the computers and users to which the rule is going to apply. You can choose to filter the rule or accept the default setting, which applies the rule to all users. Click Next.

3. Check the settings you have specified in the rule, and click Finish to save the rule.

Forward caching should now be enabled for traffic using the protocol rule. When ISA Server is installed in caching or integrated mode, forward caching is enabled by default (as shown previously in the Cache Policy section).

Reverse caching

Reverse caching is enabled using publishing rules. Unlike when ISA Server is in Firewall or Integrated mode, server publishing rules are not available in caching mode. Server publishing rules, which enable you to publish services other than HTTP and FTP, are unnecessary because these other protocols cannot be cached.

Cross-Reference   Creating a Web publishing rule is covered extensively in Chapter 17. If you are creating a rule that you want to filter, follow the directions there because the filters are also explained.

This example creates a simple rule to publish a server with no filters.

Before you create a rule, you must configure a listener. You can configure listeners individually or configure one listener for all external IP addresses on the server. Creating individual listeners is a more secure method.

Tip   On a server configured in caching mode, if there is only one network interface in the system, there may not be "external" and "internal" IP addresses as on a firewall. In this case, all IP addresses can be either external or internal.

1. Right-click the server or array in the left pane of ISA Management, and select Properties.

2. Click the Incoming Web Requests tab, ensure that the Configure listeners individually per IP address option is selected, and click the Add button to add a listener.

3. Select the server name from the Server drop-down box and the IP address on which to listen from the IP address drop-down box. This IP address should be the address referenced in the destination set configured for the publishing rule.

4. Set the authentication options as discussed in the Forward Caching section and then click OK to save the listener.

5. Ensure that no local Web servers are listening on the specified port, which will almost always be 80 for publishing Web sites, and click OK to close the server Properties dialog box.

To create a Web publishing rule, do the following:

1. Select Web Publishing Rules under Publishing in the left pane of ISA Management.

2. Click the Create a Web Publishing Rule in the right pane.

3. Enter a name for the publishing rule and then click Next.

4. The next step is to specify the server to be published using a destination set. (You must have already defined a destination set containing the external address that is being published.)

5. Select Specified destination set from the Apply this rule to drop-down box, and select the destination set to be published from the Name drop-down box. Click Next to continue.

You can now filter the rule based on client sets. A Web publishing rule is the inverse of a protocol rule in that client sets are used to define external users in the former and internal users in the latter. Destination sets, on the other hand, are used to define the server name or address to be published with a publishing rule, but contain external users in protocol rules.

Select Any request unless you want to filter the rule and then click Next. The next step is to configure how requests made to the address (or addresses) in the specified destination set are handled. You will most likely want to direct these requests to a Web server because you are configuring reverse caching. Select the Redirect the request option, as shown in Figure 18-16, and enter the name or address of the Web server to which to send the requests. Click Next to continue.

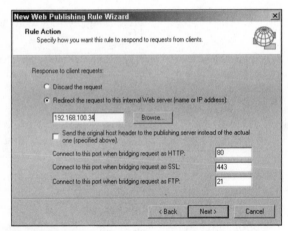

Figure 18-16: You must specify where the requests received to the address in the destination set are forwarded.

You can now review your chosen settings and then click Finish to create the rule. Requests to the address in the destination set will be forwarded to the specified server and responses will be cached.

Secure Sockets Layer bridging

SSL bridging is used to relieve the load of processing SSL encryption and decryption from a Web server. It also enables SSL content to be cached because it is not SSL encrypted as it travels between the ISA Server and Web server.

When SSL bridging is not used, SSL tunneling occurs. The client requests a secure page through the ISA Server and the server processes the request and makes the connection to the destination. Traffic between the client and destination are then tunneled through the ISA Server so that they have a clear path over which to establish SSL communications.

SSL bridging can be enabled in two directions. For server publishing, the most likely scenario, you need to have a server certificate installed on the ISA Server just as you would on the Web server. You then need to enable SSL listeners.

1. Right-click the server or array in the left pane of ISA Management, and select Properties.

2. Click Incoming Web Requests.

3. Select the Enable SSL listeners box.

4. Specify a server certificate for each listener that will accept SSL connections. Select a listener from the list and click Edit, or click Add to add a new listener if one is not already established for the IP address on which you want to listen.

5. Configure the listener as described in the Reverse Caching section, but also select the Use a server certificate to authenticate to Web clients option.

6. Click the Select button to select a certificate present on the server and then click OK.

7. Click OK to save the listener; then click OK to save the server properties.

Now that ISA Server is configured to listen for SSL requests, SSL communications from the client will be terminated at the ISA Server. With the default settings in a Web publishing rule, communications will be made via SSL from the ISA Server to the Web server. In other words, the client makes an SSL request to the ISA Server; then the ISA Server makes the request via SSL to the Web server, and returns the result via the first SSL connection from the client.

You can change this behavior, however.

1. Locate the Web publishing rule in the right pane by selecting Web Publishing Rules under Publishing in the left pane.

2. Right-click the rule for which to change SSL bridging behavior and click Properties.

3. Select the Bridging tab, as shown in Figure 18-17.

As you can see, SSL requests from clients are bridged as SSL requests to the Web server by default. To alleviate load on the Web server, you can change this setting to HTTP requests.

Setting this rule will cause ISA Server to accept SSL requests from clients as usual, but instead of requesting the data from the Web server via SSL, the request is made via HTTP. This causes the data to traverse the internal network in plain text, but reduces the load on the Web server. The Web server must also be configured accordingly because some sites may force a secure connection for some applications.

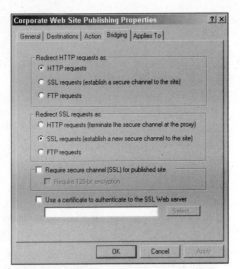

Figure 18-17: SSL Bridging behavior is configured from the Bridging tab of a Web Publishing Rule's Properties dialog box.

The Bridging tab can also be used to force SSL connections to the published site. Selecting the Require secure channel for published site option will allow only SSL connections to the site. Selecting the Require 128-bit encryption option will allow only SSL connections using 128-bit encryption.

Finally, you can select the Use a certificate to authenticate to the SSL Web server option, click Select, and choose a client certificate to have the ISA Server use the selected certificate for authentication when it makes SSL connections to the internal Web server.

Traffic Analysis and Reporting

Now that you are familiar with how to configure ISA Server for caching, let's take a look at the ISA Server tools that can be used for traffic analysis and reporting. This is important for capacity planning, as well as monitoring how clients are using the Web.

ISA Server reporting and monitoring

ISA Server provides a variety of traffic analysis features. These features are useful for looking at the overall traffic patterns on the server as well as caching efficiency.

Reporting data is generated by Report Jobs. By default, reporting is not performed automatically. You can perform a one-time report job by right-clicking Report Jobs under Monitoring Configuration in the left pane of ISA Management and selecting New, Report Job. Simply click OK in the report job Properties dialog box to run the job immediately. This will generate the required data for reports.

You may, however, want to run reporting on a schedule. To do so, follow these steps:

1. Right-click Report Jobs and select New; then select Report Job.

2. Give the report job a name and, optionally, a description, in the General tab of the report job Properties dialog box; then select the Period tab, as shown in Figure 18-18.

3. Select the reporting period for the job. The reporting period defines the time from which data is included. For example, Daily will include the previous 24 hours' data, and Weekly will include data over the previous week. You can also use a custom period. As this is a daily report, select Daily and click the Schedule tab.

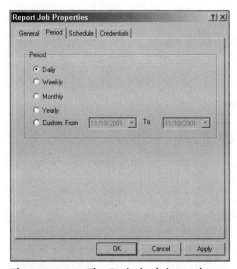

Figure 18-18: The Period tab is used to configure the amount of data collected by the reporting job.

The Schedule tab, as shown in Figure 18-19, is used to control when the job runs. The Start Report Generation section controls when the job begins. For most jobs, especially daily, you will want the report to occur at midnight so you can review the previous day's data; however, a report can be scheduled to run at any time depending on your needs and requirements.

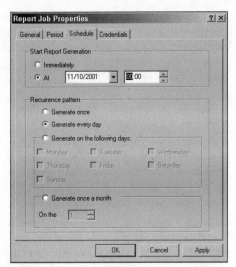

Figure 18-19: The Schedule tab is used to configure when and how often the job will run.

The Recurrence Pattern section is used to configure a recurring job. By default, the job is run only once. You may want to run a job every day, on certain days, or on a specific day of the month.

1. Select Generate every day and then choose the Credentials tab.

2. In the Credentials tab, enter a user name, domain, and password that have access to the reporting data on the server. This allows scheduled jobs to run without a user being logged in.

3. Click OK to save the job.

After the job has run at least once, you can view the report data. Expand the Reports item under Monitoring in the left pane of ISA Management, as shown in Figure 18-20. The five different reports available are as follows:

✦ Summary Report

✦ Web Usage Report

✦ Application Usage Report

✦ Traffic and Utilization Report

✦ Security Report

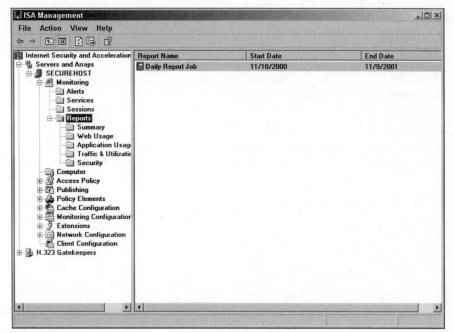

Figure 18-20: Reports in the left pane of ISA Management are used to view the data collected by the report jobs.

Select a report type in the left pane, and a list of available reports is shown in the right pane. Right-click a report in the right pane and then click Open to view the contents of the report. Reports are shown in Internet Explorer.

Summary reports

The Summary report shows a summary of all of the data in the other reports. The summary report does not go into as much detail as the others, but shows you an overall picture of activity on the server. Web usage, protocol usage, top users, and cache statistics are some of the items reported in the summary.

Web Usage report

The Web Usage report shows more detail about Web usage on the server based on the Web Proxy logs. Some of the items shown in the summary are included in this report, such as top users and top sites, but other information is also included, such as statistics pertaining to which browsers and which operating systems are connecting through the server and a breakdown of object types returned and HTTP response codes.

Application Usage report

The Application Usage report shows application usage through the server based on firewall logs. A caching server will likely not have any data in this report, but a firewall server using protocol rules will. The Application Usage report charts the applications being used over the server as well as operating system statistics and destination statistics.

Traffic and Utilization report

The Traffic and Utilization report is one of the most useful. Based on both the Web Proxy and firewall logs, this report shows overall traffic patterns on the server, including the following information:

✦ Traffic graphs and statistics

✦ Cache usage

✦ Protocol usage

✦ Connection statistics

✦ Request processing time

✦ Error statistics are all included in this report

Security report

The final report is the Security report. This report is based on the Web Proxy, firewall, and packet filter logs, and shows security statistics such as authorization failures and dropped packets.

Using all of these reports, you can better configure your ISA Server. By looking at the caching statistics, for example, you can adjust the caching configuration to better utilize the service. You can view security statistics to look for problems within the network. You can also use the Traffic and Utilization report to view traffic patterns on your network. This may allow you to adjust rules on the server to better utilize available bandwidth. Some key indicators of wasted bandwidth are protocols such as those used in instant messaging or file sharing applications being high on the list in the application usage report.

In addition to reports, the ISA Management Console provides other monitoring facilities, all under Monitoring in the left pane.

✦ **Alerts** — allows you to view ISA Server alerts in the right pane. Alerts are generated when there are problems or abnormalities in the server.

✦ **Services** — shows the ISA Server services in the right pane along with their status, the current number of sessions each service is handling, and the uptime of the service.

✦ **Sessions** — shows the current ISA Server sessions. The session type, user name, client computer name, and client IP address are all shown.

Cache performance counters

You can monitor the performance of the cache through the Windows Server Performance application. Using the System Monitor component within the Performance console you can monitor the real time performance of an ISA Server. After ISA Server is installed, counters are added to the Performance application specifically for monitoring different aspects of ISA Server performance.

1. Click Start, point to Administrative Tools, and click Performance. This opens the Performance Management Console.

2. Click System Monitor; then click the Add Counter button on the toolbar.

3. Select ISA Server Cache from the Performance object drop-down box.

A wide variety of counters are available, including the following:

✦ The URLs in Cache counter tracks the number of URLs that are being stored in the cache at any time.

✦ The Memory Cache Space Allocated and Disk Cache Space Allocated counters indicate how much of the memory or disk, respectively, is actually being used for caching. This will always be less than or equal to the total amount of space allocated for caching.

✦ The Memory URL Retrieve Rate and Disk URL Retrieve Rate display, in URLs per second, the number of URLs being served to clients from memory and disk, respectively.

✦ Memory Bytes Retrieved Rate and Disk Bytes Retrieved Rate display the number of bytes served from memory and disk.

Cache troubleshooting and optimization

You can troubleshoot and optimize the cache in a number of ways. Regular monitoring of an ISA Server using the Performance application can help you to more easily identify any problems and correct them before they become more serious and performance begins to noticeably suffer.

There are a number of indicators of a cache that is too small or is not functioning properly.

✦ Compare the URL Commit Rate counter, which tracks the attempts to cache URLs in URLs/sec to the Disk Failure Rate, which tracks failed attempts to cache URLs. If the rates are close to being equal, the cache may be too small or not functioning. Low values for Total URLs cached and URLs in Cache also indicate a problem with the caching server or a cache that is too small.

✦ Look at the Disk Cache Allocated Space counter. If this counter is close to or at the total disk space configured for caching, the cache is too small or objects are not expiring quickly enough (TTLs may be being overridden). If this value is not close to or at the limit, there is most likely a problem with the cache and more investigation is required.

✦ By looking at counters such as the Memory Usage Ratio Percent, you can determine if the memory allocation to caching is sufficient. The Memory Usage Ratio Percent counter tracks the number of URLs retrieved from memory compared to the number retrieved in total. A high value indicates that the system is using a lot of memory, and more may be allocated to the cache or added to the system to increase performance.

✦ The Cache Hit Ratio and Cache Running Hit Ratio counters in the ISA Server Web Proxy service Performance object can both show the number of requests serviced by the cache compared to the total number of requests served as a percentage. The Cache Hit Ratio counts hits from the time the Web Proxy service was started while the Cache Running Hit Ratio counts only the last 10,000 hits. Low values can indicate a cache that is too small or incorrectly configured.

Summary

The chapter looks at the caching component of ISA Server. As an ISA Server retrieves Web requests on behalf on internal clients, the results can be stored in the ISA Server cache thereby reducing network traffic and increasing response times for users. ISA Server can also be configured to perform reverse caching, where information retrieved from the internal network on behalf of Internet users is cached.

The first step in configuring ISA Server for caching is to configure the cache drive itself. The cache must be placed on an NTFS partition and should be on a drive separate from the operating system. Also, ensure the cache is large enough as per the number of users on the network. Cache policies determine the behavior of ISA Server caching. A policy is basically a collection of configured settings such as an HTTP expiration policy, and FTP expiration policy, and active caching are configured through a cache policy.

ISA Server comes with a number of different reports that can be used such things as tracking trends in Web usage and capacity planning. Each of the different reports gathers information on different aspects of ISA Server. In terms of monitoring ISA Server, the performance application included with Windows Server can be used to monitor real-time caching performance. After ISA Server is installed, ISA-specific counters are added to the performance application. Using these counters can help to identify and resolve any performance problems.

✦   ✦   ✦

Security Tools

A huge array of security tools is available. Depending on your network environment, some are excellent, some are mediocre, and some are worthless. The only way you will find out what tools are valid for your environment is to try each one in a test lab against a set of criteria that you develop. Define these criteria before you start testing so that you can find the tools that most closely fit your needs.

Security tools are available for both Microsoft Windows and UNIX. Each operating system has its own advantages for security work and it is best to use a combination of both, if possible, rather than choosing one over the other. Even when running a homogenous Microsoft Windows-based network, UNIX tools are important because, in some cases, equivalent tools are not available on Windows, and in the remainder of cases, the Windows tools are often not as comprehensive as their UNIX counterparts.

Listed below are some of the most popular tools in each category.

Windows-Based Tools

Windows-based security tools essentially have one downfall, cost. While many UNIX utilities are free, most Windows tools are quite expensive. Another negative aspect to Windows tools is the fact that many of them are made by large corporations with other large corporations in mind. For this reason many of the tools are not as flexible as the UNIX-based tools. For example, most Windows tools are used for specific testing, while many UNIX tools are available for actual penetration testing rather than simple vulnerability scanning. This is mainly because UNIX has been a more powerful tool for hackers and security professionals alike for building tools and launching attacks.

Firewalls

Microsoft Windows-based firewalls are quite common. In most cases, a Windows-based firewall is implemented when hardware firewalls are not cost effective and the environment has a large installed base of Windows systems. The only advantage to using a specific operating system for a firewall is the security of that base system. A well-secured Windows system is normally sufficient for a firewall.

✦ **Microsoft Internet Security and Acceleration Server** — Discussed in Chapters 16 through 18 of this book, Microsoft's ISA Server is a full-featured firewall and caching server. The firewall component is robust and features packet filtering, stateful inspection, and a number of application filters. You can also add third-party and custom-developed application filters. The caching component can perform both forward and reverse caching along with active caching. The one disadvantage to ISA Server is that it has been on the market for a relatively short time and has not been thoroughly tested in real-world environments. Security flaws may exist in the system that have not been worked out properly yet.

✦ **Check Point Firewall-1** — Probably the most popular software firewall on the market. Firewall-1 has been on the market for quite some time and has had the time to work out any bugs that may have existed in the system. It is well known as a very secure firewall. It also performs packet filtering, stateful inspection, and application filtering, and has a number of high availability features for load balancing and failover. Another advantage to Firewall-1 is that it runs on a number of platforms, including both Windows and several varieties of UNIX.

✦ **Symantec Enterprise Firewall (formerly known as Axent Raptor Firewall)** — Another fairly popular software firewall that has also been around for a while. It is somewhat less robust than Firewall-1, but is also less expensive. It provides the same standard security features as most firewalls, including packet filtering, stateful inspection, and application filtering, as well as some virtual private network (VPN) features.

Intrusion Detection Systems

Intrusion Detection Systems (IDSs) are not normally platform specific. A company that implements an IDS is typically a large company with a heterogeneous network that requires IDS sensors for a variety of operating systems. For this reason, IDS management consoles are normally available for a variety of platforms so that they can be implemented on whatever platform is in use for network management in your environment.

Internet Security Systems RealSecure

ISS RealSecure is one of the most common, if not the most common, IDS on the market. In fact, components of ISS RealSecure were licensed for use in Microsoft ISA Server. RealSecure provides full IDS services, including management consoles and sensors for a number of systems. These include a multitude of operating system sensors as well as network sensors. RealSecure operates on a variety of platforms, including Windows and UNIX. RealSecure can, however, become expensive on larger networks, as the number of sensors required becomes much larger.

Security scanners

A number of different security scanners are available for Microsoft Windows, and almost all of them have the same features. The advantages can be found in those that update their vulnerability database more often and are cheaper. As long as the scanner you choose has a good reputation and has the reporting features you require, it should be sufficient.

✦ **Cisco Secure Scanner** — A basic vulnerability scanner. It provides a number of user-controllable features, such as vulnerability rules and a full featured reporting system. It is moderately priced.

✦ **WebTrends NetIQ Security Analyzer** — Another basic vulnerability scanner. It also provides some level of customization and many reporting features.

✦ **Symantec Enterprise Security Manager** — Another basic vulnerability scanner. It is similar to the others listed in its feature set and reporting.

✦ **Internet Security Systems Scanners** — The ISS family of scanners differs from the others listed. ISS provides three different scanners:

- The Internet Scanner is used to scan the network for vulnerabilities, including system operating systems and routers.

- The Database Scanner is somewhat unique in that it scans database applications for security vulnerabilities.

- The System Scanner scans individual systems and applications similar to the other vulnerability scanners previously listed.

Packet sniffers

Several packet sniffers are available for Windows. Microsoft includes Network Monitor with all versions of Windows Server operating systems, and there are a number of other command line and graphical packet capture programs.

✦ **Microsoft Network Monitor**—Included with Windows Server 2003. This version is capable of scanning only traffic to and from the local host. A version of Network Monitor is included with Microsoft Systems Management Server that can scan all traffic on the network. This limited functionality is in place for security reasons but really hampers the usefulness of the product. It does not really provide an added measure of security due to the availability of other sniffers without this limitation.

That being said, Network Monitor is a fairly powerful tool. It has a wide variety of filtering capabilities, including filtering of the actual capture and filtering the display of the captured data. It is a graphical tool, but it is fairly difficult to use.

✦ **WinDump**—The Windows-based version of TCPDump. It is a command-line tool (like TCPDump) and uses the exact same command-line options as TCPDump. It provides a very thorough set of filters for the capture, but data must be captured to a file and viewed with a text editor or viewed streaming past on the command line. It is a free tool and will capture all data on the network, not just data to and from the local system.

UNIX-Based Tools

UNIX-based tools are generally more powerful than their Windows-based counterparts. UNIX operating systems have traditionally had a more robust network programming environment leading to the production of a huge number of security tools. The list is virtually endless. The major downfall to the UNIX-based tools is ease of use. These tools generally require compilation at the minimum, and may even require some code changes to work on your specific system. A different area of expertise is required to use UNIX tools, but if you have the resources, these tools are a good choice.

Firewalls

A number of firewalls are available for UNIX-based operating systems. Like Windows-based firewalls, their only advantage lies in the security of the base operating system, except for potential performance gains for those systems with more efficient network subsystems. A firewall running on Trusted Solaris, for example, would be more secure than one running on Microsoft Windows.

Check Point Firewall-1

Check Point Firewall-1 is discussed in the Windows Firewall section above. It is also available for a number of UNIX systems and is commonly found running on Sun Solaris.

OpenBSD-based firewalls

OpenBSD is not a firewall itself, but a free UNIX-like operating system based on BSD UNIX. OpenBSD was written with security in mind and full code audits have been done on the entire system. OpenBSD is known as one of the most secure free operating systems available. It may in fact be one of the most secure operating systems — period.

Included with OpenBSD are a number of utilities for the implementation of a firewall and VPN server. The latest version of OpenBSD includes Packet Filter, which is a logging packet filter with stateful inspection capability. The advantage to OpenBSD is that it is free and can be used to create fully functional firewalls and VPN routers. It is, however, fairly difficult to configure.

Intrusion Detection Systems

Many Intrusion Detection Systems, such as ISS RealSecure, are typically available for both UNIX and Windows. As previously stated, environments with the requirement or budget for an IDS will have a number of different platforms, including both UNIX and Windows.

Snort

Snort is a UNIX native IDS that also has a Windows port available. While it also provides a basic packet capture mode, it is meant to run in an IDS mode that constantly captures packets and inspects them based on a policy file. Snort is not nearly as featureful as a commercial IDS, but it is free. Its major disadvantage over the commercial products is that it lacks central administration tools.

Security scanners

The UNIX-based security scanners are usually similar in features to the Windows-based scanners but often do not have the support of a major corporation behind them and may be updated less often or development may be dropped all together. They are often less expensive or even free.

✦ **Nessus** — One of the best available security scanners. It is very robust and can scan a wide variety of systems, but updates are somewhat less reliable as it is a free product and the developers volunteer their time. The advantage of Nessus, despite it being less featureful, is in fact that it is free. Most vulnerability scanners are quite expensive.

✦ **Saint** — Another vulnerability scanner for UNIX. Originally based on the free SATAN scanner, SAINT must be purchased. Saint is similar to the Windows-based scanners in its feature set and reporting abilities. SAINT's reporting abilities are actually more powerful than most other scanners. Another product, called WebSAINT, allows you to have a single system scanned over the Internet for a fee.

Packet sniffers

The UNIX-based packet sniffers are usually command-line based, but graphical tools are also available. The major advantage to the UNIX-based packet capture utilities is that the capture results can be saved to a text file and operated on by the array of available text processing tools in UNIX.

+ **TCPDump** — Identical to WinDump (described in the Windows section), but for UNIX. TCPDump actually preceded WinDump. TCPDump is a basic packet-capture utility that captures all traffic on the local network. It has a large number of filter options and other command line options. While somewhat difficult to learn, it becomes easier once the learning curve is surpassed. There is no utility for viewing captures; you must capture to a file and view that file with a text viewing or editing program. TCPDump is free.

+ **Ethereal** — Free and available for Windows and UNIX, although it is native to UNIX. It is a graphical packet-capture utility and functions similarly to Network Monitor. It has filters for both the actual capture and the displayed data. It also has the capability to display and filter data generated in a number of other packet-capture utilities, including Network Monitor.

+ **Snoop** — Another command-line tool similar to TCPDump but with different syntax. Snoop is native to and included with Sun Solaris. It also captures all data on the local network using the packet capture driver built in to Solaris (most operating systems require a third-party packet capture driver).

+ **Dsniff** — A family of utilities that, rather than capture all data from the network in a raw format, are used to capture specific data. The Dsniff program is used to capture all plaintext and weakly encrypted passwords, and the Mailsnarf program captures e-mail messages using SMTP and POP3 protocols, for example. A large number of utilities are included with Dsniff.

The other aspect of the Dsniff package is the utilities included for DNS and ARP spoofing. These utilities allow you to capture network traffic on a switched network, among other things. These spoofing utilities are used to make other systems on the network believe that the spoofing system is actually another computer. They then forward their traffic to the spoofing system, thinking it is the actual target computer.

✦   ✦   ✦

APPENDIX

◆ ◆ ◆ ◆

In This Appendix

Web sites

Mailing lists

◆ ◆ ◆ ◆

Security Resources

A number of resources are available for security information. A search on the Internet will easily turn up thousands. Listed here are some of the most useful and most informative resources.

General Web Sites

General Web sites cover all aspects of security.

SecurityFocus

`www.securityfocus.com`

SecurityFocus, in addition to being the home of the Bugtraq mailing list and a plethora of other mailing lists, provides security-related news, editorials, and reporting on vulnerabilities and advisories. Also contained on the SecurityFocus site is a searchable archive of vulnerabilities sorted by operating system and application. This site is arguably the best security site available based on the amount of content contained within.

CERT

`www.cert.org`

The Software Engineering Institute at Carnegie Mellon University hosts the CERT coordination center. CERT is a federally funded computer security organization that investigates security vulnerabilities and attacks.

In addition to the basic vulnerability assessments, CERT also has a number of publications and documents for security best practices, performs other analysis, and provides security training.

SANS

`www.sans.org`

The SANS institute Web site also lists vulnerabilities and performs investigations. The outstanding part on the SANS site however, is the SANS Information Security Reading Room. This is a huge collection of documents, such as white papers and best practices, for security organized by operating system.

SANS also provides training and organizes a number of conferences.

Incidents.org

`www.incidents.org`

The incidents.org site is a service of the SANS institute dedicated to studying and providing information about attacks and security incidents. Incidents and vulnerabilities are listed with information about defending against them. Through a partnership with Dshield.org, this site also provides attack statistics, such as the most commonly attacked port and the top attacker.

Microsoft

The Microsoft Security Web site (`www.microsoft.com/security`) contains a good amount of Microsoft-specific security information. Some of the content on this site encompasses advisories and bulletins, as well as security toolkits, checklists, and other documentation.

Microsoft has recently changed their policies when it comes to system security and they will be releasing more toolkits for vulnerability checking and so on. This site will carry those toolkits and other updates.

Government

The U.S. Government provides a few resources on the Web with respect to Internet security. A couple of the most useful are listed in this section.

How to report Internet-Related crime

`www.usdoj.gov/criminal/cybercrime/reporting.htm`

This site, hosted by the U.S. Department of Justice, explains the procedures for reporting different types of computer crime.

IFCC

`www1.ifccfbi.gov/index.asp`

The Internet Fraud Complaint Center is a joint venture between the FBI and National White Collar Crime Center (NW3C). The purpose of this site is to allow citizens to file complaints regarding fraud on the Internet.

Cryptography

Cryptography is a fairly specific part of the computer security field and, therefore, has a number of dedicated Web sites and other resources. A couple of the most useful are listed here.

Cryptography FAQ

`www.faqs.org/faqs/cryptography-faq/`

This is the FAQ list for the sci.crypt usenet newsgroup. A huge amount of information is contained within this FAQ and the parts should be read in order.

Radiusnet.net

`http://.radiusnet.net/`

This site contains an enormous archive of cryptography information, as well as an excellent list of cryptography related books and links.

Mailing Lists

While Web sites maintain some security-related content, they have two problems in that they are updated on a relatively slow schedule and do not usually go into a lot of detail. The security-related mailing lists below are the opposite; they are often very current, go into more detail, and are very useful resources.

Bugtraq

Bugtraq is a moderated mailing list with a medium volume. It can be found at `www.securityfocus.com`. On that site, you can both subscribe to the mailing list and view and search the archives. Bugtraq is used for the release of vulnerabilities for everything, from operating systems to network equipment and beyond.

"The rest" at SecurityFocus

SecutiryFocus contains a large number of mailing lists for specific purposes. Some of the more interesting lists include the incidents list to which attacks are reported and the focus-ms list, which is dedicated to Microsoft-related security issues. The pen-test mailing list is a discussion forum for penetration testing professionals and the discussion revolves around penetration testing methods. Another interesting list is the forensics list, which discusses computer forensics procedures.

NTBugtraq

NTBugtraq is a mailing list similar to the original Bugtraq list but more specific to Microsoft Windows. NTBugtraq is found at `www.ntbugtraq.com`. The discussions on NTBugtraq pertain only to Microsoft Windows-specific security issues; other types of discussions are not allowed.

Microsoft Security Notification Service

Microsoft publishes its own security bulletins whenever a new vulnerability and fix is published. The security bulletins are published in TechNet and can be accessed at `www.microsoft.com/technet/treeview/default.asp?url=/technet/security/current.asp`. In addition to the Web site, the Microsoft Security Notification Service will e-mail the Microsoft security bulletins to you when they are released. Subscribe by sending an e-mail to `microsoft_security-subscribe-request@announce.microsoft.com`.

Crypto-Gram

Crypto-Gram is a monthly e-mail newsletter from Bruce Schneier, author of *Applied Security* and CTO and founder of Counterpane Internet Security. Crypto-Gram is less a technical mailing list and more a discussion on current events and principles relating to cryptography. Each edition includes a few short crypto-related articles by the author, as well as a number of links to applicable news articles at external sites. Also included are some editorial commentary and reader comments. This is an excellent, well-written newsletter and I recommend it for anyone with an interest in cryptography and related issues. It can be found at `www.counterpane.com/crypto-gram.html`.

✦   ✦   ✦

Standard TCP/IP Port Assignments

The Internet Assigned Numbers Association (IANA) is responsible for assigning TCP and UDP ports to specific services. The ports from 0 to 1023 are well known ports and those from 1024-49151 are registered ports. Ports above that number are free for any use and are commonly used for randomly assigned ports for data communication rather than initial connections.

This list is provided so that you can reference ports captured by your packet capture or IDS software. This list attempts to be comprehensive for the well known ports but makes no attempt to be comprehensive for the registered ports as there are far too many to list. The most common are listed.

Well-Known Ports

Well-known ports are 0 through 1023. These ports are typically only available to privileged processes or users with administrative access. Table C-1 lists many of the well-known ports.

Table C-1
Well-Known Ports

Keyword	Decimal/Description	References
	0/tcp	Reserved
	0/udp	Reserved
tcpmux	1/tcp	TCP Port Service Multiplexer
tcpmux	1/udp	TCP Port Service Multiplexer
compressnet	2/tcp	Management Utility
compressnet	2/udp	Management Utility
compressnet	3/tcp	Compression Process
compressnet	3/udp	Compression Process
rje	5/tcp	Remote Job Entry
rje	5/udp	Remote Job Entry
echo	7/tcp	Echo
echo	7/udp	Echo
discard	9/tcp	Discard
discard	9/udp	Discard
systat	11/tcp	Active Users
systat	11/udp	Active Users
daytime	13/tcp	Daytime (RFC 867)
daytime	13/udp	Daytime (RFC 867)
qotd	17/tcp	Quote of the Day
qotd	17/udp	Quote of the Day
msp	18/tcp	Message Send Protocol
msp	18/udp	Message Send Protocol
chargen	19/tcp	Character Generator
chargen	19/udp	Character Generator
ftp-data	20/tcp	File Transfer [Default Data]
ftp-data	20/udp	File Transfer [Default Data]
ftp	21/tcp	File Transfer [Control]
ftp	21/udp	File Transfer [Control]

Keyword	Decimal/Description	References
ssh	22/tcp	SSH Remote Login Protocol
ssh	22/udp	SSH Remote Login Protocol
telnet	23/tcp	Telnet
telnet	23/udp	Telnet
	24/tcp	any private mail system
	24/udp	any private mail system
smtp	25/tcp	Simple Mail Transfer
smtp	25/udp	Simple Mail Transfer
nsw-fe	27/tcp	NSW User System FE
nsw-fe	27/udp	NSW User System FE
msg-icp	29/tcp	MSG ICP
msg-icp	29/udp	MSG ICP
msg-auth	31/tcp	MSG Authentication
msg-auth	31/udp	MSG Authentication
dsp	33/tcp	Display Support Protocol
dsp	33/udp	Display Support Protocol
	35/tcp	any private printer server
	35/udp	any private printer server
time	37/tcp	Time
time	37/udp	Time
rap	38/tcp	Route Access Protocol
rap	38/udp	Route Access Protocol
rlp	39/tcp	Resource Location Protocol
rlp	39/udp	Resource Location Protocol
graphics	41/tcp	Graphics
graphics	41/udp	Graphics
name	42/tcp	Host Name Server
name	42/udp	Host Name Server
nameserver	42/tcp	Host Name Server

Continued

Table C-1 *(continued)*

Keyword	Decimal/Description	References
nameserver	42/udp	Host Name Server
nickname	43/tcp	Who Is
nickname	43/udp	Who Is
mpm-flags	44/tcp	MPM FLAGS Protocol
mpm-flags	44/udp	MPM FLAGS Protocol
mpm	45/tcp	Message Processing Module [recv]
mpm	45/udp	Message Processing Module [recv]
mpm-snd	46/tcp	MPM [default send]
mpm-snd	46/udp	MPM [default send]
ni-ftp	47/tcp	NI FTP
ni-ftp	47/udp	NI FTP
auditd	48/tcp	Digital Audit Daemon
auditd	48/udp	Digital Audit Daemon
tacacs	49/tcp	Login Host Protocol (TACACS)
tacacs	49/udp	Login Host Protocol (TACACS)
re-mail-ck	50/tcp	Remote Mail Checking Protocol
re-mail-ck	50/udp	Remote Mail Checking Protocol
la-maint	51/tcp	IMP Logical Address Maintenance
la-maint	51/udp	IMP Logical Address Maintenance
xns-time	52/tcp	XNS Time Protocol
xns-time	52/udp	XNS Time Protocol
domain	53/tcp	Domain Name Server
domain	53/udp	Domain Name Server
xns-ch	54/tcp	XNS Clearinghouse
xns-ch	54/udp	XNS Clearinghouse
isi-gl	55/tcp	ISI Graphics Language
isi-gl	55/udp	ISI Graphics Language
xns-auth	56/tcp	XNS Authentication
xns-auth	56/udp	XNS Authentication

Keyword	Decimal/Description	References
	57/tcp	any private terminal access
	57/udp	any private terminal access
xns-mail	58/tcp	XNS Mail
xns-mail	58/udp	XNS Mail
	59/tcp	any private file service
	59/udp	any private file service
ni-mail	61/tcp	NI MAIL
ni-mail	61/udp	NI MAIL
acas	62/tcp	ACA Services
acas	62/udp	ACA Services
whois++	63/tcp	whois++
whois++	63/udp	whois++
covia	64/tcp	Communications Integrator (CI)
covia	64/udp	Communications Integrator (CI)
tacacs-ds	65/tcp	TACACS-Database Service
tacacs-ds	65/udp	TACACS-Database Service
sql*net	66/tcp	Oracle SQL*NET
sql*net	66/udp	Oracle SQL*NET
bootps	67/tcp	Bootstrap Protocol Server
bootps	67/udp	Bootstrap Protocol Server
bootpc	68/tcp	Bootstrap Protocol Client
bootpc	68/udp	Bootstrap Protocol Client
tftp	69/tcp	Trivial File Transfer
tftp	69/udp	Trivial File Transfer
gopher	70/tcp	Gopher
gopher	70/udp	Gopher
netrjs-1	71/tcp	Remote Job Service
netrjs-1	71/udp	Remote Job Service
netrjs-2	72/tcp	Remote Job Service
netrjs-2	72/udp	Remote Job Service
netrjs-3	73/tcp	Remote Job Service

Continued

Table C-1 *(continued)*

Keyword	Decimal/Description	References
netrjs-3	73/udp	Remote Job Service
netrjs-4	74/tcp	Remote Job Service
netrjs-4	74/udp	Remote Job Service
	75/tcp	any private dial out service
	75/udp	any private dial out service
deos	76/tcp	Distributed External Object Store
deos	76/udp	Distributed External Object Store
	77/tcp	any private RJE service
	77/udp	any private RJE service
vettcp	78/tcp	vettcp
vettcp	78/udp	vettcp
finger	79/tcp	Finger
finger	79/udp	Finger
http	80/tcp	World Wide Web HTTP
http	80/udp	World Wide Web HTTP
www	80/tcp	World Wide Web HTTP
www	80/udp	World Wide Web HTTP
www-http	80/tcp	World Wide Web HTTP
www-http	80/udp	World Wide Web HTTP
hosts2-ns	81/tcp	HOSTS2 Name Server
hosts2-ns	81/udp	HOSTS2 Name Server
xfer	82/tcp	XFER Utility
xfer	82/udp	XFER Utility
mit-ml-dev	83/tcp	MIT ML Device
mit-ml-dev	83/udp	MIT ML Device
ctf	84/tcp	Common Trace Facility
ctf	84/udp	Common Trace Facility
mit-ml-dev	85/tcp	MIT ML Device
mit-ml-dev	85/udp	MIT ML Device

Keyword	Decimal/Description	References
mfcobol	86/tcp	Micro Focus Cobol
mfcobol	86/udp	Micro Focus Cobol
	87/tcp	any private terminal link
	87/udp	any private terminal link
kerberos	88/tcp	Kerberos
kerberos	88/udp	Kerberos
su-mit-tg	89/tcp	SU/MIT Telnet Gateway
su-mit-tg	89/udp	SU/MIT Telnet Gateway
dnsix	90/tcp	DNSIX Securit Attribute Token Map
dnsix	90/udp	DNSIX Securit Attribute Token Map
mit-dov	91/tcp	MIT Dover Spooler
mit-dov	91/udp	MIT Dover Spooler
npp	92/tcp	Network Printing Protocol
npp	92/udp	Network Printing Protocol
dcp	93/tcp	Device Control Protocol
dcp	93/udp	Device Control Protocol
objcall	94/tcp	Tivoli Object Dispatcher
objcall	94/udp	Tivoli Object Dispatcher
supdup	95/tcp	SUPDUP
supdup	95/udp	SUPDUP
Dixie	96/tcp	DIXIE Protocol Specification
Dixie	96/udp	DIXIE Protocol Specification
swift-rvf	97/tcp	Swift Remote Virtural File Protocol
swift-rvf	97/udp	Swift Remote Virtural File Protocol
tacnews	98/tcp	TAC News
tacnews	98/udp	TAC News
metagram	99/tcp	Metagram Relay
metagram	99/udp	Metagram Relay
newacct	100/tcp	[unauthorized use]
hostname	101/tcp	NIC Host Name Server
hostname	101/udp	NIC Host Name Server

Continued

Table C-1 *(continued)*

Keyword	Decimal/Description	References
iso-tsap	102/tcp	ISO-TSAP Class 0
iso-tsap	102/udp	ISO-TSAP Class 0
gppitnp	103/tcp	Genesis Point-to-Point Trans Net
gppitnp	103/udp	Genesis Point-to-Point Trans Net
acr-nema	104/tcp	ACR-NEMA Digital Imag. & Comm. 300
acr-nema	104/udp	ACR-NEMA Digital Imag. & Comm. 300
cso	105/tcp	CCSO name server protocol
cso	105/udp	CCSO name server protocol
csnet-ns	105/tcp	Mailbox Name Nameserver
csnet-ns	105/udp	Mailbox Name Nameserver
3com-tsmux	106/tcp	3COM-TSMUX
3com-tsmux	106/udp	3COM-TSMUX
rtelnet	107/tcp	Remote Telnet Service
rtelnet	107/udp	Remote Telnet Service
snagas	108/tcp	SNA Gateway Access Server
snagas	108/udp	SNA Gateway Access Server
pop2	109/tcp	Post Office Protocol - Version 2
pop2	109/udp	Post Office Protocol - Version 2
pop3	110/tcp	Post Office Protocol - Version 3
pop3	110/udp	Post Office Protocol - Version 3
sunrpc	111/tcp	SUN Remote Procedure Call
sunrpc	111/udp	SUN Remote Procedure Call
mcidas	112/tcp	McIDAS Data Transmission Protocol
mcidas	112/udp	McIDAS Data Transmission Protocol
ident	113/tcp	
auth	113/tcp	Authentication Service
auth	113/udp	Authentication Service
audionews	114/tcp	Audio News Multicast
audionews	114/udp	Audio News Multicast

Keyword	Decimal/Description	References
sftp	115/tcp	Simple File Transfer Protocol
sftp	115/udp	Simple File Transfer Protocol
ansanotify	116/tcp	ANSA REX Notify
ansanotify	116/udp	ANSA REX Notify
uucp-path	117/tcp	UUCP Path Service
uucp-path	117/udp	UUCP Path Service
sqlserv	118/tcp	SQL Services
sqlserv	118/udp	SQL Services
nntp	119/tcp	Network News Transfer Protocol
nntp	119/udp	Network News Transfer Protocol
cfdptkt	120/tcp	CFDPTKT
cfdptkt	120/udp	CFDPTKT
erpc	121/tcp	Encore Expedited Remote Pro.Call
erpc	121/udp	Encore Expedited Remote Pro.Call
smakynet	122/tcp	SMAKYNET
smakynet	122/udp	SMAKYNET
ntp	123/tcp	Network Time Protocol
ntp	123/udp	Network Time Protocol
ansatrader	124/tcp	ANSA REX Trader
ansatrader	124/udp	ANSA REX Trader
locus-map	125/tcp	Locus PC-Interface Net Map Ser
locus-map	125/udp	Locus PC-Interface Net Map Ser
nxedit	126/tcp	NXEdit
nxedit	126/udp	NXEdit
locus-con	127/tcp	Locus PC-Interface Conn Server
locus-con	127/udp	Locus PC-Interface Conn Server
gss-xlicen	128/tcp	GSS X License Verification
gss-xlicen	128/udp	GSS X License Verification
pwdgen	129/tcp	Password Generator Protocol
pwdgen	129/udp	Password Generator Protocol
cisco-fna	130/tcp	Cisco FNATIVE

Continued

Table C-1 *(continued)*

Keyword	Decimal/Description	References
cisco-fna	130/udp	Cisco FNATIVE
cisco-tna	131/tcp	Cisco TNATIVE
cisco-tna	131/udp	Cisco TNATIVE
cisco-sys	132/tcp	Cisco SYSMAINT
cisco-sys	132/udp	Cisco SYSMAINT
statsrv	133/tcp	Statistics Service
statsrv	133/udp	Statistics Service
ingres-net	134/tcp	INGRES-NET Service
ingres-net	134/udp	INGRES-NET Service
epmap	135/tcp	DCE endpoint resolution
epmap	135/udp	DCE endpoint resolution
profile	136/tcp	PROFILE Naming System
profile	136/udp	PROFILE Naming System
netbios-ns	137/tcp	NETBIOS Name Service
netbios-ns	137/udp	NETBIOS Name Service
netbios-dgm	138/tcp	NETBIOS Datagram Service
netbios-dgm	138/udp	NETBIOS Datagram Service
netbios-ssn	139/tcp	NETBIOS Session Service
netbios-ssn	139/udp	NETBIOS Session Service
emfis-data	140/tcp	EMFIS Data Service
emfis-data	140/udp	EMFIS Data Service
emfis-cntl	141/tcp	EMFIS Control Service
emfis-cntl	141/udp	EMFIS Control Service
bl-idm	142/tcp	Britton-Lee IDM
bl-idm	142/udp	Britton-Lee IDM
imap	143/tcp	Internet Message Access Protocol
imap	143/udp	Internet Message Access Protocol
uma	144/tcp	Universal Management Architecture
uma	144/udp	Universal Management Architecture

Keyword	Decimal/Description	References
uaac	145/tcp	UAAC Protocol
uaac	145/udp	UAAC Protocol
iso-tp0	146/tcp	ISO-IP0
iso-tp0	146/udp	ISO-IP0
iso-ip	147/tcp	ISO-IP
iso-ip	147/udp	ISO-IP
jargon	148/tcp	Jargon
jargon	148/udp	Jargon
aed-512	149/tcp	AED 512 Emulation Service
aed-512	149/udp	AED 512 Emulation Service
sql-net	150/tcp	SQL-NET
sql-net	150/udp	SQL-NET
hems	151/tcp	HEMS
hems	151/udp	HEMS
bftp	152/tcp	Background File Transfer Program
bftp	152/udp	Background File Transfer Program
sgmp	153/tcp	SGMP
sgmp	153/udp	SGMP
netsc-prod	154/tcp	NETSC
netsc-prod	154/udp	NETSC
netsc-dev	155/tcp	NETSC
netsc-dev	155/udp	NETSC
sqlsrv	156/tcp	SQL Service
sqlsrv	156/udp	SQL Service
knet-cmp	157/tcp	KNET/VM Command/Message Protocol
knet-cmp	157/udp	KNET/VM Command/Message Protocol
pcmail-srv	158/tcp	PCMail Server
pcmail-srv	158/udp	PCMail Server
nss-routing	159/tcp	NSS-Routing

Continued

Table C-1 *(continued)*		
Keyword	*Decimal/Description*	*References*
nss-routing	159/udp	NSS-Routing
sgmp-traps	160/tcp	SGMP-TRAPS
sgmp-traps	160/udp	SGMP-TRAPS
snmp	161/tcp	SNMP
snmp	161/udp	SNMP
snmptrap	162/tcp	SNMPTRAP
snmptrap	162/udp	SNMPTRAP
cmip-man	163/tcp	CMIP/TCP Manager
cmip-man	163/udp	CMIP/TCP Manager
cmip-agent	164/tcp	CMIP/TCP Agent
cmip-agent	164/udp	CMIP/TCP Agent
xns-courier	165/tcp	Xerox
xns-courier	165/udp	Xerox
s-net	166/tcp	Sirius Systems
s-net	166/udp	Sirius Systems
namp	167/tcp	NAMP
namp	167/udp	NAMP
rsvd	168/tcp	RSVD
rsvd	168/udp	RSVD
send	169/tcp	SEND
send	169/udp	SEND
print-srv	170/tcp	Network PostScript
print-srv	170/udp	Network PostScript
multiplex	171/tcp	Network Innovations Multiplex
multiplex	171/udp	Network Innovations Multiplex
cl/1	172/tcp	Network Innovations CL/1
cl/1	172/udp	Network Innovations CL/1
xyplex-mux	173/tcp	Xyplex
xyplex-mux	173/udp	Xyplex
mailq	174/tcp	MAILQ
mailq	174/udp	MAILQ

Keyword	Decimal/Description	References
vmnet	175/tcp	VMNET
vmnet	175/udp	VMNET
genrad-mux	176/tcp	GENRAD-MUX
genrad-mux	176/udp	GENRAD-MUX
xdmcp	177/tcp	X Display Manager Control Protocol
xdmcp	177/udp	X Display Manager Control Protocol
nextstep	178/tcp	NextStep Window Server
nextstep	178/udp	NextStep Window Server
bgp	179/tcp	Border Gateway Protocol
bgp	179/udp	Border Gateway Protocol
ris	180/tcp	Intergraph
ris	180/udp	Intergraph
unify	181/tcp	Unify
unify	181/udp	Unify
audit	182/tcp	Unisys Audit SITP
audit	182/udp	Unisys Audit SITP
ocbinder	183/tcp	OCBinder
ocbinder	183/udp	OCBinder
ocserver	184/tcp	OCServer
ocserver	184/udp	OCServer
remote-kis	185/tcp	Remote-KIS
remote-kis	185/udp	Remote-KIS
kis	186/tcp	KIS Protocol
kis	186/udp	KIS Protocol
aci	187/tcp	Application Communication Interface
aci	187/udp	Application Communication Interface
mumps	188/tcp	Plus Five's MUMPS
mumps	188/udp	Plus Five's MUMPS
qft	189/tcp	Queued File Transport

Continued

Table C-1 *(continued)*

Keyword	Decimal/Description	References
qft	189/udp	Queued File Transport
gacp	190/tcp	Gateway Access Control Protocol
gacp	190/udp	Gateway Access Control Protocol
prospero	191/tcp	Prospero Directory Service
prospero	191/udp	Prospero Directory Service
osu-nms	192/tcp	OSU Network Monitoring System
osu-nms	192/udp	OSU Network Monitoring System
srmp	193/tcp	Spider Remote Monitoring Protocol
srmp	193/udp	Spider Remote Monitoring Protocol
irc	194/tcp	Internet Relay Chat Protocol
irc	194/udp	Internet Relay Chat Protocol
dn6-nlm-aud	195/tcp	DNSIX Network Level Module Audit
dn6-nlm-aud	195/udp	DNSIX Network Level Module Audit
dn6-smm-red	196/tcp	DNSIX Session Mgt Module Audit Redir
dn6-smm-red	196/udp	DNSIX Session Mgt Module Audit Redir
dls	197/tcp	Directory Location Service
dls	197/udp	Directory Location Service
dls-mon	198/tcp	Directory Location Service Monitor
dls-mon	198/udp	Directory Location Service Monitor
smux	199/tcp	SMUX
smux	199/udp	SMUX
src	200/tcp	IBM System Resource Controller
src	200/udp	IBM System Resource Controller
at-rtmp	201/tcp	AppleTalk Routing Maintenance
at-rtmp	201/udp	AppleTalk Routing Maintenance
at-nbp	202/tcp	AppleTalk Name Binding
at-nbp	202/udp	AppleTalk Name Binding
at-3	203/tcp	AppleTalk Unused
at-3	203/udp	AppleTalk Unused

Keyword	Decimal/Description	References
at-echo	204/tcp	AppleTalk Echo
at-echo	204/udp	AppleTalk Echo
at-5	205/tcp	AppleTalk Unused
at-5	205/udp	AppleTalk Unused
at-zis	206/tcp	AppleTalk Zone Information
at-zis	206/udp	AppleTalk Zone Information
at-7	207/tcp	AppleTalk Unused
at-7	207/udp	AppleTalk Unused
at-8	208/tcp	AppleTalk Unused
at-8	208/udp	AppleTalk Unused
qmtp	209/tcp	The Quick Mail Transfer Protocol
qmtp	209/udp	The Quick Mail Transfer Protocol
z39.50	210/tcp	ANSI Z39.50
z39.50	210/udp	ANSI Z39.50
914c/g	211/tcp	Texas Instruments 914C/G Terminal
914c/g	211/udp	Texas Instruments 914C/G Terminal
anet	212/tcp	ATEXSSTR
anet	212/udp	ATEXSSTR
ipx	213/tcp	IPX
ipx	213/udp	IPX
vmpwscs	214/tcp	VM PWSCS
vmpwscs	214/udp	VM PWSCS
softpc	215/tcp	Insignia Solutions
softpc	215/udp	Insignia Solutions
CAllic	216/tcp	Computer Associates Int'l License Server
CAllic	216/udp	Computer Associates Int'l License Server
Dbase	217/tcp	dBASE Unix
Dbase	217/udp	dBASE Unix
mpp	218/tcp	Netix Message Posting Protocol

Continued

Table C-1 *(continued)*

Keyword	Decimal/Description	References
mpp	218/udp	Netix Message Posting Protocol
uarps	219/tcp	Unisys ARPs
uarps	219/udp	Unisys ARPs
imap3	220/tcp	Interactive Mail Access Protocol v3
imap3	220/udp	Interactive Mail Access Protocol v3
fln-spx	221/tcp	Berkeley rlogind with SPX auth
fln-spx	221/udp	Berkeley rlogind with SPX auth
rsh-spx	222/tcp	Berkeley rshd with SPX auth
rsh-spx	222/udp	Berkeley rshd with SPX auth
cdc	223/tcp	Certificate Distribution Center
cdc	223/udp	Certificate Distribution Center
masqdialer	224/tcp	masqdialer
masqdialer	224/udp	masqdialer
direct	242/tcp	Direct
direct	242/udp	Direct
sur-meas	243/tcp	Survey Measurement
sur-meas	243/udp	Survey Measurement
inbusiness	244/tcp	inbusiness
inbusiness	244/udp	inbusiness
link	245/tcp	LINK
link	245/udp	LINK
dsp3270	246/tcp	Display Systems Protocol
dsp3270	246/udp	Display Systems Protocol
subntbcst_tftp	247/tcp	SUBNTBCST_TFTP
subntbcst_tftp	247/udp	SUBNTBCST_TFTP
bhfhs	248/tcp	bhfhs
bhfhs	248/udp	bhfhs
rap	256/tcp	RAP
rap	256/udp	RAP
set	257/tcp	Secure Electronic Transaction
set	257/udp	Secure Electronic Transaction

Keyword	Decimal/Description	References
yak-chat	258/tcp	Yak Winsock Personal Chat
yak-chat	258/udp	Yak Winsock Personal Chat
esro-gen	259/tcp	Efficient Short Remote Operations
esro-gen	259/udp	Efficient Short Remote Operations
openport	260/tcp	Openport
openport	260/udp	Openport
nsiiops	261/tcp	IIOP Name Service over TLS/SSL
nsiiops	261/udp	IIOP Name Service over TLS/SSL
arcisdms	262/tcp	Arcisdms
arcisdms	262/udp	Arcisdms
hdap	263/tcp	HDAP
hdap	263/udp	HDAP
bgmp	264/tcp	BGMP
bgmp	264/udp	BGMP
x-bone-ctl	265/tcp	X-Bone CTL
x-bone-ctl	265/udp	X-Bone CTL
sst	266/tcp	SCSI on ST
sst	266/udp	SCSI on ST
td-service	267/tcp	Tobit David Service Layer
td-service	267/udp	Tobit David Service Layer
td-replica	268/tcp	Tobit David Replica
td-replica	268/udp	Tobit David Replica
http-mgmt	280/tcp	http-mgmt
http-mgmt	280/udp	http-mgmt
personal-link	281/tcp	Personal Link
personal-link	281/udp	Personal Link
cableport-ax	282/tcp	Cable Port A/X
cableport-ax	282/udp	Cable Port A/X
rescap	283/tcp	rescap
rescap	283/udp	rescap
corerjd	284/tcp	corerjd

Continued

Table C-1 *(continued)*

Keyword	Decimal/Description	References
corerjd	284/udp	corerjd
fxp-1	286/tcp	FXP-1
fxp-1	286/udp	FXP-1
k-block	287/tcp	K-BLOCK
k-block	287/udp	K-BLOCK
novastorbakcup	308/tcp	Novastor Backup
novastorbakcup	308/udp	Novastor Backup
entrusttime	309/tcp	EntrustTime
entrusttime	309/udp	EntrustTime
bhmds	310/tcp	bhmds
bhmds	310/udp	bhmds
asip-webadmin	311/tcp	AppleShare IP WebAdmin
asip-webadmin	311/udp	AppleShare IP WebAdmin
vslmp	312/tcp	VSLMP
vslmp	312/udp	VSLMP
magenta-logic	313/tcp	Magenta Logic
magenta-logic	313/udp	Magenta Logic
opalis-robot	314/tcp	Opalis Robot
opalis-robot	314/udp	Opalis Robot
dpsi	315/tcp	DPSI
dpsi	315/udp	DPSI
decauth	316/tcp	decAuth
decauth	316/udp	decAuth
zannet	317/tcp	Zannet
zannet	317/udp	Zannet
pkix-timestamp	318/tcp	PKIX TimeStamp
pkix-timestamp	318/udp	PKIX TimeStamp
ptp-event	319/tcp	PTP Event
ptp-event	319/udp	PTP Event
ptp-general	320/tcp	PTP General
ptp-general	320/udp	PTP General

Keyword	Decimal/Description	References
pip	321/tcp	PIP
pip	321/udp	PIP
rtsps	322/tcp	RTSPS
rtsps	322/udp	RTSPS
texar	333/tcp	Texar Security Port
texar	333/udp	Texar Security Port
pdap	344/tcp	Prospero Data Access Protocol
pdap	344/udp	Prospero Data Access Protocol
pawserv	345/tcp	Perf Analysis Workbench
pawserv	345/udp	Perf Analysis Workbench
zserv	346/tcp	Zebra server
zserv	346/udp	Zebra server
fatserv	347/tcp	Fatmen Server
fatserv	347/udp	Fatmen Server
csi-sgwp	348/tcp	Cabletron Management Protocol
csi-sgwp	348/udp	Cabletron Management Protocol
mftp	349/tcp	mftp
mftp	349/udp	mftp
matip-type-a	350/tcp	MATIP Type A
matip-type-a	350/udp	MATIP Type A
matip-type-b	351/tcp	MATIP Type B
matip-type-b	351/udp	MATIP Type B
bhoetty	351/tcp	bhoetty
bhoetty	351/udp	bhoetty
dtag-ste-sb	352/tcp	DTAG
dtag-ste-sb	352/udp	DTAG
bhoedap4	352/tcp	bhoedap4
bhoedap4	352/udp	bhoedap4
ndsauth	353/tcp	NDSAUTH
ndsauth	353/udp	NDSAUTH
bh611	354/tcp	bh611

Continued

Table C-1 *(continued)*

Keyword	Decimal/Description	References
bh611	354/udp	bh611
datex-asn	355/tcp	DATEX-ASN
datex-asn	355/udp	DATEX-ASN
cloanto-net-1	356/tcp	Cloanto Net 1
cloanto-net-1	356/udp	Cloanto Net 1
bhevent	357/tcp	bhevent
bhevent	357/udp	bhevent
shrinkwrap	358/tcp	Shrinkwrap
shrinkwrap	358/udp	Shrinkwrap
nsrmp	359/tcp	Network Security Risk Management Protocol
nsrmp	359/udp	Network Security Risk Management Protocol
scoi2odialog	360/tcp	scoi2odialog
scoi2odialog	360/udp	scoi2odialog
semantix	361/tcp	Semantix
semantix	361/udp	Semantix
srssend	362/tcp	SRS Send
srssend	362/udp	SRS Send
rsvp_tunnel	363/tcp	RSVP Tunnel
rsvp_tunnel	363/udp	RSVP Tunnel
aurora-cmgr	364/tcp	Aurora CMGR
aurora-cmgr	364/udp	Aurora CMGR
dtk	365/tcp	DTK
dtk	365/udp	DTK
odmr	366/tcp	ODMR
odmr	366/udp	ODMR
mortgageware	367/tcp	MortgageWare
mortgageware	367/udp	MortgageWare
qbikgdp	368/tcp	QbikGDP
qbikgdp	368/udp	QbikGDP

Keyword	Decimal/Description	References
rpc2portmap	369/tcp	rpc2portmap
rpc2portmap	369/udp	rpc2portmap
codaauth2	370/tcp	codaauth2
codaauth2	370/udp	codaauth2
clearcase	371/tcp	Clearcase
clearcase	371/udp	Clearcase
ulistproc	372/tcp	ListProcessor
ulistproc	372/udp	ListProcessor
legent-1	373/tcp	Legent Corporation
legent-1	373/udp	Legent Corporation
legent-2	374/tcp	Legent Corporation
legent-2	374/udp	Legent Corporation
hassle	375/tcp	Hassle
hassle	375/udp	Hassle
nip	376/tcp	Amiga Envoy Network Inquiry Proto
nip	376/udp	Amiga Envoy Network Inquiry Proto
tnETOS	377/tcp	NEC Corporation
tnETOS	377/udp	NEC Corporation
dsETOS	378/tcp	NEC Corporation
dsETOS	378/udp	NEC Corporation
is99c	379/tcp	TIA/EIA/IS-99 modem client
is99c	379/udp	TIA/EIA/IS-99 modem client
is99s	380/tcp	TIA/EIA/IS-99 modem server
is99s	380/udp	TIA/EIA/IS-99 modem server
hp-collector	381/tcp	hp performance data collector
hp-collector	381/udp	hp performance data collector
hp-managed-node	382/tcp	hp performance data managed node

Continued

Table C-1 *(continued)*

Keyword	Decimal/Description	References
hp-managed-node	382/udp	hp performance data managed node
hp-alarm-mgr	383/tcp	hp performance data alarm manager
hp-alarm-mgr	383/udp	hp performance data alarm manager
arns	384/tcp	A Remote Network Server System
arns	384/udp	A Remote Network Server System
ibm-app	385/tcp	IBM Application
ibm-app	385/udp	IBM Application
asa	386/tcp	ASA Message Router Object Def.
asa	386/udp	ASA Message Router Object Def.
aurp	387/tcp	AppleTalk Update-Based Routing Pro.
aurp	387/udp	AppleTalk Update-Based Routing Pro.
unidata-ldm	388/tcp	Unidata LDM
unidata-ldm	388/udp	Unidata LDM
ldap	389/udp	Lightweight Directory Access Protocol
uis	390/tcp	UIS
uis	390/udp	UIS
synotics-relay	391/tcp	SynOptics SNMP Relay Port
synotics-relay	391/udp	SynOptics SNMP Relay Port
synotics-broker	392/tcp	SynOptics Port Broker Port
synotics-broker	392/udp	SynOptics Port Broker Port
meta5	393/tcp	Meta5
meta5	393/udp	Meta5
embl-ndt	394/tcp	EMBL Nucleic Data Transfer
embl-ndt	394/udp	EMBL Nucleic Data Transfer
netcp	395/tcp	NETscout Control Protocol

Keyword	Decimal/Description	References
netcp	395/udp	NETscout Control Protocol
netware-ip	396/tcp	Novell Netware over IP
netware-ip	396/udp	Novell Netware over IP
mptn	397/tcp	Multi Protocol Trans. Net.
mptn	397/udp	Multi Protocol Trans. Net.
kryptolan	398/tcp	Kryptolan
kryptolan	398/udp	Kryptolan
iso-tsap-c2	399/tcp	ISO Transport Class 2 Non-Control over TCP
iso-tsap-c2	399/udp	ISO Transport Class 2 Non-Control over TCP
work-sol	400/tcp	Workstation Solutions
work-sol	400/udp	Workstation Solutions
ups	401/tcp	Uninterruptible Power Supply
ups	401/udp	Uninterruptible Power Supply
genie	402/tcp	Genie Protocol
genie	402/udp	Genie Protocol
decap	403/tcp	decap
decap	403/udp	decap
nced	404/tcp	nced
nced	404/udp	nced
ncld	405/tcp	ncld
ncld	405/udp	ncld
imsp	406/tcp	Interactive Mail Support Protocol
imsp	406/udp	Interactive Mail Support Protocol
timbuktu	407/tcp	Timbuktu
timbuktu	407/udp	Timbuktu
prm-sm	408/tcp	Prospero Resource Manager Sys. Man.
prm-sm	408/udp	Prospero Resource Manager Sys. Man.

Continued

Table C-1 *(continued)*

Keyword	Decimal/Description	References
prm-nm	409/tcp	Prospero Resource Manager Node Man.
prm-nm	409/udp	Prospero Resource Manager Node Man.
decladebug	410/tcp	DECLadebug Remote Debug Protocol
decladebug	410/udp	DECLadebug Remote Debug Protocol
rmt	411/tcp	Remote MT Protocol
rmt	411/udp	Remote MT Protocol
synoptics-trap	412/tcp	Trap Convention Port
synoptics-trap	412/udp	Trap Convention Port
smsp	413/tcp	Storage Management Services Protocol
smsp	413/udp	Storage Management Services Protocol
infoseek	414/tcp	InfoSeek
infoseek	414/udp	InfoSeek
bnet	415/tcp	BNet
bnet	415/udp	BNet
silverplatter	416/tcp	Silverplatter
silverplatter	416/udp	Silverplatter
onmux	417/tcp	Onmux
onmux	417/udp	Onmux
hyper-g	418/tcp	Hyper-G
hyper-g	418/udp	Hyper-G
ariel1	419/tcp	Ariel
ariel1	419/udp	Ariel
smpte	420/tcp	SMPTE
smpte	420/udp	SMPTE
ariel2	421/tcp	Ariel

Keyword	Decimal/Description	References
ariel2	421/udp	Ariel
ariel3	422/tcp	Ariel
ariel3	422/udp	Ariel
opc-job-start	423/tcp	IBM Operations Planning and Control Start
opc-job-start	423/udp	IBM Operations Planning and Control Start
opc-job-track	424/tcp	IBM Operations Planning and Control Track
opc-job-track	424/udp	IBM Operations Planning and Control Track
icad-el	425/tcp	ICAD
icad-el	425/udp	ICAD
smartsdp	426/tcp	smartsdp
smartsdp	426/udp	smartsdp
svrloc	427/tcp	Server Location
svrloc	427/udp	Server Location
ocs_cmu	428/tcp	OCS_CMU
ocs_cmu	428/udp	OCS_CMU
ocs_amu	429/tcp	OCS_AMU
ocs_amu	429/udp	OCS_AMU
utmpsd	430/tcp	UTMPSD
utmpsd	430/udp	UTMPSD
utmpcd	431/tcp	UTMPCD
utmpcd	431/udp	UTMPCD
iasd	432/tcp	IASD
iasd	432/udp	IASD
nnsp	433/tcp	NNSP
nnsp	433/udp	NNSP
mobileip-agent	434/tcp	MobileIP-Agent
mobileip-agent	434/udp	MobileIP-Agent

Continued

Table C-1 *(continued)*

Keyword	Decimal/Description	References
mobilip-mn	435/tcp	MobilIP-MN
mobilip-mn	435/udp	MobilIP-MN
dna-cml	436/tcp	DNA-CML
dna-cml	436/udp	DNA-CML
comscm	437/tcp	comscm
comscm	437/udp	comscm
dsfgw	438/tcp	dsfgw
dsfgw	438/udp	dsfgw
dasp	439/tcp	dasp (Thomas Obermair)
dasp	439/udp	dasp
sgcp	440/tcp	sgcp
sgcp	440/udp	sgcp
decvms-sysmgt	441/tcp	decvms-sysmgt
decvms-sysmgt	441/udp	decvms-sysmgt
cvc_hostd	442/tcp	cvc_hostd
cvc_hostd	442/udp	cvc_hostd
https	443/tcp	http protocol over TLS/SSL
https	443/udp	http protocol over TLS/SSL
snpp	444/tcp	Simple Network Paging Protocol
snpp	444/udp	Simple Network Paging Protocol
microsoft-ds	445/tcp	Microsoft-DS
microsoft-ds	445/udp	Microsoft-DS
ddm-rdb	446/tcp	DDM-RDB
ddm-rdb	446/udp	DDM-RDB
ddm-dfm	447/tcp	DDM-RFM
ddm-dfm	447/udp	DDM-RFM
ddm-ssl	448/tcp	DDM-SSL
ddm-ssl	448/udp	DDM-SSL
as-servermap	449/tcp	AS Server Mapper
as-servermap	449/udp	AS Server Mapper
tserver	450/tcp	TServer

Keyword	Decimal/Description	References
tserver	450/udp	TServer
sfs-smp-net	451/tcp	Cray Network Semaphore server
sfs-smp-net	451/udp	Cray Network Semaphore server
sfs-config	452/tcp	Cray SFS config server
sfs-config	452/udp	Cray SFS config server
creativeserver	453/tcp	CreativeServer
creativeserver	453/udp	CreativeServer
contentserver	454/tcp	ContentServer
contentserver	454/udp	ContentServer
creativepartnr	455/tcp	CreativePartnr
creativepartnr	455/udp	CreativePartnr
macon-tcp	456/tcp	macon-tcp
macon-udp	456/udp	macon-udp
scohelp	457/tcp	scohelp
scohelp	457/udp	scohelp
appleqtc	458/tcp	Apple QuickTime
appleqtc	458/udp	Apple QuickTime
ampr-rcmd	459/tcp	ampr-rcmd
ampr-rcmd	459/udp	ampr-rcmd
skronk	460/tcp	skronk
skronk	460/udp	skronk
datasurfsrv	461/tcp	DataRampSrv
datasurfsrv	461/udp	DataRampSrv
datasurfsrvsec	462/tcp	DataRampSrvSec
datasurfsrvsec	462/udp	DataRampSrvSec
alpes	463/tcp	alpes
alpes	463/udp	alpes
kpasswd	464/tcp	kpasswd
kpasswd	464/udp	kpasswd
urd	465/tcp	URL Rendesvous Directory for SSM
igmpv3lite	465/udp	IGMP over UDP for SSM

Continued

Table C-1 *(continued)*

Keyword	Decimal/Description	References
digital-vrc	466/tcp	digital-vrc
digital-vrc	466/udp	digital-vrc
mylex-mapd	467/tcp	mylex-mapd
mylex-mapd	467/udp	mylex-mapd
photuris	468/tcp	proturis
photuris	468/udp	proturis
rcp	469/tcp	Radio Control Protocol
rcp	469/udp	Radio Control Protocol
scx-proxy	470/tcp	scx-proxy
scx-proxy	470/udp	scx-proxy
mondex	471/tcp	Mondex
mondex	471/udp	Mondex
ljk-login	472/tcp	ljk-login
ljk-login	472/udp	ljk-login
hybrid-pop	473/tcp	hybrid-pop
hybrid-pop	473/udp	hybrid-pop
tn-tl-w1	474/tcp	tn-tl-w1
tn-tl-w2	474/udp	tn-tl-w2
tcpnethaspsrv	475/tcp	tcpnethaspsrv
tcpnethaspsrv	475/udp	tcpnethaspsrv
tn-tl-fd1	476/tcp	tn-tl-fd1
tn-tl-fd1	476/udp	tn-tl-fd1
ss7ns	477/tcp	ss7ns
ss7ns	477/udp	ss7ns
spsc	478/tcp	spsc
spsc	478/udp	spsc
iafserver	479/tcp	iafserver
iafserver	479/udp	iafserver
iafdbase	480/tcp	iafdbase
iafdbase	480/udp	iafdbase
ph	481/tcp	Ph service

Keyword	Decimal/Description	References
ph	481/udp	Ph service
bgs-nsi	482/tcp	bgs-nsi
bgs-nsi	482/udp	bgs-nsi
ulpnet	483/tcp	ulpnet
ulpnet	483/udp	ulpnet
integra-sme	484/tcp	Integra Software Management Environment
integra-sme	484/udp	Integra Software Management Environment
powerburst	485/tcp	Air Soft Power Burst
powerburst	485/udp	Air Soft Power Burst
avian	486/tcp	avian
avian	486/udp	avian
saft	487/tcp	saft Simple Asynchronous File Transfer
saft	487/udp	saft Simple Asynchronous File Transfer
gss-http	488/tcp	gss-http
gss-http	488/udp	gss-http
nest-protocol	489/tcp	nest-protocol
nest-protocol	489/udp	nest-protocol
micom-pfs	490/tcp	micom-pfs
micom-pfs	490/udp	micom-pfs
go-login	491/tcp	go-login
go-login	491/udp	go-login
ticf-1	492/tcp	Transport Independent Convergence for FNA
ticf-1	492/udp	Transport Independent Convergence for FNA
ticf-2	493/tcp	Transport Independent Convergence for FNA
ticf-2	493/udp	Transport Independent Convergence for FNA

Continued

Table C-1 *(continued)*

Keyword	Decimal/Description	References
pov-ray	494/tcp	POV-Ray
pov-ray	494/udp	POV-Ray
intecourier	495/tcp	intecourier
intecourier	495/udp	intecourier
pim-rp-disc	496/tcp	PIM-RP-DISC
pim-rp-disc	496/udp	PIM-RP-DISC
dantz	497/tcp	dantz
dantz	497/udp	dantz
siam	498/tcp	siam
siam	498/udp	siam
iso-ill	499/tcp	ISO ILL Protocol
iso-ill	499/udp	ISO ILL Protocol
isakmp	500/tcp	isakmp
isakmp	500/udp	isakmp
stmf	501/tcp	STMF
stmf	501/udp	STMF
asa-appl-proto	502/tcp	asa-appl-proto
asa-appl-proto	502/udp	asa-appl-proto
intrinsa	503/tcp	Intrinsa
intrinsa	503/udp	Intrinsa
citadel	504/tcp	citadel
citadel	504/udp	citadel
mailbox-lm	505/tcp	mailbox-lm
mailbox-lm	505/udp	mailbox-lm
ohimsrv	506/tcp	ohimsrv
ohimsrv	506/udp	ohimsrv
crs	507/tcp	crs
crs	507/udp	crs
xvttp	508/tcp	xvttp
xvttp	508/udp	xvttp
snare	509/tcp	snare

Keyword	Decimal/Description	References
snare	509/udp	snare
fcp	510/tcp	FirstClass Protocol
fcp	510/udp	FirstClass Protocol
passgo	511/tcp	PassGo
passgo	511/udp	PassGo
exec	512/tcp	remote process execution
comsat	512/udp	
biff	512/udp	used by mail system to notify users
login	513/tcp	remote login a la telnet
who	513/udp	maintains data bases showing who's logged in on UNIX systems on the local network
shell	514/tcpcmd	authentication
syslog	514/udp	
printer	515/tcp	spooler
printer	515/udp	spooler
videotex	516/tcp	videotex
videotex	516/udp	videotex
talk	517/tcp	like tenex link, but across
talk	517/udp	like tenex link, but across
ntalk	518/tcp	
ntalk	518/udp	
utime	519/tcp	unixtime
utime	519/udp	unixtime
efs	520/tcp	extended file name server
router	520/udp	local routing process (on site)
ripng	521/tcp	ripng
ripng	521/udp	ripng
ulp	522/tcp	ULP
ulp	522/udp	ULP
ibm-db2	523/tcp	IBM-DB2

Continued

Table C-1 *(continued)*

Keyword	Decimal/Description	References
ibm-db2	523/udp	IBM-DB2
ncp	524/tcp	NCP
ncp	524/udp	NCP
timed	525/tcp	timeserver
timed	525/udp	timeserver
tempo	526/tcp	newdate
tempo	526/udp	newdate
stx	527/tcp	Stock IXChange
stx	527/udp	Stock IXChange
custix	528/tcp	Customer IXChange
custix	528/udp	Customer IXChange
irc-serv	529/tcp	IRC-SERV
irc-serv	529/udp	IRC-SERV
courier	530/tcp	rpc
courier	530/udp	rpc
conference	531/tcp	chat
conference	531/udp	chat
netnews	532/tcp	readnews
netnews	532/udp	readnews
netwall	533/tcp	for emergency broadcasts
netwall	533/udp	for emergency broadcasts
mm-admin	534/tcp	MegaMedia Admin
mm-admin	534/udp	MegaMedia Admin
iiop	535/tcp	iiop
iiop	535/udp	iiop
opalis-rdv	536/tcp	opalis-rdv
opalis-rdv	536/udp	opalis-rdv
nmsp	537/tcp	Networked Media Streaming Protocol
nmsp	537/udp	Networked Media Streaming Protocol

Keyword	Decimal/Description	References
gdomap	538/tcp	gdomap
gdomap	538/udp	gdomap
apertus-ldp	539/tcp	Apertus Technologies Load Determination
apertus-ldp	539/udp	Apertus Technologies Load Determination
uucp	540/tcp	uucpd
uucp	540/udp	uucpd
uucp-rlogin	541/tcp	uucp-rlogin
uucp-rlogin	541/udp	uucp-rlogin
commerce	542/tcp	commerce
commerce	542/udp	commerce
klogin	543/tcp	
klogin	543/udp	
kshell	544/tcp	krcmd
kshell	544/udp	krcmd
appleqtcsrvr	545/tcp	appleqtcsrvr
appleqtcsrvr	545/udp	appleqtcsrvr
dhcpv6-client	546/tcp	DHCPv6 Client
dhcpv6-client	546/udp	DHCPv6 Client
dhcpv6-server	547/tcp	DHCPv6 Server
dhcpv6-server	547/udp	DHCPv6 Server
afpovertcp	548/tcp	AFP over TCP
afpovertcp	548/udp	AFP over TCP
idfp	549/tcp	IDFP
idfp	549/udp	IDFP
new-rwho	550/tcp	new-who
new-rwho	550/udp	new-who
cybercash	551/tcp	cybercash
cybercash	551/udp	cybercash
deviceshare	552/tcp	deviceshare

Continued

Table C-1 *(continued)*

Keyword	Decimal/Description	References
deviceshare	552/udp	deviceshare
pirp	553/tcp	pirp
pirp	553/udp	pirp
rtsp	554/tcp	Real Time Stream Control Protocol
rtsp	554/udp	Real Time Stream Control Protocol
dsf	555/tcp	
dsf	555/udp	
remotefs	556/tcp	rfs server
remotefs	556/udp	rfs server
openvms-sysipc	557/tcp	openvms-sysipc
openvms-sysipc	557/udp	openvms-sysipc
sdnskmp	558/tcp	SDNSKMP
sdnskmp	558/udp	SDNSKMP
teedtap	559/tcp	TEEDTAP
teedtap	559/udp	TEEDTAP
rmonitor	560/tcp	rmonitord
rmonitor	560/udp	rmonitord
monitor	561/tcp	
monitor	561/udp	
chshell	562/tcp	chcmd
chshell	562/udp	chcmd
nntps	563/tcp	nntp protocol over TLS/SSL (was snntp)
nntps	563/udp	nntp protocol over TLS/SSL (was snntp)
9pfs	564/tcp	plan 9 file service
9pfs	564/udp	plan 9 file service
whoami	565/tcp	whoami
whoami	565/udp	whoami
streettalk	566/tcp	streettalk
streettalk	566/udp	streettalk

Keyword	Decimal/Description	References
banyan-rpc	567/tcp	banyan-rpc
banyan-rpc	567/udp	banyan-rpc
ms-shuttle	568/tcp	Microsoft shuttle
ms-shuttle	568/udp	Microsoft shuttle
ms-rome	569/tcp	Microsoft rome
ms-rome	569/udp	Microsoft rome
meter	570/tcp	demon
meter	570/udp	demon
meter	571/tcp	udemon
meter	571/udp	udemon
sonar	572/tcp	sonar
sonar	572/udp	sonar
banyan-vip	573/tcp	Banyan vip
banyan-vip	573/udp	Banyan vip
ftp-agent	574/tcp	FTP Software Agent System
ftp-agent	574/udp	FTP Software Agent System
vemmi	575/tcp	VEMMI
vemmi	575/udp	VEMMI
ipcd	576/tcp	ipcd
ipcd	576/udp	ipcd
vnas	577/tcp	vnas
vnas	577/udp	vnas
ipdd	578/tcp	ipdd
ipdd	578/udp	ipdd
decbsrv	579/tcp	decbsrv
decbsrv	579/udp	decbsrv
sntp-heartbeat	580/tcp	SNTP HEARTBEAT
sntp-heartbeat	580/udp	SNTP HEARTBEAT
bdp	581/tcp	Bundle Discovery Protocol
bdp	581/udp	Bundle Discovery Protocol
scc-security	582/tcp	SCC Security

Continued

Table C-1 *(continued)*

Keyword	Decimal/Description	References
scc-security	582/udp	SCC Security
philips-vc	583/tcp	Philips Video-Conferencing
philips-vc	583/udp	Philips Video-Conferencing
keyserver	584/tcp	Key Server
keyserver	584/udp	Key Server
imap4-ssl	585/tcp	IMAP4+SSL (use 993 instead)
imap4-ssl	585/udp	IMAP4+SSL (use 993 instead)
password-chg	586/tcp	Password Change
password-chg	586/udp	Password Change
submission	587/tcp	Submission
submission	587/udp	Submission
cal	588/tcp	CAL
cal	588/udp	CAL
eyelink	589/tcp	EyeLink
eyelink	589/udp	EyeLink
tns-cml	590/tcp	TNS CML
tns-cml	590/udp	TNS CML
http-alt	591/tcp	FileMaker, Inc. — HTTP Alternate (see Port 80)
http-alt	591/udp	FileMaker, Inc. — HTTP Alternate (see Port 80)
eudora-set	592/tcp	Eudora Set
eudora-set	592/udp	Eudora Set
http-rpc-epmap	593/tcp	HTTP RPC Ep Map
http-rpc-epmap	593/udp	HTTP RPC Ep Map
tpip	594/tcp	TPIP
tpip	594/udp	TPIP
cab-protocol	595/tcp	CAB Protocol
cab-protocol	595/udp	CAB Protocol
smsd	596/tcp	SMSD
smsd	596/udp	SMSD

Keyword	Decimal/Description	References
ptcnameservice	597/tcp	PTC Name Service
ptcnameservice	597/udp	PTC Name Service
sco-websrvrmg3	598/tcp	SCO Web Server Manager 3
sco-websrvrmg3	598/udp	SCO Web Server Manager 3
acp	599/tcp	Aeolon Core Protocol
acp	599/udp	Aeolon Core Protocol
ipcserver	600/tcp	Sun IPC server
ipcserver	600/udp	Sun IPC server
urm	606/tcp	Cray Unified Resource Manager
urm	606/udp	Cray Unified Resource Manager
nqs	607/tcp	nqs
nqs	607/udp	nqs
sift-uft	608/tcp	Sender-Initiated/Unsolicited File Transfer
sift-uft	608/udp	Sender-Initiated/Unsolicited File Transfer
npmp-trap	609/tcp	npmp-trap
npmp-trap	609/udp	npmp-trap
npmp-local	610/tcp	npmp-local
npmp-local	610/udp	npmp-local
npmp-gui	611/tcp	npmp-gui
npmp-gui	611/udp	npmp-gui
hmmp-ind	612/tcp	HMMP Indication
hmmp-ind	612/udp	HMMP Indication
hmmp-op	613/tcp	HMMP Operation
hmmp-op	613/udp	HMMP Operation
sshell	614/tcp	SSLshell
sshell	614/udp	SSLshell
sco-inetmgr	615/tcp	Internet Configuration Manager
sco-inetmgr	615/udp	Internet Configuration Manager
sco-sysmgr	616/tcp	SCO System Administration Server

Continued

Table C-1 *(continued)*

Keyword	Decimal/Description	References
sco-sysmgr	616/udp	SCO System Administration Server
sco-dtmgr	617/tcp	SCO Desktop Administration Server
sco-dtmgr	617/udp	SCO Desktop Administration Server
dei-icda	618/tcp	DEI-ICDA
dei-icda	618/udp	DEI-ICDA
digital-evm	619/tcp	Digital EVM
digital-evm	619/udp	Digital EVM
sco-websrvrmgr	620/tcp	SCO WebServer Manager
sco-websrvrmgr	620/udp	SCO WebServer Manager
escp-ip	621/tcp	ESCP
escp-ip	621/udp	ESCP
collaborator	622/tcp	Collaborator
collaborator	622/udp	Collaborator
aux_bus_shunt	623/tcp	Aux Bus Shunt
aux_bus_shunt	623/udp	Aux Bus Shunt
cryptoadmin	624/tcp	Crypto Admin
cryptoadmin	624/udp	Crypto Admin
dec_dlm	625/tcp	DEC DLM
dec_dlm	625/udp	DEC DLM
asia	626/tcp	ASIA
asia	626/udp	ASIA
passgo-tivoli	627/tcp	PassGo Tivoli
passgo-tivoli	627/udp	PassGo Tivoli
qmqp	628/tcp	QMQP
qmqp	628/udp	QMQP
3com-amp3	629/tcp	3Com AMP3
3com-amp3	629/udp	3Com AMP3
rda	630/tcp	RDA
rda	630/udp	RDA
ipp	631/tcp	IPP (Internet Printing Protocol)
ipp	631/udp	IPP (Internet Printing Protocol)

Keyword	Decimal/Description	References
bmpp	632/tcp	bmpp
bmpp	632/udp	bmpp
servstat	633/tcp	Service Status update (Sterling Software)
servstat	633/udp	Service Status update (Sterling Software)
ginad	634/tcp	ginad
ginad	634/udp	ginad
rlzdbase	635/tcp	RLZ DBase
rlzdbase	635/udp	RLZ DBase
ldaps	636/tcp	ldap protocol over TLS/SSL (was sldap)
ldaps	636/udp	ldap protocol over TLS/SSL (was sldap)
lanserver	637/tcp	lanserver
lanserver	637/udp	lanserver
mcns-sec	638/tcp	mcns-sec
mcns-sec	638/udp	mcns-sec
msdp	639/tcp	MSDP
msdp	639/udp	MSDP
entrust-sps	640/tcp	entrust-sps
entrust-sps	640/udp	entrust-sps
repcmd	641/tcp	repcmd
repcmd	641/udp	repcmd
esro-emsdp	642/tcp	ESRO-EMSDP V1.3
esro-emsdp	642/udp	ESRO-EMSDP V1.3
sanity	643/tcp	SANity
sanity	643/udp	SANity
dwr	644/tcp	dwr
dwr	644/udp	dwr
pssc	645/tcp	PSSC
pssc	645/udp	PSSC
ldp	646/tcp	LDP

Continued

Table C-1 *(continued)*		
Keyword	**Decimal/Description**	**References**
ldp	646/udp	LDP
dhcp-failover	647/tcp	DHCP Failover
dhcp-failover	647/udp	DHCP Failover
rrp	648/tcp	Registry Registrar Protocol (RRP)
rrp	648/udp	Registry Registrar Protocol (RRP)
aminet	649/tcp	Aminet
aminet	649/udp	Aminet
obex	650/tcp	OBEX
obex	650/udp	OBEX
ieee-mms	651/tcp	IEEE MMS
ieee-mms	651/udp	IEEE MMS
hello-port	652/tcp	HELLO_PORT
hello-port	652/udp	HELLO_PORT
repscmd	653/tcp	RepCmd
repscmd	653/udp	RepCmd
aodv	654/tcp	AODV
aodv	654/udp	AODV
tinc	655/tcp	TINC
tinc	655/udp	TINC
spmp	656/tcp	SPMP
spmp	656/udp	SPMP
rmc	657/tcp	RMC
rmc	657/udp	RMC
tenfold	658/tcp	TenFold
tenfold	658/udp	TenFold
mac-srvr-admin	660/tcp	MacOS Server Admin
mac-srvr-admin	660/udp	MacOS Server Admin
hap	661/tcp	HAP
hap	661/udp	HAP
pftp	662/tcp	PFTP
pftp	662/udp	PFTP

Keyword	Decimal/Description	References
purenoise	663/tcp	PureNoise
purenoise	663/udp	PureNoise
secure-aux-bus	664/tcp	Secure Aux Bus
secure-aux-bus	664/udp	Secure Aux Bus
sun-dr	665/tcp	Sun DR
sun-dr	665/udp	Sun DR
mdqs	666/tcp	
mdqs	666/udp	
doom	666/tcp	Doom ID Software
doom	666/udp	Doom ID Software
disclose	667/tcp	campaign contribution disclosures — SDR Technologies
disclose	667/udp	campaign contribution disclosures — SDR Technologies
mecomm	668/tcp	MeComm
mecomm	668/udp	MeComm
meregister	669/tcp	MeRegister
meregister	669/udp	MeRegister
vacdsm-sws	670/tcp	VACDSM-SWS
vacdsm-sws	670/udp	VACDSM-SWS
vacdsm-app	671/tcp	VACDSM-APP
vacdsm-app	671/udp	VACDSM-APP
vpps-qua	672/tcp	VPPS-QUA
vpps-qua	672/udp	VPPS-QUA
cimplex	673/tcp	CIMPLEX
cimplex	673/udp	CIMPLEX
acap	674/tcp	ACAP
acap	674/udp	ACAP
dctp	675/tcp	DCTP
dctp	675/udp	DCTP
vpps-via	676/tcp	VPPS Via

Continued

Table C-1 *(continued)*

Keyword	Decimal/Description	References
vpps-via	676/udp	VPPS Via
vpp	677/tcp	Virtual Presence Protocol
vpp	677/udp	Virtual Presence Protocol
ggf-ncp	678/tcp	GNU Generation Foundation NCP
ggf-ncp	678/udp	GNU Generation Foundation NCP
mrm	679/tcp	MRM
mrm	679/udp	MRM
entrust-aaas	680/tcp	entrust-aaas
entrust-aaas	680/udp	entrust-aaas
entrust-aams	681/tcp	entrust-aams
entrust-aams	681/udp	entrust-aams
xfr	682/tcp	XFR
xfr	682/udp	XFR
corba-iiop	683/tcp	CORBA IIOP
corba-iiop	683/udp	CORBA IIOP
corba-iiop-ssl	684/tcp	CORBA IIOP SSL
corba-iiop-ssl	684/udp	CORBA IIOP SSL
mdc-portmapper	685/tcp	MDC Port Mapper
mdc-portmapper	685/udp	MDC Port Mapper
hcp-wismar	686/tcp	Hardware Control Protocol Wismar
hcp-wismar	686/udp	Hardware Control Protocol Wismar
asipregistry	687/tcp	asipregistry
asipregistry	687/udp	asipregistry
realm-rusd	688/tcp	REALM-RUSD
realm-rusd	688/udp	REALM-RUSD
nmap	689/tcp	NMAP
nmap	689/udp	NMAP
vatp	690/tcp	VATP
vatp	690/udp	VATP
msexch-routing	691/tcp	MS Exchange Routing
msexch-routing	691/udp	MS Exchange Routing

Keyword	Decimal/Description	References
hyperwave-isp	692/tcp	Hyperwave-ISP
hyperwave-isp	692/udp	Hyperwave-ISP
connendp	693/tcp	connendp
connendp	693/udp	connendp
ha-cluster	694/tcp	ha-cluster
ha-cluster	694/udp	ha-cluster
ieee-mms-ssl	695/tcp	IEEE-MMS-SSL
ieee-mms-ssl	695/udp	IEEE-MMS-SSL
rushd	696/tcp	RUSHD
rushd	696/udp	RUSHD
uuidgen	697/tcp	UUIDGEN
uuidgen	697/udp	UUIDGEN
olsr	698/tcp	OLSR
olsr	698/udp	OLSR
accessnetwork	699/tcp	Access Network
accessnetwork	699/udp	Access Network
elcsd	704/tcp	errlog copy/server daemon
elcsd	704/udp	errlog copy/server daemon
agentx	705/tcp	AgentX
agentx	705/udp	AgentX
silc	706/tcp	SILC
silc	706/udp	SILC
borland-dsj	707/tcp	Borland DSJ
borland-dsj	707/udp	Borland DSJ
entrust-kmsh	709/tcp	Entrust Key Management Service Handler
entrust-kmsh	709/udp	Entrust Key Management Service Handler
entrust-ash	710/tcp	Entrust Administration Service Handler
entrust-ash	710/udp	Entrust Administration Service Handler
cisco-tdp	711/tcp	Cisco TDP

Continued

Table C-1 *(continued)*

Keyword	Decimal/Description	References
cisco-tdp	711/udp	Cisco TDP
netviewdm1	729/tcp	IBM NetView DM/6000 Server/Client
netviewdm1	729/udp	IBM NetView DM/6000 Server/Client
netviewdm2	730/tcp	IBM NetView DM/6000 send/tcp
netviewdm2	730/udp	IBM NetView DM/6000 send/tcp
netviewdm3	731/tcp	IBM NetView DM/6000 receive/tcp
netviewdm3	731/udp	IBM NetView DM/6000 receive/udp
netgw	741/tcp	netGW
netgw	741/udp	netGW
netrcs	742/tcp	Network based Rev. Cont. Sys.
netrcs	742/udp	Network based Rev. Cont. Sys.
flexlm	744/tcp	Flexible License Manager
flexlm	744/udp	Flexible License Manager
fujitsu-dev	747/tcp	Fujitsu Device Control
fujitsu-dev	747/udp	Fujitsu Device Control
ris-cm	748/tcp	Russell Info Sci Calendar Manager
ris-cm	748/udp	Russell Info Sci Calendar Manager
kerberos-adm	749/tcp	kerberos administration
kerberos-adm	749/udp	kerberos administration
rfile	750/tcp	
loadav	750/udp	
kerberos-iv	750/udp	kerberos version iv
pump	751/tcp	
pump	751/udp	
qrh	752/tcp	
qrh	752/udp	
rrh	753/tcp	
rrh	753/udp	
tell	754/tcp	send

Keyword	Decimal/Description	References
tell	754/udp	send
nlogin	758/tcp	
nlogin	758/udp	
con	759/tcp	
con	759/udp	
ns	760/tcp	
ns	760/udp	
rxe	761/tcp	
rxe	761/udp	
quotad	762/tcp	
quotad	762/udp	
cycleserv	763/tcp	
cycleserv	763/udp	
omserv	764/tcp	
omserv	764/udp	
webster	765/tcp	
webster	765/udp	
phonebook	767/tcp	phone
phonebook	767/udp	phone
vid	769/tcp	
vid	769/udp	
cadlock	770/tcp	
cadlock	770/udp	
rtip	771/tcp	
rtip	771/udp	
cycleserv2	772/tcp	
cycleserv2	772/udp	
submit	773/tcp	
notify	773/udp	
rpasswd	774/tcp	
acmaint_dbd	774/udp	

Continued

Table C-1 *(continued)*

Keyword	Decimal/Description	References
entomb	775/tcp	
acmaint_transd	775/udp	
wpages	776/tcp	
wpages	776/udp	
multiling-http	777/tcp	Multiling HTTP
multiling-http	777/udp	Multiling HTTP
wpgs	780/tcp	
wpgs	780/udp	
concert	786/tcp	Concert
concert	786/udp	Concert
qsc	787/tcp	QSC
qsc	787/udp	QSC
mdbs_daemon	800/tcp	
mdbs_daemon	800/udp	
device	801/tcp	
device	801/udp	
fcp-udp	810/tcp	FCP
fcp-udp	810/udp	FCP Datagram
itm-mcell-s	828/tcp	itm-mcell-s
itm-mcell-s	828/udp	itm-mcell-s
pkix-3-ca-ra	829/tcp	PKIX-3 CA/RA
pkix-3-ca-ra	829/udp	PKIX-3 CA/RA
dhcp-failover2	847/tcp	dhcp-failover 2
dhcp-failover2	847/udp	dhcp-failover 2
rsync	873/tcp	rsync
rsync	873/udp	rsync
iclcnet-locate	886/tcp	ICL coNETion locate server
iclcnet-locate	886/udp	ICL coNETion locate server
iclcnet_svinfo	887/tcp	ICL coNETion server info
iclcnet_svinfo	887/udp	ICL coNETion server info
accessbuilder	888/tcp	AccessBuilder

Keyword	Decimal/Description	References
accessbuilder	888/udp	AccessBuilder
cddbp	888/tcp	CD Database Protocol
omginitialrefs	900/tcp	OMG Initial Refs
omginitialrefs	900/udp	OMG Initial Refs
smpnameres	901/tcp	SMPNAMERES
smpnameres	901/udp	SMPNAMERES
ideafarm-chat	902/tcp	IDEAFARM-CHAT
ideafarm-chat	902/udp	IDEAFARM-CHAT
ideafarm-catch	903/tcp	IDEAFARM-CATCH
ideafarm-catch	903/udp	IDEAFARM-CATCH
xact-backup	911/tcp	xact-backup
xact-backup	911/udp	xact-backup
ftps-data	989/tcp	FTP protocol, data, over TLS/SSL
ftps-data	989/udp	FTP protocol, data, over TLS/SSL
ftps	990/tcp	FTP protocol, control, over TLS/SSL
ftps	990/udp	FTP protocol, control, over TLS/SSL
nas	991/tcp	Netnews Administration System
nas	991/udp	Netnews Administration System
telnets	992/tcp	telnet protocol over TLS/SSL
telnets	992/udp	telnet protocol over TLS/SSL
imaps	993/tcp	imap4 protocol over TLS/SSL
imaps	993/udp	imap4 protocol over TLS/SSL
ircs	994/tcp	irc protocol over TLS/SSL
ircs	994/udp	irc protocol over TLS/SSL
pop3s	995/tcp	POP3 protocol over TLS/SSL (was spop3)
pop3s	995/udp	POP3 protocol over TLS/SSL (was spop3)
vsinet	996/tcp	vsinet
vsinet	996/udp	vsinet
maitrd	997/tcp	

Continued

Table C-1 *(continued)*		
Keyword	**Decimal/Description**	**References**
maitrd	997/udp	
busboy	998/tcp	
puparp	998/udp	
garcon	999/tcp	
applix	999/udp	Applix ac
puprouter	999/tcp	
puprouter	999/udp	
cadlock2	1000/tcp	
cadlock2	1000/udp	
surf	1010/tcp	surf
surf	1010/udp	surf
	1011-1022	Reserved
	1023/tcp	Reserved
	1023/udp	Reserved

Registered Port Numbers

Registered Ports are from 1024 to 49151. These ports can be accessed by any user. Table C-2 lists registered ports.

Table C-2 Registered Ports		
Keyword	**Decimal/Description**	**References**
	1024/tcp	Reserved
	1024/udp	Reserved
blackjack	1025/tcp	network blackjack
blackjack	1025/udp	network blackjack
cma	1050/tcp	CORBA Management Agent

Keyword	Decimal/Description	References
cma	1050/udp	CORBA Management Agent
ddt	1052/tcp	Dynamic DNS Tools
ddt	1052/udp	Dynamic DNS Tools
remote-as	1053/tcp	Remote Assistant (RA)
remote-as	1053/udp	Remote Assistant (RA)
imgames	1077/tcp	IMGames
imgames	1077/udp	IMGames
socks	1080/tcp	Socks
socks	1080/udp	Socks
webobjects	1085/tcp	Web Objects
webobjects	1085/udp	Web Objects
proofd	1093/tcp	PROOFD
proofd	1093/udp	PROOFD
rootd	1094/tcp	ROOTD
rootd	1094/udp	ROOTD
cnrprotocol	1096/tcp	Common Name Resolution Protocol
cnrprotocol	1096/udp	Common Name Resolution Protocol
sunclustermgr	1097/tcp	Sun Cluster Manager
sunclustermgr	1097/udp	Sun Cluster Manager
nfsd-status	1110/tcp	Cluster status info
nfsd-keepalive	1110/udp	Client status info
nfa	1155/tcp	Network File Access
nfa	1155/udp	Network File Access
tripwire	1169/tcp	TRIPWIRE
tripwire	1169/udp	TRIPWIRE
hp-webadmin	1188/tcp	HP Web Admin
hp-webadmin	1188/udp	HP Web Admin
kazaa	1214/tcp	KAZAA
kazaa	1214/udp	KAZAA
vpnz	1224/tcp	VPNz
vpnz	1224/udp	VPNz

Continued

Table C-2 *(continued)*

Keyword	Decimal/Description	References
dns2go	1227/tcp	DNS2Go
dns2go	1227/udp	DNS2Go
search-agent	1234/tcp	Infoseek Search Agent
search-agent	1234/udp	Infoseek Search Agent
nessus	1241/tcp	nessus
nessus	1241/udp	nessus
ibm-ssd	1260/tcp	ibm-ssd
ibm-ssd	1260/udp	ibm-ssd
dellpwrappks	1266/tcp	DELLPWRAPPKS
dellpwrappks	1266/udp	DELLPWRAPPKS
dellwebadmin-1	1278/tcp	Dell Web Admin 1
dellwebadmin-1	1278/udp	Dell Web Admin 1
dellwebadmin-2	1279/tcp	Dell Web Admin 2
dellwebadmin-2	1279/udp	Dell Web Admin 2
pacmand	1307/tcp	Pacmand
pacmand	1307/udp	Pacmand
netdb-export	1329/tcp	netdb-export
netdb-export	1329/udp	netdb-export
passwrd-policy	1333/tcp	Password Policy
passwrd-policy	1333/udp	Password Policy
icap	1344/tcp	ICAP
icap	1344/udp	ICAP
lotusnote	1352/tcp	Lotus Note
lotusnote	1352/udp	Lotus Note
apple-licman	1381/tcp	Apple Network License Manager
apple-licman	1381/udp	Apple Network License Manager
cadkey-licman	1399/tcp	Cadkey License Manager
cadkey-licman	1399/udp	Cadkey License Manager
cadkey-tablet	1400/tcp	Cadkey Tablet Daemon
cadkey-tablet	1400/udp	Cadkey Tablet Daemon
prm-sm-np	1402/tcp	Prospero Resource Manager

Keyword	Decimal/Description	References
prm-sm-np	1402/udp	Prospero Resource Manager
prm-nm-np	1403/tcp	Prospero Resource Manager
prm-nm-np	1403/udp	Prospero Resource Manager
ibm-res	1405/tcp	IBM Remote Execution Starter
ibm-res	1405/udp	IBM Remote Execution Starter
mloadd	1427/tcp	mloadd monitoring tool
mloadd	1427/udp	mloadd monitoring tool
ms-sql-s	1433/tcp	Microsoft-SQL-Server
ms-sql-s	1433/udp	Microsoft-SQL-Server
ms-sql-m	1434/tcp	Microsoft-SQL-Monitor
ms-sql-m	1434/udp	Microsoft-SQL-Monitor
infoman	1451/tcp	IBM Information Management
infoman	1451/udp	IBM Information Management
ibm_wrless_lan	1461/tcp	IBM Wireless LAN
ibm_wrless_lan	1461/udp	IBM Wireless LAN
pipes	1465/tcp	Pipes Platform
pipes	1465/udp	Pipes Platform
ms-sna-server	1477/tcp	Microsoft SNA Server
ms-sna-server	1477/udp	Microsoft SNA Server
ms-sna-base	1478/tcp	Microsoft SNA base
ms-sna-base	1478/udp	Microsoft SNA base
dberegister	1479/tcp	dberegister
dberegister	1479/udp	dberegister
ica	1494/tcp	ica
ica	1494/udp	ica
sybase-sqlany	1498/tcp	Sybase SQL Any
sybase-sqlany	1498/udp	Sybase SQL Any
saiscm	1501/tcp	Satellite-data Acquisition System 3
saiscm	1501/udp	Satellite-data Acquisition System 3
shivadiscovery	1502/tcp	Shiva
shivadiscovery	1502/udp	Shiva

Continued

Table C-2 *(continued)*

Keyword	Decimal/Description	References
utcd	1506/tcp	Universal Time daemon (utcd)
utcd	1506/udp	Universal Time daemon (utcd)
wins	1512/tcp	Microsoft's Windows Internet Name Service
wins	1512/udp	Microsoft's Windows Internet Name Service
ingreslock	1524/tcp	Ingress
ingreslock	1524/udp	Ingress
orasrv	1525/tcp	Oracle
orasrv	1525/udp	Oracle
prospero-np	1525/tcp	Prospero Directory Service non-priv
prospero-np	1525/udp	Prospero Directory Service non-priv
pdap-np	1526/tcp	Prospero Data Access Prot non-priv
pdap-np	1526/udp	Prospero Data Access Prot non-priv
tlisrv	1527/tcp	Oracle
tlisrv	1527/udp	Oracle
coauthor	1529/tcp	Oracle
coauthor	1529/udp	Oracle
laplink	1547/tcp	laplink
laplink	1547/udp	laplink
xingmpeg	1558/tcp	xingmpeg
xingmpeg	1558/udp	xingmpeg
pay-per-view	1564/tcp	Pay-Per-View
pay-per-view	1564/udp	Pay-Per-View
rdb-dbs-disp	1571/tcp	Oracle Remote Data Base
rdb-dbs-disp	1571/udp	Oracle Remote Data Base
oraclenames	1575/tcp	oraclenames
oraclenames	1575/udp	oraclenames
radio	1595/tcp	radio
radio	1595/udp	radio
radio-sm	1596/tcp	radio-sm

Keyword	Decimal/Description	References
radio-bc	1596/udp	radio-bc
icabrowser	1604/tcp	icabrowser
icabrowser	1604/udp	icabrowser
shockwave	1626/tcp	Shockwave
shockwave	1626/udp	Shockwave
oraclenet8cman	1630/tcp	Oracle Net8 Cman
oraclenet8cman	1630/udp	Oracle Net8 Cman
cert-initiator	1639/tcp	cert-initiator
cert-initiator	1639/udp	cert-initiator
cert-responder	1640/tcp	cert-responder
cert-responder	1640/udp	cert-responder
kermit	1649/tcp	Kermit
kermit	1649/udp	Kermit
xnmp	1652/tcp	xnmp
xnmp	1652/udp	xnmp
groupwise	1677/tcp	groupwise
groupwise	1677/udp	groupwise
xmsg	1716/tcp	xmsg
xmsg	1716/udp	xmsg
h323gatedisc	1718/tcp	h323gatedisc
h323gatedisc	1718/udp	h323gatedisc
h323gatestat	1719/tcp	h323gatestat
h323gatestat	1719/udp	h323gatestat
h323hostcall	1720/tcp	h323hostcall
h323hostcall	1720/udp	h323hostcall
pptp	1723/tcp	pptp
pptp	1723/udp	pptp
cisco-net-mgmt	1741/tcp	cisco-net-mgmt
cisco-net-mgmt	1741/udp	cisco-net-mgmt
3Com-nsd	1742/tcp	3Com-nsd
3Com-nsd	1742/udp	3Com-nsd

Continued

Table C-2 *(continued)*		
Keyword	**Decimal/Description**	**References**
remote-winsock	1745/tcp	remote-winsock
remote-winsock	1745/udp	remote-winsock
oracle-em1	1748/tcp	Oracle em1
oracle-em1	1748/udp	Oracle em1
oracle-em2	1754/tcp	Oracle em2
oracle-em2	1754/udp	Oracle em2
ms-streaming	1755/tcp	ms-streaming
ms-streaming	1755/udp	ms-streaming
tftp-mcast	1758/tcp	tftp-mcast
tftp-mcast	1758/udp	tftp-mcast
femis	1776/tcp	Federal Emergency Management Information System
femis	1776/udp	Federal Emergency Management Information System
hello	1789/tcp	hello
hello	1789/udp	hello
msmq	1801/tcp	Microsoft Message Que
msmq	1801/udp	Microsoft Message Que
oracle-vp2	1808/tcp	Oracle-VP2
oracle-vp2	1808/udp	Oracle-VP2
oracle-vp1	1809/tcp	Oracle-VP1
oracle-vp1	1809/udp	Oracle-VP1
radius	1812/tcp	RADIUS
radius	1812/udp	RADIUS
radius-acct	1813/tcp	RADIUS Accounting
radius-acct	1813/udp	RADIUS Accounting
etftp	1818/tcp	Enhanced Trivial File Transfer Protocol
etftp	1818/udp	Enhanced Trivial File Transfer Protocol
direcpc-video	1825/tcp	DirecPC Video

Keyword	Decimal/Description	References
direcpc-video	1825/udp	DirecPC Video
net8-cman	1830/tcp	Oracle Net8 CMan Admin
net8-cman	1830/udp	Oracle Net8 CMan Admin
direcpc-dll	1844/tcp	DirecPC-DLL
direcpc-dll	1844/udp	DirecPC-DLL
vrtstrapserver	1885/tcp	Veritas Trap Server
vrtstrapserver	1885/udp	Veritas Trap Server
unix-status	1957/tcp	unix-status
unix-status	1957/udp	unix-status
dxadmind	1958/tcp	CA Administration Daemon
dxadmind	1958/udp	CA Administration Daemon
tivoli-npm	1965/tcp	Tivoli NPM
tivoli-npm	1965/udp	Tivoli NPM
hsrp	1985/tcp	Hot Standby Router Protocol
hsrp	1985/udp	Hot Standby Router Protocol
licensedaemon	1986/tcp	Cisco license management
licensedaemon	1986/udp	Cisco license management
tr-rsrb-p1	1987/tcp	Cisco RSRB Priority 1 port
tr-rsrb-p1	1987/udp	Cisco RSRB Priority 1 port
tr-rsrb-p2	1988/tcp	Cisco RSRB Priority 2 port
tr-rsrb-p2	1988/udp	Cisco RSRB Priority 2 port
tr-rsrb-p3	1989/tcp	Cisco RSRB Priority 3 port
tr-rsrb-p3	1989/udp	Cisco RSRB Priority 3 port
stun-p1	1990/tcp	Cisco STUN Priority 1 port
stun-p1	1990/udp	Cisco STUN Priority 1 port
stun-p2	1991/tcp	Cisco STUN Priority 2 port
stun-p2	1991/udp	Cisco STUN Priority 2 port
stun-p3	1992/tcp	Cisco STUN Priority 3 port
stun-p3	1992/udp	Cisco STUN Priority 3 port
ipsendmsg	1992/tcp	Ipsendmsg
ipsendmsg	1992/udp	Ipsendmsg

Continued

Table C-2 *(continued)*

Keyword	Decimal/Description	References
snmp-tcp-port	1993/tcp	Cisco SNMP TCP port
snmp-tcp-port	1993/udp	Cisco SNMP TCP port
stun-port	1994/tcp	Cisco serial tunnel port
stun-port	1994/udp	Cisco serial tunnel port
perf-port	1995/tcp	Cisco perf port
perf-port	1995/udp	Cisco perf port
tr-rsrb-port	1996/tcp	Cisco Remote SRB port
tr-rsrb-port	1996/udp	Cisco Remote SRB port
gdp-port	1997/tcp	Cisco Gateway Discovery Protocol
gdp-port	1997/udp	Cisco Gateway Discovery Protocol
x25-svc-port	1998/tcp	Cisco X.25 service (XOT)
x25-svc-port	1998/udp	Cisco X.25 service (XOT)
tcp-id-port	1999/tcp	Cisco identification port
tcp-id-port	1999/udp	Cisco identification port
nfs	2049/tcp	Network File System — Sun Microsystems
nfs	2049/udp	Network File System — Sun Microsystems
event-port	2069/tcp	HTTP Event Port
event-port	2069/udp	HTTP Event Port
veritas-ucl	2148/tcp	Veritas Universal Communication Layer
veritas-ucl	2148/udp	Veritas Universal Communication Layer
apc-cms	2160/tcp	APC Central Mgmt Server
apc-cms	2160/udp	APC Central Mgmt Server
apc-agent	2161/tcp	APC Agent
apc-agent	2161/udp	APC Agent
raw-serial	2167/tcp	Raw Async Serial Link
raw-serial	2167/udp	Raw Async Serial Link
directplay	2234/tcp	DirectPlay

Keyword	Decimal/Description	References
directplay	2234/udp	DirectPlay
cpq-wbem	2301/tcp	Compaq HTTP
cpq-wbem	2301/udp	Compaq HTTP
manage-exec	2342/tcp	Seagate Manage Exec
manage-exec	2342/udp	Seagate Manage Exec
compaq-https	2381/tcp	Compaq HTTPS
compaq-https	2381/udp	Compaq HTTPS
ms-olap3	2382/tcp	Microsoft OLAP
ms-olap3	2382/udp	Microsoft OLAP
ms-olap4	2383/tcp	Microsoft OLAP
ms-olap4	2383/udp	Microsoft OLAP
3com-net-mgmt	2391/tcp	3COM Net Management
3com-net-mgmt	2391/udp	3COM Net Management
ms-olap1	2393/tcp	MS OLAP 1
ms-olap1	2393/udp	MS OLAP 1
ms-olap2	2394/tcp	MS OLAP 2
ms-olap2	2394/udp	MS OLAP 2
fmpro-fdal	2399/tcp	FileMaker, Inc. — Data Access Layer
fmpro-fdal	2399/udp	FileMaker, Inc. — Data Access Layer
sybasedbsynch	2439/tcp	SybaseDBSynch
sybasedbsynch	2439/udp	SybaseDBSynch
owwdb	2447/tcp	OpenView NNM daemon
owwdb	2447/udp	OpenView NNM daemon
netadmin	2450/tcp	netadmin
netadmin	2450/udp	netadmin
netchat	2451/tcp	netchat
netchat	2451/udp	netchat
giop	2481/tcp	Oracle GIOP
giop	2481/udp	Oracle GIOP
giop-ssl	2482/tcp	Oracle GIOP SSL
giop-ssl	2482/udp	Oracle GIOP SSL

Continued

Table C-2 *(continued)*

Keyword	Decimal/Description	References
ttc	2483/tcp	Oracle TTC
ttc	2483/udp	Oracle TTC
ttc-ssl	2484/tcp	Oracle TTC SSL
ttc-ssl	2484/udp	Oracle TTC SSL
netobjects1	2485/tcp	Net Objects1
netobjects1	2485/udp	Net Objects1
netobjects2	2486/tcp	Net Objects2
netobjects2	2486/udp	Net Objects2
citrixima	2512/tcp	Citrix IMA
citrixima	2512/udp	Citrix IMA
citrixadmin	2513/tcp	Citrix ADMIN
citrixadmin	2513/udp	Citrix ADMIN
adaptecmgr	2521/tcp	Adaptec Manager
adaptecmgr	2521/udp	Adaptec Manager
ms-v-worlds	2525/tcp	MS V-Worlds
ms-v-worlds	2525/udp	MS V-Worlds
compaq-wcp	2555/tcp	Compaq WCP
compaq-wcp	2555/udp	Compaq WCP
clp	2567/tcp	Cisco Line Protocol
clp	2567/udp	Cisco Line Protocol
spamtrap	2568/tcp	SPAM TRAP
spamtrap	2568/udp	SPAM TRAP
citriximaclient	2598/tcp	Citrix MA Client
citriximaclient	2598/udp	Citrix MA Client
netmon	2606/tcp	Dell Netmon
netmon	2606/udp	Dell Netmon
connection	2607/tcp	Dell Connection
connection	2607/udp	Dell Connection
sybaseanywhere	2638/tcp	Sybase Anywhere
sybaseanywhere	2638/udp	Sybase Anywhere
hp-nnm-data	2690/tcp	HP NNM Embedded Database

Keyword	Decimal/Description	References
hp-nnm-data	2690/udp	HP NNM Embedded Database
sms-rcinfo	2701/tcp	SMS RCINFO
sms-rcinfo	2701/udp	SMS RCINFO
sms-xfer	2702/tcp	SMS XFER
sms-xfer	2702/udp	SMS XFER
sms-chat	2703/tcp	SMS CHAT
sms-chat	2703/udp	SMS CHAT
sms-remctrl	2704/tcp	SMS REMCTRL
sms-remctrl	2704/udp	SMS REMCTRL
msolap-ptp2	2725/tcp	Microsoft OLAP PTP2
msolap-ptp2	2725/udp	Microsoft OLAP PTP2
compaq-scp	2766/tcp	Compaq SCP
compaq-scp	2766/udp	Compaq SCP
www-dev	2784/tcp	World Wide Web development
www-dev	2784/udp	World Wide Web development
media-agent	2789/tcp	Media Agent
media-agent	2789/udp	Media Agent
f5-globalsite	2792/tcp	f5-globalsite
f5-globalsite	2792/udp	f5-globalsite
livestats	2795/tcp	LiveStats
livestats	2795/udp	LiveStats
veritas-tcp1	2802/tcp	Veritas TCP1
veritas-udp1	2802/udp	Veritas UDP1
citrix-rtmp	2897/tcp	Citrix RTMP
citrix-rtmp	2897/udp	Citrix RTMP
wap-push	2948/tcp	WAP PUSH
wap-push	2948/udp	WAP PUSH
wap-pushsecure	2949/tcp	WAP PUSH SECURE
wap-pushsecure	2949/udp	WAP PUSH SECURE
wimd	2980/tcp	Instant Messaging Service
wimd	2980/udp	Instant Messaging Service

Continued

Table C-2 *(continued)*

Keyword	Decimal/Description	References
veritas-vis1	2993/tcp	VERITAS VIS1
veritas-vis1	2993/udp	VERITAS VIS1
veritas-vis2	2994/tcp	VERITAS VIS2
veritas-vis2	2994/udp	VERITAS VIS2
realsecure	2998/tcp	Real Secure
realsecure	2998/udp	Real Secure
cifs	3020/tcp	CIFS
cifs	3020/udp	CIFS
xbox	3074/tcp	Xbox game port
xbox	3074/udp	Xbox game port
njfss	3092/tcp	Netware sync services
njfss	3092/udp	Netware sync services
ms-dotnetster	3126/tcp	Microsoft .NETster Port
ms-dotnetster	3126/udp	Microsoft .NETster Port
ms-slipstream	3132/tcp	MS-Slipstream
ms-slipstream	3132/udp	MS-Slipstream
jpegmpeg	3155/tcp	JpegMpeg Port
jpegmpeg	3155/udp	JpegMpeg Port
stvp	3158/tcp	SmashTV Protocol
stvp	3158/udp	SmashTV Protocol
msft-gc	3268/tcp	Microsoft Global Catalog
msft-gc	3268/udp	Microsoft Global Catalog
msft-gc-ssl	3269/tcp	Microsoft Global Catalog with LDAP/SSL
msft-gc-ssl	3269/udp	Microsoft Global Catalog with LDAP/SSL
admind	3279/tcp	admind
admind	3279/udp	admind
mysql	3306/tcp	MySQL
mysql	3306/udp	MySQL
directv-web	3334/tcp	Direct TV Webcasting

Keyword	Decimal/Description	References
directv-web	3334/udp	Direct TV Webcasting
directv-soft	3335/tcp	Direct TV Software Updates
directv-soft	3335/udp	Direct TV Software Updates
directv-tick	3336/tcp	Direct TV Tickers
directv-tick	3336/udp	Direct TV Tickers
directv-catlg	3337/tcp	Direct TV Data Catalog
directv-catlg	3337/udp	Direct TV Data Catalog
dsc	3390/tcp	Distributed Service Coordinator
dsc	3390/udp	Distributed Service Coordinator
ibm3494	3494/tcp	IBM 3494
ibm3494	3494/udp	IBM 3494
suucp	4031/tcp	UUCP over SSL
suucp	4031/udp	UUCP over SSL
vrts-auth-port	4032/tcp	VERITAS Authorize Server
vrts-auth-port	4032/udp	VERITAS Authorize Server
sanavigator	4033/tcp	SANavigator Peer Port
sanavigator	4033/udp	SANavigator Peer Port
wap-push-http	4035/tcp	WAP Push OTA-HTTP port
wap-push-http	4035/udp	WAP Push OTA-HTTP port
wap-push-https	4036/tcp	WAP Push OTA-HTTP secure
wap-push-https	4036/udp	WAP Push OTA-HTTP secure
rwhois	4321/tcp	Remote Who Is
rwhois	4321/udp	Remote Who Is
f5-iquery	4353/tcp	F5 iQuery
f5-iquery	4353/udp	F5 iQuery
rfe	5002/tcp	radio free ethernet
rfe	5002/udp	radio free ethernet
fmpro-internal	5003/tcp	FileMaker, Inc. — Proprietary transport
fmpro-internal	5003/udp	FileMaker, Inc. — Proprietary name binding

Continued

Table C-2 *(continued)*		
Keyword	*Decimal/Description*	*References*
aol	5190/tcp	AmericaOnline
aol	5190/udp	AmericaOnline
aol-1	5191/tcp	AmericaOnline1
aol-1	5191/udp	AmericaOnline1
aol-2	5192/tcp	AmericaOnline2
aol-2	5192/udp	AmericaOnline2
aol-3	5193/tcp	AmericaOnline3
aol-3	5193/udp	AmericaOnline3
sun-mc-grp	5306/tcp	Sun MC Group
sun-mc-grp	5306/udp	Sun MC Group
cfengine	5308/tcp	Cfengine
cfengine	5308/udp	Cfengine
apc-tcp-udp-4	5454/tcp	apc-tcp-udp-4
apc-tcp-udp-4	5454/udp	apc-tcp-udp-4
apc-tcp-udp-5	5455/tcp	apc-tcp-udp-5
apc-tcp-udp-5	5455/udp	apc-tcp-udp-5
apc-tcp-udp-6	5456/tcp	apc-tcp-udp-6
apc-tcp-udp-6	5456/udp	apc-tcp-udp-6
pcanywheredata	5631/tcp	pcANYWHEREdata
pcanywheredata	5631/udp	pcANYWHEREdata
pcanywherestat	5632/tcp	pcANYWHEREstat
pcanywherestat	5632/udp	pcANYWHEREstat
openmail	5729/tcp	Openmail User Agent Layer
openmail	5729/udp	Openmail User Agent Layer
wbem-rmi	5987/tcp	WBEM RMI
wbem-rmi	5987/udp	WBEM RMI
wbem-http	5988/tcp	WBEM HTTP
wbem-http	5988/udp	WBEM HTTP
wbem-https	5989/tcp	WBEM HTTPS
wbem-https	5989/udp	WBEM HTTPS
cvsup	5999/tcp	CVSup

Keyword	Decimal/Description	References
cvsup	5999/udp	CVSup
x11	6000-6063/tcp	X Window System
x11	6000-6063/udp	X Window System
softcm	6110/tcp	HP SoftBench CM
softcm	6110/udp	HP SoftBench CM
spc	6111/tcp	HP SoftBench Sub-Process Control
spc	6111/udp	HP SoftBench Sub-Process Control
gnutella-svc	6346/tcp	gnutella-svc
gnutella-svc	6346/udp	gnutella-svc
gnutella-rtr	6347/tcp	gnutella-rtr
gnutella-rtr	6347/udp	gnutella-rtr
apc-tcp-udp-1	6547/tcp	apc-tcp-udp-1
apc-tcp-udp-1	6547/udp	apc-tcp-udp-1
apc-tcp-udp-2	6548/tcp	apc-tcp-udp-2
apc-tcp-udp-2	6548/udp	apc-tcp-udp-2
apc-tcp-udp-3	6549/tcp	apc-tcp-udp-3
apc-tcp-udp-3	6549/udp	apc-tcp-udp-3
font-service	7100/tcp	X Font Service
font-service	7100/udp	X Font Service
pmdmgr	7426/tcp	OpenView DM Postmaster Manager
pmdmgr	7426/udp	OpenView DM Postmaster Manager
oveadmgr	7427/tcp	OpenView DM Event Agent Manager
oveadmgr	7427/udp	OpenView DM Event Agent Manager
ovladmgr	7428/tcp	OpenView DM Log Agent Manager
ovladmgr	7428/udp	OpenView DM Log Agent Manager
opi-sock	7429/tcp	OpenView DM rqt communication
opi-sock	7429/udp	OpenView DM rqt communication
xmpv7	7430/tcp	OpenView DM xmpv7 api pipe
xmpv7	7430/udp	OpenView DM xmpv7 api pipe
pmd	7431/tcp	OpenView DM ovc/xmpv3 api pipe
pmd	7431/udp	OpenView DM ovc/xmpv3 api pipe

Continued

Table C-2 *(continued)*		
Keyword	*Decimal/Description*	*References*
sun-lm	7588/tcp	Sun License Manager
sun-lm	7588/udp	Sun License Manager
apc-snmptrap	7845/tcp	APC SNMP Trap Proxy
apc-snmptrap	7845/udp	APC SNMP Trap Proxy
apc-snmp	7846/tcp	APC SNMP Proxy
apc-snmp	7846/udp	APC SNMP Proxy
http-alt	8008/tcp	HTTP Alternate
http-alt	8008/udp	HTTP Alternate
http-alt	8080/tcp	HTTP Alternate (see port 80)
http-alt	8080/udp	HTTP Alternate (see port 80)
xprint-server	8100/tcp	Xprint Server
xprint-server	8100/udp	Xprint Server
wap-wsp	9200/tcp	WAP connectionless session service
wap-wsp	9200/udp	WAP connectionless session service
wap-wsp-wtp	9201/tcp	WAP session service
wap-wsp-wtp	9201/udp	WAP session service
wap-wsp-s	9202/tcp	WAP secure connectionless session service
wap-wsp-s	9202/udp	WAP secure connectionless session service
wap-wsp-wtp-s	9203/tcp	WAP secure session service
wap-wsp-wtp-s	9203/udp	WAP secure session service
wap-vcard	9204/tcp	WAP vCard
wap-vcard	9204/udp	WAP vCard
wap-vcal	9205/tcp	WAP vCal
wap-vcal	9205/udp	WAP vCal
wap-vcard-s	9206/tcp	WAP vCard Secure
wap-vcard-s	9206/udp	WAP vCard Secure
wap-vcal-s	9207/tcp	WAP vCal Secure
wap-vcal-s	9207/udp	WAP vCal Secure
msgsys	9594/tcp	Message System

Keyword	Decimal/Description	References
msgsys	9594/udp	Message System
pds	9595/tcp	Ping Discovery Service
pds	9595/udp	Ping Discovery Service
domaintime	9909/tcp	domaintime
domaintime	9909/udp	domaintime
ndmp	10000/tcp	Network Data Management Protocol
ndmp	10000/udp	Network Data Management Protocol
scp-config	10001/tcp	SCP Configuration Port
scp-config	10001/udp	SCP Configuration Port
mvs-capacity	10007/tcp	MVS Capacity
mvs-capacity	10007/udp	MVS Capacity
amanda	10080/tcp	Amanda
amanda	10080/udp	Amanda
entextxid	12000/tcp	IBM Enterprise Extender SNA XID Exchange
entextxid	12000/udp	IBM Enterprise Extender SNA XID Exchange
entextnetwk	12001/tcp	IBM Enterprise Extender SNA COS Network Priority
entextnetwk	12001/udp	IBM Enterprise Extender SNA COS Network Priority
entexthigh	12002/tcp	IBM Enterprise Extender SNA COS High Priority
entexthigh	12002/udp	IBM Enterprise Extender SNA COS High Priority
entextmed	12003/tcp	IBM Enterprise Extender SNA COS Medium Priority
entextmed	12003/udp	IBM Enterprise Extender SNA COS Medium Priority
entextlow	12004/tcp	IBM Enterprise Extender SNA COS Low Priority
entextlow	12004/udp	IBM Enterprise Extender SNA COS Low Priority

Continued

Table C-2 *(continued)*

Keyword	Decimal/Description	References
vnetd	13724/tcp	Veritas Network Utility
vnetd	13724/udp	Veritas Network Utility
bpcd	13782/tcp	Veritas NetBackup
bpcd	13782/udp	Veritas NetBackup
mtrgtrans	19398/tcp	mtrgtrans
mtrgtrans	19398/udp	mtrgtrans
webphone	21845/tcp	webphone
webphone	21845/udp	webphone
netspeak-is	21846/tcp	NetSpeak Corp.Directory Services
netspeak-is	21846/udp	NetSpeak Corp. Directory Services
netspeak-cs	21847/tcp	NetSpeak Corp. Connection Services
netspeak-cs	21847/udp	NetSpeak Corp. Connection Services
netspeak-acd	21848/tcp	NetSpeak Corp. Automatic Call Distribution
netspeak-acd	21848/udp	NetSpeak Corp. Automatic Call Distribution
netspeak-cps	21849/tcp	NetSpeak Corp. Credit Processing System
netspeak-cps	21849/udp	NetSpeak Corp. Credit Processing System
snip	24922/tcp	Simple Net Ident Protocol
snip	24922/udp	Simple Net Ident Protocol
quake	26000/tcp	quake
quake	26000/udp	quake
traceroute	33434/tcp	traceroute use
traceroute	33434/udp	traceroute use
mbus	47000/tcp	Message Bus
mbus	47000/udp	Message Bus
bacnet	47808/tcp	Building Automation and Control Networks
bacnet	47808/udp	Building Automation and Control Networks

✦   ✦   ✦

Index

Continued

Continued

Continued

Continued

DATE DUE